W9-DGU-619

Bloom's Modern Critical Views

Bloom's Modern Critical Views

HERMAN MELVILLE
New Edition

Edited and with an introduction by
Harold Bloom
Sterling Professor of the Humanities
Yale University

BLOOM'S
LITERARY CRITICISM
An imprint of Infobase Publishing

Editorial Consultant, John Wenke

Bloom's Modern Critical Views: Herman Melville—New Edition
Copyright ©2008 by Infobase Publishing

Introduction ©2008 by Harold Bloom

Bloom's Literary Criticism
An imprint of Infobase Publishing
132 West 31st Street
New York NY 10001

Library of Congress Cataloging-in-Publication Data

Herman Melville / edited and with an introduction by Harold Bloom. — New ed.
    p. cm. — (Bloom's modern critical views)
Includes bibliographical references and index.
ISBN 978-0-7910-9621-5 (acid-free paper) 1. Melville, Herman, 1819–1891—
Criticism and interpretation. I. Bloom, Harold.

  PS2387.H4135 2008
  813'.3—dc22

                            2008007595

You can find Bloom's Literary Criticism on the World Wide Web at
http://www.chelseahouse.com.

Cover design by Ben Peterson

Printed in the United States of America
Bang BCL 10 9 8 7 6 5 4 3 2 1

This book is printed on acid-free paper.

All links and Web addresses were checked and verified to be correct at the time of
publication. Because of the dynamic nature of the Web, some addresses and links may
have changed since publication and may no longer be valid.

Contents

Editor's Note

My introduction begins with a reading of "The Bell-Tower" in *The Piazza Tales*, and then moves to some of the visionary centers of *Moby-Dick*, particularly Chapter 119, "The Candles," and Chapter 42, "The Whiteness of the Whale."

Milton R. Stern perspectivizes the uncannily Kafkan parable of "Bartleby the Scrivener," finding in Bartelby a coming-together of several fictive selves a customary Melvillian *praxis*.

The problem of Being—Neoplatonic, Spinozan, Coleridgean, Emersonian—is shown as haunting Meville and his *Moby-Dick*, in an erudite essay by Sanford E. Marovitz.

An extraordinary tale, "Benito Cereno," is characterized by Sandra A. Zagarell as a crucial testimony to our inability to divide exploration from colonization, "free enterprise from slavery, profit from plunder."

A very problematic work, *The Confidence-Man*, receives illuminating observations from John Bryant, after which Bryan C. Short praises *Typee* as a complex and energetic first novel.

Nancy Fredricks traces Melville's attempts, after the very masculine *Moby-Dick*, to portray women characters for a partly feminine audience.

Redburn is studied by Stephen Mathewson as an autobiographical narrative, while *Israel Potter* is found by Bill Christopherson to be Melville's most compassionate book.

Judith Hiltner subtly traces a pattern of male intrusion into realms of female suffering in a number of Melvillean texts, after which the plenitude of *Mardi* is explored by John Wenke.

Whether the prime protagonist of *Moby-Dick* is Ishmael, Captain Ahab, or the White Whale is judiciously weighed by Merton M. Sealts, Jr., while Stanton Garner interestingly presents Melville's strong reaction to the police state of Bourbon Naples, a repulsion that helped contribute to *Billy Budd*.

The psychological weavings of *Billy Budd* are followed by Thomas Hove, after which Melville's maddening (to me) *Pierre* is bravely confronted by Cindy Weinstein.

In this volume's final essay, Peter Bellis takes us into the harsh world of *White-Jacket*, where the cat-o'-nine tails dominates.

HAROLD BLOOM

Introduction

I

Melville's *The Piazza Tales* was published in 1856, five years after *Moby-Dick*. Two of the six tales—"Bartleby, The Scrivener" and "Benito Cereno"—are commonly and rightly accepted among Melville's strongest works, together with *Moby-Dick* and (rather more tenuously) *The Confidence-Man* and *Billy Budd, Sailor*. Two others—"The Encantadas, or Enchanted Isles" and "The Bell-Tower"—seem to me even better, being equal to the best moments in *Moby-Dick*. Two of the *The Piazza Tales* are relative trifles: "The Piazza" and "The Lightning-Rod Man." A volume of novellas with four near-masterpieces is an extraordinary achievement, but particularly poignant if, like Melville, you had lost your reading public after the early success of *Typee* and *Omoo*, the more equivocal reception of *Mardi*, and the return to a wider audience with *Redburn* and even more with *White Jacket*. *Moby-Dick* today is, together with *Leaves of Grass* and *Huckleberry Finn*, one of the three candidates for our national epic, but like *Leaves of Grass* it found at first only the one great reader (Hawthorne for Melville, Emerson for Whitman) and almost no popular response. What was left of Melville's early audience was killed off by the dreadful *Pierre*, a year after *Moby-Dick*, and despite various modern salvage attempts *Pierre* certainly is unreadable, in the old-fashioned sense of that now critically abused word. You just cannot get through it, unless you badly want and need to do so.

1

The best of *The Piazza Tales* show the post-*Pierre* Melville writing for himself, possibly Hawthorne, and a few strangers. Himself the sole support of wife, four children, mother and several sisters, Melville was generally in debt from at least 1855 on, and Hawthorne and Richard Henry Dana, though they tried, could not get the author of *Pierre* appointed to a consulate. In the late 1850s, the tormented and shy Melville attempted the lecture circuit, but as he was neither a pulpit-pounder like Henry Ward Beecher, nor a preternaturally eloquent sage like Ralph Waldo Emerson, he failed rather badly. Unhappily married, mother-ridden, an apparent literary failure; the author of *The Piazza Tales* writes out of the depths. Steeped, as were Carlyle and Ruskin, in the King James Bible, Melville no more believed in the Bible than did Carlyle and Ruskin. But even as *Moby-Dick* found its legitimate and overwhelming precursors in the Bible, Spenser, Shakespeare and Milton, so do *The Piazza Tales*. Melville's rejection of Biblical theology, his almost Gnostic distrust of nature and history alike, finds powerful expression in *The Piazza Tales,* as it did throughout all his later fictional prose and his verse.

II

"The Bell-Tower" is a tale of only fifteen pages but it has such resonance and strength that each rereading gives me the sense that I have experienced a superb short novel. Bannadonna, "the great mechanician, the unblest foundling," seeking to conquer a larger liberty, like Prometheus, instead extended the empire of necessity. His great Bell-Tower, intended to be the noblest in Italy, survives only as "a stone pine," a "black massed stump." It is the new tower of Babel:

> Like Babel's, its base was laid in a high hour of renovated earth, following the second deluge, when the waters of the Dark Ages had dried up, and once more the green appeared. No wonder that, after so long and deep submersion, the jubilant expectation of the race should, as with Noah's sons, soar into Shinar aspiration.
>
> In firm resolve, no man in Europe at that period went beyond Bannadonna. Enriched through commerce with the Levant, the state in which he lived voted to have the noblest Bell-Tower in Italy. His repute assigned him to be architect.
>
> Stone by Stone, month by month, the tower rose. Higher, higher; snail-like in pace, but torch or rocket in its pride.
>
> After the masons would depart, the builder, standing alone upon its ever-ascending summit, at close of every day saw that he overtopped still higher walls and trees. He would tarry till a late hour there, wrapped in schemes of other and still loftier

piles. Those who of saints' days thronged the spot—hanging to the rude poles of scaffolding, like sailors on yards, or bees on boughs, unmindful of lime and dust, and falling chips of stone—their homage not the less inspirited him to self-esteem.

At length the holiday of the Tower came. To the sound of viols, the climax-stone slowly rose in air, and, amid that firing of ordnance, was laid by Bannadonna's hands upon the final course. Then mounting it, he stood erect, alone, with folded arms; gazing upon the white summits of blue inland Alps, and whiter crests of bluer Alps off-shore—sights invisible from the plain. Invisible, too, from thence was that eye he turned below, when, like the cannon booms, came up to him the people's combustion of applause.

That which stirred them so was, seeing with what serenity the builder stood three hundred feet in air, upon an unrailed perch. This none but he durst do. But his periodic standing upon the pile, in each stage of its growth—such discipline had its last result.

We recognize Captain Ahab in Bannadonna, though Ahab has his humanities, and the great mechanician lacks all pathos. Ahab plays out an avenger's tragedy, but Bannadonna's purpose lacks any motivation except pride. His pride presumably is related to the novelist's, and the black stump that is the sole remnant of the Bell-Tower might as well be *Pierre*, little as Melville would have welcomed such an identification. The sexual mortification of the image is palpable, yet adds little to the comprehensiveness of what will become Bannadonna's doom, since that necessarily is enacted as a ritual of castration anyway. Melville's Prometheans, Ahab and Bannadonna, have an overtly Gnostic quarrel with the heavens. Melville's narratives, at their strongest, know implicitly what Kafka asserted with rare explicitness in his great parable:

The crows maintain that a single crow could destroy the heavens. Doubtless that is so, but it proves nothing against the heavens for the heavens signify simply: the impossibility of crows.

In Melville, the heavens signify simply: the impossibility of Ahab and of Bannadonna. Ahab is a hunter and not a builder, but to destroy Moby-Dick or to build the Bell-Tower would be to pile up the Tower of Babel and get away with it:

If it had been possible to build the Tower of Babel without ascending it, the work would have been permitted.

Kafka's aphorism would be an apt title for Melville's story, with Bannadonna who has built his tower partly in order to ascend it and to stand "three hundred feet in air, upon an unrailed perch." Kafka could have told Bannadonna that a labyrinth underground would have been better, though of course that too would not have been permitted, since the heavens would have regarded it as the pit of Babel:

> What are you building?—I want to dig a subterranean passage. Some progress must be made. My station up there is much too high.
> We are digging the pit of Babel.

Bannadonna is closest to the most extraordinary of the Kafkan parables concerning the Tower, in which a scholar maintains that the Great Wall of China "alone would provide for the first time in the history of mankind a secure foundation for the new Tower of Babel. First the wall, therefore, and then the tower." The final sentence of "The Great Wall and the Tower of Babel" could have impressed Melville as the best possible commentary upon Bannadonna-Melville, both in his project and his fate:

> There were many wild ideas in people's heads at that time—this scholar's book is only one example—perhaps simply because so many were trying to join forces as far as they could for the achievement of a single aim. Human nature, essentially changeable, unstable as the dust, can endure no restraint; if it binds itself it soon begins to tear madly at its bonds, until it rends everything asunder, the wall, the bonds and its very self.

The fall of Bannadonna commences with the casting of the great bell:

> The unleashed metals bayed like hounds. The workmen shrunk. Through their fright, fatal harm to the bell was dreaded. Fearless as Shadrach, Bannadonna, rushing through the glow, smote the chief culprit with his ponderous ladle. From the smitten part, a splinter was dashed into the seething mass, and at once was melted in.

That single blemish is evidently Melville's personal allegory for whatever sense of guilt, in his own pained judgment, flawed his own achievement, even in *Moby-Dick*. More interesting is Bannadonna's creation of a kind of *golem* or Frankensteinean monster, charmingly called Haman, doubtless in tribute to the villain of the Book of Esther. Haman, intended to be the bell-ringer, is meant also: "as a partial type of an ulterior creature," a titanic helot who would be called Talus, like the rather sinister iron man who wields an iron flail against the rebellious Irish in the savage Book V of Spenser's *The Faerie Queene*. But Talus is never created; Haman is quite enough to immolate the ambitious artist, Bannadonna:

> And so, for the interval, he was oblivious of his creature; which, not oblivious of him, and true to its creation, and true to its heedful winding up, left its post precisely at the given moment; along its well-oiled route, slid noiselessly towards its mark; and aiming at the hand of Una, to ring one clangorous note, dully smote the intervening brain of Bannadonna, turned backwards to it; the manacled arms then instantly upspringing to their hovering poise. The falling body clogged the thing's return; so there it stood, still impending over Bannadonna, as if whispering some post-mortem terror. The chisel lay dropped from the hand, but beside the hand; the oil-flask spilled across the iron track.

Which of his own works destroyed Melville? Juxtapose the story's deliberately Addisonian or Johnsonian conclusion with the remarkable stanza in Hart Crane's "The Broken Tower" that it helped inspire, and perhaps a hint emerges, since Crane was a superb interpreter of Melville:

> So the blind slave obeyed its blinder lord; but, in obedience, slew him. So the creator was killed by the creature. So the bell was too heavy for the tower. So that bell's main weakness was where man's blood had flawed it. And so pride went before the fall.

> The bells, I say, the bells break down their tower;
> And swing I know not where. Their tongues engrave
> Membrane through marrow, my long-scattered score
> Of broken intervals . . . And I, their sexton slave!

Crane is both Bannadonna and Haman, a complex fate darker even than Melville's, who certainly had represented himself as Bannadonna. The Bell-Tower of Bannadonna perhaps was *Pierre* but more likely *Moby-Dick* itself, Melville's "long-scattered score / of broken intervals" even as *The Bridge* was Hart Crane's. This is hardly to suggest that Haman is Captain Ahab. Yet Melville's "wicked book," as he called *Moby-Dick* in a famous letter to Hawthorne, indeed may have slain something vital in its author, if only in his retrospective consciousness.

III

"Canst thou draw out Leviathan with a hook?," God's taunting question to Job, can be said to be answered, by Captain Ahab, with a "Yes!" in thunder. Job's God wins, Ahab loses, and the great white Leviathan swims away, harpooned yet towing Ahab with him. But Ahab's extraordinary last speech denies that Moby-Dick is the conqueror:

> I turn my body from the sun. What ho, Tashtego! let me hear thy hammer. Oh! ye three unsurrendered spires of mine; thou untracked keel; and only god-bullied hull; thou firm deck, and haughty helm, and Pole-pointed prow,—death-glorious ship! must ye then perish, and without me? Am I cut off from the last fond pride of meanest shipwrecked captains? Oh, lonely death on lonely life! Oh, now I feel my topmost greatness lies in my topmost grief. Ho, ho! from all your furthest bounds, pour ye now in, ye bold billows of my whole foregone life, and top this one piled comber of my death! Towards thee I roll, thou all-destroying but unconquering whale; to the last I grapple with thee; from hell's heart I stab at thee; for hate's sake I spit my last breath at thee. Sink all coffins and all hearses to one common pool! and since neither can be mine, let me then tow to pieces, while still chasing thee, though tied to thee, thou damned whale! *Thus,* I give up the spear!

Beyond the allusions—Shakespearean, Miltonic, Byronic—what rings out here is Melville's own grand self-echoing, which is of Father Mapple's sermon as it concludes:

> He drooped and fell away from himself for a moment; then lifting his face to them again, showed a deep joy in his eyes, as he cried out with a heavenly enthusiasm,—"But oh! shipmates! on the starboard hand of every woe, there is a sure delight; and higher the top of that delight, than the bottom of the woe is deep. Is not the main-truck higher than the kelson is low? Delight is to him—a far, far upward, and inward delight—who against the proud gods and commodores of this earth, ever stands forth his own inexorable self. Delight is to him whose strong arms yet support him, when the ship of this base treacherous world has gone down beneath him. Delight is to him, who gives no quarter in the truth, and kills, brns, and destroys all sin though he pluck it out from under the robes of Senators and Judges. Delight,—top-gallant delight is

to him, who acknowledges no law or lord, but the Lord his God, and is only a patriot to heaven. Delight is to him, whom all the waves of the billows of the seas of the boisterous mob can never shake from this sure Keel of the Ages. And eternal delight and deliciousness will be his, who coming to lay him down, can say with his final breath—O Father!—chiefly known to me by Thy rod—mortal or immortal here I die. I have striven to be Thine, more than to be this world's, or mine own. Yet this is nothing; I leave eternity to Thee, for what is man that he should live out the lifetime of his God?"

Father Mapple's intensity moves from "a sure delight, and higher the top of that delight" through "a far, far upward, and inward delight" on to "Delight,—top-gallant delight is to him," heaven's patriot. Ahab's equal but antithetical intensity proceeds from "unsurrendered spires of mine" through "my topmost greatness lies in my topmost grief" to end in "top this one piled comber of my death." After which the *Pequod* goes down with Tashtego hammering a hawk to the mainmast, an emblem not of being "only a patriot to heaven" but rather of a Satanic dragging of "a living part of heaven along with her." Admirable as Father Mapple is, Ahab is certainly the hero, more Promethean than Satanic, and we need not conclude (as so many critics do) that Melville chooses Mapple's stance over Ahab's. William Faulkner, in 1927, asserted that the book he most wished he had written was *Moby-Dick*, and called Ahab's fate "a sort of Golgotha of the heart become immutable as bronze in the sonority of its plunging ruin," characteristically adding: "There's a death for a man, now."

As Faulkner implied, there is a dark sense in which Ahab intends his Golgotha, like Christ's, to be a vicarious atonement for all of staggering Adam's woes. When Melville famously wrote to Hawthorne: "I have written a wicked book," he was probably quite serious. The common reader does not come to love Ahab, and yet there is a serious disproportion between that reader's awe of, and admiration for, Ahab, and the moral dismissal of the monomaniacal hero by many scholarly critics. Ahab seems to provoke academic critics rather more even than Milton's Satan does. Ishmael, presumably speaking for Melville, consistently emphasizes Ahab's greatness. And so does Ahab himself, as when he confronts the corposants or St. Elmo's fire, in the superb Chapter 119, "The Candles":

Oh! thou clear spirit of clear fire, whom on these seas I as Persian once did worship, till in the sacramental act so burned by thee, that to this hour I bear the scar; I now know thee, thou clear spirit, and I know that thy right worship is defiance. To neither love nor reverence wilt thou be kind; and e'en for hate thou canst but kill; and all are killed. No fearless fool now fronts thee. I own thy speechless, placeless power; but to the last gasp of my earthquake life will dispute its unconditional, unintegral mastery in me. In the midst of the personified impersonal, a personality stands here. Though but a point at best; whensoe'er I came; wheresoe'er I go; yet while I earthly live, the queenly personality lives in me, and feels her royal rights. But war is pain, and hate is woe. Come in thy lowest form of love, and I will kneel and kiss thee; but at thy highest, come as mere supernal power; and though thou launchest navies of full-freighted worlds, there's that in here that still remains indifferent. Oh, thou clear spirit, of thy fire thou madest me, and like a true child of fire, I breathe it back to thee.

If Ahab has a religion, it is Persian or rather Parsee, and so Zoroastrian. But Melville has not written a Zoroastrian hymn to the benign light for Ahab to chant. Ahab's invocation is clearly Gnostic in spirit and in substance, since the light is hailed as being both ambiguous and ambivalent. Ahab himself knows that the clear spirit of clear fire is not from the Alien God but from the Demiurge, and he seems to divide the Demiurge into both the "lowest form of love" and the "highest . . . mere supernal power." Against this dialectical or even self-contradictory spirit, Ahab sets himself as personality rather than as moral character: "In the midst of the personified impersonal, a personality stands here." As a personality, Ahab confronts "the personified impersonal," which he astonishingly names as his father, and defies, as knowing less than he, Ahab, knows:

I own thy speechless, placeless power; said I not so? Nor was it wrung from me; nor do I now drop these links. Thou canst blind; but I can then grope. Thou canst consume; but I can then be ashes. Take the homage of these poor eyes, and shutter-hands. I would not take it. The lightning flashes through my skull; mine eye-balls ache and ache; my whole beaten brain seems as beheaded, and rolling on some stunning ground. Oh, oh! Yet blindfold, yet will I talk to thee. Light though thou be, thou leapest out of darkness; but I am darkness leaping out of light, leaping out of thee! The javelins cease; open eyes; see, or not? There burn the flames! Oh, thou magnanimous! now I do glory in my genealogy. But thou art but my fiery father; my sweet mother, I know not. Oh, cruel! what hast thou done with her? There lies my puzzle; but thine is greater. Thou knowest not how came ye, hence callest thyself unbegun. I know that of me, which thou knowest not of thyself, oh, thou omnipotent. There is some unsuffusing thing beyond thee, thou clear spirit, to whom all thy eternity is but time, all thy creativeness mechanical. Through thee, thy flaming self, my scorched eyes do dimly see it. Oh, thou foundling fire, thou hermit immemorial, thou too hast thy incommunicable riddle, thy unparticipated grief. Here again with haughty agony, I read my sire. Leap! leap up, and lick the sky! I leap with thee; I burn with thee; would fain be welded with thee; defyingly I worship thee!

The Gnosticism here is explicit and unmistakeable, since "some unsuffusing thing beyond thee, thou clear spirit, to whom all thy eternity is but time, all thy creativeness mechanical" is certainly what the Gnostics called the true or alien God, but off from our cosmos. But who is Ahab's sweet mother"? Ahab scarcely recognizes a benign aspect of our cosmos, so that his mother, in Gnostic terms, must be the original abyss, preceding the Demiurge's false creation. But, as Melville knew, that motherly abyss, in Gnosticism, is also the forefather or Alien God. Echoing the Gnostics' savage reading of the opening of Genesis, Ahab insinuates that his father, the Demiurge, begat him upon the true God, or abyss, his mother. Rebelling (though equivocally) against his father, Ahab proudly asserts his mother's knowledge of origins against his father's ignorance. When Ahab cries out that he wishes to be welded with his father, we rightly should flinch, because hat is the book's true wickedness. Ahab, like Bannadonna, like Melville himself, desires to be one with the Demiurge.

IV

The visionary center of *Moby-Dick,* and so of all Melville, as critics always lave recognized, is Chapter 42, "The Whiteness of the Whale." It is Ishmael's meditation, and not Ahab's, and yet how far is it from Ahab? Ishmael is himself half a Gnostic:

Though in many of its aspects this visible world seems formed in love, the invisible spheres were formed in fright.

Closer to Carlyle than to Emerson, this extraordinary sentence is he prelude to the final paragraph of Ishmael's reverie:

But not yet have we solved the incantation of this whiteness, and learned why it appeals with such power to the soul; and more strange and far more portentous—why, as we have seen, it is at once the most meaning symbol of spiritual things, nay, the very veil of the Christian's Deity; and yet should be as it is, the intensifying agent in things the most appalling to mankind.

Is it that by its indefiniteness it shadows forth the heartless voids and immensities of the universe, and thus stabs us from behind with the thought of annihilation, when beholding the white depths of the milky way? Or is it, that as in essence whiteness is not so much a color as the visible absence of color, and at the same time the concrete of all colors; is it for these reasons that there is such a dumb blankness, full of meaning, in a wide landscape of snows—a colorless, all-color of atheism from which we shrink? And when we consider that other theory of the natural philosophers, that all other earthly hues—every stately or lovely emblazoning—the worst tinges of sunset skies and woods; yea, and the gilded velvets of butterflies, and the butterfly cheeks of young girls; all these are but subtile deceits, not actually inherent in substances, but only laid on from without; so that all deified Nature absolutely paints like the harlot, whose allurements cover nothing but the charnel-house within; and when we proceed further, and consider that the mystical cosmetic which produces every one of her hues, the great principle of light, for ever remains white or colorless in itself, and if operating without medium upon matter, would touch all objects, even tulips and roses, with its own blank tinge—pondering all this, the palsied universe lies before us a leper; and like wilful travellers in Lapland, who refuse to wear colored and coloring glasses upon their eyes, so the wretched infidel gazes himself blind at the monumental white shroud that wraps all the prospect around him. And of all these things the Albino whale was the symbol. Wonder ye then at the fiery hunt?

Ishmael's "visible absence of color" becomes the trope of whiteness, "a dumb blankness," similar to its descendant in the beach-scene of Wallace Stevens's "The Auroras of Autumn":

> Here, being visible is being white,
> Is being of the solid of white, the accomplishment
> Of an extremist in an exercise . . .
> The season changes. A cold wind chills the beach.
> The long lines of it grow longer, emptier,
> A darkness gathers though it does not fall.
>
> And the whiteness grows less vivid on the wall.
> The man who is walking turns blankly on the sand.

Melville and Stevens alike shrink from "a colorless, all-color of atheism," not because they are theists, but precisely because they both believe in and fear the Demiurge. When Ishmael cries out: "Wonder ye then at the fiery hunt?", he refutes all those critics, moral and psychoanalytic, who condemn Ahab as being immoral or insane. It was Melville, after all, who wrote two memorable quatrains, in the mode of Blake, which he entitled "Fragments of a Lost Gnostic Poem of the 12th Century":

> Found a family, build a state,
> The pledged event is still the same:
> Matter in end will never abate
> His ancient brutal claim.
>
> Indolence is heaven's ally here,
> And energy the child of hell:
> The Good Man pouring from his pitcher clear,
> But brims the poisoned well

There the Gnosticism is overt, and we are left a little cold, since even an heretical doctrine strikes us as tendentious, as having too clear a design upon us. Perhaps "The Bell-Tower" is a touch tendentious also. *Moby-Dick,* despite its uneven rhetoric, despite its excessive debt to Shakespeare, Milton and Byron, is anything but tendentious. It remains the darker half of our national epic, complementing *Leaves of Grass* and *Huckleberry Finn,* works of more balance certainly, but they do not surpass or eclipse Melville's version of darkness visible.

MILTON R. STERN

Towards "Bartleby the Scrivener"

When Ishmael asserted that the changefulness of life 'requires a strong decoction of Seneca and the Stoics to enable you to grin and bear it,' he was offering a jocular way to handle the shock and horror that accompany the discovery of our human oneness in our common, mortal victimization by the conditions of life. "Bartleby the Scrivener" is a tale of that discovery, not by seafarers in the vastness of natural force and space, but by landlubbers in claustral immurement.

Some critics are tempted to find stoic heroism in the pallid law-office clerk and to dismiss the lawyer-narrator as merely a wicked victimizer. Other critics more wisely sense a more complex connection between the two men. When I follow the lead offered by a view of Bartleby as stoic hero, I find that treating the tale as an example of Bartleby's stoicism results in oversimplifications and dead ends that do not account for tone and imagery. The insistence on stoicism is negatively useful because it leads to the conclusion that Melville was playing with other, deeper aspects of victimization than grinning and bearing it. Attempts to heroine Bartleby with ideological particularity diminish the dimensions of this perennially fascinating tale, so central among Melville's works. All such attempts seem to arise from the readers' desires to identify and secure Melville within their own rather than his contexts. A

The Stoic Strain in American Literature, edited by Duane J. Macmillan (Toronto: University of Toronto Press, 1979): pp. 19–41. © 1979 University of Toronto Press.

review of "Bartleby" criticism is a useful approach to critical caveats which define the directions that future readings might usefully take.

Melville made mirrors. No other writer in English since Shakespeare has assumed so many protean shapes, and so invitingly, for his readers. "Bartleby" especially is one of the weird pieces in which readers find whatever they came to seek. The ideological possibilities of "Bartleby" are enormous: the seer of psychiatric, political, literary, metaphysical, or religious positions is sure to find in the tale a paradigm for his own advocacy. So, a critic reading critics becomes like Ishmael contemplating water as the mirror of the self: 'And still deeper the meaning of that story of Narcissus, who because he could not grasp the tormenting, mild image he saw in the fountain, plunged into it and was drowned. But that same image, we ourselves see in all rivers and oceans. It is the image of the ungraspable phantom of life; and this is the key to it all.' What image could be more tormenting and mild than that of the tormenting, mild Bartleby? The critical literature concerning "Bartleby" exposes the process of interpretative criticism as very often a narcissistic operation in which each reader sees the tale as a mirror of the Gestalt within his own mind.

But the story itself is a fixed thing; it undergoes no more revision by Melville. Though each reader shifts it, unlike water it does not shift itself. Some Gestalts fix more of the story's details than do others. If much criticism is foolish, not all criticism is useless. And each critic knows that although he too will find the key to it all in a version of his own vision, there are priorities of value to be found in a criticism of the criticism; some visions are better than others.

The political Gestalt of Leo Marx's "Melville's Parable of the Walls,"[1] for instance, remains a valuable mirroring because it illuminates more details within the story than does a set of literary parallels like Egbert S. Oliver's "A Second Look at 'Bartleby,'"[2] which sees the pallid scrivener as a type of Thoreau. When we move beyond the story to the references the criticism furnishes, Marx provides a more usably wide focus: his Gestalt expands rather than contracts the area within which the story exists. For all its gratuitous contumaciousness, an essay like Kingsley Widmer's "'Bartleby' and Nihilistic Resistance"[3] fixes many more details in a brilliantly suggestive and useful mirror than does the pendantically narrow angle of vision of works like Mario L. D'Avanzo's "Melville's 'Bartleby' and Carlyle,"[4] which, in effect, makes Carlyle the ghostwriter of "Bartleby."

When George Bluestone commented on the making of his film out of the tale, he provided pertinent caveats for critics precisely because he had to specify details in order to recreate them in another medium, and therefore had to examine closely the components of his own Gestalt. His activities led him quickly to a concentration on what was usable for translation, and this process led him, in turn, to an important conclusion about the puzzling scrivener: one cannot specify in event, in historical of literary parallel, or in psycho-biography, exactly what made Bartleby the way he was. Bluestone realized that his film would lose power if it attempted to show the cause of Bartleby's depression precisely because in this area Melville provided no usable details. The film would have to centre on what Melville did provide, which was the effect of whatever it was that turned Bartleby into Bartleby: 'To explain the malaise is to explain it away.'[5] In accounting for the criticism available to him it 1962, when he made the film, Bluestone summed up his findings as follows: 'Critics, have seen . . . ["Bartleby"] as a tale (1) of exorcism, in which Bartleby figures as surrogate for Melville, the artist protesting the killing demands of hack work; (2) of psychosis, a classic case of depression, or catatonic schizophrenia,[6] with overtones of homosexuality; (3) of the alter ego, Bartleby as a projection of the death-urge in the Lawyer, a kind of early 'Secret Sharer'; (4) of social criticism, a critique of industrial America symbolized by an implacable Wall Street. Certainly there are overtones of all these.[7] There is, however, another category at least as important as any that Bluestone has listed, and that is the Gestalt in which the tale is seen as a metaphysical treatise in which man is a homeless wanderer in a universe of indifference, meaninglessness, and absence of moral point or purpose. This last critical vision often merges with Bluestone's first and fourth categories, and provides one of the few general areas of critical agreement.

When we look at the criticism that appeared up to the time of Donald M. Fiene's bibliography,[8] which includes work published through 1965, and add to it a few pieces published later, we become aware that the "Bartleby" mirror attracts and reflects more water-gazers in certain areas than in others.[9] When many disparate individuals begin to fix the tale into one or two dominant shapes, and especially when those shapes encompass and account for the greatest number of details in the tale, the cumulative effect is to make criticism a useful act as it incrementally defines areas of agreement and, more important, the areas that are problematical and require more and new attention. Accumulated criticism spotlights the points at which we must try to shift our own Gestalts and begin anew with a basic experience of the details in question.

Those who see Bartleby as a type of the writer living in but alienated by a heartless bourgeois society join at many points with those who see the tale as a metaphysical and psychological examination of the terrible loneliness that results from a vision of the universe as empty of meaning: Bartleby becomes the typal figure who repudiates established society, its shallow vision of human experience, and its concomitant easy beliefs. For both groups of readers the lawyer and Bartleby represent conflicting opposites: the lawyer represents the establishment, the unexamined life, the surface vision with its facile hopes; and Bartleby is his rebellious, stoic victim. Depending upon the critic's Gestalt, the lawyer represents (1) the selfish capitalist society; (2) the repressive world of law and order; (3) the world of rationality, (3a) the world of self-deceiving rationalization, (3b) the world of genteel consciousness; (4) the world of orthodoxy; (5) the world of surfaces; (6) all of the above. Bartleby represents (1) the man who will no longer conform to the standards of the capitalist world; (2) Christianity, or Christliness, or—sometimes—Christ; (3) the unconscious, (3a) the hidden recognition of the world as meaningless chaos, as the absurd, (3b) the lawyer's conscience, (3c) the world of preferences, will, and revolution; (4) the stoic tragic view; (5) the defeated stoic writer-artist-rebel; (6) the heroic stoic writer-artist-rebel; (7) the defeat of the stoic human will; (8) the stoic triumph of human will; and (9) any of the above that are not too obviously mutually contradictory.

Many of those who see Bartleby as a redemptive challenger of the lawyer see him as a type of Christ,[10] while those who see him as a passive or defeated challenger may make him a type of the absurd itself.[11] The view of him as Christ is as much a catch-all as any other category, ranging from a rather rigid and silly assertion that the lawyer is Jehovah, Bartleby is Christ, Turkey is Michael, Nippers is Lucifer, and Ginger Nut—the poor little kid—is Raphael (see John Gardner, note 9), to Bruce Franklin's much more useful and suggestive considerations of the mythic possibilities within the tale (see note 9). It is also possible to see Bartleby as Christ, even though passive and defeated, if one sees him as an 'emasculated' Christ (see William Stein, note 10). But whether he is seen as active or passive, almost all critics agree that he typifies the principle of *non serviam* in whatever world he is said to inhabit.[12] The line of logic leads critics from the *non serviam* relationship Bartleby maintains with his employer to a speculation about Bartleby as a kind of *doppelgänger* or, at least, a conscience for the lawyer. Here too there is a range of opinion, from Bartleby as the embodiment of the principle of the English Court of Chancery, 'the Keeper of the King's Conscience,' to Bartleby as the lawyer's hidden death-wish.[13]

Three firm agreements emerge from the welter of hermeneutics, propaedeutics, and ephemera. One is that Bartleby becomes the repudiator of the civilization and vision that the lawyer stands for. The second is that Bartleby cannot be defined except through a definition of the lawyer. The third is that the lawyer, at least at the beginning of the story, is the bad guy. I delay discussion of the first until I look at Bartleby a bit later in this essay. The second should be obvious, by virtue of the narrative method, without any critical aids. The third is fixed through a series of self-revelations that every critic who has examined the lawyer has noted.

The revelations always cited are the lawyer's 'conviction that the easiest way of life is the best'; that he never suffers any real involvement in his law cases to invade his peace; that he loves the 'cool tranquillity' of his

'snug retreat' as he does 'a snug business among rich men's bonds, and mort-
gages, and title-deads'; that he is considered to be an 'eminently safe man';
that he loves being associated with John Jacob Astor, that he loves Astor's
name, which 'hath a rounded and orbicular sound to it, and rings like unto
bullion'; that he is proud that John Jacob Astor has named the lawyer's two
grand points as prudence and method; that he is greedy about the Court of
Chancery and is upset only when easy income from the Master's office is
denied him through dissolution of the court—*that* invades his peace if equity
and justice do not; that he uses people—his clerks—selfishly, putting up with
their vagaries not out of any really compassionate humanity but only out of
his sense that they are 'most valuable' to him; that he is concerned only with
the appearances of things and desires decorum and seemliness at all human
costs; that he tolerates Bartleby at first not out of real compassion or fraternal
feeling, but because to humour Bartleby 'in his strange wilfullness, will cost
me little or nothing while I lay up in my soul what will eventually prove a
sweet morsel for my conscience'; that he betrays and abandons Bartleby while
mouthing pious and/or legalistic rationalizations for refusing responsibility
and running away. In short, the lawyer reveals in every way that he is a smug
and heartless man of small vision and hypocritical Christianity, that he is a
respectable, bourgeois cannibal, a conformist to all the surfaces, gentilities,
selfishnesses, and human enormities of established values, law, and order. He
is mindless of pain, soulless to real suffering, compassionless to any possible
vision that sees the establishment's world as a lie. Whether he discloses his
consciousness as a factor of political, economic, social, metaphysical, or psychological reality, he is a shallow and complacent man of easy optimism.

In detailing the lawyer there is critical agreement that the world he rules
dooms human activity to a walled-in (almost all critics, especially since Leo
Marx, have specified the imagery of the walls: that need not be done again)
round of alternating acquiescence and frustration (almost all critics have
noted the complementary ante- and post-meridian changes in the behaviour
and personalities of Turkey and Nippers: that need not be done again). People
struggle between desire and submission in the lawyer's world—if Bartleby's
opting-out is characterized by 'I prefer not to,' Turkey's key phrase is 'with
submission, sir'—and spend half their lives conforming to their lot and half
their lives raging against it. Yet, the established world is inhabited by people
whose very vision is walled-in for, despite their longings for freedom from
their hated rounds of monotonous sameness in which everything and everyone is a copy and a repetition, they uphold the system: what they aspire
to is the lawyer's top-dog position in the walled-in world. The narrator is
interested only in containing and repressing the periods of resentment in
which people do not engage in profit-making labour for the boss, in which
they turn against the symbols of their monotonous lives (Turkey blots his

papers in steaming fury, Nippers grinds his teeth and fights with his hated desk), and in which people have no real individuality—no real names, but only nicknames—but merely alternatingly duplicate each other with fits that differentiate them only so that they reflect each other. The lawyer wants to see all activity and appearances buttoned up into law, order, decorum, and profitable routine: everyone is to spend his life copying the law indeed. Whenever the lawyer confronts Bartleby in a serious showdown, he buttons things up. 'I buttoned up my coat, balanced myself, advanced slowly towards him . . .' 'What shall I do? I now said to myself, buttoning up my coat to the last button.' The buttoning is itself an enactment of a contemporary slang phrase, 'button up,' meaning 'shut up,' 'shape up.' The phrase, like the action, is one of repression, suppression, conformity.

If the walled-in workers yearn, like Nippers, 'the truth of the matter was, Nippers knew not what he wanted. Or, if he wanted anything, it was to be rid of his scrivener's table altogether.' However, Nippers thinks that the way to be rid of his table is by taking on even more of the same, by succeeding, like the lawyer, by continuing the system, not by opting-out of or by destroying it. His twin vices of ambition and indigestion (Turkey's twin characteristics are, similarly, submission and insolence), are indicators of his impatience with how far he has come in a system in which he too wants to be a lawyer. His ambition 'was evinced by a certain impatience at the duties of a mere copyist, an unwarrantable usurpation of strictly professional affairs, such as the original drawing up of legal documents.' Thus Turkey, also, when presented with a token of status—fittingly, the lawyer's cast-off coat 'which buttoned straight up from the knee to the neck'—becomes insolently and snobbishly restive not with the world he lives in but merely with his position within it. And Ginger Nut, the little son of a carter, also plays at being a lawyer with his little desk in the corner. In sum, the ordinary population, in its fits and frustrations and frenzies and alternations, acquiesces, with submission, sir, to the values of the world epitomized by the lawyer. Melville's metaphors for the populace, like Shakespeare's, never give us a picture of a revolutionary mass with class consciousness despite several wistful critical attempts to find in Melville a major literary neo-Marxian voice.

Given the nature of the world's common inhabitants, the snug lawyer becomes even more the enemy of human freedom when he blandly and civilly views the inhabitants of his world not as people but in the way he first views Bartleby—as 'a valuable acquisition.' Committing the unforgivable sin of reducing people to things, he thinks that, like any acquisition, people can be bought. Twice, while trying to get Bartleby out of his life, he gives him money. Commercializing all human relations, he is yet smug enough to feel that Bartleby's 'perverseness seemed ungrateful, considering the undeniable good usage and indulgence he had received from me.' He 'trembled to think' of what might happen to his world if the implications of 'prefer' were to become the basis of human conduct—button up, boy. Contemplating Bartleby's incredible and fantastic plight, the lawyer allows 'necessities connected with my business' to 'tyrannize over all other considerations.' He congratulates himself that his assumptions about Bartleby's departure will get rid of Bartleby in a seemly and decorous way: he can do something that nags at his conscience, but is satisfied as long as appearances and the *status quo* remain undisturbed. He indulges in 'sweet charity's sake' only as a guarantee of his own safety—he continues to buy human beings and human actions. He is constantly concerned that Bartleby is 'scandalizing [his] professional reputation,' and even in the Tombs he tries to placate his conscience by attempting to talk Bartleby into enjoying the sky and the grass—in prison. In sum, that is the case against the lawyer-narrator, and up to this point almost all critics agree.[14]

A quantitative overview of the criticism suggests that this, too, is ground that need not be gone over yet once more, and can be taken as a given in the tale. But just beyond this agreement lies one of the rocks upon which criticism splits, and that is the question of whether or not the narrator changes. Some see that modifications must be made in the condemnation of the lawyer.[15] Generally, the arguments favouring the proposition that the lawyer undergoes a change of vision insist (1) that there is no possibility of salvation for Bartleby, no matter how great his lonely integrity may be, and that there is a possibility of salvation for the narrator, whose increasingly pained awareness of what Bartleby might be gives him a new sense of the connectedness of all humanity no matter how smug and shallow he was at the beginning; (2) that when all is said and done, it is a vast act of sentiment to see Bartleby as a rebel-hero only, for he effects no rebellion. All he does is to commit an ultimate withdrawal. So, too, it is dangerous to see Bartleby as stoic hero for, as we shall see, it is questionable at best that there are positive moral values shoring up Bartleby's bearing of his burden and, in any event, Bartleby does not in any positive way indicate how life may be borne. Just the opposite, in fact. But the narrator comes to feel the agony of the world at last: Melville is as much the lawyer as he is Bartleby, and to divide him into allegiance to only one aspect of himself is to oversimplify Melville's sense of reality by substituting a straw-man for the narrator who actually exists in the story. (3) For all that is wrong with the lawyer, Bartleby, finally, is socially irresponsible: he leads only towards death. All arguments that would modify the agreement about the initial self-presentation of the narrator depend upon the narrator's sympathetic acts and thoughts concerning Bartleby, upon the tone of the narratorial voice when the lawyer describes the Tombs and murmurs, 'with kings and counselors,' upon the section presenting the Dead Letters Office, and upon the tone of the narrator's final cry, 'Ah Bartleby! Ah humanity!'

Those who see the narrator as unredeemable and a total villain all denigrate as maudlin the lawyer's feelings when he begins to react deeply to Bartleby; they dismiss the epilogue as the 'thick Victorianism' of an attempt to furnish a liberal 'hard times' explanation for Bartleby, and refuse to see the narrator's last cry as anything but 'a last sentimental gesture.'[16] It is significant, for instance, that the most uncompromising view of the lawyer as villain not only sees him as 'incapable of moral regeneration' but fails to deal with or even mention the narrator's final cry.[17] The Dead Letters epilogue is seen suddenly and somehow as 'Melville's' rather than as the narrator's, for to attribute sensitivity and pained compassion to the narrator would ruin the thesis of unmixed villainy. In fact, all views of the narrator as unchanging villain sweep away every instance in which Melville makes the narrator's villainy problematical without ever distinguishing in terms of tone between the narrator's moments of smugness and his moments of pain.

Well, I find that there is no arguing about tone. If there is any one aspect of literary art that is crucial to comprehension it is tone, and of all aspects of art it is the one most encysted by the Gestalt in which the reader sees the parts. As just one more critic I can only assert that a quick juxtaposition of parts will establish tone. Read the opening passages through the Turkey and Nippers episodes. Then immediately read the entire Sunday morning sequence detailing the narrator's 'overpowering stinging melancholy' as distinct from the mere sentimentality of 'a not unpleasant sadness' and his consequent Melvillean awareness of human fraternity in mortal woe. Then read the episode in the Tombs. Then read the epilogue. The juxtaposition must—should—create at least a sense of uneasiness in the critics who assert that the narrator never changes. There is, I submit, a palpable shift in Melville's presentation of the narrator, and it is discernible at the crucial episode—almost exactly half way through the story—of the narrator's Sunday morning visit to his office. Up to that moment Melville has the narrator disclose only those self-revelatory ironies and pseudo-sympathies that destroy the lawyer's assumed image. He is indeed the bad guy. But for the remaining half of the story Melville has the narrator vacillate between continued self-exposing hypocrisy and puzzled concern and pain, with the power of the sympathetic passages—the Tombs, the epilogue—gaining ascendency over the others. The nature of the narrator's consciousness begins to change. Does he still worry about being scandalized? Does he still try to explain Bartleby away? Is he still self-seeking and self-protective? Does he still fly into a rage? Does he still try to evade Bartleby? Of course. That is the truth. It is nothing but the truth. But it is not the whole truth. In the first half of the story there are no expressions of pain (astonishment, outrage, anger, and bewilderment, yes, but not the pain of his own deepest self's contact with Bartleby) or of confusion deeper than those of the law office proprieties. The last half of the story is full of them, including among them such awarenesses as the fact that 'I might give alms to his body; but his body did not pain him; it was his soul that suffered, and his soul I could not reach.' It is the narrator, after all, who becomes aware of Bartleby as 'alone, absolutely alone in the universe. A bit of wreck in the mid-Atlantic.' Continuing to act the hypocritical burgher, nevertheless, the narrator now has his consciousness focused on the knowledge that he has to wrench himself, almost in tears, 'from him whom I had so longed to be rid of.' Nowhere in the first half is there a physico-psychic jolt of current running between the narrator and Bartleby as there is in the death scene in the Tombs. And in the context of the Tombs the grub-man, fittingly named Mr. Cutlets in the original *Putnam's* version, makes even the lawyer's attempt to cheer Bartleby by pointing to grass and sky less a matter of blind smugness than one of pathetic failure. (Food as a pervasive motif in "Bartleby" should be the subject of a short critical essay, for the story is filled with instances of food and feeding. The negative relationship of oral gratification to total separation is a psychological rendition of the central question of nourishment and sustenance for human hope, for the ability of the human spirit to bear consciousness and pain and still live and remain human.) The narrator's reply to the grub-man, 'With kings and counselors,' draws the clear and distinct distance in insight, sympathy, and pain between the lawyer and the grub-man. At the beginning the lawyer was to Bartleby as the grub-man now is to the lawyer. One can refuse to recognize a meaningful change in the lawyer only by refusing to recognize that the second half of the story does prepare for an undeniable difference between the lawyer and the grub-man. Were there no change there could be no difference between the lawyer and the grub-man, for Mr. Cutlets is but a meaty, mindless, and relatively moneyless version of what the lawyer was at the beginning. Mr. Cutlets is an official grub inhabiting the same world of grubby morality that the lawyer's walled-in office does, and he can no more supply sustenance for Bartleby than can the lifeless bust of Cicero in the lawyer's office—the Cicero, no doubt, of *De officiis*. Yet, at the end of the story the difference between the grub-man and the narrator is a qualitative difference, not a mere difference in manner and education, but a difference in insight and sympathy, which is exactly what is denied by an unmixed view of the narrator. Even before the midpoint of the tale the narrator is not unmixed in his given qualities. Consider the following passage:

> He lives, then, on ginger-nuts, thought I; never eats a dinner, properly speaking; he must be a vegetarian, then; but no; he never eats even vegetables, he eats nothing but ginger-nuts. My mind then ran on in reveries concerning the probable effects upon the human constitution of living entirely on ginger-nuts. Ginger-nuts are so called, because they contain ginger as one of their peculiar

constituents, and the final flavoring one. Now, what was ginger? A hot, spicy thing. Was Bartleby hot and spicy? Not at all. Ginger, then, had no effect upon Bartleby. Probably he preferred it should have none.

This passage can be and has been fitted into ideologies that polemicize against the narrator. Yet all such critical ingenuity always misses one humble, simple, tonal, surface fact: the passage is mildly funny. The narrator has a sense of humour. The presentation of the clerks discloses an observer with a sense of humour that makes his paternalistic relationship to their vagaries not totally and solely a matter of selfish exploitation. Scattered throughout the tale on either side of the midpoint are small instances of humour which create the expectation that this same smug narrator might yet be a man with enough sensibilities to recognize a connection with Bartleby. As that metaphysical wanderer-narrator, Ishmael, from the very beginning is hintingly given qualities which will enable him to see the Ahab he admiringly repudiates as an extended aspect of his own human identity, so too that prudentially selfish lawyer-narrator from the very beginning is hintingly given qualities which will enable him to see that the Bartleby he will compassionately leave is inextricably interrelated with his own human identity. Surely there is a tonal difference not only between the narrator and the grub-man but also between the lawyer and all the other inhabitants and landlords and lawyers who do not for a moment see Bartleby as anything but a nuisance to be got rid of. The difference between the lawyer and the successors to his chambers is scanted or ignored by critics who fix the narrator as a single moral quantity, and for the same reasons that make them miss the intermittent humour of the tale.[18]

But, as I say, the tonal aspect of change in the lawyer cannot be argued: either you hear it or you do not. Rather, I would open a question which seems to me quite pertinent. Why has there been so much commentary on "Bartleby"? Why so much varied and fascinated response beyond the agreement about the preliminary characterization of the lawyer and of Bartleby as his opponent? Clearly one answer must be that there is something about the tale that creates Melvillean nuance; *something* about this story must offer ambiguity and multiplicities of meaning. But what is the effect of a rigid definition of the lawyer as unmixed villain? The effect is to remove ambiguity, multiplicity, and subtlety by reducing the story to a simple tale of good versus evil (defined by whatever Gestalt). Problems of meaning remain in the superimposition of Gestalts upon the story and in conflicts between Gestalts—lots of room for explicators still—but moral ambiguity, moral evaluation is removed as a problem. And is not that problem precisely the central one that remains to puzzle the reader and itch in his mind? Remove shiftings of moral evaluations, and all that is left is the working out of equivalents to hang around the lawyer and Bartleby—which is what, I think, accounts for so much critical cleverness and narrowness in much of the criticism of "Bartleby." To see the lawyer as a fixed value is to remove him as a source of that itch that engages the reader in the first place and that the spate of criticism undeniably announces. And to remove the narrator as a source is to be quite tricky indeed, not only because the narrator is the only source of information we have about Bartleby but also because the narrator is the only continuing source of response to Bartleby. To fix the narrator is to place the burden for *all* the creation of multiple meaning in the story on Bartleby alone. Yet, why do all readers come away from the story with the impression that in the narrator they have met a person—whether they scorn him or not—and that in Bartleby they have met—what?—a quality? And embodied in a repetitious cadaver, at that?

There is in this question a serious matter that must be met, but which is all but unmentioned in "Bartleby" criticism, and that is the matter of types of characterization. It is neither accidental nor insignificant that all critics confront the story by characterizing the narrator in social, political, religious, and economic, as well as moral, terms, and by characterizing Bartleby in typal or mythic terms. Furthermore, all readers come away from the story with the sense that it is weird. The sense of weirdness is a result of the same factor that accounts for the ways in which critics characterize the lawyer and Bartleby. That is, the lawyer and Bartleby are characters from two distinctly different modes of fiction. The narrator comes from a recognizable world and can be measured in terms of that world: he is the kind of character who inhabits the province of realistic fiction. Bartleby, however, in every way inhabits a world other than the narrator's. He comes from the province of allegorical fiction, or romantic fiction, or both. The narrator is a human character; Bartleby is a metaphor. The narrator is sociologically explicable; Bartleby is no more sociologically explicable than is Ahab. The vehicle for the realistic character is verisimilitude; the lawyer, like his clerks, is given human, peculiar characteristics by which he is recognized, and the verisimilitude of characterizing human peculiarities is the vehicle for individuation, regardless of purpose—sentiment, rebellion, reportage—in realistic fiction. The narrator and his clerks come from the fiction of a writer like Dickens. But the vehicle for the allegorical character is typalism. Bartleby is given metaphoric weightings by which he is recognized, mysterious qualities independent of verisimilitude or realistic statistication. He comes from the fiction of a writer like Bunyan turned into Kafka—the emblematic quality of characterization remains, but all the rubrics have been erased from the labels for which the character is beast of burden. The science-fiction and gothic impingement of alien worlds gives "Bartleby" its weirdness. One does not expect the preternatural or the preternaturalistic to be accommodated into simultaneous existence with the realistic or the naturalistic. It is the calm intrusion of one world into another that gives "Bartleby" its Kafkan tones and makes it seem so very modern in its techniques and surfaces. In terms of action within the recognizable or naturalistic or Dickensian world the realistic character has dynamic dimensions: his fate and his character may both change along with his insights and experiences. But the inhabitant of the typal world is fixed. In speech, action, and possibility Bartleby *as character* is as rigidly fixed as a corpse. In the problem of moral evaluation, when the question is, what should the character do? Bartleby offers the narrator no world in which to do anything. He offers only the possibility of becoming like Bartleby, which is to say the possibility of leaving altogether the world of reality as it is defined for characterization within the demands of realistic fiction. The very nature of the differences in fictive worlds, fictive methods, and fictive characterization suggests that if either of the characters may undergo change, it is the lawyer, not Bartleby. I submit that in relation to Bartleby, it is the narrator who is not the fixed value. Nor, I should add, does this suggestion make a freak of "Bartleby the Scrivener" within the canon of Melville's works. The mixing of characters from different worlds of fictive mode is a constant Melvillean technique and always accounts for the element of weirdness in his fiction. For instance, is not the magnificently created sense of displacement, discontinuity of worlds, and disproportion in the confrontations between Ahab and Starbuck attributable to the fact that they are confrontations between a raging myth and a man from Nantucket, Massachusetts? And Melville's typal characters are disconnected from the humanity of verisimilitude and the world of its realities. What is Ahab's past? A hint from Elijah. And as for Bartleby, there is only an uncertain rumour about the Dead Letters Office. Consistently and pervasively Melville's typal characters are not of woman born, have no dimensions taken from realistic fiction's world of verisimilitude. They are characters without a past and without social measurements.[19]

In fact, what do we know of Bartleby? Only what the lawyer tells us, and he warns us from the very beginning that Bartleby does not inhabit the same dimensions as other scriveners, about whom he could write some amusing and sentimental vignettes. 'While of other law-copyists I might write the complete life, of Bartleby nothing of that sort can be done. I believe that no materials exist for a full and satisfactory biography of this man . . . Bartleby was one of those beings of whom nothing is ascertainable, except from the original sources, and in his case, those are very small. What my own astonished eyes saw of Bartleby, that is all I know of him, except, indeed, one vague report, which will appear in the sequel.' The appropriate question to ask, since Melville obviously knew he would furnish no sudden world of verisimilitude out of Bartleby's past, is why Melville chose to add the 'sequel' about the Dead

Letter Office; and in order to answer that question it becomes necessary to ask what it is we know of Bartleby without the epilogue.

Here again, the body of criticism gives us a solid agreement: Bartleby is the *isolato* who has come to the nadir of pallid despair in which all things are equal ('I am not particular') and all things are pointless ('I prefer not to'). The ordinary world that demands reasonableness is seen by Bartleby to be a dead end of meaninglessness that mocks all attempts to copy a non-existent law and order ('At present I prefer not to be a little reasonable'). There is at least this much preliminary bedrock of agreement. The criticism divides on the identification and evaluation of Bartleby. To some he is entirely heroic; to some he is mixed in his qualities. As is to be expected, those critics who see the lawyer as all villainous tend to see Bartleby as all good; those critics who see the lawyer as a changing quality tend to see unchanging Bartleby as a quality demanding a mixed response. If we are to be thrown on Bartleby as the sole source of ambiguity and multiplicity, we find that the criticism provides ample evidence that we cannot settle on a fixed response to him. Readers who conclude that Bartleby is the type of the hero, the rebel of whatever—art, nihilism, Christian morality, political honesty, metaphysical awareness—never satisfactorily handle those hard stumbling-blocks of facts which are the specifics whereby Bartleby is shown to us.

Would we have him stand as a life-principle, a rebellion against claustrophobic immurement in the dehumanizing world of the respectable lawyer? Would we have him the representative of true Christianity, true art, or the true revolution in his nay-saying to the mechanical world of law-copyists? To do so goes beyond the basic recognition that Bartleby prefers not to participate in any activity whatsoever; to do so assigns meanings to him that are not verifiable in the actual facts of the story. Because Melville is so heavily involved in metaphysical ideas, because Melville makes mirrors, the temptation is great to assign meanings out of the Gestalt of the critic, but to do that is to reduce criticism to a game of filling in the blanks: the lawyer equals —— ; Bartleby equals —— . But when we look at the specific details through which Bartleby is in fact presented, it becomes a bit difficult to turn our impression of a pallid, sick, corpse-like, motionless, silent fixed being into the life-principle or the humanity-principle or the rebel-principle or the reality-principle or an active body of moral principles. What are the specific terms that actually present Bartleby? In this long short story the catalogue surprisingly is not so long that the salient facts cannot be listed conveniently; and when the concrete instances are precisely isolated, they become quite instructive in the revelation of what is repeated.

Bartleby's movements are most often accompanied by the word 'gliding,' and his voice is most often described as 'mild.' He is 'pallidly neat, pitiably respectable, incurably forlorn'; 'he wrote on silently, palely, mechanically'; his face is 'leanly composed; his gray eye dimly calm'; he has absolutely no 'agitation, uneasiness, anger, or impertinence,' nor is there 'anything ordinarily human about him'; his corner is called a 'hermitage' (four times); he is 'gentle' or totally silent; he appears 'like a very ghost'; he is 'a pale young scrivener'; he is characterized by 'his steadiness, his freedom from all dissipation, his incessant industry (except when [in a] . . . standing revery . . .) , his great stillness, his unalterableness of demeanor'; his is a 'lean visage'; he is an 'apparition'; he has a 'cadaverously gentlemanly nonchalance'; he is 'eminently decorous'; he will not be seen in dishabille and would not 'by any singular occupation violate the proprieties' of Sunday; although he has very few belongings, he owns a blacking box and brush to keep his shoes shined; although he does not care for money (he does not touch the conscience money twice given him by the narrator), he frugally saves his salary and keeps it knotted in a handkerchief 'bank' hidden in the recesses of his desk; he has no interest in or apparent need for food or drink; he has a 'pale form' that appears as though 'laid out, among uncaring strangers, in its shivering winding-sheet'; he is 'thin and pale' with an air of 'pallid haughtiness'; his tones are 'mildly cadaverous'; he 'would prefer to be left alone here'; 'he seemed alone, absolutely alone in the universe [like] . . . a bit of wreck in the mid-Atlantic'; his triumph over the narrator is a 'cadaverous triumph'; he becomes both totally silent and totally motionless; he 'silently acquiesced' in 'his pale, unmoving way'; and he is 'prone to a pallid hopelessness.'

It will not do to object that these are only the narrator's vision of Bartleby, for everything we know about Bartleby is given through the narrator's vision, regardless of the meanings we would affix to Bartleby. Melville could have chosen to give us, through the narrator, other kinds of details for constant repetition, but he did not. What he did choose to give was a repetition of details that result in two major categories of impression. One is that of a silent, motionless, emaciated, pale, cadaverous negativism and withdrawal, a suggestion of the implacable stubbornness of a corpse, of death itself. The other is that of a mechanically industrious, mild, and seemly respectability. Just as the details that present the narrator begin to change at that crucial Sunday morning mid-point of the story, so they change for Bartleby, too. On the Tuesday following that Sunday Bartleby announces, 'I have given up copying' and abandons his industry altogether. From that moment the details of presentation begin to emphasize the characteristics of silence, motionlessness, and death much more than those of respectability. In short, just as the narrator's responses begin to be mixed with anguish and sympathy, Bartleby's characteristics begin to be associated with total withdrawal and extinction.

It is also important to note that from the mid-point on, the lawyer's strange sense of private connection with Bartleby also intensifies. 'I never feel so private as when I know you are here,' he says, thinking of Bartleby. The lawyer discovers that it is Bartleby who mysteriously has the unaccounted-for key to his private chambers. The lawyer has to tear himself away from the Bartleby he had longed to be rid of. And, finally, when the lawyer touches the hand of Bartleby's foetally curled corpse, 'a tingling ran up my arm and down my spine to my feet.' Melville has the lawyer supply ample hints that Bartleby has an essential, interior, and intimate connection with him. When one considers that up to the mid-point the lawyer was smugly, snugly, and actively respectable and that Bartleby was pallidly, forlornly, and mechanically respectable, there is an opening for speculation about Bartleby as an inversion, or at least a version, of the narrator. And after the mid-point the more the narrator becomes agonizingly aware of his connection with Bartleby, yet fails to give up his way of life, the more Bartleby repudiates him ('I know you, and I want nothing to say to you'), and retreats into suicide by refusing any of the food of this world. It is as though the lawyer came to learn that in seeing the repressed and negativistic Bartleby he saw himself, the logical, or at least spiritual extension of his very life which offers neither nourishment nor hope for everything within us that is buttoned up beneath the surfaces of conventional acquiescence to forms and values. It is just this possibility that leads some critics to contend that the narrator is changeless, unredeemed, and unredeemable: he does not, after all, give up his life when confronted with the apparition of Bartleby. But when religious or political meanings are affixed to Bartleby, the nagging questions fail to disappear. If Bartleby is the narrator's conscience or the spirit of true Christianity, why should he tend more towards death, isolation, withdrawal, and silence than towards strength, activity, and expression, as the narrator becomes increasingly tortured by the pain of sympathy? If Bartleby is the spirit of rebellion against the culture that is, why should he droop, fail, and withdraw just as the narrator becomes aware in anguish of a strange kind of justice in Bartleby's existence—just as the narrator finds he *cannot* rationalize Bartleby away with charges of vagrancy or any other charges?

   I am convinced that the explications that tend towards a one-to-one identification of Bartleby and the critic's political or religious Gestalt fail and will continue to fail to satisfy the logic, the psychological demands, that the story sets up. On the level of metaphysical points of view, there is, at least, a general basic agreement in the critical canon. As the narrator, at least at first, represents the materialistic world of hypocritical and blind bourgeois selfishness, Bartleby is the woebegone representative of a view of existence that denies all the shallow rationality and expectations of predictability, purpose, law, and meaning that the comfortably mindless and selfish commercial world self-justifyingly assumes to be the nature of the universe: God's in his heaven and all's right with the world. On this level there is general agreement that the lawyer, at least at the beginning, and Bartleby are the conflicting and obverse sides of human vision and human experience. If one is a vision of orthodox optimism and institutionalized belonging, the other is a vision of existential absurdity, the vision of the outcast stranger. This vision reduces to absurd meaninglessness all the activities of the lawyer's institutionalized world. On the level of metaphysical vision the psychological expectations are satisfied: as there are no alternatives in the institutionalized world for Bartleby's vision and no point in any kind of action on his part, pallid and silent withdrawal follows.

But when we parallel the level of metaphysical vision with the tempting levels of politics, the psycho-logics are not satisfied. On this level the narrator is the capitalist boss who exploits those who work for him, denying them full human existence and identity; Bartleby is the nay-sayer who refuses to copy the law-and-order of the narrator's world any longer. But on this level the story must remain psychologically frustrating, especially because there is certainly enough material that 'fits.' One might expect the fury of an Ahab or the activity of a Joe Hill or even the unaware, protesting dissoluteness of the *Lumpenproletariat,* but hardly the ghost of a motionless cadaver. The fictive mode from which Bartleby characterologically comes is not that which satisfies in any way the demands of realistic fiction. On this level "Bartleby" criticism becomes confused about the difference between the victim and the victim-rebel. Even if Bartleby were to be seen as victim only, what the story would then need would be something like a Hurstwood, or a Clyde Griffiths, but what we have is—Bartleby. And, on the political level, the story certainly does not psychologically support the view of Bartleby as rebel-hero if the type of pure victim is to be abandoned.

The same is true of the view of Bartleby as hero-artist. One might think of Joyce's silence, exile, and cunning as fitting Bartleby, but the 'fit' squeezes a bit with the cunning, and it does not take too much thinking before one runs into equally tight fits with the differences between Joyce's—or even Stephen Dedalus's—silence and exile and Bartleby's. Again, if Bartleby is to be 'the artist,' he is victim rather than victim-hero-rebel, closer to Kafka's hunger artist than to Dedalus. And, even at that, unlike the hunger artist Bartleby has no art of his own (he is himself either a mail-clerk or a copyist) that is sacrificed: abstemiousness is certainly not treated in Melville's story as it is in Kafka's. All that one can say is that Bartleby finds no food for his sustenance or values worth copying in the established world—and we are back to the one area of agreement, which is on the level of metaphysical vision, and which cannot really be specified in a one-to-one relationship to 'the artist.'

And if the ideologies of Christianity replace those of politics or artistic identity as the something further that is to parallel the level of metaphysical vision, psychological expectations run into further difficulty in the basic question of why Bartleby should choose suicide just as he has begun to make some meaningful impact upon the lawyer. What the specifics of the story and the inflexibly unrelenting characterology of Bartleby suggest in tandem with the strengths and weaknesses of critical commentary is either that there is no really useful particular level with which to parallel the level of metaphysical vision, or that if there is, the fruitful directions are to be found in the psycho-logics rather than the political logic or Christian logic of the critic's Gestalt. What remains, I suggest, for "Bartleby" criticism that will not be merely an-other repetition of what has already been said too often is not a one-to-one connection between Bartleby and a clinical category of psychopathology, but an exploration of psychological theory concerning various aspects of the self, theory that will provide a parallel to the metaphysical connections between the lawyer and Bartleby as somehow interrelated beings.

The matter of the epilogue bears strongly upon my view of approaches to "Bartleby." For those who see no change in the narrator the epilogue is unsatisfactory because it creates too sympathetic a perspective for the narra-tor to possess; or, alternatively, the epilogue becomes one more irony in which Melville creates a merely sentimental perspective with which to establish the narrator's shallowness. In fact, the epilogue does sound like any number of sentimental pieces in the gift-book and periodical literature of the nineteenth century. But even if one were to isolate a 'Dead Letters Office' tradition in sentimental literature, the basic question would still remain: how does Mel-ville use it? The fact of the tradition is much less important than its function within this tale, especially when one is cognizant of the fact that in *Pierre,* written only a little more than a year before the writing of "Bartleby," Melville had used various elements of the popular sentimental literary tradition for very unpopular and unsentimental reasons. Let us consider the epilogue for a moment from the point of view of the writer rather than from the desire for interpretation.

What were Melville's necessities by the time he came to the epilogue? He had promised the epilogue at the very beginning of the story, when he obviously had the entire tale clearly in mind. One thing is certain: by the end of the tale Melville has not 'explained' Bartleby. He had planned, from the very beginning of the first installment, not to say what happened to Bartleby to make him that way. But what could he say to answer this question? What events could he invent which would be horrible enough? And suppose he invented something truly hideous enough so that the character of Bartleby himself were not simply maudlin. In that event, the details of the destruction of all hope, all meaning, and all purpose—all life itself—would demand the writing of another story, something like the day-to-day to day-to-day incre-mental buildup of the horrors of an Auschwitz, or some other hell. But that was not the story Melville had in mind, and the story he told was the story he wanted to tell. All he could do was suggest, and merely suggest at that, a vision of some sort that would hint at universal possibilities of dead hopes, closed lives, pointless endeavours, and missed connections. Moreover, he had to avoid a hint so lurid that it would shift the emotional emphasis, dragging the weight of the story and the reader's attention from all that had preceded the epilogue to the epilogue itself. Consciously or not, Melville was evidently aware that a hint that really tried to account for Bartleby's life would defeat the very purpose it was there for: to prevent a shift of the reader's engagement to a demand for seeing *more*. The mild, brief universal so lightly hinted about the affairs of mortal men, the Dead Letter[s] Office, says, in effect, 'there is no more.' That is, the uncertain rumour about the Dead Letters Office at once universalizes Bartleby and keeps the focus exactly where Melville wants it—on the effect of Bartleby's condition, not on the cause of it.

Bartleby as a victim of the established world also comes to seem a victim of existence itself, and this, I think, is at the centre of what I take to be Melville's purpose—a speculation not about stoicism but about victimization. In much of his fiction he is anguished by victimization, compassionate with it, fascinated by it, and yet he also finds that in inexplicable ways the victim acquiesces in his victimization and intensifies the process. It is to ask the question, 'What else could Bartleby do?' Neither the universe nor the established world of the lawyer allowed him any alternatives. He could only assume his victimization and accept the death that is the consequence of it in his uncompromisingly honest view of a world empty of real alternatives—and thereby expose the nature of the world. But if the lawyer is to be attacked as the dehumanized organization man, is not Bartleby presented as dehumanized both explicitly and implicitly throughout the story, saying to the life around him, 'I prefer not to live it'?

My contention is that if one is willing to accept the facts of the story's characterization rather than attempt to fit those facts into an ideology, one has to conclude that Melville found not only heartbreak and terror in human victimization but also something mysteriously acquiescent and repelling about the dehumanized victim. The human possibilities for inhumanity construct rationalizations for the perverse desire to barbarize the victim precisely because of his passive victimization: the smug narrator burns to be rebelled against in order to justify his own sense of *separation* from the victim: the bastard is getting what he deserves. I suggest that Melville's psychological insights are too keen, when he puts them in the lawyer's mind that crucial Sunday morning, to dismiss them as merely more instances of the lawyer's selfishness—especially since those insights occur, as they do, in the context of the true melancholy that the narrator, deeply shaken for the first time in his life, experiences for the first time in his life. 'My first emotions,' he says, 'had been those of pure melancholy and sincerest pity; but just in proportion as the forlornness of Bartleby *grew and grew in my imagination,* did that same melancholy merge into fear, that pity into repulsion. *So true it is, and so terrible, too,* that up to a certain point the thought or sight of misery enlists our best affections; but, in special cases, beyond that point it does not. They err who would assert that invariably this is owing to the inherent selfishness of the human heart. It rather proceeds from a certain hopelessness of remedying excessive and organic ill' [italics added]. The lawyer's naked glimpse of Bartleby is as though one could imagine the anachronistic possibility of the good, Christian, prudent, American businessman doing a thriving, profitable business with the Nazis and suddenly becoming soul-shakingly aware of the death-camps at Auschwitz. The lawyer's speech is partly self-defensive. But it also expresses the horror that goes beyond a defence of one's self in shallow selfishness and becomes a fearful revulsion that includes the victim—take it away, make it not be. Yet what could the victim do but be? Either he must *be,* in the face of the observer's desperate desire for him to go away, not to be, or he himself must also prefer not to be. The first choice can only increase the observer's shock and horror; the second can only increase the observer's guilt and remorse because of his own psychological complicity in the victim's death. The more Bartleby preferred not to, the more the lawyer wished him to vacate the premises. The intimate, interior oneness of Bartleby and lawyer must be contemplated in the intricate and complex context of victimization.

But once a consideration is admitted into evidence, it cannot be used by the prosecution only. If we ask the question, but what else could he do? we must be willing to apply it to the lawyer as well. In the longest and most intelligent attack on the narrator and defence of Bartleby as hero, Kingsley Widmer (see note 3) concludes that the 'narrator never . . . changes his view and way of life.' It is a charge that subsumes within it the many narrower, less thoughtful, and less suggestive attacks on the lawyer and defences of Bartleby. But in terms of Bartleby as the only alternative to the lawyer, what, indeed, could the lawyer do? To apply equal sanctions to Bartleby and narrator is to create no contest. As metaphor Bartleby simply is not subject to the kinds of reality that are inevitable for the lawyer, who is derived from realistic characterology. Arguing from his own political and philosophical Gestalt, Widmer asserts that because culture is the product of the inhuman lawyer's world and serves only to civilize that world's enormities, against which Bartleby rebels, it is a sign of the dehumanizing failure of meliorism. As the lawyer's culture is a lie in human terms, culture up to the total revolution of Bartleby is to be repudiated. Bartleby's nay-saying unto death is the truly revolutionary response. In sum, not only is the present to be put to death as a sacrifice to a metaphor of the liberated future, but so is the past as well. (Is it not fitting that Bartleby, who is heroic to Widmer, and who has no emulative present, is a man with no past?) But to me there is a familiar Melvillism in the fact that, being totally committed to his vision and thus isolating himself from all connections with the shallow lee-shore present, Bartleby in his monomania leads not to full life in the future but pallidly to death. It is clear to me that if Melville does not condone the culture of *is,* neither does he advocate a destruction of *was.* Not, at least, the multiple Melville, the mirror-maker, that we know in the totality of his works. One cannot make the corpselike Bartleby a sign of life without wrenching that cadaver out of Melville's presentation of him and into the polemics of one's own Gestalt.

Widmer's charge is extra-literary, for, like all strong art, "Bartleby the Scrivener" leads strong readers beyond the literary fact itself, and Widmer is justified in stepping beyond. In my disagreement with his view I wish simply to meet him on his own grounds. True, within the story itself, one can find instances to rebut the charge against the narrator. One instance that is always either slighted or virtually ignored in attacks on the narrator is the moment in which he does offer to open his life to Bartleby, to support him, to stay with him, and to assume responsibility for him: "'Bartleby,' said I, in the kindest tone I could assume under such exciting circumstances, "will you go home with me now—not to my office, but my dwelling—and remain there till we can conclude upon some convenient arrangement for you at our leisure? Come, let us start now, right away.'" At this point it is more than clear that were Bartleby to accompany the narrator, he would never leave for 'some convenient arrangement' elsewhere. The narrator offers no less than a lifelong 'arrangement.' And he does not offer gradualism either; the delays, assumptions, and illusions are gone: 'Come, let us start now, right away.' But even with this evidence those who wish to simplify the story into a totalistic choice of Bartleby-hero versus narrator-villain can argue that the lawyer wishes only to get Bartleby out of the public building and into his private home—as though the connection between public and private, outer and inner, were not the essence of the connection in victimization between the lawyer and Bartleby in the first place.

So we return to the question, what else could the narrator do? What life could the narrator change to, other than Bartleby's? And again Melville gives us no alternatives other than the lawyer and Bartleby. With this inescapable given, then, let us abandon the evidences within the story for a moment and step outside it with Widmer to the arguments beyond. Widmer identifies the true essence of humanity as nihilism, 'that simply recurrent human reality—the vital desire to angrily negate [sic] things as they are' (Widmer, p. 128). It is significant that Widmer feels it necessary to intrude that word 'angrily,' for it provides the human and psychological necessary dimension that the characterologically typal Bartleby most patently lacks. But, given Widmer's premise, the story 'reveals the confession of a decent, prudent, rational "liberal" who finds in his chambers of consciousness the incomprehensible, the perverse, irrational demon of denial, and of his own denied humanity'

(Widmer, p. 119). 'The attempt to wryly force [sic] benevolent American rationalism to an awareness of our forlorn and walled-in humanity provides the larger purpose of the tale' (Widmer, p. 120). But if we must assume that the spirit of denial is deeply human, must we assume, then, that it is the only deep or true humanity, much less the total essence of humanity, as Widmer assumes? Is not the need for self-deception as human as the desire for denial? Is not the conscious as *real* as the unconscious? Is not the invention of predictable meaning as human as the nihilistic response to the revelation of cosmic absurdity? By what fiats may critics *assume*, like that man of assumptions, the lawyer, total categories of the really human and the falsely human in human behaviour and in human history and in human perception? What is true is that we wish to identify as human what affirms life rather than what denies it, what enlarges personality rather than what claustrophobically walls it in. It is also true that as a repressive principle the narrator in the first half of the tale is dehumanizing. But can the denials of Bartleby really be held up as a model of what affirms life and enlarges personality? For Widmer Bartleby becomes 'a small wan Ahab' who 'defiantly butts all . . . blind walls' (Widmer, pp. 106–107). Thus Bartleby becomes an 'abstract personification of the attorney's own humanity' (Widmer, p. 107), as though, again, the principle of defiance were the totality subsumed under the category 'human.' Will, preference, in and of itself, and not rationality—certainly not rationality—becomes the true human characteristic. The true morality, therefore, is the demonic, not the common morality. 'The scrivener provides the human completion, the rage [and here again, significantly, is Widmer's response to the demands of psycho-logic and he invents for Bartleby a characteristic of which Bartleby is, in fact, completely devoid] to the restraint, the covert rebellion to the conviction that "the easiest way of life is the best," the assertion of *human* preferences against depersonalized assumptions, and the melancholy pessimism to balance the bland optimism' (Widmer, pp. 112–113, italics added). For Widmer anything less than Bartleby's willingness to go to death in his denials of the present points away from the true morality on the other side of the nihilistic revolution and is merely meliorism. Again, there is nothing the narrator can do short of becoming Bartleby. But the good world on the other side of Bartleby's pallid and unvarying negations comes from Widmer's Gestalt, not from Melville's story. For not only is Bartleby no small, wan Ahab, he is the complementary opposite of Ahab, and offers none of the Ahabian rage that Widmer consequently has to supply for him. Moreover, the imputation to Melville of millennial views of history is most strange in the context of invoking Ahab's spirit. For surely if Melville saw anything in that context, it was Ahab's murderous miscalculations about the possibilities of experience. If our context is Melville's rather than Widmer's Gestalt, what we have is not the total rebel ushering in the ultimate revolution, but the endless, indeterminate continuations of history, as repetitive and as illuminating of human limitation as the great shroud of the sea that rolls on as it did five thousand years ago. The totalistic critical view makes demands and meanings that entirely subvert and are deaf to the despairing tone of the tale as well as to its indeterminateness.

It is precisely at the point of turning everyone into Bartleby, which for Widmer would be the salvation of the revolution accomplished, that Melville draws back—the same Melville who looks askance at romantic and nihilistic versions of history and the human essence; the same Melville who says that if oysters and champagne are the foods of the body, get you your oysters and champagne; the same Melville who warmly sees the inescapable necessity of the lee shore for all that is kindly to our mortalities even as he urges Bulkington to keep the open independence of his soul's sea from the lee shore's lawyer-like slavish and shallow copy-assumptions; the same Melville who would repudiate the mast-head visions in order to ameliorate the ship's course with the first hint of the hitching tiller; the same Melville who has Ishmael learn that man must eventually learn to lower or at least shift his conceit of attainable felicity. He is, to the point, the same Melville who leaves the stage to the lawyer, not to Bartleby. Because he is the Melville who is so gnarledly aware that the only operable human actuality is the despised and limited *now* trapped between absolutes of infinity and eternity, he draws back from the absolutist prescriptions of totalistic literary criticism that would have the world go even unto death for salvation in the future. He will not annihilate the limited human existence within mortal history, the source of realistic fiction, for the triumph of the absolute quality of typalism, even when heroic. Much less does he do so for idea, the bloodless universal, the pallid metaphor. In "Bartleby" the problems of fictive characterization *are* the problems of metaphysics and psychology. If Edwards on the will and Priestly on necessity, if Locke and Paley are not justifications of necessity that Melville accepts, the deathlessness of the white whale and the deathfulness of Bartleby are. I take it that the real agony of the story comes from Melville's seeing that man must smash the surfaces of respectable and established vision to become fully human, but that if, in doing so, truth turn out to be the frozen absurd or the new vision become the monomania of totalistic defiance, man is plunged into even more deadly and deathly dehumanization. Both Bartleby and the lawyer are victims of human limitation; both suffer dehumanizations, and "Bartleby" is indeed a speculation about the process of victimization. The cosmic truth kills. The comfortable lies blind us and destroy our hearts that should be enlarged by woe. Both the defiant vision and the lee shore are needed, both are inescapable, and to wake from the world of one into the world of the other is mortal despair, overpowering, stinging melancholy. It is this impingement of worlds that is Melville's constant technique in mingling the characters of different fictive modes to suggest his view of the dilemma of men.

Ah, Bartleby! Ah, humanity!

Perhaps it is a deep knowledge that one possible corollary of the total revolution is generational suicide—*that* as a possibility at least as much as the good world that is supposed to lie beyond the revolution of total negation—that continues to make the masses, who desire nothing so much as a secured present, the despair of the total revolutionaries. I do not mean for a moment that Melville endorses the status quo he presents in the narrator's world. I do mean that through his vision of Bartleby the narrator is awakened to the perception of vulnerable nakedness and woe that makes us all monkey-rope brothers. Paradoxically it is 'revolutionary' Bartleby, not the narrator, who is the one-dimensional man.

When I called "Bartleby" a speculation, I meant just that. To see it as a polemic rather than as a query is to substitute the Gestalt of the critic for the Gestalt of the story. To reduce the narrator to a fixed moral quantity is to deny the extent to which the story continues to nag and itch after you have read all the criticism that affixes weightings, labels, answers, to what Melville created as lasting question marks. To insist upon ideological equivalents for the details of the story is to lose the suppleness and openness of the story, which is, I think, why critiques of the story always seem to be so much more rigid than the tale itself. To fix an ideology upon this tale is to substitute a desire for a satisfying *quod erat demonstrandum* in place of the continuing perturbation left by the tale, and which is a mark of its particular art. The substitution of polemical answers for Melville's questions is merely to discover the face in the mirror[20]—it is, finally, to substitute the lesser imagination behind fixed quantities for the greater imagination behind the tale. The paradox, as I see it, is that the critics who dismiss the narrator as merely smug and bad in his narrow solipsism are guilty of exactly the same sin of which they indict him.

I suggest that as a speculation about human victimization "Bartleby the Scrivener" is a despairing recognition that neither the lee-shore life nor the truth-piercing total vision that repudiates it provides adequate sustenance for our hungry humanity. Yet, a glimpse of the victim's woe can become the woe that is wisdom, and, given that, a man is on his way to becoming human even in his only present world, for that world will never be the same to him again. Perhaps that is the birth of revolution. (I suspect, in my memory of his works, that Melville would say, 'No, no—that *is* the unending revolution.') When I say, then, that we can declare a blessed moratorium on saying certain kinds of things about Bartleby and the narrator, I do not mean that we can declare a moratorium on speculations that continue to explore the story both within and beyond itself. All readers provide that 'beyond' out of their own times and visions and will continue to know the headache of trying to explore the story in that beyond. On errands of contemplation art speeds to—contemplation, and leaves is—ah, Melville! ah readers!—with our own dead letters offices. And with kings and counsellors.

Notes

1. *Sewanee Review,* 61 (1953): 602–627. This essay is one of the earliest and most comprehensive of the many articles that see "Bartleby" as a story of the worker, particularly the literary worker, within the entrapments of a capitalistic, commercialized society.

2. *College English,* 6 (1945): 431–439. In the criticism that deals with literary parallels, Oliver's is one of the most engaging examples, which is why I choose it to stand for a genre which, it seems to me, tends to lead to its own closed, walled-in world as far as 'opening up' a piece of literature is concerned.

3. Chapter 4 of *The Ways of Nihilism: Herman Melville's Short Novels* (California State Colleges Publications, 1970), pp. 91–125. Widmer's Gestalt is one of 'new left' nihilism, deriving strongly from Marcuse, especially from *One Dimensional Man.* Bartleby emerges as the nihilistic hero who refuses to participate in the lawyer's inhuman and philosophically blind world and thereby demonically points toward the true revolution beyond middle-class 'liberal' rationality.

4. In "Bartleby the Scrivener," *Melville Annual 1965 Symposium,* edited by Howard P. Vincent (Kent State University Press, 1966), pp. 113–139.

5. "'Bartleby': The Tale, the Film" in Vincent, ed., p. 47.

6. The psychologist-critic, Henry A. Murray, says that there is no psychiatric category for Bartleby. 'Bartleby is unprecedented, an invention of Melville's creative spirit, the author's gift to psychology, a mythic figure who deserves a category in his own name: "Bartleby and I,"' in Vincent, ed., p. 23.

7. In Vincent, ed., p. 49.

8. *A Bibliography of Criticism of "Bartleby the Scrivener,"* in Vincent, ed., pp. 140–190, esp. pp. 151–190.

9. If we adopt the necessary luxury of detached hindsight and impose approximately a ten-year hiatus between ourselves and the twenty-year development of "Bartleby" scholarship up to the beginning of the past decade, we can derive a chronological overview from a survey of some selected critics who see the tale as a parable of Melville himself and/or of the artist generally. These include, among others, Lewis Mumford, *Herman Melville* (New York, 1929; rev. 1962), pp. 162–164; Alexander Eliot, 'Melville and "Bartleby,"' *Furioso,* 3 (1947), 11–21; Willard Thorp, 'Herman Melville,' *Literary History of the United States,* ed. R. E. Spiller, et al. (New York, 1948; rev. 1955), I, 463; Richard Chase, *Herman Melville: A Critical Study* (New York, 1949), pp. 143–193, 267, 280; also Chase's 'Introduction,' *Selected Tales and Poems of Herman Melville* (New York, 1950), pp. vii–viii; Newton Arvin, *Herman Melville* (New York, 1950), pp. 242–244; Eugene Current-Garcia and R. W. Patrick, eds., 'Introduction' and note, *American Short Stories* (Chicago, 1952), pp. xxiv, 109–110; Marx, n. 1 above; Norris Merchant, 'The Artist and Society in Melville,' *Views,* 4:3 (University of Louisville, 1957), pp. 56–57; Harry Levin, *The Power of Blackness* (New York, 1958), pp. 187–188; Jean-Jacques Mayoux, *Melville,*

translated by John Ashberry (New York, 1960), pp. 111–112, 158–186; Norman E. Hoyle, *Melville as a Magazinist* (Duke University Press, 1960), pp. 85–86, 89–94, 102; Hugh W. Hetherington, *Melville's Reviewers* (University of North Carolina Press, 1960), pp. 265–276; J. J. Boies, 'Existential Nihilism and Herman Melville,' *Transactions of the Wisconsin Academy of Science, Arts, and Letters,* 50 (1960): 307–320; Marvin Felheim, 'Meaning and Structure in "Bartleby,"' *College English,* 23 (1962): 369–370, 375–376; John Gardner, '"Bartleby": Art and Social Commitment,' *Philogical Quarterly,* 43 (1964): 87–98; Murray (see n. 6 above), pp. 3–24; and D'Avanzo (see n. 4 above). For a view of "Bartleby" as a tale of existential alienation, isolation, or negation, some of the many essays to consult are F. O. Marthiessen, *American Renaissance* (New York, 1941), p. 493; R. E. Watters, 'Melville's *Isolatos,*' *PMLA,* 60 (1945): 1138–1148; Alfred Kazin, 'Ishmael in His Academic Heaven,' *The New Yorker,* 24 (12 February, 1949): 84–89; Newton Arvin, *Herman Melville* (New York, 1950), pp. 242–244; Jack Ludwig and Richard Poirier, 'Instructor's Manual,' *Stories: British and American* (Boston, 1953), pp. 6–8; Merlin Bowen, *The Long Encounter* (Chicago, 1960), pp. 133–134; William M. Gibson, 'Herman Melville's "Bartleby the Scrivener" and "Benito Cereno,"' *Die Neueren Sprachen,* 9 (1960): 107–116; James E. Miller Jr., *A Reader's Guide to Herman Melville* (New York, 1962), pp. 13, 160–161; Roy R. Male, *Types of Short Fiction* (Belmont, California 1962), pp. 438–439; Joseph Schiffman, ed., *Three Shorter Novels of Herman Melville* (New York, 1962), pp. 229, 235–237; Maurice Friedman, *Problematical Rebel* (New York, 1963), pp. 77–98; Norman Springer, '"Bartleby" and the Terror of Limitation,' *PMLA,* 80 (1965): 410–418; John Haag, '"Bartleby"—in for the Camera,' in Vincent, ed. pp. 55–63; Maurice Friedman, '"Bartleby" and the Modern Exile,' in Vincent, ed. pp. 64–81; Marjorie Dow, 'The Attorney and the Scrivener,' in Vincent, ed., pp. 94–103; Peter E. Firchow, '"Bartleby": Man and Metaphor,' *Studies in Short Fiction,* 5 (1968): 342–348; and Kingsley Widmer, see n. 3 above, as well as 'The Negative Affirmation: Melville's "Bartleby,"' *Modern Fiction Studies,* 8 (1962): 276–86.

10. Among several who assign a Christly role to Bartleby are Chase (see n. 9 above); Nathalia Wright, *Melville's Use of the Bible* (Duke University Press, 1949), p. 128; G. A. Knox, 'Communication and Communion in Melville,' *Renascence,* 9 (1956): 26–31; Bowen (see n. 9 above); H. Bruce Franklin, *The Wake of the Gods* (Stanford University Press, 1963), pp. 126–136, 150–153, 188–190, 205–206; Gardner (see n. 9 above); and William Bysshe Stein, in Vincent, ed., pp. 104–112.

11. See Robert D. Spector, 'Melville's "Bartleby" and the Absurd,' *Nineteenth Century Fiction,* 16 (1960): 175–177; and Firchow, n. 9 above.

12. See also Stanley Edgar Hyman, 'Melville the Scrivener,' *New Mexico Quarterly,* 23 (1953): 381–415; and Richard Harter Fogle, 'Melville's "Bartleby": Absolutism, Predestination, and Free Will,' *Tulane Studies in English,* 4 (1954): 125–135.

13. For the first, see Herbert F. Smith, 'Melville's Master in Chancery and His Recalcitrant Clerk,' *American Quarterly,* 17 (1965): 734–741. The main difficulty with Smith's thesis is that Melville most decidedly does not introduce the New York Court of Chancery in the context to which Smith wrenches it. For one thing, Bartleby refuses to engage in chancery work, the addition of which to his regular business causes the lawyer to hire Bartleby in the first place. Chancery in "Bartleby" is used not as a model for ideal conscience but exactly as Dickens had used it in *Bleak House.* If one considers the dates of composition and publication of "Bartleby," the model provided by Dickens becomes extremely visible. *Bleak House*

was serialized from March 1852 to September 1853. It was shipped to and read in the United States in 'parts,' the last of which was a double installment. It was well known to Melville and his audience. It was reviewed in *Putnam's* in November 1853, the same issue in which the first installment of "Bartleby" appeared. For Bartleby as death-wish, see Mordecai Marcus, 'Melville's "Bartleby" as a Psychological Double,' *College English*, 23 (1962): 365–368.

14. For one of the rare exceptions, see Patricia Lacy, 'The Agatha Theme in Melville's Stories,' *University of Texas Studies in English*, 35 (1956): 96–105. Lacy sees the narrator as sympathetic and a voice for Melville, and sees Bartleby as the long-suffering humanity exemplified in the Agatha letter to Hawthorne, in *Cock-a-Doodle-Doo!* and in the sketch of Hunilla, the Chola widow, in *The Encantadas*.

15. In addition to Lacy, some representative points of view may be found in Marx (see n. 1 above); Chase (see n8 above); Robert L. Gale, '"Bartleby"—Melville's Father-in-Law' Anneli Instituto Universitario Orientate, *Sczione Germanica*, 5 (1962): 57–72; and F. W. Davidson, '"Bartleby": A Few Observations,' *Emerson Society Quarterly*, no. 27 (1962): 25–32.

16. Widmer, p. 118.

17. Stein (see n. 10), pp. 104–112.

18. I am indebted for some of these observations to Irving Cummings of the University of Connecticut and Frank Hodgins of the University of Illinois. When Hodgins's long-awaited study of psychology and American literature appears, it will contain the kind of reading I call for in this essay.

19. R. H. Broadhead's *Hawthorne, Melville, and the Novel* (Chicago, 1976) contains an excellent discussion of this problem. See esp. pp. 11–12.

20. I cannot resist the appositeness of Melville's warning in *Moby-Dick*. That book cautions repeatedly that because value and meaning are a projection of human perceptions, humans must be careful not to identify those values and meanings as objective, external realities, for all we discover is ourselves. The 'mild,' 'tormenting' Bartleby is a critical face seen in the mirror, into which some critics fall, thinking they are catching THE ungraspable phantom of single meaning. Ishmael warns that 'still deeper' is 'the meaning of that story of Narcissus, who because he could not grasp the tormenting, mild image he saw in the fountain, plunged into it and was drowned. But that same image, we ourselves see in all rivers and oceans. It is the image of the ungraspable phantom of life; and this is the key to it all.'

SANFORD E. MAROVITZ

Melville's Problematic "Being"

Shortly after reading *The House of the Seven Gables* early in 1851, Melville wrote to Hawthorne what is now one of the most familiar of his letters in praise of the romance. He followed his commendation with profound observations on Hawthorne's tragic insights as an artist and on his sense of autonomy, even defiance, with respect to those who would in any way restrict his independence. As has often been recognized by critics, Melville appears to have had his own artistic ideals in mind at least as much as Hawthorne's while writing this letter, just as he had been probing his own motives in "reviewing" Hawthorne's *Mosses* the previous year for Duyckinck's *Literary World*. That he envisioned his own image behind Hawthorne's as he wrote to his friend of still less than a year is strikingly apparent in his shift within a few sentences from the third person to the first, from reference to "the tragicalness of human thought" and "intense feeling of the visable *[sic]* truth" in "this man's" "recorded mind" to the hypothesis that although select "Powers [may] choose to withhold certain secrets," they can nevertheless not "impair my sovereignty in myself" nor "make me tributary."[1]

Although the thrust of Melville's letter is clear, despite the confusion in person, certain passages are not; highly suggestive, they nevertheless remain ambiguous and at times even cryptic. One in particular is worth close consideration largely *because* of its ambiguity in that it testifies to the author's

ESQ: A Journal of the American Renaissance, Volume 28, Number 1 (1982): pp. 11–13. © 1982 Sanford E. Marovitz.

ambivalence over the foundation of religious and philosophical Truth as he struggled with the "Whale" "in his flurry" (*L*, pp. 128–129; June 1?, 1851) and moved toward the completion of *Moby-Dick*. In this passage, which concludes the long middle paragraph of his letter, Melville wrote:

> But it is this *Being* of the matter; there lies the knot with which we choke ourselves. As soon as you say *Me, a God, a Nature,* so soon you jump off from your stool and hang from the beam. Yes, that word is the hangman. Take God out of the dictionary, and you would have Him in the street.[2]

It is especially the word *"Being,"* which Melville capitalized and underscored—"the puzzle of puzzles," as Whitman would call it a few years later[3]—that warrants specific attention. What did he mean by it—for there is a range of possibilities—in the immediate context of the letter? Also, how do suggested definitions comport with ideas presented elsewhere in Melville's work, especially in *Moby-Dick* and *Pierre*? Correspondences between his ideas on the nature of *Being* and those from a multitude of likely philosophical sources from which he drew—from Plato and the Neoplatonists through Coleridge and Emerson—evince the extent to which his mind was first opened, then thrown into turmoil by the intellectual nourishment he absorbed during his formative period as a writer. Variously stimulated, frustrated, and disgusted by diverse and often conflicting viewpoints, Melville employed the word *Being* ambivalently, manifesting his confusion when the moral and religious Truths he longed to accept conflicted with the empirical truths that belied them.

Melville may have been applying that word in either a substantive sense (as a noun) or an active sense (as a participle), for in context it connotes both. He was unquestionably familiar, either directly or indirectly, with both philosophical uses of the term. At first, a reader of Melville's letter is strongly tempted to accept his use of the word *Being* as substance, or principle, because each of the three italicized words in the sentence which follows it appears to be in apposition, and all three are substantive: *"Me, a God, a Nature."* Moreover, his reference to *"a God"* in that sentence is probably tied to "God" and "Him" in the second sentence after it, and these latter two words are also substantive. *"Being,"* then, appears to be a general term that subsumes the others.

Is there anything outside of those remarks to Hawthorne which supports the notion of *Being* here as principle? Possibly. There is, for one thing, a letter Melville wrote to Duyckinck about two years earlier, in the spring of 1849, informing him that he had recently purchased a set of Pierre Bayle's *Dictionary* and that he expected to "go to sleep on them thro' the summer, with the Phaedon in one hand & Tom Brown[e] in the other" (*L*, pp. 83–84; April 5, 1849). Although he may have been too busy writing *Redburn* and *White-Jacket* during that spring and summer to become drowsy over Browne, Bayle, and Plato, evidence abounds that he had read all three well before sending *The Whale* to press, soon after his letter to Hawthorne was written. Particularly relevant in the letter to Duyckinck is that all three of those writers looked upon *Being* as one or more principles of existence. According to Merton Sealts, Plato was the most important of Melville's ancient philosophical sources.[4] That he was reading the *Phaedo* at this time is especially noteworthy because in that dialogue "more than elsewhere, Plato preaches withdrawal from the world. . . . The theory of ideas here assumes its most transcendental aspect," the Rev. Lewis Campbell writes, and "a long step is made in the direction of pure idealism."[5] It is precisely this withdrawal into the ideal that Melville is deriding in *Moby-Dick* when Tashtego, baling spermaceti from the case, falls into the severed head of a sperm whale which throbs and heaves with the Indian's struggles "as if that moment seized with some momentous idea."[6] Shortly before the accident, which almost proves fatal to the harpooner, Ishmael ponders over the suspended "Platonian" head (*M-D*, p. 284), with its eyes, one on either side of the vast skull, "effectually divided" and "surround[ed] each by a circle of profound darkness" (*M-D*, p. 279), as if the ideal world of the one side and the shadow world of the other were eternally removed from one another and beyond hope of reconciliation. This "Platonian" head, with its broad placid brow and an expression "born of a speculative indifference as to death" (*M-D*, p. 284)—like that of Socrates in the *Phaedo* as the moment of his own death approaches—is metaphorically conjoined to "Plato's honey head" (*M-D*, p. 290), which entraps the unwary with the seductive sweetness of its thought. In the next year, it would also tie in with the expansive brow and cool disposition of Plotinus Plinlimmon in *Pierre*, though the tone of Melville's irony then will have become considerably darker and more caustic.

Tashtego's fall into the "Platonian" head recalls Ishmael's earlier admonition to "young Platonists" (*M-D*, p. 139), that they need beware of losing themselves in a reverie over "that deep, blue, bottomless soul, pervading mankind and nature" lest they return with a misstep to the cold, mechanically indifferent material world of "Descartian vortices" and drop into the sea, "no more to rise for ever" (*M-D*, p. 140). In this passage, Melville may have been responding less directly to Plato and his pantheistic disciples than to Thomas Carlyle, whose *Sartor Resartus* he had borrowed from Duyckinck in 1850. Time and all things affected by it are but shadows, Carlyle wrote; "only . . . Time-shadows . . . are perishable; . . . the real Being of whatever was, and whatever is, and whatever will be, *is* even now and forever."[7] Earlier, in the whaleman's chapel, Ishmael, echoing Socrates in the *Phaedo* (Sealts, diss. p. 50), affirmed this belief when he said, "Methinks my body is but the lees of my better being" (*M-D*, p. 41), but now, with a fall from the masthead in his mind, he seems to be implying that the "young Platonist" who drop into the sea will remain there forever—presumably *Being* and all. Ahab, on the other hand, retains his Socratic /Carlylean view throughout, asserting on the second day of the chase that nothing earthly can affect him "in his own proper and inaccessible being" (*M-D*, p. 458). The quest for ultimate Reality beyond time is addressed comprehensively and ambivalently, of course, throughout both *Moby-Dick*, one of the central issues of which is Ahab's quest for immortality while locked into a temporal world, and with increasing skepticism in *Pierre*, where the principal moral dilemmas are presented and discussed metaphorically in terms of time—specifically the chronometrical/horological conflict in Plinlimmon's pamphlet.

The conflicts are resolved in the idea traced by Arthur Lovejoy as "the Great Chain of Being." Describing the theoretical background that led to the development of that idea, Lovejoy distinguishes the two antithetical conceptions of God held by the Western world historically under the influence of Platonism; these two conceptions are identified as one God of two aspects. First is the absolute and other-worldly aspect, which is perfect and self-contained, beyond time, space, and human comprehension; the other is that of the contingent Being, which is this-worldly, creative, generative, dependent upon all other forms of existence for its own fulfillment, and within the order of time and space. Values based on the first aspect conformed with the notion of a transcendent spirit to emulate, adore, or obey and an afterlife to anticipate, whereas values based on the second were in keeping with the contingent, generative nature of the God—that is, they were based on a love of the world and its possibilities within which divine meaning could be found. Lovejoy points out, further, that this distinction evolved as a result of two completely different ideas of what constituted the Good. With respect to the absolute and self-contained aspect of God, the Good necessarily means that what is all-perfect can make neither itself nor anything else better than it is; nor can anything new be created for a better existence because everything is already perfect. On the other hand, for the creative aspect of God, the Good requires continuous generation and emanation for, the self-fulfillment of divine potentiality.[8] Both aspects originated with Plato in his distinction between two kinds of supernal existence: universal, essential Ideas, which were "eternal objects of pure thought"; and individual Souls, which were "everlasting conscious and thinking beings." Although the two fundamentally different concepts would seem to be irreconcilable, Lovejoy believes that Plato probably unified them at their highest point (p. 48). Later they would be more definitely and systematically related by Plotinus.

When one thinks of Platonic philosophy, one's mind usually turns first to the ideal theory, and it is this aspect of Plato's thought that most directly influenced Melville in his writing. While at work on *Mardi* he was becoming acquainted with Plato and Platonism in the Taylor-Sydenham translation of Plato, in Thomas Taylor's translation of Proclus' *On the Theology of Plato*, and possibly in one or more of Taylor's translations of Plotinus.[9]

Although the basic ideas of the great chain of being were initially formulated by Plato and developed to some extent by Aristotle—who established a continuum of categories among the diverse forms of *being* he recognized—the grand concept was not fully fashioned until Plotinus and his disciples added the principle of gradation to the continuum and thus applied a scale of evaluation upon all of existence from the highest to the lowest. According to Merton Sealts, Melville may well have read Taylor's introduction to *Select Works of Plotinus*, in a footnote to which Taylor provided a clear and extensive exposition of the chain metaphor, thus showing to what a great extent the idea still held currency early in the nineteenth century. Taylor's description of the chain graphically reveals the extremely important social implications of the concept as well as the philosophical ones:

> In every class of beings in the universe . . . there is a first, a middle, and a last, in order that the progression of things may form one unbroken chain, originating from deity, and terminating in matter. In consequence of this connection, one [small] part of the human species naturally coalesces, through transcendency, with beings of an order superior to man; another [larger] part, through diminution, unites with the brutal species; and a third part ["a countless multitude"], which subsists as the connecting medium between the other two, possesses those properties which characterize human nature in a manner not exceeding but exactly commensurate to the condition of humanity. . . . In consequence of this beautiful gradation, the most subordinate part of mankind are only to be benefited by good rulers, laws, and customs, through which they become peaceable members of the communities in which they live. . . . Hence the present efforts to enlighten by education the lowest class of mankind is an attempt to break the golden chain of beings, to disorganise society, and to render the vulgar dissatisfied with the servile situations in which God and nature intended them to be placed. In short, it is an attempt . . . to subvert all order [and] introduce anarchy.[10]

Even if Melville did not see this striking passage in Taylor, with its feudalistic implications, he certainly would have been familiar with the angel

Raphael's depiction to Adam of the chain in which the concept of emanation is clearly derived from Plotinus, and which just as clearly anticipates Emerson's "subtle chain of countless rings," the opening lines of his epigraph to the 1849 edition of *Nature.* Raphael says, in the fifth book of *Paradise Lost:*

> O Adam, one Almightie is, from whom
> All things proceed, and up to him return,
>   . . . created all
> Such to perfection, one first matter all,
> Indu'd with various forms, various degrees
> Of substance, and in things that live, of life. [V. 469–474]

And in his reading of Thomas Browne's *Religio Medici,* possibly during the summer of 1849, Melville found, "there is in this Universe a Staire, or manifest Scale of creatures, rising not disorderly, or in confusion, but with a comely method and proportion. . . ."[11] Moreover, Melville would have recognized that, like Taylor, Browne believed that "to remove one rung from the Scale of Nature were to dismantle the entire scheme, and abrogate order."[12] Finally, Melville surely read Ulysses' well-known monologue on "degree" in Shakespeare's *Troilus and Cressida,* in which the crafty, Ithacan tells his compatriots:

>   O! when degree is shak'd,
> Which is the ladder to all high designs,
> The enterprise is sick. . . .
> ....
> Take but degree away. . . .
> And, hark! what discord follows; . . .
> ....
> Then every thing includes itself in power,
> Power into will, will into appetite;
> And appetite, a universal wolf,
> So doubly seconded with will and power,
> Must make perforce a universal prey,
> And last eat up himself. . . . [13]

Although Ishmael replaces the wolf with the shark, the basic concept and the imagery that clothes it correspond to much in *Moby-Dick,* including one of the most directly and obviously related appearances of the gradation concept in that novel, Ishmael's classification of the crew of the *Pequod,* from the "grand, ungodly, god-like" Ahab to Pip (*M-D,* p. 76), whom the narrator calls "the most insignificant of the *Pequod*'s crew" (*M-D,* p. 344). Particularly relevant are the chapters entitled "Knights and Squires," "The Specksynder," and, most especially, "The Cabin-table," in which the Caucasian officers' dining protocol according to rank is described and followed by the sharply contrasting behavior, or as Ishmael phrases it, "the almost frantic democracy of those inferior fellows" (*M-D*, p. 133), the three non-Caucasian harpooners. This "almost frantic democracy," represented by, again in Ishmael's words, "the periodical tumultuous visitations of these three savages" (*M-D*, p. 133), manifests the subversion and abrogation of order, the discord and "universal wolf" feared by Taylor, Browne, and Shakespeare's Ulysses when anomalies occur in the chain of Being. Between "Knights and Squires" and "The Specksynder" five chapters intervene, four of which—"Ahab," "Enter Ahab; to Him, Stubb," "The Pipe," and "Queen Mab"—emphasize Ahab's omnipotence on the *Pequod*. Ishmael describes him in "The Pipe," for example, as seated on a stool fashioned of whale ivory and asks how he could sit there "without bethinking him of the royalty it symbolized? For a Khan of the plank, and a king of the sea, and a great lord of Leviathans was Ahab" (*M-D*, p. 114). The fifth chapter of that group is "Cetology," in which Ishmael attempts to categorize "the constituents of a chaos" (*M-D*, p. 117) by classifying the whales, nominally according to size but also according to value with respect to the quality and quantity of oil as well as to the availability of the various species. All of these nine chapters from 26 to 34 reflect the conceptual scheme of the chain of Being.

That cosmological chain is predicated, of course, upon the existence of one original Being, a benign cause or creator of everything including itself, and whoever bolds to another principle—a principle of evil—on equal footing with the first cannot accept the Platonic cosmology in either the original form or in its diversified development. If a thinking person with a will to believe cannot accept one of the many variations of the argument alleging that God created evil for the sake of ultimate good, he is left, then, with limited alternatives: to accept the principle of evil as a reality, to take existentially the empirical world for what it is and nothing more, to seek the nature of existence with the eye and ear of a skeptic, or to turn inward and brood over the inscrutability of one's own relation to the cosmos, a turn which often has very dark and even deadly results.

Pulled toward the latter two of these choices, Melville found confirmation of his contradictory inclination toward both faith and doubt in the *Historical and Critical Dictionary* of Pierre Bayle.[14] In her superb study of Melville's use of Bayle, Millicent Bell indicates that Melville was particularly attracted to the portraits of Zoroaster—whose universe required the existence of two sovereign beings, one Good and the other Evil—and of Pyrrho, the skeptic, a contemporary of Alexander who denied knowledge of absolutes altogether and asserted that all we can know even of things themselves is "some relations they have to one another" (p. 648). Bayle despised the pantheism of Spinoza, "whose 'absurd and monstrous hypothesis' it was," he said, "that 'there is one Being and one Nature, and that Being produces in itself and by an immanent action, whatever goes by the name of creatures'" (Bell, p. 628). Melville's skeptical outlook on the alleged benignity of nature led him to follow Bayle's line of thought and to satirize Spinoza in conjunction with Plato, for Ishmael hypothesizes that the placidity and speculative indifference of the sperm whale, evident in the physiognomy of its severed head, gives him the aspect not only of a "Platonian, [but one] who might have taken up Spinoza in his latter years" (M-D, p. 284).

Whereas in *Pierre*, Melville would have his hero tell Isabel that "Virtue and Vice are trash,"[15] shadows in a dream, both before and after that novel he gave those moral qualities a more positive state of existence and made them more distinct—even approaching absolutism at times with regard to evil— by personifying them. Although Fedallah, for example, may be seen as a manifestation of a Jungian shadow figure or an alter ego in a psychological reading, on a moral level he represents both Satanism and the Zoroastrian principle of evil which Melville found in Bayle, but which is also, though to a lesser extent, embodied in the character of Ahab. Just as it would be naive to assert that the evil element in the monomaniacal captain was derived from a single source, so would it be equally foolish to suggest that it is attributable to one "tragic flaw" in a colossal mortal being—pride, defiance, heresy, alienation, the seeking after forbidden knowledge, the lust for vengeance, or whatever. Clearly, however, the over-application of intellect to matters better suited for sympathetic or spiritual openness underlies much of Ahab's evil quest, an intellectual journey that carries him, in Coleridge's phrase, beyond the point of "morbid excess."[16] Though Fedallah says little to him during the course of the novel, his cryptic prophecies and evil beckoning give Ahab "reasonable" cause to move ever onward to his quest and ever deeper into what Emerson in "The Sphinx" called "the pit of the Dragon."[17] The Devil, of course, as well as being the arch-liar, is the arch-reasoner; Hawthorne's Young Goodman Brown learns that to his dismay in a tale which much impressed Melville. Momentarily Brown has his doubts as he walks through the forest, but his smiling companion of the ophidian staff tells him, "Let us walk on, nevertheless, reasoning as we go, and if I convince thee not, thou shalt turn back."[18] Indeed, the convincing devil here makes an excellent confidence-man.

In the heavens as Milton describes them, there is no need of such reasoning, for pure love, acceptance, willingness to serve, and desire to obey characterize the attitude of the angels toward the Lord. When Melville, on his way to England in 1849, sat up late on the second night out, talking with his new friend, George Adler, about "'Fixed Fate, Free will, foreknowledge absolute' &c,"[19] he was carrying on a pastime of the fallen angels, not the heavenly ones. After Satan has left Pandaemonium on his evil mission, some of the fallen angels who remain behind sit apart philosophizing over

Fixt Fate, free will, foreknowledge absolute,
And found no end, in wand'ring mazes lost.
Of good and evil much they argu'd then,
Of happiness and final misery,
Passion and Apathie, and glory and shame,
Vain wisdom all, and false Philosophic:
Yet with a pleasing sorcerie could charm
Pain for a while or anguish, and excite
Fallacious hope, or arm th' obdured brest
With stubborn patience as with triple steel. [II, 560–569]

Ultimately Melville's profound questioning with no hope of satisfactory answers inevitably led to despair, only occasionally ameliorated by brief periods of satisfaction or even elation. But the doubts were imperious. As early as 1851, his own uncertainty is reflected in his fiction through Ahab's comment to Starbuck, "Sometimes I think there's naught beyond" (*M-D*, p. 144), which directly echoes a passage in his letter to Hawthorne suggesting, "perhaps, after all, there is *no* secret" (*L*, p. 125; April? 16?, 1851).

The skepticism becomes certainty in *Pierre*, where it approaches sacrilege as the narrator describes his young hero's rapid awakening to disillusionment: "By vast pains we mine into the pyramid; by horrible gropings we come to the central room; with joy we espy the sarcophagus; but we lift the lid—and no body is there!—appallingly vacant as vast is the soul of a man!" (*P*, p. 285). But Melville goes further in *Pierre* than his ostensible rejection of spiritual Being; as Twain was to do half a century later, he treats it with sarcastic scorn. In *Paradise Lost* he had read God's words to His son explaining His nature as "uncircumscrib'd" divinity: "I am who fill / Infinitude, nor vacuous the space" (VII, 168–170), and he played upon this description when exposing Pierre's mockery of religious faith. Awaiting Lucy's arrival at the Church of the Apostles, Pierre is bitter over everything that has gone wrong: a "vague, fearful feeling stole into him, that, rail as all atheists will, there is a mysterious, inscrutable divineness in the world—a God—a Being positively present everywhere;—nay, He is now in this room; the air did part when I here sat down. I displaced the Spirit then—condensed it a little off from this spot" (*P*, p. 317). Of this incident William Braswell pointedly remarks, "Displacement of the Holy Ghost by a human rump is hardly the sort of humor that one finds in an author wholly reverent toward the Deity."[20] That, of course, is an understatement. Pierre ultimately commits suicide as a result of his overwhelming rage, defiance, and disillusionment, and by the time

Melville had completed his seventh novel, he had already entered what was to become the darkest period of his life.

If Melville could be specific in his reference to *Being* as a universal presence—as he was in *Pierre*—he could also, even in the same novel, suggest that divinity was to be found more in energy than in principle. Isabel, for example, explains to Pierre, "I had been taught no God—I thanked the bright human summer, and the joyful human sun in the sky [for the kindness of an old woman] . . . and I would sometimes steal away into the beautiful grass, and worship the kind summer and the sun" (*P,* p. 123). Here Isabel partially reflects Hawthorne's portrait of Hester Prynne, who is no nature worshipper but who does lack divine guidance though she dwells in a Puritan community; her *love* for Dimmesdale, she reminds him, "had a consecration of its own,"[21] which suggests her finding sanctity in energy and action rather than in principle, a quality that characterizes Isabel as well. Moreover, if there is a clear implication of *Being* as substance in Melville's letter of 1851 to Hawthorne, through its proximity to nouns in apparent apposition, there is also in that letter a possible confirmation of its connoting *activity,* by virtue of its correspondence with the word "exists" several sentences above. In that passage, Melville asserts that the absolutely fearless man "declares himself a sovereign nature (in himself) amid the powers of heaven, hell, and earth. He may perish; but so long as he *exists* he insists upon treating with all Powers upon an equal basis" (*L,* pp. 124–125; April?, 16?, 1851; my emphasis). Here it seems that the defiant "Nay sayer" is sovereign by virtue of his existence alone, or in other words, his *being* a nature in himself.

Where might Melville have found this application of the term? One of the most likely places is Coleridge's *Biographic Literaria,* which he is known to have read early in 1848. Furthermore, his profound interest in the writing of Coleridge was maintained through the next few highly crucial years of his career.

For example, when he discussed with George Adler "Fixed Fate, Free will," and so forth, he had Coleridge as well as Milton in mind. In his journal entry for the following day, Melville wrote that Adler's "philosophy is Coleridgean: he accepts the Scriptures as divine, & yet leaves himself free to inquire into Nature. . . . He believes that there are things *out* of God and independent of him,—things that would have existed were there no God," such as mathematical facts.

Hence Melville was familiar with the theological and philosophical thought of Coleridge at least two and a half years before he wrote to Hawthorne of sovereign natures and *Being* early in 1851. Although Melville's journal entry specifies a nominal God when referring to Adler's "Coleridgean" philosophy, Owen Barfield succinctly notes that Coleridge's faith "was a Christianity of energy, or . . . of the *energeia* of the Pauline Epistles; a doctrine of the sovereign independence and initiative of the human spirit."[22] Indeed, a climactic passage from Coleridge's *Theory of Life* (1848) so clearly anticipates Melville's phrasing as well as thought in his assertion of autonomous man that it is difficult to believe he was not himself familiar with that essay by the time he wrote to Hawthorne in 1851. *"Porphyrigeniti sumus!,"* Coleridge wrote, explaining,

> In Man the centripetal and individualizing tendency of all Nature is itself concentred and individualized—he is a revelation of Nature! Henceforward, he is referred to himself, delivered up to his own charge; and he who stands the most on himself, and stands the firmest, is the truest, because the most individual, Man. In social and political life this acme is inter-dependence; in moral life it is independence; in intellectual life it is genius.[23]

Melville's introduction to the prose of the British romantic, however, more than likely came through not *The Theory of Life* but the *Biographia*, which is more philosophically and aesthetically than theologically oriented, and in the twelfth chapter of which Coleridge, who uses the word in both senses, is distinctly emphasizing the nature of *Being*. He writes, for instance, that philosophy is the search for Truth, and "Truth is the correlative of Being; . . . both are *ab initio,* identical and co-inherent; . . . intelligence and being are reciprocally each other's substrate."[24] Again, anticipating Emerson's Yankee brand of transcendentalism, he describes philosophy as the "science of BEING altogether" (111, 335), a union of the speculative with the practical. Finally and most explicitly, Coleridge indicates that he is investigating an absolute principle of *knowing ("cognoscendi"),* not of *being ("essendi"),* for, he says, to seek the principle of *being* would mean that "philosophy would pass into religion, and religion become inclusive of philosophy. We begin with the I KNOW MYSELF, in order to end with the absolute I AM. We proceed from the SELF, in order to lose and find all self in GOD" (111, 348). Here he concludes with the basically Spinozan idea that generated Pierre Bayle's derision of pantheism, though unlike Spinoza, Coleridge found Self in a God of love rather than in an emotionally detached universal divinity.

With this implicit reference to Spinoza, however, Coleridge was in step with the Germanic philosophy of his time. Several Coleridgean scholars have shown that he drew heavily from post-Renaissance British and European philosophy as well as from that of his German contemporaries in attempting to construct a system of his own. Lovejoy points out that as the two aspects of the dual God—other-worldly and this-worldly—broke apart in the eighteenth century, God began to be identified with Nature in its progenitiveness, its fecundity, and its variety; by the end of the century, God was being thought of as an evolutionary and self-realizing life-force in Nature instead of as a source of emanation and creation (pp. 316–318). In Friedrich Schelling, both sides of God remain, but the first is only a vestige, and the second, the evolutionary life-force, is predominant. For Schelling, God is necessarily self-actualizing, consistently "becoming," and thus achieving His "Being" through that process (Lovejoy, p. 318).

The debt of Coleridge to Schelling in the *Biographia* is substantial, and one would be hard put not to say that Melville's was, also, had Melville been able to read German. Evidently, what he may have derived from Schelling came largely through Coleridge, for no little of the German pantheist's thought may be found in the *Biographia*, sometimes translated verbatim, and certain echoes which appear in Melville's fiction are little short of astonishing;[25] clearly, they document the dynamic effects of the *Zeitgeist* upon the fertile literary mind. The correspondences between Schelling's *Of Human Freedom* (1809) and *Moby-Dick* provide a case in point. Not only elements of the thought but at times even the images are similar. In that tract, Schelling explains in very complex and paradoxical language the manner in which cosmic order and reason have been created from chaos and unreason; although disorder was then submerged, a residue remains below. Schelling depicts this with images of light and darkness—what would be for Melville "love" and "fright"—showing how man's conceit (which Melville might have personified in Ahab) is disruptive: "Without . . . preceeding [sic] gloom, creation would have no reality; darkness is its necessary heritage. Only God—the Existent himself—dwells in pure light; for he alone is self-born. Man's conceit opposes this origin from the depths and even seeks out moral reasons against it."[26] Schelling describes the "primal longing" that eventuates in the creation of the cosmos as a longing which "moves in anticipation like a surging, billowing sea" (p. 35). Later he distinguishes between universal and individual Will, indicating that in combination they seem self-contradictory; whereas the universal Will strives for union, the ego longs for autonomy and freedom. In describing their seeming opposition, Schelling anticipates Melville's well-known image which concludes chapter 58—"Brit." According to Schelling, "The terror of life drives man out of the center in which he was created; for being the lucid and pure essence of all will[,]" this is consuming fire for each particular will; in order to be able to live in it man must mortify all egotism, which almost makes necessary the attempt to leave it and to enter the periphery in order to seek peace for his selfhood there (p. 59). In a similar vein, Ishmael asks his readers to ponder over the "eternal war" in existence since the world began:

> Consider all this; and then turn to this green, gentle, and most docile earth; consider them both, the sea and the land; and do you

not find a strange analogy to something in yourself? For as this appalling ocean surrounds the verdant land, so in the soul of man there lies one insular Tahiti, full of peace and joy, but encompassed by all the horrors of the half known life. God keep thee! Push not off from that isle, thou canst never return!

Again the "consuming fire" for each particular will presages the auto-consumptive Ahab: "the very light of life which shines in the depths of darkness in every single man is fanned in the simmer into a consuming fire" (p. 70).

In his *Stuttgart Private Lectures* of the following year, 1810, Schelling might have provided the philosophical framework for Melville's ambiguous letter of 1851, praising the autonomous individual. Schelling wrote that "since man occupies a middle place between the non-being [that is, "unawakened-ness"] of nature and the absolute Being, God, he is free from both. He is free from God through having an independent root in nature; free from nature through the fact that the divine is awakened [only] in him, that which in the midst of nature is above nature. One may call the former, man's own (natural) aspect through which he is an individual, a personal being; the latter may be called his divine aspect."[27] Embracing such a philosophy of liberation, a man could be a colossus, a demi-god—a Taji, let us say, or an Ahab. "I almost believe," wrote Friedrich Schlegel, in keeping with the same idea, "that a wise self-limitation and moderation of the mind is not more necessary to man than the inward, ever restless, almost voracious, participation in all life, and a certain feeling of the sanctity . . . of an abounding fullness."[28] From here it is but a short step to an ebullient Melville approaching the climax of his first risky romance: "better to sink in boundless deeps, than float on vulgar shoals; and give me, ye gods, an utter wreck, if wreck I do."[29] This is the dynamic *Being* in Melville which pressed him onward and provided the motivating force behind the pilgrimage of *Clarel*, the *Being* which persistently reminded him of his mortality in a universe where immortality was but a word.

Not only in his fiction but also in his letters of the early 1850's Melville betrays his deep brooding over the problem of increasing age—and at the time he was not much beyond thirty. Among many examples, two stand out, as much for their context as their content. Responding exuberantly to Hawthorne's letter praising *Moby-Dick*, Melville acknowledged the "pantheistic" feeling he had enjoyed while reading it: "your heart beat in my ribs and mine in yours, and both in God's," he wrote. A moment later on an Emersonian tack, he asked, "Lord, when shall we be done growing?" and ended the paragraph optimistically: "Leviathan is not the biggest fish;—I have heard of Krakens." But after only a few lines his mood has become melancholy: "Lord, when shall we be done changing? Ah! it's a long stage, and no inn in sight, and night coming, and the body cold. . . . Knowing you persuades me more than the Bible of our immortality" (*L,* pp. 142–143; November 17?, 1851). Two months later he wrote to Sophia, pleased that she had recognized a certain allegorical significance, in *Moby-Dick* and telling her, with extraordinary myopia for Melville, that his next book —*Pierre*—will be "a rural bowl of milk," that he hopes the children are content, and that her husband's writing is deserving of abundant praise; suddenly he turns once more to the theme of mortality, though with a touch of whimsy in the tone: "Life is a long Dardenelles [*sic*] . . . the shores whereof are bright with flowers, which we want to pluck, but the bank is too high; & so we float on & on, hoping to come to a landing-place at last—but swoop! we launch into the great sea!" (*L,* pp. 145–147; January 8, 1852). Even in his more light-hearted moments the chronic sense of mortality seems to him irrepressibly like a steady bass rhythm in his consciousness, and it effects at times inexplicable changes of mood. Gradually the theme became more prevalent in his fiction, as may be seen in the number of aging protagonists and narrators who people his short stories of the 1850's.

The sharp contrasts of mood evident in Melville's letters exemplify a constant theme in Emerson's essays—that everything is subject to change but the intrinsic permanence of the universal soul. "Our moods do not believe in each other," Emerson wrote and, as if anticipating Melville's letter to Hawthorne of a decade later added, "I am God in nature; I am a weed by the wall."[30] But for him, such inconsistency was merely a matter of mood, something readily transcended in a man of character. For Melville, however, it was not so simple. Like Emerson, Melville was well aware of the apparent incongruity between the two worlds of Descartes, that of the *"cogito ergo sum"* and that of the vortices (Ishmael's "universal thump" in an entirely mechanistic and material cosmos). But whereas Descartes could find a way to unify them in, strange to say, the human pineal gland, and Emerson could see them merge in the context of nature or the metaphor of the circle, Melville found them irreconcilable. Unlike Emerson, in "Circles," who said that although "We grizzle every day. . . . old age ought not to creep on a human mind [because] . . . every moment is new" (p. 189), Melville could not satisfactorily reconcile the chronometrical with the horological in terms of life and death any more than he could do so with respect to heavenly and earthly mortality.

This fundamental difference between them cannot be disregarded, of course, though it has too often led readers to overlook equally important correspondences in their thought.[31] That Melville was highly impressed with Emerson upon first hearing him speak is very clear from his letter to Evert Duyckinck of early 1849; he wrote, "Say what they will, he's a great man" (*L,* p. 77; February 24, 1849). That his next letter, only a week later, is more restrained can be attributed more to his confidant's attitude than to a genuine change of view on Melville's part. "Nay," he begins, "I do not oscillate in Emerson's rainbow"; instead, he says, he prefers intellectual autonomy; nevertheless, he acknowledges that Emerson "is more than a brilliant fellow, . . . an uncommon man"; and he implies further that Emerson is a "thought-diver" worthy of admiration despite his presumptuousness (*L*, pp. 78–79; March 3, 1849). This partial disclaimer was quickly sent after his earlier letter of unqualified praise had drawn an immediate rejoinder from Duyckinck, who charged Emerson with aloofness. Why? In fact, Duyckinck had never held much affection for Emerson, and during the late 1840's he was especially irritated with the Transcendentalist, who persistently refused to accept his invitation to contribute a collection of essays or verse to Wiley and Putnam, for whom he was editing the "Library of American Books." (He had been especially anxious to acquire publication rights to *Representative Men*.)[32] Melville paid homage to Duyckinck's sarcastic criticism but still found much to admire in Emerson, though he could never hold faith in Transcendental optimism and would occasionally subject it to caustic satire in later years.

And yet the very existence of that satire strongly implies that something in Emersonian thought continued to remain alive for Melville.[33] Why else, in the late 1850's, for example, did it warrant such extensive attention as he gave it in *The Confidence-Man*? Although perhaps she goes too far in making her point, Nina Baym touches upon the issue when she proposes that Melville was probably closer to Emerson than to Hawthorne in his writing because of Melville's overriding concern with side moral content of his work.[34] Indeed, all three writers show a profound underlying consideration of truth and faith. "We are natural believers," Emerson wrote in "Montaigne" (IV, 170); and in "Experience," the great fact in history is not *what* man believes about the soul, "but *the universal impulse to believe*" at all in some Ideal, some spiritual power (III, 74–75). Melville was not immune to this impulse. When he traveled to England and the Continent late in 1849, he made it a point to see churches and cathedrals of all sizes, kinds, and ages—and not for their art and architecture alone, for while overseas he spent most of his Sundays at church often attending more than one full service in a day and commenting upon the sermons in his journals. When he returned to England in 1856, Hawthorne testified to the presence of this "impulse to believe" in Melville, and the whole of *Clarel* documents his continuous exploration for a ground on which to base it—a Sacred Ground of Being, as it were. Emerson points out that although the "First Cause" has been called many different things through the ages, it "refuses to be named." "In our more correct writing," he says, "we give to this generalization the name of Being."[35] Melville never ascertained the truth of this *Being*; like Rolfe in *Clarel*, he felt "cut off" from faith, sensing "all the depths of Being moan, / Though luminous on every hand" (II, xxi, 94–97). Truth for him, well before the writing of *Clarel*, was no longer simply elusive, but worse; it was silent.

Early in 1877, less than a year after the publication of *Clarel,* he wrote to John C. Hoadley, the husband of his sister Catherine, "Life is so short, and so ridiculous and irrational . . . that one knows not what to make of it, unless—well, finish the sentence for yourself" (*L,* 260; March 31, 1877)—unless, in other words, there is nothing to be made of it at all. Like Clarel himself near the end of the journey, with no understanding of the mortal world, Melville asks, how can one expect to comprehend *"that* alleged, which is afar?"[36] Ultimately, Shakespeare's Lafeu, in *All's Well That Ends Well,* seems effectively to express Melville's philosophy of *Being* from the beginning of his career as a romancer to the end of his life; he triple marked these revealing lines in his edition of Shakespeare:

> They say miracles are past; and we have our philosophical persons,
> to make modern and familiar, things supernatural and causeless.
> Hence is it that we make trifles of terrors, ensconcing ourselves
> into seeming knowledge, when we should submit ourselves to an
> unknown fear. [II, iii, 1–6]

At the end Melville submitted not to fear but to life and doubt; then as always, however, one feels, if *Billy Budd* is a fair indication, his submission was not without reservations.

NOTES

An earlier version of this paper was presented at a meeting of the Melville Society, Houston, Texas, on December 29, 1980. I wish to express my appreciation here to Professor Merton M. Sealts Jr., for his care in reading and generously commenting upon that original version.

1. *The Letters of Herman Melville,* ed. Merrell R. Davis and William H. Gilman (New Haven: Yale University Press, 1960), pp. 124–125; letter dated April? 16?, 1851; hereafter cited parenthetically in the text by *L,* followed by page number (s) and date of letter.

2. *L.,* p. 125; April? 16?, 1851. Some textual uncertainty exists regarding the quoted passage in that the original letter, which has never been found, may not have been transcribed correctly by Julian Hawthorne. Nevertheless, his text is the earliest one available. A question may be raised, however, as to how far one should or can reasonably go in attempting to grasp the significance of this oddly phrased passage of questionable authenticity. In response, it may be suggested, first, that such a question would probably be raised chiefly *because* of the unexpected and somewhat cryptic phrasing. Second, Melville was evidently writing rapidly and in a highly charged emotional state as he drafted this personal letter to a friend and confidant whose mind he believed to be in intimate rapport with his own. Surely, he could assume that Hawthorne would catch his meaning readily enough.

Finally, the two alternate readings proposed by Davis and Gilman do not significantly change the meaning of the phrase in context (*L.* p. 125 n. 6); the principal word—*"Being"*—to which Melville redirects our attention again two sentences later (with reference to "that word") is the same in all three. Melville is addressing here the fundamental difference between an ideal substance, divinity, or spiritual energy underlying existence and man's verbalization of the same. On the one hand, with Emerson, he resents the conversion of the living God to a mere word in the dictionary; on the other, very unlike Emerson, he believes that to assume he or any other human being—is himself divine would lead one toward self-destruction, for such a conviction would be too much for a sane mortal to bear. Unless it can be demonstrated that Julian Hawthorne grossly misread or purposely altered the original text of the letter, there is no sound reason to doubt that the present phrasing in the Davis-Gilman edition conveys at least a good sense of Melville's intended meaning as well as his ambivalence over the whole matter of divinity in relation to human existence—especially his own.

3. "Song of Myself," section 26, ll. 609–610, *Leaves of Grass: A Textual Variorum of the Printed Poems,* ed. Sculley Bradley *et al.* (New York: New York University Press, 1980), I, 38.

4. Sealts, "Herman Melville's Reading in Ancient Philosophy," Diss. Yale, 1942, pp. 35, 120–122, 192. For a rewarding discussion of Melville's link to Platonic thought, especially with respect to *Moby-Dick,* also see Michael E. Levin, "Ahab as Socratic Philosopher: The Myth of the Cave Inverted," *American Transcendental Quarterly,* No. 41 (Winter 1979), pp. 61–73.

5. Campbell, "Plato," *Encyclopaedia Britannica,* 11th ed. (1910–1911), XXI, 814–815.

6. *Moby-Dick,* ed. Harrison Hayford and Hershel Parker (New York: W. W. Norton, 1967), p. 288; hereafter cited parenthetically in the text by *M-D* and page number(s).

7. *The Works of Thomas Carlyle,* ed. H. D. Traill (1896; rpt. New York: AMS Press, 1969), I, 209.

8. Lovejoy, *The Great Chain of Being* (1936; rpt. New York: Harper & Brothers, 1960), pp. 82–83, 316–317.

9. Merton M. Sealts, Jr., has made a detailed study of Melville's knowledge of and response to Plato and his successors among philosophical idealists, including a consideration of previous scholarship. See "Melville's 'Neoplatonical Originals,'" *MLN,* 67 (1952), 80, and "Melville and the Platonic Tradition," in his *Pursuing Melville, 1940–1980: Chapters and Essays* (Madison: University of Wisconsin Press, 1982), pp. 278–336. I am especially indebted here to Prof. Sealts for making available to me details and observations from the latter essay prior to its publication.

10. Thomas Taylor, ed. and trans., "Introduction" to *Select Works of Plotinus,* ed. G. R. S. Mead (London: G. Bell & Sons, 1914), pp. lxix–lxx, n. 1.

11. *The Works of Sir Thomas Browne,* ed. Geoffrey Keynes (London: Faber & Faber, 1964) I, 43.

12. C. A. Patrides, ed., Introduction to *Sir Thomas Browne: The Major Works* (Harmondsworth, Middlesex: Penguin Books, 1977), p. 27.

13. I, iii, 101–103, 110, 119–124. Evidently, Melville liked to think of himself as reading Shakespeare in the manner of "philosophers" rather than as do "those mistaken souls" who regard him as "a mere man of Richard-the-Third humps, and Macbeth daggers" ("Hawthorne and His Mosses," in *M-D,* p. 541).

14. Millicent Bell, "Pierre Bayle and *Moby-Dick,*" *PMLA,* 66 (1951), 628–629.

15. *Pierre; or, The Ambiguities,* ed. Harrison Hayford, Hershel Parker, and G. Thomas Tanselle, *The Writings* (Evanston and Chicago: Northwestern University

Press and Newberry Library, 1971), pp. 273-274; hereafter cited parenthetically in the text by *P* and page number(s).

16. Leon Howard now believes that Melville may have been familiar with Coleridge's phrase as applied to Hamlet prior to completing *Moby-Dick;* see Tom Quirk, "More on the Composition of *Moby-Dick:* Leon Howard Shows Us Ahab's Leg," *Melville Society Extracts,* No. 46 (May 1981), p. 6.

17. *The Complete Works of Ralph Waldo Emerson* (Boston: Houghton Mifflin, 1903), IX, 23, I. 75; hereafter this edition is cited parenthetically in the text by volume and page number.

18. Hawthorne, *Mosses from an Old Manse,* ed. William Charvat et al. (Columbus: Ohio State University Press, 1974), p. 76.

19. Melville, *Journal of a Visit to London and the Continent . . . 1849–1850,* ed. Eleanor Melville Metcalf (Cambridge: Harvard University Press, 1948), p. 5; entry dated October 13, 1849.

20. Braswell, *Melville's Religious Thought* (1943; rpt. New York: Pageant Books, 1959), p. 71.

21. *The Scarlet Letter* (Columbus: Ohio State Univ. Press, 1971), p. 195.

22. Owen Barfield, *What Coleridge Thought* (London: Oxford University Press, 1971), p. 8; Barfield's emphasis.

23. *The Complete Works of Samuel Taylor Coleridge,* ed. [W. G. T.] Shedd (New York: Harper & Brothers, 1853), I, 412.

24. *Biographic Literaria . . . , in Complete Works,* III, 249.

25. Thomas McFarland, *Coleridge and the Pantheist Tradition* (London: Oxford Univ. Press, 1969), pp. 24–26; ch. 1 *passim.*

26. Friedrich Wilhelm, Joseph Schelling, *Philosophical Inquiries into the Nature of Human Freedom* trans. and ed. James Gutmann (Chicago: Open Court Publishing Co., 1936), p. 34.

27. Quoted by Gutmann, ed., "Introduction" to Schelling, p. xliii.

28. Quoted and translated by Lovejoy, pp. 304–305, from *Ueber die Philosophic: An Dorothea, in Athenaeum, II,* 1, 15–16 (as cited by Lovejoy, p. 370, n. 29).

29. *Mardi and A Voyage Thither,* ed., Harrison Hayford, Hershel Parker, and G. Thomas Tanselle, *The Writings* (Evanston and Chicago: Northwestern University Press and Newberry Library, 1970), p. 557.

30. "Circles," in *The Collected Works of Ralph Waldo Emerson,* ed. Alfred R. Ferguson *et al.* (Cambridge, Mass. and London: Belknap of Harvard University Press, 1971–), II, 182.

31. Nevertheless, the association of Melville with Emerson's thought and writing has been widely studied. A recent comprehensive and convincing account appears in Merton M. Sealts, Jr., "Melville and Emerson's Rainbow," *ESQ,* 26 (1980), 53–78.

32. See Emerson's letters to Duyckinck and Rusk's annotations in *The Letters of Ralph Waldo Emerson,* ed. Ralph L. Rusk (New York: Columbia University Press, 1939), III, 296–297, 301–302, 307–308, 308 n. 108.

33. Sealts, "Melville and Emerson's Rainbow," pp. 63, 69–71.

34. Baym, "Melville's Quarrel with Fiction," *PMLA,* 94 (1979), 914.

35. "Experience," III, 73; according to Sealts, Melville may well have read "Experience" early in 1849 ("Melville and Emerson's Rainbow," p. 63).

36. *Clarel,* ed. Walter E. Bezanson (New York: Hendricks House, 1960), IV, iii, 118.

SANDRA A. ZAGARELL

Reenvisioning America:
Melville's "Benito Cereno"

"How unlike we are made!" thinks Amasa Delano, the American captain of Herman Melville's "Benito Cereno," about the weak and sickly Spanish captain Benito Cereno.[1] Through national and racial appellations, Delano constantly marks differences between himself and others. He perceives the black slaves aboard the Spanish ship the *San Dominick* as animals; he so frequently labels Cereno "the Spaniard" that the epithet comes to imply indelible and tainted national characteristics; he thinks himself possessed of superior energy and decisiveness that emanate from his privileged nationality. Delano's smugness is characteristic of the prevailing American political and cultural climate of the 1850's, for Melville was writing at a time when many Americans insisted on their country's superiority and saw its destiny as historically unique. In 1854–1855, when he composed "Benito Cereno,"[2] such feelings were taking political expression in the doctrine of Manifest Destiny and the Young America movement, which had just had their heyday, in the American Party and Know-Nothingism, which were at their peak, and in the glorification of the revolutionary fathers, who were viewed as having freed America from a decadent Europe.[3]

In "Benito Cereno," Melville challenges his countrymen's Delano-like sense of superiority by showing how very like other nations America was. In fact, he turns inside out some of nineteenth-century America's most cherished

ESQ: A Journal of the American Renaissance, Volume 30, Number 4 (1984): pp. 245–259. © 1984 Sandra A. Zagarell.

visions of itself by portraying the country not as an historical clean slate but as the unwitting perpetuator of forms of commercialism, colonialism, and slavery that began centuries earlier in the Old World from which Delano holds himself disdainfully aloof. In a painstaking anatomy of the mind of the American captain, he lays bare the elaborate ideology by means of which Americans denied the historical implications of such practices, and he presents slavery and the rationalizations that justified it not simply as discrete phenomena but as powerful synecdoches for economic activities and cultural disjunctions that threatened the country's stability at every level. In short, "Benito Cereno" implicitly portrays the United States as a nation—to borrow from a description of the *San Dominick*—whose "every inch of ground" was "mined into honey-combs" (p. 138). Like *Pierre*, it attacks American values and institutions; like *Israel Potter* it revises Americans' sense of their own history; and it does so, this essay argues, by destabilizing a range of cultural conventions from Americans' self-proclaimed benevolence to their unconscious authoritarianism.

Critics have long been interested in the historicity of "Benito Cereno," many of them focusing on issues connected with slavery in the Old World and the New.[4] Recent studies have expanded the scope of that interest, seeing the novella as comprising a broad reenvisioning of antebellum America. Michael Paul Rogin's *Subversive Genealogy: The Politics and Art of Herman Melville*, while interpreting the novella in terms of slavery, sees it as a sort of meditation on contemporary political theory, a realization that neither prevalent model of race relations, not the natural rights argument of Abolitionists nor the paternalism favored by slaveholders and their apologists, provided a safe and peaceful way out of the violent conflict that, as Melville saw, slavery would soon produce. While Rogin demonstrates Melville's concern with both the character of American society and with the ways Americans conceptualized that character, Allan Moore Emery in "'Benito Cereno' and Manifest Destiny" establishes a hitherto unrecognized historical frame of reference, American expansionism, and demonstrates how "Benito Cereno" exposes with almost allegorical precision both the expansionist, anti-Catholic, Anglo-Saxonist mentality of America in the 1850's and the ironic fact that this expansionism mirrored the earlier colonialism of the very country—Spain—whose New World presence was being contested.[5] The fruitfulness of each of these very different readings attests to how stubbornly "Benito Cereno" resists being keyed to any single historical referent.[6] The present study—which is indebted to the many critics who have demonstrated the extent and historicity of Melville's indictment of slavery—profits especially from Emery's renewed attention to historical context and Rogin's focus on Melville as a kind of social theorist, and it attempts to extend these arguments by showing that the novella contains a keen analysis of the *cultural* dimensions of the ways social systems are interpreted.

In particular, this paper maintains that in "Benito Cereno" Melville subjects a panoply of American cultural codes and assumptions to intense critical pressure in order to expose gaps in his countrymen's knowledge and characteristic modes of thought. If his vision is radical, his approach is wide-ranging. The portrayal of Amasa Delano, to be considered in the first section, is, as most readers assume, that of a representative northerner, but it is at once denser and more dynamic than has been realized. Elaborating a complex ideology, it also dramatizes the epistemological fancy footwork Delano must perform in order *not* to understand what is amiss on the *San Dominick,* and it ominously doubles Delano's ideology with that of the Spanish captain, Benito Cereno. In elucidating the means by which Melville structures his portrait of Delano, this section explores one level on which "Benito Cereno" discloses what Americans did not know, why they did not know it, and the potential consequences of that ignorance.

The second section examines a more theoretical aspect of Melville's critique in "Benito Cereno," its presentation of the extensive cultural discontinuities that prevail under an unstable social order. In presenting Delano's ideology with a situation it cannot explain—the slaves' revolt and subsequent pretense of enslavement—Melville reveals that the conventions whose fixity men like Delano take for granted are actually exceedingly fluid. In social orders built on inequity, disempowered groups like the black slaves convert such conventions into unspoken languages of dissent and, when possible, insurrection. This section focuses on Melville's explication of the multivalent indeterminacy of these conventions. The last section addresses Melville's indirect but powerful effort to destabilize the existing social order by undermining the sort of authority on which it rests. This section attempts, first, to establish how Melville links accession to social-cultural authority with incapacity for independent, clear-sighted interpretation.[7] For different reasons, none of the characters, black or white, can genuinely resist the hierarchical social system that circumscribes him, and therefore none can achieve the kind of disinterested analysis that "Benito Cereno" itself accomplishes. Finally, a comparison of "Benito Cereno" with its source, the eleventh chapter of the historical Amasa Delano's *Narrative of Voyages and Travels in the Northern and Southern Hemispheres,* illustrates how Melville's composition of the novella itself amounted to a symbolic dismantling of the kind of authority which perpetuates hierarchical social systems. Melville revises the *Narrative* to put Delano, and America, in a context that damns the American system; he also reverses the real Delano's portrait of himself as moral innocent, recasting him as a minor originator of the self-celebrating hypocrisy that allowed Americans to think themselves historically unique.

I

Through the thought processes of Amasa Delano, Melville critiques northern antebellum thought by letting it speak for itself. Delano's sentimental
racism, which prevents him from perceiving the blacks' hatred of slavery,
and his expansionist mentality and chauvinism[8] are only two of his ideology's many components: the code of gentility, debased romanticism, and sensational melodrama are developed with equal care. In fact, Delano's ideology
is meticulously keyed to Melville's America, each aspect being drawn from
specific motifs and linguistic registers prominent in contemporary culture.

Charity and courtesy, predominant among Delano's values, were central to Victorian America's emphasis on gentility. From first to last, and in
sharp contrast to Melville's other captains, Delano judges acts and gestures
in accordance with how they measure on a scale of politeness. This code is
conspicuously irrelevant to the situation he actually faces, and his persistent
faith in it obscures the real problem by preventing him from seeing clues
as clues. Critical though Delano is of Cereno's apparent indifference to all
the routines of ship life and to the arrival of an American rescuer, he labels
such behavior "unfriendly," quickly ascribes Cereno's attitude "in charity" to
ill health, and soon thereafter castigates himself for not exercising "charity
enough" in making allowances for the Spanish captain (p. 63). After being
subjected to a highly suspicious cross-examination about security measures
on his own ship, he leaves the suddenly taciturn Cereno alone because he is
"unwilling to appear uncivil even to incivility itself" (p. 80). Because he values
gentility, he is fooled by the crude parody enacted by the steward Francesco,
whose excessive shuffling and bowing cause Babo to look "askance" (p. 105),
and declares himself pleased with the man's "nods, and bows, and smiles; a
king indeed—the king of kind hearts and polite fellows" (p. 106). Even at the
end of a day filled with doubts about Cereno's motives, Delano is gratified
to discover the Spanish captain recovering from an anguished silence, which
the American thinks merely a "recent discourtesy," and to hear his own name
"courteously sounded" as Cereno advances toward him; in consequence, he
"self-reproachfully" dismisses his suspicions on the grounds that Cereno had
not "meant to offend" (p. 116).

Like the code of gentility, Delano's chauvinism undercuts his ability to
discover what is amiss on the *San Dominick* and to analyze his suspicions
about Cereno. Embroidering upon the epithet "Spaniard" to explain the
captain on the basis of national characteristics, he thinks Cereno afflicted
with "Spanish spite" when he appears to have mistreated Babo (p. 105).
When Delano's suspicions about a plot against him multiply, he comforts
himself with the chauvinistic thought that "as a nation . . . these Spaniards
are all an odd set; the very word Spaniard has a curious, conspirator, Guy-
Fawkish twang to it" (p. 94). Likewise, his racism, identified by most critics

as a northern variety,[9] usually surfaces when he is confronted by something unsettling. It too functions as an epistemological smoke screen, dispelling his suspicions by reaffirming his comfortable ideology about the blacks' docile inferiority. He assuages his anxieties by envisioning all blacks as "odd-looking" and sees the oakum pickers, who are disguised figures of authority, as "bedridden old knitting women" (p. 82); he perceives a black mother as a "dam" nursing her "wide-awake faun" (p. 87). When Babo shaves Cereno, Delano has what he terms an "antic conceit" (p. 101) that the black is an executioner, then quickly takes refuge in the platitudes of racism. Attributing the black's seditious use of the Spanish flag as a barber's cloth to his love of color, Delano lays his own fears to rest once more (p. 102).

Delano also sometimes indulges in a debased romanticism, the closest he comes to a conscious philosophy. This romanticism—reminiscent of Melville's double parody of Wordsworth's "Resolution and Independence" and of American Transcendentalism in "Cock-A-Doodle-Doo!"[10]—is linked to Delano's racism, enabling him also to view blacks as noble savages. Delano revises the romantic view of the child as the father of the man: he thinks the (white) man enjoys heavenly protection because he was once a child. When his fears of being murdered mount, he calms himself with the thought that because he was formerly a boy, "little Jack of the Beach," "some one above" will shield him from harm (p. 92). Such complacency culminates in his late declaration to Cereno about the uselessness of drawing conclusions from their experiences, because "the past is passed . . . yon bright sun has forgotten it all, and the blue sea, and the blue sky; these have turned over new leaves."[11] Whereas Emerson invokes nature partly as a medium through which the individual is transported beyond personal and social mediocrity, Delano does so to avoid the responsibility of understanding human experience. Emerson's "liv[ing] in nature in the present, above time" degenerates into an escape from time, history, and inquiry.[12]

Despite its multiple components, Delano's ideology finally fails him, forcing him, however reluctantly, to modify his complacent interpretation of the San Dominick as a ship in distress with the darker view of it as a pirate ship with Cereno masquerading as a legitimate captain.[13] The theme of piracy, which dominated antebellum sea fiction in such an influential novel as Cooper's The Red Rover, had become popularized and sentimentalized by the 1840's.[14] It is a sensationalist tale that Delano produces; he "had heard of [tales of pirates]—and now, as stories, they recurred" (p. 81). He imagines a lurid scenario in which, "[o]n heart-broken pretense of entreating a cup of cold water, fiends in human form had got into lonely dwellings, nor retired until a dark deed has been done," and recalls tales of Malay pirates who lure unsuspecting seamen aboard ships that look empty, while beneath the decks "prowled a hundred spears with yellow arms ready to upthrust them through the mats" (p. 81). These fantasies relieve him of the need to think inductively, for personally threatening though they are, they do not admit of any significant threat to the social order. Moreover, Delano's sensationalist explanation of the *San Dominick* as a pirate ship complements his sentimental racism: not only are both informed by cliché, but the two are also interchangeable. When Delano finally discovers the true nature of the blacks' position, he shifts effortlessly from sentimentalizing them to brutalizing them as monsters, "flourishing hatchets and knives, in ferocious piratical revolt" (p. 119).

Because they filter out information which could challenge his ideology, Delano's modes of perception keep his faith in the social order intact. The content of his ideology, moreover, actively supports that order. All its parts have a common denominator, a belief in that unequal distribution of power which "Benito Cereno" shows as perilously unstable. Thus genteel regard for proper conduct, the racist justification of the subordination of blacks to whites, chauvinistic assumptions about the inferiority of other nations, the pseudo-romantic insistence on the natural order of present arrangements, and even the melodramatic scenario in which a sickly white captain controls a crew composed of a few renegade whites and an enormous supporting cast of blacks, all depend on a stable social hierarchy. Delano quite openly advocates such hierarchy. He assumes that "good order" should prevail in "armies, navies, cities, families, in nature herself" (p. 61) and defines that order in terms of the absolute authority of those at the top. As in so many of Melville's works, "the top" is symbolized by the ship's captain, in whom, as Delano thinks approvingly, is "lodged a dictatorship beyond which, while at sea, there is no earthly appeal" (p. 63).

The American's complacent piety and smug compassion, then, overlie a vigorous dedication to the personal exercise of authority: he tells Cereno by way of example how, in order to maintain discipline, he relentlessly kept his crew busy "thrumming mats for my cabin" during a three-day storm when survival seemed impossible (p. 71). As Rogin points out, the rhetoric of paternal relations characterized nineteenth-century American public discourse about the organizations of institutions like the navy, the asylum, and the educational system;[15] along these lines, Delano thinks of his ship, with its "quiet orderliness," as a "comfortable family of a crew" (p. 64). The authoritarianism underlying this family model becomes apparent when he observes the contrasting "noisy confusion" of the *San Dominick*. Noting the troublesome character of "living freight," he attributes the blacks' unruliness to the absence of "the unfriendly arm of the mate, . . . [of] stern superior officers" (pp. 64–65). His plan to reestablish order by withdrawing Cereno's command and placing his own surrogate, his second mate, in charge until Cereno is well enough to be "restored to authority" (p. 83) indicates just how important the hierarchy of command is to him: to depose another captain, however gently and temporarily, is to assume that the proper wielding of authority takes precedence over considerations of national sovereignty or private ownership of a vessel. Uppermost for Delano is a strong-minded devotion to preserving a highly vertical institutional organization.

If "Benito Cereno" lays American ideological limitations bare in Amasa Delano, it also undermines notions of American uniqueness by depicting Delano as parallel to the foreigner Cereno in many regards. Each man is a cultural type—the hearty Yankee Delano is balanced by the effete Spaniard.[16] "[B]rother captain[s]" (p. 61), both are merchants, engaging in free trade in economies dependent on slavery.[17] Each is also an established representative of the social order: Cereno belongs to "one of the most enterprising and extensive mercantile families" in South America (p. 77), while the historical Delano is from a prominent New England family whose descendants would eventually include Franklin Delano Roosevelt. Most important, placed in a situation which could throw their beliefs into disarray, they exhibit equal fervor in preserving their ideologies and their commitments to social order.

Cereno's "foreign" ideology has clear parallels in Delano's American beliefs; their values are strikingly similar. When the Spaniard finally speaks in his own voice, in the deposition and in the third section of the novella, he echoes Delano's racism and morality. The American articulates racial differences as a matter of "species" (p. 90); Cereno divides the *San Dominick*'s population into "men" and "negroes" (p. 124). Each man embraces a rigid, absolutist morality, Delano operating according to "certain general notions which, while disconnecting pain and abashment from virtue, invariably link them with vice" (p. 86) and Cereno making a similarly fixed distinction between the blacks, with their "malign machinations and deceptions" and his own position as "an innocent . . . the most pitiable of all men" (p. 139). Even more fundamentally, by juxtaposing Cereno's deposition, the second section of "Benito Cereno," with Delano's interpretations of events in the first, Melville emphasizes that for each captain, the "story" of "Benito Cereno" is an interpretation shaped and structured by ideology.

Cereno's narrative is more obviously ideological than is Delano's interpretation. Cereno's voice is almost never personal: primarily expressed through his deposition, it is a voice sanctioned by, and sanctioning, the Spanish legal system. His narrative, a declaration "against the negroes of the ship San Dominick" (p. 124), serves the express purpose of perpetuating slavery. Despite its seeming neutrality of tone and its apparent factuality, it is a sharply limited account of what Cereno has witnessed, and its limits are set by unquestioned assumptions. The deposition accepts as synonymous the legality and the moral rightness of the whites' ownership of and trade in blacks. Thus it presents the statistics of the case—names, ages, status of whites and blacks—in scrupulous detail, as though the facts speak for themselves, and speak for the innocence of the white owner, Aranda, and his entourage of clerks and cousins, and against the large group of slaves whose labor supports them. Although the narrative fails to connect its stated facts about the slaves with their revolt, it shows that Aranda's slaves epitomize the atrocities their race has suffered since the commencement of black slavery, for this group includes "raw" blacks and mulattos, old men, young men, a black chieftain, mothers and children, all uprooted, all massed together. Nor does Cereno ever question how this miscellany developed the resources to forge itself into a disciplined, purposeful organization. Even the deposition's ennumerative syntax, which Melville preserved from the original, discourages the recognition of causal connections among the events it details and thus serves to preserve the social order, not to inquire why it has failed.

The human results of this repression are manifested in Cereno's final mystification of the figure of Babo. Placing Babo in a metaphysical category, "the negro," which conflates racial and moral connotations, Cereno haunts himself with the slave. When he faints under the court's pressure to confront the black, his swoon is a double avoidance: fainting in fear, he is also fainting to escape having to explain "the negro" institutionally or historically, as "Benito Cereno" itself does. Because he chooses to mystify rather than clarify, Cereno exemplifies the price of this self-elected incapacity. Retreating further, first into silence, then into death, he becomes the victim of his ideology by remaining its spokesman.

II

In contrast to the whites, the blacks have no ideology; they are simply opposed to the social order. "Benito Cereno" incorporates their stance into the stunning depiction of the instability of any culture emanating from a fluctuating social order. The novella demonstrates that the hierarchy and the characteristics of both race and gender, thought to be natural by ante-bellum Americans, are merely conventions; it also implies that all culture is a human creation, subject to change and frequently unstable.[18] The novella pivots upon a major reversal in racial relations, the blacks' inversion of the usual master-slave conditions. Presenting blacks as enslavers, whites as slaves, it goes beyond challenging the slave system's literal hegemony, as an actual slave revolt like the Nat Turner rebellion did, to show racial characteristics as cultural constructs. Not only does the intelligence of the blacks turn prevalent white supremacy on its head, as Karcher and others have noted, but the doublings between Cereno and Babo demonstrate that racial dominance is a matter of circumstance. Approximately the same age, one the former captain of the ship, the other former captain of the slaves turned leader of the ship, Babo and Cereno encircle each other in a perpetual embrace in which ruler plays ruled, ruled plays ruler, and from which racial authority emerges as a question of context only.

By playing on the intense physical contact between Babo and Cereno, Melville also dramatizes gender as a cultural convention. Readers have sometimes detected a homoerotic coloring to Delano's perceptions of the two men,[19] but grounded as it is in a reversal of power, the relationship actually reveals the literal instability of gender. In cultures where the status of women is low, subordinated people are often feminized in order to perpetuate and to justify their inferiority. "Benito Cereno" frequently refers to nineteenth-century America's version of this practice, which blended feminization and domestication, as in the observation, made from Delano's perspective, that "most negroes" are peculiarly fitted for "vocations about one's person" because they are "natural valets and hair-dressers" (pp. 100–101). When the blacks reverse power relations, forcing the whites into captivity, they impose on the white leader, Cereno, feminine attributes like those conventionally imposed on them. They emasculate the former master, forcing him to wear an empty scabbard, "artificially stiffened" (p. 140), and feminize him by casting him in a powerless role which often renders him speechless, sickened, and swooning—a parody of the fragile, genteel lady. Cereno evinces the consequences of his emasculation by responding as though he has been raped. Indeed, his inability to face Babo after the normal order has been restored resembles many rape victims' inability to name or confront their assailants.

Melville goes beyond portraying race and gender as cultural constructs, moreover, to suggest that *all* meaning in his readers' world derives from convention, and that meaning itself is therefore unfixed. In the blacks' revolt, Melville may represent his increasing sense of the fluidity of meaning which, as Nina Baym has pointed out, was a ground for profound despair.[20] He may also have seen this fluidity to result from the essential instability of a social order based on a highly unequal distribution of power. "Benito Cereno" suggests that even under normal circumstances, at least in a slave society, conventional ideologies like Delano's remain coherent only at the price of vast oversimplification. In reality, mutability prevails. Even artifacts are cultural markers lacking inherent properties. This contingency is half-apparent to Delano, who muses that the *San Dominick*'s rusty main-chains are "more fit for the ship's present business," transporting slaves, than for its original purposes as a war vessel (p. 89). Once the slaves' revolt has demonstrated the instability of the social order, many other artifacts also acquire new functions. Tar is no longer just a preservative but a medium by which the blacks degrade and punish recalcitrant white sailors (pp. 85, 136). Hatchets—presumably to have been used by slaves in clearing land for cultivation—become weapons against the whites; the whites' sealing-spears are also transformed into weapons.

Even more dramatically, unexceptional parts of the cultural fabric emerge as unspoken languages which encode mutually exclusive meanings, some of them seditious. Babo's properly slave-like ministrations to Cereno appear solicitous to Delano but communicate veiled threats to Cereno; Cereno's moments of faintness betoken ill health to Delano, passive resistance to Babo.[21] Clothing is a particularly mutable form of visual language. Babo's near-nakedness projects the image of a submissive, powerless servant, but it also potently signifies his power and intelligence in appropriating the connotations of the rags which inscribe his former subjugation. Cereno's elaborate apparel is a traditional sign of status and the intricacy of protocol in Spain's colonial government—Delano thinks his "toilette . . . not beyond the style of the day among South Americans of his class" (pp. 68–69)—as well as a token of the wealth derived from an economy dependent on slavery. In his present circumstances, however, his adornment also bespeaks the blacks' ability to convert these traditional signs into the means of deceiving one white while degrading another.

Meaning within a culture ultimately rests on a consensus. When basic opposition to the social order prevails, as it is bound to in a slave society, the lack of such consensus produces radically divergent assumptions about meaning and communication. Those who are privileged, like Delano, will simply assume—as Delano does—that their culture is stable and determinate; disempowered groups such as black slaves will be alert to and intent on exploiting every ambiguity. "Benito Cereno" not only reveals cultural markers such as gestures and clothes to be heavily laden codes of communication, but it shows the blacks' genius in disrupting the meaning of such markers. They so increase the normal ambiguity of gestures, for example, that they seem on the verge of reversing commonly accepted meanings altogether. Thus Francesco's smiles and bows appeal to Delano, mock Cereno, and signal pleasure in their shared masquerade to Babo; Atufal appears strategically as a shackled slave to calm Delano, alarm Cereno, and support Babo. And Babo's every smile threatens Cereno while reassuring Delano on one level and the other blacks on quite another. After he cuts Cereno while shaving him, Babo's body language becomes strikingly multivalent. As he directs the Spaniard to answer questions about the *San Dominick*'s difficulties, "his face was turned half round, so as to be alike visible to the Spaniard and the American, and seemed, by its expression, to hint, that he was desirous, by getting his master to go on with the conversation, considerably to withdraw his attention from the recent annoying accident" (p. 103). Babo's single gesture conveys consideration to Delano, menace and malice to Cereno; on another level, it communicates to the reader Babo's extraordinary skill at appropriating and subverting all the nuances of the traditional role of the black body servant. More generally, his practices also cast new light on the double signification frequently employed by American slaves, "puttin' on ole Massa." Being in a position of unusual power, Babo can pitch his gestures to three different readings at once. If this slave's silent communication comprises a richer language than Delano's spoken platitudes, it also implies that a slaveholding society is a minefield of reversed meanings and unuttered languages.

III

The assumption in "Benito Cereno" that culture and ideology are imperiled human creations extends with equally destabilizing results to Americans' attitudes toward authority. Not only laying bare the authoritarianism of a Delano, the novella also implies that Americans accede to authority on all levels, from the literal authority of public officials and public records to the more abstract, even more powerfully culture-shaping authority which inheres in standard versions of the country's origins and values. Such accession bears heavily on the country's present and future, for unquestioning acceptance of authority discourages disinterested interpretation. Interpretation is part of the process of producing a literal or metaphoric text, and these texts— Cereno's deposition, the blacks' masquerade, the real Delano's *Narrative*, Melville's novella—are instrumental in perpetuating or modifying social structures. This conception of authority anticipates twentieth-century associations between authority and authorship; it is also distinctly political. The white captains accept all institutionalized authority because of their privileged status; though the blacks contest such authority, taking advantage of the instability of existing cultural codes, the literal power of the social order denies them the possibility of true creative achievement.

The backbone of the ideologies which limit the white captains' interpretations is the equation of authority with meaning. For both men, the official truth is the complete truth. When Delano boards the *San Dominick*, he encounters a "shadowy tableau" that seems "unreal" (p. 59) and in need of interpretation, but he sees only the need to get the facts, "details" (p. 65). Taking for granted that "the best account would, doubtless, be given by the captain" (p. 65)—the proper authority—he seeks out Cereno. When Cereno finally gives all the details that Delano seeks, he does so in as authoritative a mode as the American could possibly desire, speaking under oath and before the Spanish king's councilor. "Benito Cereno" of course, repudiates such modes of interpretation: after Cereno's testimony is given, the narrator even asserts that "If the Deposition have served as the key to fit into the lock of the complications which precede it, then . . . the *San Dominick*'s hull lies open today" (p. 138). By allying themselves with the authority they serve, embody, and perpetuate, Delano and Cereno have ceded to that authority control of their own capacity to interpret. Rather than unlock the complications of the actual events on the *San Dominick*, rather than face the multivalent meanings of the symbols of lock and key to which the narrator also alludes here, they will turn out documents like Cereno's deposition—and Delano's *Narrative*—which dutifully enshrine the status quo.

So heavy is the weight of social authority that conscious interpreters must also always take it into account. They, however, can question the authority which upholds the existing order, turning it against itself through illicit acts of creative rewriting. In one sense, as commentators have suggested, both Melville and Babo perform these acts,[22] Melville rewriting Chapter Eleven of Delano's *Narrative,* Babo attempting to refashion a socio-cultural script which embodies the social order. Indeed, Babo's consummate artistry appears to grant him stunning success. Readers have often remarked on how the novella's theatricality reproduces the slave system in order to destroy it. With its tableaux, its stark images, the ominous symmetry of the four oakum pickers and the six hatchet-sharpeners, "Benito Cereno" looks forward uncannily to the subversive metamorphoses of Black Arts agitation-propaganda dramas such as Amiri Baraka's "Slave Ship." Babo is brilliant as the impressario of the *San Dominick*'s drama because he can read through the white authorities and therefore thwart their objective of sustaining slavery. Yet he can achieve no authority on his own terms. As a social actor, he essentially perpetuates the slave system; he destroys the authority of the whites only to claim the same authority for himself, unleashing terror and murder likened to those of the Inquisition, while his later plan to pirate Delano's ship would entangle him in an economic web which ties free enterprise to slavery. His script, too, duplicates rather than goes beyond the old order—it is, for all its grandeur, only a masquerade. Melville makes clear that Babo can produce no genuinely new rewritings of the old script because he is completely circumscribed by the slave system. Slavery prevails so thoroughly in South America that the blacks are afraid to venture on shore for desperately needed water; moreover, though they recognize that their only chance for freedom lies in getting to a "negro country" (p. 126), their choice, Senegal is—in a detail Melville added to his source—a country where blacks enslave blacks.

All of the novella's characters are, then, claustrally restricted by pre-existing authority. Discourse within "Benito Cereno," with its echoes and tautologies, reflects this entrapment,[23] as do the images of chains and knots, the recurring motifs of becalmed ships and becalmed minds, the many types of doubling. The central symbol of the stern-piece explicates the levels of this confinement. The "shield-like" "oval," "intricately carved with the arms of Castile and Leon," is decorated with mythological figures, the central pair consisting of a masked figure whose foot grinds the "prostrate neck of a writhing figure, likewise masked" (p. 58). The stern-piece distills the essence of the social structure. All the characters literally or figuratively play the roles of both victors and victims. No other roles are structurally possible. The antiquity of the stern-piece, moreover, bespeaks the longevity of the social relations it depicts, for though the might of Castile and Leon had diminished by 1799, when "Benito Cereno" takes place, its characters continue to

enact the traditional historic parts. That Delano finally and most conspicuously assumes the posture of victor, clutching the unconscious Cereno and
grinding the "prostrate" Babo with his foot (p. 118), suggests that Americans
are the latest to inherit this social structure. Finally, the medallion's status as a
heraldic device reflects on the functions of official art: as a synecdoche of the
social order which predates the characters, it prescribes the roles they must
play. The social system becomes, in effect, a text which writes the characters.
All of them are inside it, imprisoned within its oval. No one, not even Babo,
can rewrite it.

In contrast, Melville himself, as an author, inherits a tangible, literal
document, not a social script. Delano's *Narrative* purports to be a representation of certain historical events, but it is, as Melville recognizes, an interpretation, open to reinterpretation. While he must reckon with its authority, he
can transform such reckoning into recreation. Taking off from *Moby-Dick*'s
playful spoofing of its authorities, he enters into a subversive dialogue with
Delano's *Narrative* which furthers the project he had undertaken in *Israel
Potter:* he turns an historical document reflective of America's sense of identity on its head. In both pieces he also specifically undermines the authority
of American forefathers, though "Benito Cereno" attacks a minor progeni-
tor rather than such luminaries as Benjamin Franklin and John Paul Jones;
Delano's ancestor, Phillipe de la Noye, came to America in 1621, and both
Delano and his father fought in the Revolutionary War.[24] Highlighting the
gaps in Delano's *Narrative* and playing on its unacknowledged inconsistencies, Melville indicts Delano as a minor author of the Americanism which
was straightjacketing his contemporaries.

The major hiatus in the original Delano's *Narrative* is its lack of historical
consciousness; its author was given instead to reflecting on the transcultural,
transhistorical traits common to all humanity.[25] This same lack was implicit
in the assumption of many of the country's founders that America's connection with Europe had been contractual, not organically historical. It was also
shared by Melville's contemporaries, whose sense of history was consonant
with their belief that they were superior to the rest of the Western world; as
George B. Forgie and others have suggested, they were inclined to foreshorten
America's past by imagining the founding fathers as their first ancestors.[26] For
many, their greatest tie to Europe consisted in freeing themselves from it.
Melville rebukes the ahistoricism of his source and of his contemporaries by
weaving into his text a rich tapestry of historical allusion and analogy which
challenges the idea of America's uniqueness. It specifies unsettling similarities between the Old and New Worlds and locates America's history within
a general expansionist trend among Western nations that began with the first
great European marriage between commerce and the sea in Venice.

Melville's framework far exceeds the Spanish-American connection critics have reconstructed.[27] Embellishing Delano's *Narrative* by blending expansive analogies with compressed symbols, Melville fuses mercantilism, free enterprise, and the slave trade. The novella's comparisons range throughout modern Western history, often pivoting, as if in warning, on the rebelliousness of subordinated populations.[28] At the same time, the Spanish slave ship—rechristened the *San Dominick* to allude to the slaves' revolts in Santo Domingo—becomes a condensation of this revisionary history. A "Spanish merchantman," the *San Dominick* is a "very large, and, in its time, a very fine vessel, such as in those days were at intervals encountered along that main; sometimes superseded Acapulco treasure-ships, or retired frigates of the Spanish king's navy, which, like superannuated Italian palaces, still, under a decline of masters, preserved signs of former state" (p. 57). The reference to Acapulco treasure calls attention to the raiding parties transported by the Spanish ships that followed on Columbus' discovery of the New World; the paralleling of the Conquistadores' ships with the vessels of a naval fleet famous for its bellicosity connects Spain's aggressive posture in the Old and New Worlds. Generalizing the example of Spain, the capping comparison to superannuated Italian palaces, later expanded through a reference to the ship's "Venetian-looking balustrade," specifically links the Spanish empire with the Italian city-state where early modern mercantilism flourished, while the *San Dominick*'s concealed slave revolt warns of a continuing cycle of violent enmity.

By reconstructing Delano's *Narrative* to accommodate this historical vision, Melville implicitly indicts Delano as an ironically fit ancestor for a country which preferred to regard slavery within its borders as an ahistorical institution peculiar to one of its regions. He also mines inconsistencies in Delano's text to subject Delano to a witty, historically resonant character assassination.[29] The historical Delano had been stung by the "misery and ingratitude" he had suffered at the hands of the "very persons to whom [he] had rendered the greatest services"—particularly the real Cereno, who, by besmirching his character, had treacherously tried to avoid recompensing him for saving the Spanish ship.[30] Chapter Eleven of Delano's *Narrative* is in a sense its author's character reference for himself. He carefully presents himself as an honorable and blameless man. At pains to establish his rectitude, he corroborates his version of events by including numerous testimonies to his disinterested goodness, among them his own letters to the Spanish king's emissaries insisting that "the services rendered off the island of St. Maria were from pure motives of humanity" (p. 528, repeated in substance, p. 529) and two versions of the Chilean Tribunal's official recommendation that the king be informed of his "generous and benevolent conduct" in succoring Cereno (pp. 526, 527). In his own deposition, which he also includes, Delano reports himself to have woven humanitarian appeals into the monetary pitch he made to his crew when encouraging them to retake the Spanish ship: he told them, he says, that they could return half the value of the ship to Cereno "as a present" and reminded them of the suffering of the Spaniards still on board (pp. 509–510).

Melville reformulates the terms of this presentation so as to expose Delano's self-interest. Eliminating all documents praising Delano except Cereno's ideologically biased deposition, Melville also discredits Delano's claims to disinterest and subtly reduces his motives to the sheer, unacknowledged drive for profit. In "Benito Cereno," the sailors are urged to recapture the *San Dominick* by being told only that they stand to gain a good part of the "ship and her cargo, including some gold and silver . . . worth more than a thousand doubloons" (p. 120). Taking off on the real Delano's protestations that he is an innocent, Melville's Delano holds himself above slavery—"Ah, this slavery breeds ugly passions in man," he thinks (p. 105)—while his drive for profit actually implicates him in the slave trade. The "cargo" his crew is to liberate includes one hundred and sixty slaves—Melville doubled his source's figures—and the American stands to gain from their sale.[31]

Far beyond this reversal of Delano's character, Melville reinterprets the *Narrative* to show that Delano's pursuit of profit implicates him in illegitimate as well as legitimate economic activities. Without acknowledging it, the historical Delano revealed a significant blurring of such boundaries. He reported that he had trouble with his crew because many were escaped convicts. The real Cereno exploited Delano's use—however unwilling—of sailors who were outlaws: Cereno got testimony from some of them "to injure [Delano's] character," including, an offended Delano reports, their affirmation that "I was a pirate" (p. 511). Melville plays with this accusation of piracy most adroitly. Aside from being one of the ideological categories Delano uses to stereotype others, it becomes emblematic of his economic activities. Although Melville ironically makes his Delano fear that Cereno may be a pirate, the novella strongly hints that it is Delano himself who is a pirate, or very like one—just as the real Cereno claimed. Changing Delano's ship from the Yankee-sounding *Perseverance* to the *Bachelor's Delight,* the name of the ship of buccaneer William Ambrose Cowely,[32] is only the most obvious aspect of Melville's indictment. In order to flesh out the accusation, he plays on the real Delano's failure fully to separate legitimate free enterprise from illegal activities. Persuaded by his men not to go after the *San Dominick* himself, Melville's Delano has the attack headed by a surrogate, his chief mate. This man, we are told, "had been a privateer's-man" (p. 120). Melville may be referring obliquely to the fact that Delano himself served on the privateer *Mars* during the Revolutionary War. In any case, since privateering is legalized piracy in time of war, Melville suggests guilt by association to establish a definite tie between the American captain and the practice of piracy. He also expands this association between the honest trader and his ex-privateer mate to show that the boundaries separating national histories are as indistinct as the boundaries supposedly separating types of illegal activity. Leading Delano's men in their attack on the *San Dominick,* Melville's mate cries, "Follow your leader." Literally, the cry is in response to seeing the ship's hull, with this epithet chalked beneath Aranda's bleached skeleton. Contextually, its echoes connect the New World conclusively with the Old. "Leader" refers to Aranda, whose death will be avenged, but also to Columbus, whose figure his skeleton replaces, to Babo, who led the slaves' revolt and caused the words to be chalked, to the mate himself, who leads the American crew, and to the captain he represents. In the traditions Melville's Delano carries forward, exploration is inseparable from colonization, free enterprise from slavery, profit from plunder.

Because Melville's reversals of Delano's *Narrative* are apparent only through close study of a fairly obscure source, it may seem that he deliberately concealed his reenvisionment rather than offering it as an instance of creative reinterpretation. Yet "Benito Cereno" is more deliberately accessible than many of Melville's other tales, for even without knowing Delano's text, those who read Melville as closely as Melville read Delano could profit from his challenge. Indeed, Melville explicitly proffers his reinterpretation to his contemporaries in the final passage of "Benito Cereno": Babo's severed head looks out over a plaza toward the church "in whose vaults slept *then, as now,* the recovered bones of Aranda" and toward the monastery where Benito Cereno, in dying, "did indeed follow his leader" (p. 140, emphasis added). By echoing the earlier appearances of this resonant phrase, this last sentence once more connects Old and New Worlds, blacks and whites; the reference to the present, the only reference in the entire novella, openly includes antebellum America in the novella's vision. Focusing on three characters who have all been victors and victims in the social structure framed by the stern-piece, "Benito Cereno" also faintly but clearly sounds the possibility for change. The grim fates of these three characters are given some closure by being past, while the conspicuous absence of Amasa Delano raises the possibility that his descendants might still avoid the fate of blindly following the lead of the Old World. If, like Melville rather than his characters, they queried their culture-bound encoding of texts of social and racial roles, if they queried their inadequate histories and hierarchical ideologies, they might at last sever the chains that bind their interpretations of their world to the authority of an old, unjust, unstable order. Only by seeing how like the Old World they had made their own, "Benito Cereno" suggests, could they genuinely begin to ask how the New World could, indeed, be made "new."

Notes

1. Herman Melville, *Piazza Tales,* edited by Egbert S. Oliver (New York: Hendricks House, Farrar Straus, 1948), p. 73; hereafter cited parenthetically in the text.

2. Merton M. Sealts, Jr., *Pursuing Melville, 1940–1980* (Madison: University of Wisconsin Press, 1982), pp. 230–231, documents the probable composition of "Benito Cereno" during the winter of 1854–1855.

3. Allan Moore Emery, "'Benito Cereno' and Manifest Destiny," *Nineteenth-Century Fiction,* 39 (1984): 48–68, addresses the issues of Manifest Destiny and Know-Nothingism but places the novella exclusively in the context of the United States' expansionist desires with regard to Latin America. I am indebted to this discussion, but I maintain that "Benito Cereno" refers to a much broader political and cultural climate; moreover, I find that, directly and indirectly, slavery is, as earlier critics recognized, central to the novella.

4. Among the many critics who have seen "Benito Cereno" as a cautionary work, I have found the following particularly useful: Jean Fagin Yellin, "Black Masks: Melville's *Benito Cereno,*" *American Quarterly,* 22 (1970): 678–689; Joyce Adler, "Melville's *Benito Cereno:* Slavery and Violence in the Americas," *Science and Society,* 38 (1974): 19–48; and Carolyn L. Karcher, *Shadow over the Promised Land: Slavery, Race, and Violence in Melville's America* (Baton Rouge & London: Louisiana State University Press, 1980). More generally, Eric J. Sundquist, "Suspense and Tautology in 'Benito Cereno'" *Glyph 8, Johns Hopkins Textual Studies* (Baltimore: Johns Hopkins University Press, 1981), pp. 101–126, connects the novella's context, a social order poised on the verge of conflict yet keeping conflict at bay, with its pattern of suspense and tautology. Allan Moore Emery, "The Topicality of Depravity in 'Benito Cereno,'" *American Literature,* 55 (1983): 316–331, summarizes earlier work on the novella's references to slavery and reads it as the portrayal of universal human depravity, black and white. Barbara J. Baines, "Ritualized Cannibalism in 'Benito Cereno,'" *ESQ,* 30 (1984): 163–169, interprets cannibalism as a "central event and metaphor" by means of which Melville portrays slavery as an institution that consumes white master and black slave, body and soul. Marianne DeKoven, "History as Suppressed Referent in Modernist Fiction," *ELH,* 15 (1984), 137–152, sees "Benito Cereno" as a work which, though making little explicit reference to the historical reality of slavery, contains powerfully oblique historical political referents. Ann Douglas, *The Feminization of American Culture* (New York: Alfred A. Knopf, 1977), pp. 292–320, gives an excellent account of Melville's general opposition to contemporary American culture.

5. Rogin, *Subversive Genealogy: The Politics and Art of Herman Melville* (New York: Alfred A. Knopf, 1983); Emery, "'Benito Cereno' and Manifest Destiny."

6. DeKoven makes the important point that the novella's historical referents are indirect. While DeKoven links the novella solely to slavery, her method—elucidating how "Benito Cereno" inscribes its historical framework through allusion, imagery, and diction—underscores the fact that many readers have reduced its figures of speech, which are not usually one-dimensional, to markers for colonial Spain and/or the slaveholding United States.

7. For an important discussion of other aspects of authority, including its connection with authorship, see Edward W. Said, *Beginnings: Intention and Method* (New York: Basic Books, 1975), especially Chapter Three, "The Novel

as Beginning Intention." Said argues that in novels authority, or invention, is inseparable from molestation, or constraint, that texts always both assert and usurp their own authority.

8. Karcher, for instance, reads the novella primarily as "an exploration of the white racist mind and how it reacts in the face of a slave insurrection" (p. 128). Emery, "'Benito Cereno' and Manifest Destiny," sees Delano as Melville's exemplification of American expansionist attitudes toward Latin America. He points out that Delano's "Anglo-Saxonism" causes him to stereotype Cereno as a certain kind of Spaniard but finds Delano's prejudices tangential to Melville's purpose of indicting Americans for following Spain in becoming dogmatically imperialist (pp. 61–63).

9. Karcher, however, feels that Delano often exhibits the language of the southern apologist for slavery (p. 132).

10. See, for example, Edward H. Rosenberry, *Melville and the Comic Spirit* (Cambridge, Mass: Harvard University Press, 1955), p. 163; and R. Bruce Bickley, Jr., *The Method of Melville's Short Fiction* (Durham, N.C.: Duke University Press, 1975), pp. 58–59 and 62–66.

11. P. 139. Compare pp. 113, 115, where Delano finds solace in a parodic conversion of romanticism into cliché. Cereno's black spirits become a natural phenomenon: the "foul mood was now at its depths, as the fair wind was at its heights" (p. 113).

12. "Self-Reliance" in *The Collected Works of Ralph Waldo Emerson*, edited by Alfred R. Ferguson *et al.* (Cambridge, Mass. & London: Belknap of Harvard University Press, 1971), II: 39.

13. See p. 77 for the first instance, pp. 81, 90, 92, 115, 117 for later ones.

14. Thomas Philbrick, *James Fenimore Cooper and the Development of American Sea Fiction* (Cambridge, Mass: Harvard University Press, 1961), especially pp. 116–203. Rogin, pp. 3–11, discusses connections between piracy and slavery and analyzes Melville's references to Cooper's novel in Delano's piracy fantasies; his focus, however, is on antebellum distinctions between (illegitimate) piracy and (legitimate) slavery.

15. Rogin, p. 22. In an interesting alternative reading, Emery, "'Benito Cereno' and Manifest Destiny," pp. 52–54, sees the American's plan to take over the Spanish ship as a mirroring of Americans' conviction that their Anglo-Saxon energy would succeed in bringing order to Latin America where Spain's enervation had brought only disaster.

16. H. Bruce Franklin, *The Wake of the Gods: Melville's Mythology* (California: Stanford University Press, 1963), examines the parallels between Cereno and William Sterling's portrayal of the Spanish monarch Charles V in *Cloister Life of the Emperor Charles the Fifth* (pp. 136–152); Karcher identifies in Cereno the stereotype of the effete southern plantation owner (p. 136).

17. Adler notes the economic similarity between the two (p. 45); Karcher identifies the ideological, unanalytic nature of Cereno's deposition (p. 135).

18. I am indebted here to Rogin's view that in portraying the master-slave relation in terms of a charade, "Benito Cereno" reveals that the bond between the two, regarded as "natural" by apologists for slavery, is a social construct (pp. 208–220). Emery, "The Topicality of Depravity in 'Benito Cereno,'" argues that Melville challenges cultural assumptions about blacks and whites, men and women, for the moral purpose of exposing universal human depravity.

19. See, for instance, Harold Beaver's comment in his edition of *Billy Budd, Sailor, and Other Stories*, (Middlesex, U.K. & New York: Penguin Books, 1970), pp. 33–34. While Delano may feminize the blacks, as Beaver, Karcher (p. 134), and others have suggested, Melville also shows that the blacks likewise deny Cereno status. I am indebted to Lauren Shohet, "Discovering Oppression in Melville's *Benito Cereno*," unpublished paper written for American Romanticism, Oberlin College, 1983, for noticing that the blacks emasculate Cereno, whose response is similar to a rape victim's.

20. Baym, "Melville's Quarrel with Fiction," *PMLA*, 94 (1979): 910, maintains that "Melville's Emerson-derived notion of language [proceeded] from a divine Author or Namer," and his "loss of belief in an Absolute entailed the loss not only of truth in the universe but also of coherence and meaning in language."

21. In an interesting reading, DeKoven sees the "false appearances" of the blacks 'masquerading as proper slaves' to contain "the actual truth of the social order": its despotism and irrationality, and its destructiveness of whites as well as blacks (see pp. 139–143).

22. Adler associates the playwright Babo with the poet Melville (p. 491). Sundquist sees Babo and the narrator as silent figures who carry out "plots" and express their authority over Cereno and Delano, respectively, with razor-sharp rituals (pp. 111, 119).

23. See Sundquist, especially p. 116, on this discourse.

24. John D. Wade, "Delano, Amasa," *DAB* (1934).

25. Delano reflected that "virtue and vice, happiness and misery, are much more similarly distributed to nations than those are permitted to suppose who have never been from home" (quoted in Wade, p. 217).

26. Forgie, *Patricide in the House Divided: A Psychological Interpretation of Lincoln and His America* (New York: W. W. Norton, 1979), especially pp. 3–54; Rogin, pp. 33–41.

27. Franklin was among the first to establish Melville's careful evocation of Spanish history. Among more recent researchers, Gloria Horsely-Meacham, "The Monastic Slaver: Image and Meaning in 'Benito Cereno,'" *New England Quarterly*, 56 (1983): 262–266, develops connections between the American slave trade, the Church, and the campaign for Christian dominion.

28. The novella's first extended simile establishes a resemblance between the half-shadowed slave ship and a "Lima intriguante's one sinister eye peering across the Plaza from the Indian loop-hole of her dusk *saya-y-manta*" (p. 56); the last comparison suggests that the wounds the whites inflict on the blacks as they retake the slave ship are like "those shaven ones of the English at Preston Pans, made by the poled scythes of the Highlanders" (p. 122). In between, comparisons are made between Cereno and the tyrannical James I of England (p. 103): North Americans forcing slave women to bear their children and Spanish planters' similar treatment of enslaved Indians (p. 106); Delano's sailors, as they fight the blacks, and "troopers in the saddle" (p. 122); the blacks' hatchets and the weapons of Indians and woodsmen (p. 121); the *San Dominick* and a decaying Italian palace (pp. 58, 88).

29. Despite a confusion between Ledyard and Mungo Park, Melville similarly discredits the authority of both as sources of information about Africa. In a passage adapted by Park, Ledyard, in his *Proceedings of the Association for Promoting the Discovery of the Interior Parts of Africa*, described the generosity of African women; Melville indicates Ledyard's inaccuracy by stressing how fiercely the women oppose

the whites. He also exposes Ledyard's celebration of the black women's hospitality as a useful rationalization for their enslavement, for Delano takes special pleasure in thinking that the female slaves on the *San Dominick* might be the same women who were so gracious to Ledyard. See Emery, "The Topicality of Depravity in 'Benito Cereno,'" for a discussion that summarizes earlier work on Melville's emendation of these sources and contains new information on his adaptations of material in *Harper's* and *Putnam's*.

30. All citations are to Amasa Delano, *Narrative of Voyages and Travels in the Northern and Southern Hemispheres* (Boston, 1817), Chapter Eleven, reprinted in Horace Scudder, "Melville's *Benito Cereno* and Captain Delano's Voyages," *PMLA*, 43 (1928): 502–532; here 513.

31. These textual associations between New England merchants and Spanish slave traders are rooted in facts of which Adler gives a concise account (p. 38).

32. Beaver, p. 435.

JOHN BRYANT

Allegory and Breakdown in The Confidence-Man: Melville's Comedy of Doubt

1

The reviewer for the *London Illustrated Times* did not much care for *The Confidence-Man;* in fact, it nauseated him. He did not know what the book meant, and, worse, he could not tell what it was—a "novel, comedy, collection of dialogues, repertory of anecdotes, or whatever it is." A colleague at the *Westminster Review* was able to locate a meaning in the book's apparent theme ("the gullibility of the great Republic"), but he would have had to agree with the *Illustrated Times* that Melville's work was, indeed, "a sad jumble."[1] The assessment has proved prophetic, for recent critics have still not reached a consensus on "whatever it is." *The Confidence-Man* has been labelled allegory, "new novel," comedy, picaresque, satire, romance, and even "picaresque satiric romance."[2] As might be expected, Melville offers few clues in untangling the jumble. At the end of Chapter 14, for instance, his narrator announces that he will "pass from the comedy of thought to that of action,"[3] suggesting that the book comprises, in the broadest sense, both didactic and mimetic forms. How these modes blend and what effect they have on readers are questions scholars are only beginning to address.

The modern critical impulse has been to read *The Confidence-Man* didactically as either a social, religious, or philosophical commentary. And the notion that Melville wrote an allegory or satire remains deeply embedded in the scholarly community, even to the degree that general studies of allegory

Philological Quarterly, Volume 65 (Winter 1986): pp. 113–130. ©1986 University of Iowa.

have used the book as a crucial example.[4] Although the case for allegory is strong, it seems in some sense to be a reading of last resort stemming from an obdurate text that refuses to yield anything truly mimetic or novelistic. Foster, for instance, observes that "the surface story is an aimless string of episodes, without tension, suspense, variation in pace, or climax." But when seen as an allegory, "when the allegory surfaces," the book becomes "as formal as a fugue [and] richly patterned." As a "cipher" to be "decoded," it is "tight, ingenious, and rational."[5] Foster's orientation has persisted. Parker calls *The Confidence-Man* a "consistent" and "carefully structured allegory" with the Devil as the title character.[6] And recently, less satanic, more elaborate allegorical readings correlate the fiction's seemingly haphazard development of plot and character to the growth of abstract human consciousness.[7] For these readers, then, the entire novel is clearly "a comedy of thought."

But the didactic approach, in which a fiction develops along the lines of an external argument or idea rather than the probable and necessary forces inherent in human action, does not account for the novel's full effect.[8] To begin with, its unreliable narrator, not usually found in allegory, seems to abdicate any responsibility for interpreting motives or guiding the reader through events. As a result, Melville's argument seems to disintegrate for lack of a resolute voice, and readers must float between "maybe yes, maybe no"; it all becomes a "carefully-constructed muddle," according to Lawrence Buell.[9] Moreover, as the novel progresses into its second half, social satire diminishes and our involvement in a human comedy expands; the allegorical opening yields a mimetic end.

The difference between these two halves is as dramatic as the broad disparity exemplified in the mute who opens the novel and the cosmopolitan who puts it to rest. Clearly an allegorical figure, the colorless mute (emblematic of ineffectual Christianity) engages our emotions only at a minimum. The colorful and talkative cosmopolite, Frank Goodman, however, excites deeper sympathies. A flesh and blood character with dubious motives seeking confidence for either positive or malicious ends, he arouses our anxieties and to use Wayne Booth's words, "force[s] the reader into thought about his own moral dilemma."[10] To the degree, then, that Goodman's story awakens us to our "own moral dilemma" of faith, *The Confidence-Man* is as mimetic as it is didactic. Ultimately, Melville's novel cannot be confidently classified as strictly a didactic comedy of thought or a mimetic comedy of action; it is somehow both.

Melville's blending of comic thought and action begins as early as Chapter 14 in which Melville uses his digression on fiction to enhance the audience's involvement in the action. The merchant Roberts, who has been diddled twice already, and a Mr. Truman, who is about to diddle him again, stand poised, champagne in hand, when the simple merchant suddenly sees the truth and calls off all bets. As the two principals remain frozen on stage with lines of pain and wonder etched on their brows, Melville discusses the ramifications of "the queer, unaccountable caprices of [Roberts's] natural heart" (p. 68). The chapter, therefore, interrupts the climactic backfiring of a confidence game: the effect is twofold. On the one hand, Melville is telling his readers how to read, or more specifically, how we may empathize with Roberts. The merchant's inconsistency derives from a "natural heart." If our hearts, too, are "natural," we must know his dilemma well. The digression is also a "delay tactic" intensifying suspense by forestalling the resolution of vital questions that have grown out of the action. Will Roberts clarify the nature of his doubt, expose Truman, and provide useful warnings for future victims of larceny (the reader included)? Will Truman reveal his motives or fabricate a cover up? Is confidence, we finally ask, merely a wine-induced fantasy? Melville's interruption heightens action *and* thought. It is as suspenseful as it is idea bound, as mimetic as it is didactic.

This mixing of modes, sustained throughout Melville's larger drama, is best understood in the context of the evolving interrelationship of text and reader. In earlier days, Melville encouraged readers to become what Wolfgang Iser calls "partners in a process of communication."[11] When, for instance, Sophia Hawthorne found a "subtile significance" in *Moby-Dick*'s spirit spout image, the author replied with emphasis that he did not *mean* it." The creation was hers: "You . . . see more things, . . . and by the same process, refine all you see, so that they are . . . things which while you think you but humbly discover them, you do in fact create them. . . ."[12] Reading (seeing and refining) is an act of creation, a sharing in, indeed completion of, the author's dynamic creative process. Ishmael proclaims as much in his familiar declaration of independence from aesthetic completion: ". . . grand [erections], true ones, ever leave the copestone to posterity."[13] Posterity's readers, more than the writer, supply the copestone of coherence to a fiction like *Moby-Dick*.

But this symbiotic partnership between text and reader erodes almost entirely in *The Confidence-Man*. Although Melville seems to invite us to create "subtile significances," especially with the procession of confidence men and victims in the first half of the novel, the reader's ability to "allegorize" confidently seems thwarted by the end of the work. The confidence man may be God, Devil, or Man, or any two, or all three. Eventually the reader's mind short circuits. Just as Melville's sentences frequently collapse under the weight of too many nested subordinations, we are left confounded and confused. In Chapter 18, for instance, a chorus of three gentlemen interrupts the drama with their confusion: is the herb doctor a knave, fool, original genius, or all three, or perhaps an agent for the pope? All three perspectives are mere "suspicions." And if "True knowledge comes but by suspicion or revelation" and if it is a "wise" man who waits for suspicions to "ripen into knowledge," our chorus of three must wait indefinitely for their deliverance from doubt, for their "triangular duel" ends "with but a triangular result" (p. 92). There is no ripeness here, nor "True knowledge." Melville then does not invite us to supply a "copestone" to this fiction. We are not partners with his text; like the chorus, we are its victims.[14] It seems clear, though, that Melville's point is that we share in the confusion. This, however, is risky business for a dramatist.

Indeed, unrelieved doubt or confusion is generally taken as a fatal flaw in both didactic and mimetic fictions. To be sure, defenders of allegory such as Angus Fletcher have convincingly demonstrated the form's capacity for fluidity and ambivalence in conveying "the action of the mind." But despite this potential for ambiguity, allegory's ultimate function is to purge doubt: it "'carries off' the threat of ambivalent feelings." Moreover, "its enigmas show . . . an obsessive battling with doubt. It does not accept the world of experience and senses; it thrives on their overthrow, replacing them with ideas."[15] Unrelieved doubt is equally problematic in mimetic fiction. As Booth observes, a certain consequence of the kind of unreliable or "inconscient" narrator Melville uses is that the author may be misunderstood.[16] The fate of irony is misreading and audience alienation. But this is a risk Melville was willing to take. In Chapter 14 he argues that while nature is inconsistent, "experience is the only guide," and that, by logical extension, fiction is an experience that can guide us only to the degree that its "twistings" (no matter how confusing) parallel nature's. Thus, by inflicting upon his reader triple-layered suspicions and refusing to supply a trigonometry that will triangulate "True knowledge," Melville engages us in a process of doubt that mimics life. In short, its fictive confusion has a moral function. It only remains, then, to show how the author combines the didactic and mimetic modes in creating this complex reading experience.

2

The Confidence-Man clearly possesses the trappings of allegorical plot, character, and setting. It works within a highly schematized time frame, moving from sunrise to midnight with sunset occurring just as the cosmopolitan enters precisely half way into the action. The aptly named steamboat *Fidele* falls into the *narrenschiff* tradition; it is a ship of fools, a microcosm of humanity.[17] The title character (a protean, supernatural figure typical of allegory) bears allegorical names such as Goodman, Truman, and Noble. He is what Fletcher would call a "daemonic agent" or half human, half divine character "possessed" by a single idea and "act[ing] free of the usual moral restraints, even when he is acting morally. . . ." Moreover, Goodman engages in both Quest and Battle, the "radically reductive" patterns of action found in allegory, for his search for confidence progresses from one philosophical "debate" or "Socratic dialogue" to another.[18]

Fletcher observes that allegories display rhythmic, ritualistic plots (such as the pattern of repeated shipwrecks in *Gulliver's Travels*) and what he calls the "fractionated" character.[19] Briefly, the allegorical hero generates one or more doubles of himself, and the repeated actions of these "fractionated" or "partial characters" enhance both the rhythm and symmetry of the plot, which accordingly engender in the reader expectations of allegory. Fletcher's ritualized patterns occur in the first half of *The Confidence-Man* but are sedulously thwarted in the second, leaving readers vaguely suspicious of the author's reliability and confused as to the final shape of Melville's apparent allegory. A well-known problem in the novel, the failure of Black Guinea's prophetic list of confidence men to be fully realized, illustrates the point.

Melville begins "fractionating" in Chapter 3 when he has Black Guinea list eight "ge'mmen" who will vouch for his integrity. As the novel progresses through the first half, each gentleman appears in the order in which he is listed, and each, of course, is clearly an "avatar" or "fraction" of the confidence man. But, as readers of *The Confidence-Man* know, the list of "fractionated" characters breaks down upon the cosmopolitan's entrance. Two of the predicted confidence men, one in a "yaller west" another in a "wiolet robe," seem not to appear. Scholars have tried to account for this lapse noting that if the colors were interchanged the resultant "wiolet west" might refer to Charlie Noble and the "yaller robe" to a minor figure in the last scene or even (because he wears a traveling robe) to the cosmopolitan Frank Goodman. But if the men in Black Guinea's list are, in fact, the serial guises of one "daemonic agent," and if (through a rational emending of the text) Noble were admitted to that list, and if Goodman is, as many assume, *the* confidence man *par excellence,* Goodman and Noble's crucial encounter (chs. 25–35) would be logically impossible. Two "avatars" cannot occupy one stage at the same time. Even if the Devil could pull off this trick, it seems unlikely that he would waste his time trying to talk himself into having a drink or giving himself a loan. Given the problems of Black Guinea's list, the allegory becomes dramatically absurd.[20]

In the final analysis, the non-fulfillment of Black Guinea's list leads to an arrhythmic, asymmetric, and necessarily incomplete allegory. Whereas six confidence men in the first half of the novel follow each other in almost ritualized rhythm, only one suspected confidence man, the cosmopolitan, occupies the stage in the slower paced second half. H. Bruce Franklin notes a number of crucial differences between Goodman and his allegorical predecessors, intimating that the cosmopolitan may not be an operator at all. He takes no money, but, in fact, gives away two shillings; he exposes a confidence man, Charlie Noble; he grows in stature as the novel progresses.[21] By reason of Goodman's departure from the anticipated allegorical mold, the entrance of this cosmopolitan seems to work against allegorical plot symmetry and form. The failure of Black Guinea's list is only one of many recurring patterns of breakdown in Melville's allegory. Here I shall note nine other broken patterns contained within an overall two-part structure.

Readers rarely fail to recognize that Melville's text is divided into two sections. The first half includes six confidence men (seven, if you count the mute) who engage in eighteen interactions with fourteen minor characters while the second half follows one man, the cosmopolitan, through five encounters with five interlocutors. Whereas the first half leaps rapidly from one episode to the next, each spotlighting a single confidence man, the second half creeps through extended dialogues on friendship and confidence. To accentuate the bifurcation, Melville sets the first half mostly outdoors and in sunlight and the second indoors and in darkness from sunset to midnight. The two halves, then, are as distinct as the many and the one, outside and in, day and night. Clearly, the text asks us to play one half against the other. The first encourages the reader to formulate empirical judgments on the nature of confidence men, and the second carefully disintegrates our confidence in those judgments. Melville's one-two punch, then, is itself a confidence game complete with *set-up* and *sting*.

Each half of the novel is organized upon a single, dramatically compelling question. In the first we ask "What is a confidence man?" This is a relatively easy problem to solve: one merely observes. Here, Melville pre-sents a complex but comprehensible world of knaves and fools; our task is to gather information about that world. The reader discerns clear patterns of behavior which when consolidated constitute a distinct syndrome of larcenous activity. By the time we reach the sixth Mississippi operator, the Philosophical Intelligence Officer, we have had our fill of pious pretenders, genial panhandlers, and enthusiastic faith healers. We know a confidence man when we see one. In the first half, then, Melville educates us to survive in the self-contained, allegorical world of confidence men. Like the three gentlemen in Chapter 18, we are bemused by our suspicions but relatively secure in the knowledge Melville has created and passed along. "True knowledge" of the confidence man's motives may not be possible, but our suspicions about his larceny approach certitude, for as each of the six confidence men enters, his behavior corresponds to and confirms the larcenous activity of his predecessors. Even the narrator's use of irony and circuitous phrasing contributes to this process of familiarization. In a way, Melville conditions us to respond to certain signs that identify the confidence man. Although the world he portrays is duplicitous, even "triangular," it appears to be knowable and the reader is trained to understand that world.

If the first half establishes a reliable set of correspondences earmarking the confidence man's allegorical identity, and if the reader is conditioned to recognize those signs, the second half challenges the reader's newly acquired knave-detecting ability. The second overwhelming question that propels us to the end of the novel is whether Goodman is, in fact, a confidence man. Given our conditioning, the solution should be easy. But ultimately, our training fails us. As Goodman moves from scene to scene, our early expectations of nabbing yet another diddler dissolve. The signals of larceny are only partially transmitted. The effect upon the reader, then, is not so much confusion as tension over the issue of when Goodman will somehow slip and reveal his duplicity. But solid evidence never arrives, and the suspense grows until the last, dim, anti-climactic scene. Our failure to identify Goodman conclusively as a confidence man forces us to reconsider our expectations, or in a more radical mental leap, to doubt the efficacy of Melville's early signals and the validity of such correspondences in general.

Nine patterns of behavior (both ritualized and aesthetic) recur throughout the first half of the novel and condition the reader's responses to the second half. Three of these patterns bear directly upon the characteristics of the confidence men. To begin with the most obvious, a confidence man reveals his true identity when he (1) initiates a *confidence game.* Such fishy propositions as the appeal to charity, the bogus stock deal, and the herbal panacea were as familiar to Melville's first readers as they are to us today. Once a character plays a game, his guilt is confirmed, and by this yardstick there is little doubt that Black Guinea, Ringman, the man in gray, Truman, the herb doctor, and the PIO man are all con artists. Equally suspicious although less conclusive is (2) a character's *shape shifting* ability. Like any actor, a confidence man assumes many roles and is an excellent rhetorician who molds himself and his arguments to fit the needs of a particular audience.[22] A third pattern of behavior is that the six confidence men (3) adopt the benevolent mask of a *simpleton* (Black Guinea, PIO man), *enthusiast* (man in gray, herb doctor), or *genialist* (Truman).

Three more patterns hint that the confidence men are in cahoots with one another. Melville first of all links his characters primarily through (4) an elaborate network of *set-ups;* that is, one knave prepares a potential victim to be duped by another.[23] In the same vein, a confidence man will acknowledge the existence of other confidence men or (5) *confirm* their good will or veracity.[24] Furthermore, Melville uses (6) *physical resemblances* and *spatial linkages* to suggest a conspiracy.[25]

In addition to these six characteristic patterns, we find three distinct patterns in the narrator's treatment of the confidence men. A well-known pattern is (7) *the dual imagery* used in describing the sometimes angelic (mute, herb doctor) sometimes satanic (PIO man) confidence men. Moreover, Melville often introduces a new confidence man with a new chapter that begins with (8) *the dialogue of one or two unidentified speakers.* Chapter 19 is a case in point:

"Mexico? Molino del Rey? Resaca de la Palma?"
"Resaca de la *Tombs.*"

Not until the middle of the chapter do we fully understand that the second speaker's bitter response to the herb doctor refers to its (the soldier of fortune's) crippling incarceration in New York's municipal prison and not to any wound received during the Mexican War. Melville's use of dialogue generates a complex reading experience which forces us to suspend judgment, read on, re-read, and re-evaluate. His refusal to identify speakers makes it difficult to distinguish the confidence man's words from his victim's. In a way, the process engages us in an excursion through the intricacies of acquiring knowledge.[26] Finally, when Melville does identify speakers, he often refers to them as either (9) *"the stranger"* or *"the other."* For the most part, this subtle stylistic pattern is reserved exclusively for the confidence men.[27] These nine features are part of the confidence man's talisman. But in the second half of the novel, the identifying emblem fails us; the allegory breaks down, and we must move from a confident didactic mode into doubt.

3

"who in thunder are you?"

The speaker is Pitch, a skeptical Missourian, now moved to truculence by a series of confidence games. What has happened to him has happened before; it is all a recurring dream. Just as Roberts has been set up and stung by Black Guinea then Ringman then Truman, Pitch has endured the serial onslaught of the herb doctor and the PIO man. Now, too, the reader anticipates the arrival of "Jeremy Diddler No. 3." Thus, it is with equal vehemence that the reader asks along with Pitch, "who in thunder are you" (p. 132) when Frank Goodman, the genial cosmopolitan, enters the stage.

For Pitch, the issue is clear: Goodman is "another of them": a "metaphysical scamp" (p. 136). And the reader, conditioned to recognize a confidence man's patterns of larceny, readily concurs. Goodman first appears as an unidentified speaker (pattern 8). Like those before him, his faceless rhetoric precedes any physical or moral description. With "philanthropical pipe" in hand, he quickly assumes the role of a genialist (pattern 3), inveighs against too much "soberness," and invites Pitch "to tipple a little" (p. 134). In this regard, Goodman bears a strong physical resemblance (pattern 6) to another genialist, the ruddy-faced confidence man Mr. Truman. Moreover, his geniality takes on a satanic flavor (pattern 7), for he loves man so much that he could eat the "racy creature" (p. 133). Finally, like Melville's confidence men,

Goodman is referred to as "stranger" and "the other" (pattern 9) five times throughout the scene (pp. 131, 136, 138).

On the other hand, the cosmopolitan does not appear on Black Guinea's list, nor is he "set up" (pattern 4) by any other earlier confidence man. He does not himself "set up" other potential victims, nor does he "confirm" (pattern 5) other confidence men. Thoroughly uncharacteristic of his predecessors are his denial of knowing another confidence man, the herb doctor (p. 136), and his disparagement of the PIO man's ill-fitting coat (p. 133). Goodman does not seem to be a part of any conspiracy of confidence men, nor does he attempt any confidence games. In fact, he is a miserable specimen of con artistry. He openly confesses himself an eavesdropper (p. 133), admits to perpetrating a "little stratagem" (p. 135) against Pitch, and revels in play acting (p. 133). Finally, Goodman, who eschews "Irony, and Satire" (p. 136), is himself the victim of Pitch's ironic wordplay. When the cosmopolitan states his preference for Diogenes' sociable misanthropy over Timon's antisocial behavior, Pitch purposefully misconstrues the point, salutes Goodman as a fellow misanthrope, and exits triumphantly. Goodman, then, plays the dupe; his presumed victim, the knave.

In all, Goodman's first scene leaves us confused. He follows some of the behavior patterns perfectly, some ambiguously, and some not at all. Our expectations thwarted, we slowly grow to entertain the possibility that Goodman is not a diddler but a true believer in man, seeking friendship or merely human interaction amidst a boat load of untrusting souls. As Goodman progresses through his remaining scenes, Melville's novel acquires a new and forceful coherence. No longer a series of disjointed episodes, the comedy becomes unified by our search for the evidence that will prove or disprove Goodman's alleged infidelity. But at this juncture our thinking is so strongly set against Goodman that Melville's ambiguous signals only introduce a passing doubt. Goodman's next encounter enhances our admiration for the cosmopolitan.

The ten chapters of well-modulated dialogue with Charlie Noble "should" reveal Goodman to be a confidence man. But, in fact, we quickly perceive that Noble is our "operator" and the cosmopolitan his intended victim. Here, the comedy revolves around Noble's ineptitude and Goodman's ability to "con the con man." Noble fits many of the most damning patterns of larceny. He attempts to "fuddle" Frank (p. 174) by plying him with wine and cigars while refraining himself from the narcotics (pattern 1). He professes geniality (pattern 3), but, like his false teeth which are too good to be true, he harbors uncharitable moods. Having just eaten a "diabolic ragout" (p. 169), he is associated with the Devil (pattern 7) and is as well a shapeshifter (pattern 2) comparable to "Cadmus glid[ing] into the snake" (p. 180). But the most intriguing evidence against Noble is that he is referred to as "stranger" or "the other" more often than any other single character in the book (29 times), while the cosmopolitan, who has told Pitch that "No man is a stranger," is never in this scene called "stranger" and only twice called "the other" (pp. 142 and 163).

In contrast, Goodman exhibits few, if any, of these questionable traits and grows from an apparent simpleton to a sage humorist. Charlie Noble's opening gambit is to gain Goodman's esteem by inviting a vicious comparison between Pitch and the barbarous Indian hater, Moredock. By reducing the surly Pitch to Moredock's level, he hopes to validate his own geniality. But the cosmopolitan denies the existence of such depravity, calls Moredock a fiction, and warns Noble against his "one-sided" view of man (p. 175). Normally, such naivete would only make Charlie's game easier, but Frank's good nature has a sting to it. As a "genial misanthrope," Goodman uses his benevolence both to subsume and conceal a deeper awareness of iniquity. For him, humor is "so blessed a thing" that it can "neutralize" the "sting" of a "wicked thought" (pp. 163–164). By containing his misanthropy within a philanthropic heart, he can acknowledge the likes of Noble and even fight back. This balanced sensibility allows Goodman his genial aspirations while it guards him against duplicity. It is a "saving grace" indicating moral as well as intellectual superiority. By asking Noble, then, for the very loan that Noble was intending to extract from Goodman, our cosmopolitan beats the confidence man at his own game, vanquishes false wit, and gives us a small taste of "genial misanthropy."

How is the reader to take this frank, good man? His dramatic growth as a character necessarily subverts the criteria we have come to rely upon for discerning the confidence man. His "air of necromancy" rather than being sinister is amusing, even attractive. He seems to be a different order of operator, "a new kind of monster," a victim who fights back and succeeds where Roberts and Pitch have failed. And yet Goodman's ability to play Noble's game must give us pause. How well and to what end can a genial misanthrope repress his misanthropy? Will he use his "wisdom" to guard against the likes of Noble or is he capable himself of Indian crimes? If we invert his genial pipe, will we find a tomahawk? Such lingering doubts typify the reader's response to the second half of Melville's novel. When Goodman fails to conform in lock step to his predecessors, we must "see" the character in new light, "refine" our expectations, and "create" a new understanding of his role. On to a fresh start, the reader warily anticipates who in thunder Goodman might be.

4

"Egbert, this . . . is, like all of us, a stranger" (p. 197).

The speaker is Mark Winsome; Egbert, his disciple; and "this" is Goodman himself. Winsome has observed Noble and hopes to warn the cosmopolitan of the obvious: Noble is a "Mississippi operator" (p. 196). And yet this mystic philosopher, a cross between "a Yankee peddler and a Tartar priest" (p. 189), appears to be a satanic operator himself (pattern 7). He admits, for instance, to a curious desire to "change personalities" with a rattlesnake (p. 190). He is a "metaphysical merman" (p. 191) whose "tempting" discourse "bewitch[es]" Goodman (p. 193). And as with Noble, he (not Goodman) is referred to repeatedly (19 times) as "stranger" and "the other."

Winsome and Goodman are precise opposites. One is cool and transcendental, the other warmly genial; one a stranger, the other "nowhere a stranger."[28] Despite the evidence against Winsome he is, in fact, too disinterested to be the confidence man he seems to be. Once establishing his doctrine of universal estrangement, he leaves all further discussion to Egbert who reenacts with Goodman the scene in which Frank asks Charlie for a loan. Egbert will be Charlie, and Frank will play himself. In the psychodrama that follows, Frank/Frank resorts to numerous rhetorical ploys to get Charlie/Egbert to surrender. He creates a common heritage for the two (they are, he imagines, boyhood and college chums). He portrays himself as a business associate, a personal friend in need, and finally as a "fellow-being." But Charlie/Egbert will not budge from his maddening argument that a friend in need is no friend at all: "no man drops pennies into the hat of a friend. . . . If you turn beggar, . . . I turn stranger" (p. 223). In this play within a play, Goodman is a humanist and dramatist, taking many parts, each a projection of himself; he explores a full spectrum of human vicissitudes and desires. His histrionics deepen his humanity. Egbert, however, is only a spokesman of another man's one-sided principle. Goodman fails to win his point, drops his masks, and leaves enraged. Both defeat and rage are uncharacteristic of those confidence men we have already met. Indeed, it is the confidence man's victims who often stalk off in anger. Goodman, the victim of a harsh philosophy, has played his part for real. Egbert has only played a game (pattern 1).

This is Goodman's darkest hour. His humor and humanism have failed to dissolve stony distrust or enlighten blind orthodoxy. But out of his many defeats, Goodman has gained the reader's sympathy. More of a knave killer than a knave, he has not fulfilled the behavior patterns that would label him a confidence man. In fact, he has become the victim or intended victim of various game players who bear more of a resemblance to earlier operators than he. Moreover, his suspiciously simple-minded faith in man has evolved into the more pragmatic notion of genial misanthropy. But, sadly, this sagacity is more effective as a safeguard against diddlers (Noble) than as a means for winning friends (Egbert). He is as ineffectual as the mute who opens the novel. But the novel is not over.

Thus far, in applying our understanding of confidence men to Goodman, we have moved from the reasonable suspicion that he is a confidence man to a willingness to accept the cosmopolitan as another Roberts or Pitch. But at the eleventh hour, when Goodman greets the barber, Melville turns the table. Suddenly, the larcenous signals return. Chapter 42 begins with an unidentified speaker (later revealed to be Goodman) whose form might represent either an angel or the devil. By shifting point of view, Melville now refers to Goodman as "the stranger" and "the other" (pp. 225, 226, 229). Once the good-natured humorist, he is now the false wit quibbling, as would the PIO man or Noble, that a man's wig is not a sign of falsity, for it is genuinely "his" hair in that he has purchased it. But most damning, of course, is that he finally plays a confidence game. Insuring the barber against "a certain loss" if he removes his "No Trust" sign, Goodman leaves without paying for his shave. Rarely does an insurer become the cause of his insuree's first claim.

In "shaving" the barber, the cosmopolitan reveals his duplicity. But the sudden reversal does not prove that Goodman is a diddler. Goodman has not, in fact, broken his contract. Paradoxically, his request for credit is the necessary "burning" that allows the contract to become binding and for the barber then to exercise the necessary human emotion of confidence. Thus, an irresolvable, comic question remains: Will Goodman make good on the "certain loss" he has perpetrated? Will he pay the debt or redeem the loss? The barber knows; he replaces his sign. The reader, however, amused by the barber's absurd business predicament and bemused by the larger human dilemma it provokes, continues to doubt. Thus, all of Melville's episodes—the early introduction to the confidence man's varied patterns of behavior and the later inspection of the cosmopolitan in the light of that pathology—lead the reader to the final, anti-climactically comic scene in which "True knowledge" of Goodman's identity should, with certainty, be revealed, but is not.

Goodman rushes below decks to the gentlemen's cabin where passengers sleep fitfully beneath a dying, smoky lamp. "Dispens[ing] a sort of morning" in this dark "place full of strangers," the ebullient cosmopolitan himself harbors "a disturbing doubt" (pp. 241, 240, 242). The barber has quoted scriptures which condone distrust, and which consequently erode Goodman's argument for confidence in man. By chance, an old man points out that because the lines are from the Apocrypha, they lack validity and true wisdom. Goodman's relief is expressed as an apparent rejection of "wisdom" altogether: "What an ugly thing wisdom must be! Give me the folly that dimples the cheek, say I, rather than the wisdom that curdles the blood" (p. 243). At this point, readers are left to endure a final round of their own "disturbing doubts" about the cosmopolitan's character. Why should the barber's appeal to a minor scriptural citation bother Goodman? If he is a confidence man, he should have no problem arguing around the quotation. If he is a genuine seeker of confidence, his sudden doubt would seem to belie his earlier expressions of rock-bed faith. His equally precipitous relief over the lines' apocryphal source seems naive, for the damaging bit of wisdom would be no less wise because of its source. In fact, the cosmopolitan has typically argued from "experience" not "authority"; hence, he seems, here, to be out of character. The reader is left with yet another "triangular" conclusion: (1) Goodman's worry is an act, more histrionics to lure more victims; and yet (2) with no victims in sight at this late hour, these histrionics seem genuine; his own faith, having withstood the "curdling" onslaughts of Pitch, Noble, Winsome, and Egbert, has finally, sadly, begun to erode; and yet (3) his quick recovery suggests he may be a pious, "dimpled" booby, utterly naive in his view of the world. Is Goodman a knave, fool, or "quite an original"? The matter seems past knowing.

But Goodman's apparent rejection of "ugly" wisdom (seen in the context of his notion of the genial misanthrope) takes on deeper meaning. His words resonate with the mediating language of the man with a weed: "there is sorrow in the world, but goodness too; and goodness that is not greenness, either, no more than sorrow is" (p. 24). In *Moby-Dick*, Ishmael uses the same cadences to perform a similar triangulation: "There is a wisdom that is woe; but there is a woe that is madness" (*MD*, p. 355). In *The Confidence-Man*, Melville replays these chords but in a comic key. Goodness and sorrow can be tempered without greenness or madness. Thus, to survive in "a place full of strangers," one must combine folly and wisdom in such a way as to steer clear of what is too naive (greenness) and that which is too wise (disintegrative madness).

Our "disturbing doubt" about Goodman's motive is never resolved. When the old man asks the way to his stateroom, the cosmopolitan offers assistance: "I have indifferent eyes, and will show you" (p. 251). Are these the eyes of a balanced wisdom that can penetrate darkness, or are they the optics of a knave who spares no victim? What "may follow of this Masquerade," however, is not as important as what has happened to the reader. We have experienced the breakdown of an allegory and the failure of an empirical process. But the disintegration has proved instructive. We have found patterns of iniquity keyed to a larger pattern of allegory which we assume will be sustained throughout the novel; we have been forced to revise our assumptions when Goodman fails to conform to those allegorical requisites; and having once revised, we have learned (ironically) that our original suspicions are perhaps (but only perhaps) correct. By having us adopt, challenge, and finally reject a set of assumptions about the nature of confidence men, the comedy thwarts our understandably human desire to discover "True knowledge." Ineluctably, Melville's willful creation and negation of norms pushes us beyond authority and certitude into a world of perpetual questioning. As Melville puts it in Chapter 14, fiction is like a "true delineation" of old Boston; it should show us "the twistings of the town." It may be said, then, that fiction succeeds only in the degree to which it makes the reader twist. In reading *The Confidence-Man*, we are made to live the kinds of philosophical inconsistencies of human nature that Melville's characters merely project. We play them "to the life" (p. 181). Melville subverts easy allegorical correlations by thrusting us into an action that engages our sympathies. Finally, the mixture of didactic and mimetic modes exercises those necessary twistings of doubt that help us achieve the full ripeness of being or what Ishmael calls "manhood's pondering repose of If" (MA, p. 406).[29]

Notes

1. Watson G. Branch, *Melville: The Critical Heritage* (London: Routledge & Kegan Paul, 1974), pp. 380 and 385.

2. These positions are argued, respectively, in the following critiques: Hershel Parker, "The Metaphysics of Indian-hating," *Nineteenth-Century Fiction*, 18 (September, 1963): 165–173; Christopher W. Sten, "The Dialogue of Crisis in *The Confidence-Man:* Melville's 'New Novel,'" *Studies in the Novel*, 6 (Summer 1974): 165–185; Lawrence Buell, "The Last Word on *The Confidence-Man?*" *Illinois Quarterly*, 35 (November 1972): 15–29; John Seelye, *Melville: The Ironic Diagram* (Northwestern University Press, 1970); Elizabeth S. Foster, Introduction, *The Confidence-Man: His Masquerade* (New York: Hendricks House, 1954); Michael Davitt Bell, *The Development of American Romance: The Sacrifice of Relation* (University of Chicago Press, 1980); and Daniel Hoffman, *Form and Fable in American Fiction* (Oxford University Press, 1961), p. 311.

3. *The Confidence-Man: His Masquerade,* edited by Harrison Hayford, Hershel Parker, and G. Thomas Tanselle (Northwestern University Press and The Newberry Library, 1984), p. 71. Subsequent parenthetical references are to this text.

4. Edwin Honig, *Dark Conceit: The Making of Allegory* (Oxford University Press, 1966); and Stephen A. Barney, *Allegories of History, Allegories of Love* (Hamden, Conn.: Shoestring Press, 1979).

5. Foster, pp. xci, xviii, xlvi.

6. Parker, pp. 324 and 322.

7. Honig, p. 84, and Barney, p. 158.

8. Sheldon Sacks elaborates this distinction between the mimetic and didactic in his discussion of satire, apologue and represented actions in *Fiction and the Shape of Belief: A Study of Henry Fielding, with Glances at Swift, Johnson, and Richardson* (University of California Press, 1964), pp. 1–69. See also R. S. Crane, *The Languages of Criticism and the Structure Poetry* (U. of Toronto Press, 1953), pp. 122–123; and Bainard Cowan, *Exiled Waters:* Moby-Dick *and the Crisis of Allegory* (Louisiana State University Press, 1981), p. 30.

9. Buell, p. 20. John G. Cawelti argues a similar position in "Some Notes on the Structure of *The Confidence-Man,*" *American Literature*, 29 (November, 1957): 278–288. Finding clear, normative values amidst such ambiguities are Walter Dubler, "Theme and Structure in Melville's *The Confidence-Man,*" *American Literature*, 33 (November 1961): 307–319, and Merlin Bowen, "Tactics of Indirection in Melville's *The Confidence-Man,*" *Studies in the Novel*, 1 (Winter 1969): 401–420.

10. *The Rhetoric of Fiction* (University of Chicago Press, 1961), p. 293.

11. Wolfgang Iser, *The Act of Reading: A Theory of Aesthetic Response* (Johns Hopkins University Press, 1978), p. 54.

12. Merrell R. Davis and William H. Gilman, eds., *The Letters of Herman Melville* (Yale University Press, 1960), p. 146.

13. *Moby-Dick* (New York: Norton, 1967), pp. 127–128.

14. R. W. B. Lewis was one of the first to call Melville's narrator a confidence man. See "Afterword," *The Confidence-Man: His Masquerade* (New York: Signet, 1964). See also Edgar A. Dryden, *Melville's Thematics of Form: The Great Art of Telling the Truth* (Johns Hopkins University Press, 1968).

15. Angus Fletcher, *Allegory: The Theory of a Symbolic Mode* (Cornell University Press, 1964), pp. 278, 343, 322.

16. Booth, p. 378.

17. Edward Rosenberry, "Melville's Ship of Fools," *PMLA*, 75 (December 1960): 604–608.

18. Fletcher, pp. 68 and 151. Warwick Wadlington also likens the con man to Socrates. See *The Confidence Game in American Literature* (Princeton University Press, 1975), p. 19.

19. Fletcher, pp. 172, 190, and 195.

20. Black Guinea's list may be explained away as incomplete due to authorial oversights (See Watson G. Branch, "The Genesis, Composition, and Structure of *The Confidence-Man*," *Nineteenth-Century Fiction*, 28 [March, 1973]: 432). But if Melville intended a "consistent allegory" keyed to a single list established early in the narrative, this would be a major blunder indeed, suggesting that Melville did not check back to Chapter 3 or the kind of detail he had followed so faithfully with his previous con men. It is just as logical to assume that the flaw is a printer's error undetected by the author who, according to the Northwestern-Newberry editors, did not supervise proofs (p. 313). Or perhaps this well-known inconsistency reveals an author who had grown away from or lost interest in his initial allegorical schema. Perhaps, too, as I argue here, Melville allowed the "error" to signal a pattern of the allegorical breakdown that eventually dominates the novel's second half.

21. Others arguing for the cosmopolitan's distinctive nature include Franklin (p. 164) and Buell (pp. 15–29). See also Philip Drew, "Appearance and Reality in Melville's *The Confidence-Man*," *ELH*, 31 (December 1964): 442; and, in particular, Elizabeth Keyser, "'Quite an Original': The Cosmopolitan in *The Confidence-Man*," *TSLL*, 15 (Summer 1973): 279. Most recently, Tom Quirk has found Goodman to be the culmination of the "evolving significances" of the confidence man figure in Melville's imagination (*Melville's Confidence Man: From Knave to Knight* [University of Missouri Press, 1982], pp. 11 and 17).

22. Ringman, for instance, moves from amiable to serious with the troubled merchant Roberts (p. 21) and returns to heightened sociability with the shallow collegian (*CM*, p. 25). The same pattern occurs with the man in gray (pp. 38 and 43) and Truman (p. 64).

23. Black Guinea sets Roberts up for Ringman and the Episcopalian for the man in gray (p. 19). Ringman sets up Roberts and the collegian for Truman (p. 22), who in turn sets the miser up for the herb doctor (p. 74).

24. Ringman vouches for Black Guinea to Roberts (p. 19): Truman assures the collegian of the man in gray and Ringman's good nature; the man in gray (we learn from Roberts) has confirmed Ringman (p. 59); and the PIO man tells Pitch that the herb doctor looks "like a very mild Christian sort of person" (p. 115). The man in gray confirms Black Guinea to the Episcopalian (p. 29); the herb doctor confirms

the man in gray to the passengers (p. 90), Black Guinea to the soldier of fortune (p. 99), and Truman to the miser (p. 102).

25. The early confidence men are invariably associated with the ship's forward section where the mute sleeps, Black Guinea performs, and Ringman first appears. Ringman, Truman, and the PIO man are associated with the gang plank, and along with the mute are said to come from the East.

26. Similar openings occur in Chapters 4, 5, 6, 9, 21, and 22.

27. Parenthetical notations after each character indicate the number of times that character is referred to as "the stranger" or "the other," respectively, Mute (8, 0) Ringman (9, 1), Man in Gray (4, 1), Truman (6, 6), Herb Doctor (1, 3), PIO Man (1, 8), Cosmopolitan (5, 9), Noble (14, 15), Winsome (17, 3), and Egbert (1, 0).

28. Although Melville does not use this phrase, which is Noah Webster's primary definition of "Cosmopolite," his almost excessive use of "stranger," especially in the latter half of the novel, suggests his familiarity with the dictionary entry. Melville owned the 1846 edition of *An American Dictionary of the English Language* (See John Bryant, "'Nowhere a Stranger': Melville and Cosmopolitanism," *Nineteenth-Century Fiction*, 39 [December 1984]: 275–291).

29. I would like to thank the Institute for Arts and Humanistic Studies at The Pennsylvania State University for providing funds that allowed me time to write this essay.

BRYAN C. SHORT

"The Author at the Time": Tommo and Melville's Self-Discovery in Typee

> There are some things related in the narrative which will be sure to appear
> strange, or perhaps entirely incomprehensible, to the reader; but they
> cannot appear more so to him than they did to the author at the time.[1]

One prominent, ongoing trend in *Typee* criticism focuses attention on the
thematics of cross-cultural contact and other social concerns in the novel.[2]
Another views it as the representation of gathered forces in Melville's preliterary life.[3] From the beginning *Typee* has transcended the inconsistent
application of conventional literary forms noted by Melville's own family[4] to
command respect on the basis of a vigorous and seemingly unguarded social
and psychological perspicacity. Thus Tommo has often been taken either as
representing Melville's earlier self—"the author at the time"—or else Western
culture in general. Sometimes the two are combined, as in E. H. Miller's
characterization of him as "child in cannibal land."[5] Such approaches, revealing as they are, turn attention away from what I shall argue to be the central
experience narrated in *Typee,* the compelling tale of Melville's self-discovery
as a writer. This perspective mediates between extrinsic approaches and the
accomplishments of such intrinsically oriented treatments as those of Stern
and Dryden;[6] it clarifies a number of the inconsistencies in Tommo's narrative
standpoint and the thematics of the novel, and it offers a new insight into the
importance, both for *Typee* and for Melville, of style.

Texas Studies in Literature and Language, Volume. 31, Number. 3 (Fall 1989): pp. 386–405. ©
1989 University of Texas Press.

Three well-known factors shaped Melville's experience of *Typee*. First, he came to the novel, in Newton Arvin's words, "not after long and conscious preparation, but with a kind of inadvertence."[7] Second, as evidenced by responses to the novel beginning with its publisher John Murray and climaxing in Charles R. Anderson's *Melvlle in the South Seas,* its truth claims are complex and debatable.[8] Third, the success of *Typee* hangs largely on Melville's style: both Murray and a reviewer for the London *John Bull* wondered that a sailor could write so well (286); other reviewers praised the work as "so graceful, so graphic," "brilliantly colored," and "lightly but vigorously written."[9] These factors determine the manner in which Melville's self-discovery as an author informs *Typee*. Melville's inexperience explains the contradictory blend of truth and fancy in the novel: in order to legitimate his authorship, he concurrently privileges and denies his preliterary past.[10] This ambivalence toward the sources of his authority as a storyteller initiates a dialectic which both figures and realizes the emergence of his narrative voice out of the background of his early experiences. "The author at the time" is a trope possible only in a preface that looks with hindsight on the finished novel as well as on Tommo's adventures and that thus unifies the double narrative perspective noted by critics.[11] It announces Melville's emergent confidence in the power of an effective literary style to resolve his ambivalent feelings and the complex of thematic oppositions that they generate. Tommo is not an "author" "at the time" of his experiences, but Melville's style pxxermits him to read authorial functionality back into the plot and incidents of the tale.[12] Thus, the operation of style on theme in *Typee* reveals the meaning for Melville's career of both the blend of sympathy and ethnocentrism in Tommo's attitudes toward the natives and of his at times headlong and at times dilatory movement toward final denial of their claims on his feelings.[13]

The preface of *Typee* documents Melville's impulse to attribute the charisma of his text to the experiences of a preliterary past. "Sailors are the only class of men who now-a-days see anything like stirring adventure," it asserts; a tale which has excited the "warmest sympathies of the author's shipmates" can thus "scarcely fail to interest" ordinary readers (xiii). On the other hand, Melville rapidly tires of his status as a man who lived among cannibals and in 1848 praises *Mardi* as a "*real* romance" unsullied by the "dull common places" of his earlier work. He eagerly trades "the unvarnished truth" (xiv) for "that play of freedom & invention accorded only to the Romancer & poet."[14] *Typee* holds out the claim of verisimilitude against a rapidly surfacing impulse to deny the value of an earlier life that Melville associates with the creative freedom of romance, with authorship rather than seamanship.

The conflict between experience and romance, adventuresome past and literary present, gives *Typee* its basic thematic opposition, clearly reflected in Tommo. On the one hand, by braving the perils and charms of Typee

Valley, Tommo effectively represents the background of objective experience against which Melville defines the imaginative freedom of romance. This side of Tommo draws heavily on Richard Henry Dana, Jr., in his role as narrator of *Two Years before the Mast* (1840), a book which, Melville later wrote to Dana, made him feel "tied & welded to you by a sort of Siamese link of affectionate sympathy" (*Letters*, 106). On the other hand, a different Tommo gives experience a subjective coloring, the force of which has been well outlined by Dryden.[15] Tommo's narrative subjectivity draws on an equally important source, Poe's *Narrative of A. Gordon Pym* (1838).[16] Both Tommo and Pym avow an exorbitant love of adventure, undergo figurative death and rebirth, confront the terrors of cannibalism, and register numerous sensations of the sort to which Dana's unflappable persona seems immune.

The conflict in Tommo's narrative standpoint mirrors Melville's own conflicting views of the fictional process. Dana's narrator submits calmly to circumstances; his responses give interest but not direction to the plot of *Two Years before the Mast*. At one point, lowered off a sheer cliff, he reports, "I could see nothing below me but the sea and rocks upon which it broke, and a few gulls flying in mid-air. I got down, in safety, pretty well covered with dirt; and for my pains was told, 'What a d—d fool you were to risk your life for half a dozen hides.'"[17] His account, utterly believable, conveys little sense of "that play of freedom and invention" to which Melville aspires. Pym, in a similar situation, falls victim to his own unfettered imagination:

> At length arrived that crisis of fancy, so fearful in all similar cases, the crisis in which we begin to anticipate the feelings with which we *shall* fall—to picture to ourselves the sickness, and dizziness, and the last struggle. . . . And now I found these fancies creating their own realities, . . . in the next my whole soul was pervaded with *a longing to fall*; a desire, a yearning, a passion utterly uncontrollable.[18]

Pym's fancies do not simply color experience but create "their own realities." As a result, Pym cannot trust himself; his horror of cannibalism is not of being eaten but of becoming a cannibal. His narrative crosses the line between romance and phantasmagoria.

Descending into Typee valley, Tommo controls his vertigo by shutting out the immediate sensations on which his imagination, unlike Pym's, seems to depend: "My brain grew dizzy with the idea of the frightful risk I had just run, and I involuntarily closed my eyes to shut out the view of the depth beneath me" (61). Similarly, Tommo balances Pym's compulsive adventurousness against Dana's prim desire for home. However, where Dana fears time lost from his Boston future, Tommo, having no clear future, fears only entrapment in a repeated past:

> There is scarcely anything when a man is in difficulties that he
> is more disposed to look on with abhorrence than a right-about
> retrograde movement—a systematic going over of the already
> trodden ground; and especially if he has a love of adventure, such
> a course appears indescribably repulsive. (54)

Tommo's anxiety vis-à-vis the past makes him a fitting vehicle for Melville's
ambivalence toward the sources of his own literary authority. The progress
of his life continually bows to Melville's search for persuasiveness, for the
grounds of belief in his own verbal creativity; and his mix of the characteristics of Dana and Pym keeps Melville's contrasting impulses in suspension.

Tommo's controlled imagination and fear of the past blur the line between
native and "civilized" culture. The threat of entrapment in Typee Valley
echoes the prior threat of an interminable sea voyage; indeed the basic nature
of Tommo's responses is determined before he reaches land; the Edenic
harmony of valley life duplicates the experience of sailing for the Marquesas
during which the lazy felicity brought on by sun, waves, teeming ocean life,
and the all-encompassing blue of sea and sky calls forth some of Melville's
most transcendental prose. What finally attracts about the sea is exactly that
quality that Melville as author and Tommo as narrator must escape—its
silence: "But the most impressive feature of the scene was the almost upbro-
ken silence that reigned over sky and water" (10). The charms of the sea are
mute and, under its spell, language is foreclosed; one hesitates to intrude on
the quietude, and one cannot read without falling asleep. In order to break
into voice, Melville must imagine a mediate realm, Typee Valley, where the
charms of inarticulate experience and linguistic authority coexist.

Typee Valley, in contrast to the sea, offers little indigenous animal life,
shows the scars of age-old paths and ruins, and is colored a pervasive green
that, as has been noted, betokens not timelessness but decay.[19] In order to
cast his valley experiences in a romantic light, Tommo exaggerates vague and
groundless dangers:[20]

> In looking back to this period, and calling to remembrance the
> numberless proofs of kindness and respect which I received from
> the natives of the valley, I can scarcely understand how it was that,
> in the midst of so many consolatory circumstances, my mind should
> still have been consumed by the most dismal forebodings. (118)

Without both Tommo's "most dismal forebodings" and the contrasting
Edenic cast which he gives to his surroundings, Typee Valley would lose
the suggestiveness that raises it above Tommo's earlier maritime experiences
as a source of inspiration. Typee Valley is organized by Melville in order to

provide a theater for the exercise of a literary imagination calculated to save him from a shipboard identity that undercuts his power of articulation.

Typee history and society also reveal a contradictory structure: Melville allows the reader to imagine that the Typees are largely innocent of contact with whites; still only the Typees' elaborately sophisticated response to European culture preserves them from it—they remain constantly alert to the movements of the French in Nukuheva Bay and carefully cultivate xenophobia. Typee life is characterized not by natural innocence but rather by numerous systems of articulation and differentiation—by talk and taboo—which Tommo only superficially acknowledges.

While ignoring the historical circumstances of the Typees in order to present them as innocent children of nature, Tommo takes the further step of imposing on them a romance history. In his eyes their charm lies partly in the doom that hangs over them: they are the last unsullied tribe; Hawaii, Tahiti, even Nukuheva, have fallen into hopeless corruption. Typee's timelessness and peace exist in a fragile, fleeting moment poised between an endless natural past and an imminent, hopeless future. Tommo views corruption as an absolute state of being; he projects onto the culture of the islanders an imaginary gulf between innocence and degradation. Intensely aware of and indignant over results, he remains blind to processes, to his own corrupting influence.[21] Tommo's blindness creates a further stage for his own "play of freedom and invention"; Typee society is charmed because it is timeless, and timeless because Tommo "closes his eyes" to change and causality during his stay—as if "involuntarily" to "shut out the view" of the cultural movement in which he participates.

The pattern of relationships informing Tommo's responses, the state of nature and life in Typee Valley, and the sense of history in the work can be summarized as follows: a situation claimed as a source of coherent authority in Tommo's narrative turns out to be self-contradictory; the novel, in order to tell Tommo's tale, imposes a series of imaginary gaps—between past and present, art and experience, sea and valley, "civilization" and primitivism, corruption and innocence—which clear a space for "freedom and invention" manifested in the operation of Melville's style. Tommo's "consciousness of self," noted by Stern, and the concomitant "progressive unfolding of the self" mentioned by Dryden[22] turn out to be ruses of fiction dependent on Melville's assertion of authorship. By sustaining the thematic oppositions in *Typee,* Melville justifies the overriding, synthetic power which style comes to accrue in the novel, and thus the undeniable proof of his own authorial identity. What Tommo seeks to escape from is Melville's own entrapment in a mute and impotent past. That escape can never be realized because its ongoing enactment figures Melville's emergence into authorship, and his emergence dominates the work. Tommo cannot grow because he tropes, on the one hand, the need for growth on Melville's part and, on the other hand, the achieved growth indicated by the existence of his story; he is not "the author at the time" but a vehicle by which "the author at the time" can be incarnated in the operation of style; thus he remains a static and dichotomous figure.

Tommo's surprise at the happiness of Typee Valley life simulates Melville's surprise at finding himself suddenly wielding the authority of a masterful style. To be in charge of such a style makes its earlier lack equally surprising. A phenomenological gap opens between Melville's vocal and voiceless selves, a gulf that inspires his sense of wonder and delight in being a writer. *Typee* images the preliterary self of its author in terms of a regression that can only be spoken figuratively, an authority in words emerging out of that which is prior to words (his experience of the sea), an image of growth possible only if, like the figures on Keats's urn, willfully and gracefully frozen. In *Typee*, Melville's style comes to mediate the contradictions of the fictional world. The textual history of the work gives a unique insight into Melville's growing identification with an authority residing in the powers of literary voicing.

Typee was published first in London and almost simultaneously in New York. Between the American copyright date of 17 March 1846 and August of that year, Melville prepared a second American edition, incorporating Toby's story and making numerous excisions. Melville's letters suggest the excisions to have been made in response to his American publisher's objections over antimissionary sentiment and certain "sea freedoms" in the first edition (*Letters*, 39). However, several factors suggest that the excisions reflect Melville's own growing authorial identity. First, Melville's letters express the opinion that the excisions give the book "a unity . . . which it wanted before" (*Letters*, 39). Second, many of the removed passages bear only minimally on the publisher's ostensible objections. Third, comparison of the original and excised editions with Melville's sources and with the newly discovered manuscript pages in the New York Public Library shows a continuous trend of development toward the "play of freedom and invention" of which Melville wrote in regard to *Mardi*. Finally, Melville made no move to restore any of the excised material in later editions during his lifetime.

The excisions have the effect of simplifying both the language and the world of *Typee*, and of giving freer play to Melville's dominant style. In many of the excised passages, Melville speaks with an aggressive wit backed up by hindsight, the citing of sources, or historical data not immediately relevant to Tommo's adventures. The passages are often strong and delightful, and modern readers tend to prefer the first edition; still, these segments draw attention away from Tommo's half-innocence and the essential contradictions in his situation. Interestingly, the manuscript pages show the first edition to benefit from corresponding "purifications of style," excision of numerous colorful metaphors and allusions, and softening of tone. Once they become widely available, many readers will undoubtedly prefer them to the first edition.

Melville's excisions weigh particularly heavily on the first four chapters, which are reduced by about half in the second American edition. The first chapter loses its famous "Oh! ye state-room sailors" passage and two humorous incidents: the natives' curious disrobing of a missionary's wife and the embarrassment of the French over the public display of "her own sweet form" by Mowanna's consort. The history of French occupation of the islands in chapter 3 vanishes entirely. Chapter 4 loses a disquisition on the brutalization of the natives by European violence, a description of Tior, and a meditation on the relative happiness of native and civilized humankind. With the excisions disappears all reference to the genuine, historical world of the islands and the aggressive play of Melville's satire—directed in turn against genteel voyagers, the French, missionaries, civilization, and the childish immodesty of the natives. Between the two editions, the beginning of the novel changes from a rhapsodic history, Voltairean in its witty superiority of tone, to a much more unified account of supposedly personal experiences. The story of Tommo's arrival at Nukuheva, immediate escape, life among the Typees, and rescue by the *Julia* leaves little time for his learning about the French presence in the islands so prominent in the removed material. Excision of the incident involving Mowanna's consort cancels a humorous treatment of the theme of tattooing which makes overt the similarity between native and sailor. Removal of the "state-room sailors" passage dispels an early belligerence out of tune with Tommo's narrative personality in the rest of the work.

Melville's excisions deemphasize the historical world within which the narrative takes place, leaving a more uniform sense of the timelessness and innocence of Typee life. As T. Walter Herbert concludes, "Revisions of *Typee* had the effect of rendering the work more 'romantic.'"[23] They blur, on the one hand, the sharpness of Melville's contrasts between civilization and savagery and, on the other, the moralistic indignation of the narrative voice. The second American edition permits Tommo's experiences to speak more on their own terms; comparisons between European and Typee emerge from the context of happenings in the tale rather than seeming laid on ex post facto. The narrative voice of the second American edition is left to seek the meaning of observed events without reference to a library of sources. A similar effect can be attributed to the omission in the first edition of a number of biblical, classical, and literary allusions and a degree of humorous elaboration, notable, for example, in the description of Kory-Kory's speech at the end of chapter 14, which enliven Melville's manuscript. As Melville moves from manuscript to printed text, excisions significantly outnumber additions, a further indication of his sharpening focus. In numerous places he softens his references to the Typees, referring to them, for example, as men rather than as savages.

The key distinction between *Typee* and earlier treatments of native life in the Marquesas—such as those of Stewart, Porter, Langsdorff, and Ellis—is the degree of intimacy with the islanders that it evokes. The history of Melville's text demonstrates his growing willingness to, on the one hand, romanticize the natives and, on the other hand, bring Tommo into closer contact with them. As the dual effects of romance and immediacy become more pronounced, the conflict between them (and in Tommo's responses) is heightened, leaving a more serious task for the narrative voice. Tommo's contact with the Typees produces a weight of detail potentially inimical to "that play of freedom and invention accorded only to the Romancer and poet," yet it threatens Tommo's supposed objectivity. Thus, the problematic structure of Tommo's involvement, amplified by successive versions of the text, results from Melville's calculated departure from the models available to him—a departure that shows itself to be even more extraordinary under the light of stylistic analysis.

As mentioned above, one of the chief effects of Melville's emphasis on the closeness of Tommo's involvement in a romanticized native world is the sense of timelessness that tints Typee Valley. Interestingly, the uncertain temporality of Tommo's own experiences is a fact that Melville finds important enough to justify in the preface. No Robinson Crusoe, Tommo counts the days only when he expects Toby to return with help. The obverse side of Tommo's attenuated time sense is the heightened spatialization of experience in which he participates. Spatialization, as Joseph Frank defines it,[24] operates in *Typee* to create a theater for the operation of style. The timelessness of Tommo's life, once Toby leaves and Tommo's leg begins to heal, brings to a halt the progress of the narrative from Tommo's entry into the head of the valley toward his ultimate escape by sea at the narrative's far end. Timelessness also puts out of play his sense of the causal processes by which the Typees adjust to European encroachment, his own included. In rhetorical terms it signals a move from a metaphorical to a metonymic perspective,[25] from a system of external comparisons to associations justified by contiguity within a uniform, static field. As Tommo loses his compulsion to escape, he wanders the valley, inescapably enfolded in a closed, undifferentiated space, "nothing but a labyrinth of foot-paths twisting and turning among the thickets without end" (194); and yet he continually encounters new sources of wonder—ruins, idols, natural phenomena, structures, activities—included with little regard to the temporal movement of plot.

Tommo's entrapment within a timeless, nonprogressive, metonymic world focuses attention on the visual quality of his experiences—their incongruousness, beauty, or shock value—apart from their meaning in relation to external systems of value. This focus is clear in regard to the theme of tattooing. Scholars have pointed out that the Typees are tattooed with marks of their own status and that Tommo must avoid being inscribed with a native identity envisioned, like the bars etched across Kory-Kory's face, as a prison.[26] Yet Tommo is willing to have his arms tattooed, an act which would signal, in the same metaphoric terms, acceptance of the identity of a sailor—equally threatening to Melville's authorial selfhood. Tommo must remain free from tattoos, from metaphorical determination, because the unspecified nature of his identity is figuratively crucial to *Typee*. Tattooing, like the operation of a literary style, is "so beautifying an operation" (219) which has the ability to fix the essential identity of something by working on its surface. Melville does not exercise his authority by giving *Typee* the powerful underlying drive or symbolic architecture of a *Mardi* or *Moby-Dick;* instead he takes individual scenes and events and colors them vividly. The central sections of the novel present a series of intensely visual tableaux that could be rearranged without loss. Tommo himself often becomes one of the figures within such a tableau, as when he reclines among bathing "nymphs," sails on the lake with Fayaway, or dresses for a native gala. Tommo's relationships with the natives are presented in the same visual, spatialized, metonymic terms as the world of the valley: a description of native music can lead by association into an account of Tommo delighting the Typees by singing a sea chanty; a sense of kinship with Marheyo is built up out of bits of description of his incessant, happy, aimless movements near the mat where Tommo lies. Tommo's intimacy with the natives is predominantly picturesque; Melville's descriptive style makes that intimacy seem much more profound.

Melville's style draws its power from a variety of techniques not normally associated with description—the main reason, I believe, for his style's synthetic power. These techniques, although on one level evocative of a defensiveness vis-à-vis the pure, mute nature of experience, become in Melville's hands the tools for a rapacious linguistic appropriation of it. Unlike Poe, who turns inward and thereby loses the face of reality in his narrative, Melville fills his descriptions with a teeming world of obliquely associated detail. His style turns frequently on a visual hyperbole that annexes sensation to voice. Consider the beginning of the novel as it remains in the second American edition:

> Six months at sea! Yes, reader, as I live, six months out of sight of land; cruising after the sperm-whale beneath the scorching sun of the Line, and tossed on the billows of the wide-rolling Pacific—the sky above, the sea around, and nothing else! Weeks and weeks ago our fresh provisions were all exhausted. There is not a sweet potatoe left; not a single yam. Those glorious bunches of bananas which once decorated our stern and quarter-deck have, alas, disappeared! and the delicious oranges which hung suspended from our tops and

stays—they, too, are gone! Yes, they are all departed, and there is nothing left us but salt-horse and sea-biscuit.

Oh! for a refreshing glimpse of one blade of grass—for a snuff at the fragrance of a handful of loamy earth! Is there nothing fresh around us? Is there no green thing to be seen? Yes, the inside of our bulwarks is painted green; but what a vile and sickly hue it is, as if nothing bearing even the semblance of verdure could flourish this weary way from land. Even the bark that once clung to the wood we use for fuel has been gnawed off and devoured by the captain's pig; and so long ago, too, that the pig himself has in turn been devoured. (3–4)

Rarely has a novel opened with such an exuberant rhapsody on the subject of that which is no longer present. The passage, rather than paining the reader with a vision of the privation experienced on the voyage, eulogizes the richness of fare seemingly available on a South Sea cruise; the prose overwhelms the reader with the pure joy of describing. Hyperbole has the effect of drawing attention to the telling rather than the message; it suggests the imaginative vigor of a mind capable of marshaling any amount of detail, of spinning a chain of associated signifiers that might stretch on indefinitely no matter what the limits of actual experience. The privation experienced by the sailors is represented by a fictional plenitude that evokes an imaginary sensual world, a world of gustatory relish that preempts the thematics of feasting in the valley. Melville's humorous longing for the sacrifice of Pedro, the captain's rooster, as both Clark and Tolchin have noted,[27] combined with the reference to "*heathenish rites and human sacrifice*" (5), introduces later fears as a by-product of the voicing of freely associated images. Before we know it, Melville's narrative voice has, characteristically, enfolded many of the issues that will later determine Tommo's responses to the natives. That they will prove to be just like the sailors, like Tommo himself, and cannibalize their prisoner out of hunger or exuberance is a possibility, despite his own tabooed status, which Tommo can never dispel from his mind.

The beginning of *Typee* displays another of Melville's techniques, what can be called promiscuous apostrophe. He begins by addressing the reader directly, fades into soliloquy, and in subsequent paragraphs addresses the rooster, another sailor, and the "poor old ship" itself. The impression created is of a voice ready to fix on any imaginable auditor. The world of *Typee* gets personified, made immediate, by being talked to or by being talked—to someone. Even when Melville is not employing direct address, his style has the power to make its current topic take on an air of momentary intimacy between author and reader. Melville's dissertations on the distinction between primitive and civilized life almost always have a mediating quality which, under the pennant of voicing—the placing of the fictional world in a close relation to the act of its articulation—bridges the gaps seemingly emphasized. Frequently the gaps bridged are temporal; what was "so long ago" is made current or projected into a near future: "but courage, old lass, I hope to see thee soon within a biscuit's toss of the merry land" (5).

The mediating nature of Melville's style is clear in the famous passage in which Kory-Kory lights a fire. Tommo signals the start of his tableau by announcing to the reader that, because the act "was entirely different from what I had ever seen," he will describe it. He then shifts to the present tense, as if, in spite of his generalizations, he were addressing a scene taking place right in front of him. As Kory-Kory speeds up, Melville's style becomes more vivid, concrete and hyperbolic, but such phrases as "amazing rapidity" and "this is the critical stage of the operation" maintain the presence of an auditor in the description. In the final sentences, Melville's vocal force comes to reside in two strong metaphors, the second of which has been anticipated earlier in the passage:

> His hands still retain their hold of the smaller stick, which is pressed convulsively against the further end of the channel among the fine powder there accumulated, as if he had just pierced through and through some little viper that was wriggling and struggling to escape from his clutches. The next moment a delicate wreath of smoke curls spirally into the air, the heap of dusty particles glows with fire, and Kory-Kory almost breathless, dismounts from his steed. (111)

The point is not that the metaphorical structure of the passage makes it an allegory of masturbation—a theory reinforced by the intimate tone but complicated by the existence of additional comparisons between Kory-Kory and both a locomotive and a steamship that appear in the manuscript pages. Melville's metaphor of the viper is so unusual, indeed catachrestic, and yet visually pointed, that it breaks down the structure of external reference which the subsequent native-civilized comparisons seem to produce. Because of the violence of the viper image, the physical impact of the passage refuses to rest within the confines of an easy humor. In the manuscript Melville ends his suggestion for a "college of vestals," to keep valley fires lit, with a rather abstract sentence making it clear that the "special difficulties" mentioned in conjunction with this scheme refer to the lack of virgins among native women. In revising, he decided to give the subject a more serious and pointed treatment. At stake is the outlay of "good temper," "toil," and "anxiety" and a process undertaken for the purpose of lighting Tommo's pipe takes on the weight of duties that would drive a "European artisan" "to his wits' end." The coloring given by the viper image is picked up, as

Melville comes to realize that the intimacy of visual detail in the passage prevents the use of a cooler or more condescendingly humorous tone.

In "Kory-Kory strikes a light a la Typee," Melville begins with a paragraph of colorful, present-tense description in which an unusual image creates a swerve in tone and reference; he then moves to a paragraph of understated humor containing his suggestion for a "college of vestals"; finally he compares European with island life in a way that reflects the disconcerting note introduced by the viper image. The entire passage mediates thematically between the two societies as it integrates three distinct and characteristic temporal modes—present-tense immediate ("Kory-Kory goes to work quite leisurely . . ."), retrospective reflection ("had I possessed a sufficient intimacy with the language to have conveyed my ideas upon the subject, I should certainly have suggested . . ."), and generalized commentary ("What a striking evidence does this operation furnish . . ."). Melville's style draws together the "striking evidence" of the third paragraph—which discusses relative obligations faced by native and European—with the initial motive for the passage: "often he was obliged to strike a light for the occasion." The "intimacy with the language" that Tommo lacks in the second paragraph evokes the extraordinary physical intimacy of the preceding passages, in which Tommo's body is rubbed down with "aka" by the native girls. The various aspects of the whole scene come together in an act of address where visual content, speaking voice, and audience intermix and cohere closely in an integrated yet complex locutionary act.

The mediatory nature of Melville's voice in "Kory-Kory strikes a light a la Typee" critically involves the handling of time in the passage. Melville deliberately elides the distinctions between the time of the event and the time of writing about it. The fact that the prose relates associatively—metonymically—to its context helps; the passage is presented as a contiguous part of the prior domestic scene, a natural prelude to musings on family obligations. It has no determinate temporal position. The same use of style to shape the timeless time sense of *Typee* appears in bolder outline in a later passage:

> For hours and hours during the warmest part of the day I lay upon my mat, and while those around me were nearly all dozing away in careless ease, I remained awake, gloomily pondering over the fate which it appeared now idle for me to resist. When I thought of the loved friends who were thousands and thousands of miles from the savage island in which I was held a captive, when I reflected that my dreadful fate would for ever be concealed from them, and that with hope deferred they might continue to await my return long after my inanimate form had blended with the dust of the valley—I could not repress a shudder of anguish.

How vividly is impressed upon my mind every minute feature of the scene which met my view during those long days of suffering and sorrow! . . .

Just beyond the pi-pi, and disposed in a triangle before the entrance of the house, were three magnificent bread-fruit trees. At this moment I can recal to my mind their slender shafts, and the graceful inequalities of their bark, on which my eye was accustomed to dwell day after day in the midst of my solitary musings. It is strange how inanimate objects will twine themselves into our affections, especially in the hour of affliction. Even now, amidst all the bustle and stir of the proud and busy city in which I am dwelling, the image of those three trees seems to come as vividly before my eyes as if they were actually present, and I still feel the soothing quiet pleasure which I then had in watching hour after hour their topmost boughs waving gracefully in the breeze. (243–244)

This passage so clearly presages a host of others in Melville's later works —Redburn's memories of his model ship, Ishmael's commentary on the "Counterpane" experience, the memorable, damned tortoises of *The Encantadas*—that it deserves careful attention. It is the only passage in *Typee* where Tommo suggests a past (loved friends) prior to his experiences on ship or the future circumstances of his life ("the proud and busy city in which I am dwelling"). It dramatically oversteps the temporal boundaries of the rest of the novel, but it does so in a way that specifies the novel's temporality.[28]

At the beginning of the passage, Tommo places himself in exactly the position that he imagines the Typees to be in—suspended between an indeterminate innocent past and an endless, hopeless future. His anguish derives not from fear of approaching events, of which he has no sense, but rather fear of silence—that his "dreadful fate would for ever be concealed." As with the novel itself, the gap between past and future is a theater for imaginatively articulated experience: "How vividly is impressed upon my mind every minute feature of the scene which met my view during those long days of suffering and sorrow" (243). Here the present tense indicates the time of writing or reflection, so the whole experience is projected forward to a moment that replaces the original point of sensation: "at this moment I can recal. . . ." This instant then opens out further into a sense of the process of the author's continuing life: "Even now, amidst all the bustle and stir . . . , the image of those trees seems to come as vividly before my eyes. . . ." The memory of images from Tommo's tale, inspired by a state of mind brought on in turn by a memory of "loved friends," gives time and substance to Melville's authorial personality. The passage presents an indeterminate fictional moment that involves a looking back that enables a looking forward, both perspectives outside the fictional bounds of the novel, both therefore aspects of voice rather than theme. The same figure lies hidden behind the assertion, "I can never forget . . ." which opens the description of the sea in the second chapter and which Melville repeats throughout *Typee*—for example, in the final line of chapter 6 (40), twice in chapter 7 (45, 46), and three times in the final chapter (248 twice, 252). In this case the moment of telling is eclipsed by a going back—remembering—which goes endlessly forward—never to be forgotten.

The backward and forward movement of time in *Typee* corresponds to the trope of metalepsis which, in the intertextual analysis of Harold Bloom, permits a poem to imagine itself as prior to, enfolding, and misreading, its own precursor.[29] In *Typee* it enables the existence of "the author at the time"—a consciousness free to range beyond the boundaries of the work and thus beyond the limits of its own existence as figured by Tommo. "The author at the time" is an author who appropriates time to voicing. Metalepsis tends to show up throughout Melville's writings wherever the substance of authorial identity, the relation between author and materials, and the imaginative generation of discourse are in question. It integrates theme and style, content and form, in a way that sets *Typee* apart from both its nonfiction sources and earlier sea novels from Defoe through Marryat; it is precisely the narrative function that Poe fails to control in attempting to get Pym's story told.

The mediating or synthetic nature of Melville's style is enabled by its key functional qualities: metonymy, the proleptic enfolding or preempting of thematic materials, hyperbole, apostrophe, catachresis, and metalepsis. The ending of *Typee* resolves its contradictions through the achieved powers of style and realizes Melville's emergence from silence into his particular, compelling voice. The final chapter begins by canceling the sense of timelessness outlined above; in returning Tommo to time, it also returns him to the portentous silence mentioned in Melville's early description of the sea: "Nearly three weeks had elapsed since the second visit of Marnoo, and it must have been more than four months since I entered the valley, when one day about noon, and whilst everything was in profound silence. . . ." (245). Melville establishes directly that Tommo's escape must come by way of return to the sea, a sea which for the moment suspends its power to suffocate Tommo's sense of self:

> Having been prohibited from approaching the sea during the whole of my stay in the valley, I had always associated with it the idea of escape. Toby too—if indeed he had ever voluntarily deserted me—must have effected his flight by the sea; and now that I was drawing near to it myself, I indulged in hopes which I had never felt before. (246)

"Hopes which I had never felt before" repeats the metalepsis responsible for the enabling timelessness of Typee Valley—now attached to the idea of the sea. At issue is the ability, in escaping from the island, to avoid a relapse into the world of silence, muteness, which it supplanted. Tommo is, at this point, still trapped in the Typee world of static space and corresponding articulation, and his progress toward the beach is agonizingly delayed by a throng of gesturing, talking, shouting, and arguing islanders. Finally, his own "eloquence of gesture" prevails on the otherwise hostile Mow-Mow to permit him to struggle onward, now with no help from his surrogate family. Within the world of the valley, Tommo can only gesture, not speak, and he exists under a pseudonym which as much indicates a lack of identity as a created one. Gesture must give way to real articulation, to the projection of an authorship which Tommo can never genuinely figure, before he will be free to go.

At this point, in a mirror image of the process by which the contradictions in the thematic world of *Typee* were earlier seen to open a space for articulation, the talk of the natives divides to open a space for Tommo's escape:

> To my surprise I was suffered to proceed alone, all the natives remaining in front of the house, and engaging in earnest conversation, which every moment became more loud and vehement; and to my unspeakable delight I perceived that some difference of opinion had arisen between them; that two parties, in short, were formed, and consequently that in their divided counsels there was some chance of my deliverance. (248)

Immediately after this passage, Marheyo, with an expression that Tommo says he "shall never forget," articulates, on behalf of the mute Tommo, the space between the "divided counsels" of the natives by pronouncing the words "home" and "mother" to him. Six lines later, Tommo nears the sea:

> Never shall I forget the extacy I felt when I first heard the roar of the surf breaking upon the beach. Before long I saw the flashing billows themselves through the opening between the trees. Oh glorious sight and sound of ocean! with what rapture did I hail you as familiar friends! By this time the shouts of the crowd upon the beach were distinctly audible, and in the blended confusion of sounds I almost fancied I could distinguish the voices of my own countrymen. (248)

Marheyo's words give way to the noise of the surf and the voices on the beach: the babble of the arguing natives conflicts and blends with sounds that Tommo can understand. It is another experience that he can "never for-get"; the metaleptic device that has informed the suspended time of the val-ley now relates Tommo to the sea, which, in the guise of "familiar friends," echoes the "loved friends" of Tommo's musings in the valley. By evoking the figure that permits authorial transcendence of the fictional time in *Typee*, the waves momentarily transcend their own threatening past. The "opening between the trees" yields in the next paragraph to "the open space between the groves and the sea" (249). Tommo's escape is staged in the in-between space of the beach, an image that will retain its significance for Melville even to the "Pebbles" which end *John Marr and Other Sailors:*

> But Orm from the schools to the beaches strays,
> And, finding a Conch hoar with time, he delays
>   And reverent lifts it to ear.
> That Voice, pitched in far monotone,
>   Shall it swerve? Shall it deviate ever?[30]

Tommo, bounced between images of transcendence and suppression in time, fears that he has arrived "too late" when again the available space is occupied by a mark of enabling articulation—the sound of his "own name shouted out by a voice from the midst of the crowd" (249).

It is, of course, "Tom," not "Tommo," that he hears (unless, as Wither-ington has suggested, that too is a pseudonym),[31] since Karakoee would not have known his native name, and the word prompts Tommo to two crucial acts: he recognizes and he remembers. A page later, after the "detestable word 'Roo-ne'" threatens to take over the theater of articulation opened by the "op-posing counsels" of the natives on the beach, a second reference to Tommo's ability to remember leads into the exertion of all his strength in plunging toward Karakoee, who now stands "to the waist in the surf." Tommo's success is signaled by Fayaway, who is rendered "speechless" with sorrow and im-mediately described as "retired from the edge of the water." The other natives may follow Tommo "into the water," but the power of those who are key in-gredients in the romance world of Typee Valley ends at the shore. Mow-Mow is the only recognizable native who swims after the boat, and his "ferocious expression" at being defeated is the final thing of which Tommo says "never shall I forget" (252).

The entry of the natives into the water in pursuit of Tommo elides, once and for all, the valley-sea distinction that Melville has pretended to maintain throughout. He is able to give up such an important locus of vocal enablement because the distinction bows, in the final moments of the story, to another more central to Melville's later works—being afloat as opposed to being im-mersed. The natives would overturn Tommo's boat; to be swamped in the sea is the last threat of residence in Typee Valley; it signals the allegiance which the realms share in figuring the dangers of the past, experience, and silence to the emergence of Melville's authorial identity. The natives, unaccountably more formidable in the water than on land, usher into Melville's fiction the fear of immersion associated with the end of *Mardi,* with White-Jacket's plunge, and with the tragedy of Pip in *Moby-Dick.*

It is not, of course, "Tommo" who is pulled on board the *Julia,* since that appellation has not appeared in the novel since he has heard "my own name" shouted by Karakoee. "Tom" (the real name is not crucial) now represents a narrative voice that mediates between Melville and Tommo, and he tells us that "on reaching the 'Julia' I was lifted over the side, and my strange appearance and remarkable adventure occasioned the liveliest interest" (252–253). His phrase echoes the assertion of the preface that the narrator's story "could scarcely fail to interest those who are less familiar than the sailor with a life of adventure." The echoed language constitutes a final metaleptic figure which permits the end and beginning of the book to evoke each other and complete its narrative circle. The circle is closed not by Tommo's adventures but by the "interest" displayed by auditors in the accomplished tale. Melville's new narrative persona never takes substantial form, for to do so would be for him to traduce the allegorical focus of the work. On one level, then, nothing has been solved; Tommo faces another problematic sea voyage. On another level, everything has been solved, for Melville's simulacrum has discovered his voice. The tale does not end; it tails off into an appendix, a sequel, the story of Toby, another sequel, *Omoo,* and Melville's subsequent literary career, a career during the entire scope of which his strong sense of authorial identity and his strong style never leave him. Melville's self-discovery in *Typee* carries the force of a conversion experience, an inconceivable but undeniable election; *Typee* is the first in a series of instances in which voicing and salvation interweave to produce a texture of thematic and formal concerns characteristic of Melville's fictional method. It is hard to imagine a first novel that does more to enable the mature, complex, and durable creative energy of its author.

NOTES

1. Herman Melville, *Typee,* ed. Harrison Hayford, Hershel Parker, and G. Thomas Tanselle (Evanston and Chicago: Northwestern University Press and Newberry Library, 1968), xiv. Subsequent references to *Typee* will be cited from this edition in the text. I would like to thank the Northern Arizona University Organized Research Committee for supporting the writing of this article.

2. See James Duban, *Melville's Major Fiction: Politics, Theology, and Imagination* (De Kalb: Northern Illinois University Press, 1983) 3–11; John Wenke, "Melville's *Typee:* A Tale of Two Worlds," in *Critical Essays on Herman Melville's –"Typee,"* ed. Milton R. Stern (Boston: G. K. Hall, 1982), 250–258; T. Walter Herbert, Jr.,

Marquesas Encounters: Melville and the Meaning of Civilization (Cambridge: Harvard University Press, 1980); 149–191; A. N. Kaul, "Herman Melville: The New-World Voyageur," in *The American Vision: Actual and Ideal Society in Nineteenth-Century Fiction* (New Haven: Yale University Press, 1963), 222–235; Charles R. Anderson, *Melville in the South Seas* (New York: Columbia University Press, 1939), 69–195.

3. See Neal L. Tolchin, *Mourning, Gender, and Creativity in the Art of Herman Melville* (New Haven: Yale University Press, 1988) 36–58; Michael Paul Rogin, *Subversive Genealogy: The Politics and Art of Herman Melville* (New York: Knopf, 1983) 43–49; Edwin Haviland Miller, *Melville* (New York: Braziller, 1975) 118–135; Lawrance Thompson, *Melville's Quarrel with God* (Princeton: Princeton University Press, 1952), 43–55.

4. Tolchin, 36.

5. Miller, *Melville*, 118.

6. Milton R. Stern, *The Fine-Hammered Steel of Herman Melville* (Urbana: University of Illinois Press, 1957) 29–65; Edgar A. Dryden, *Melville's Thematics of Form: The Great Art of Telling the Truth* (Baltimore: Johns Hopkins University Press, 1968), 37–46.

7. Newton Arvin, *Herman Melville* (New York: William Sloane, 1950), 77.

8. On Murray's suspicions, see Leon Howard, Historical Note, in *Typee*, 279; Anderson (191) concludes that Melville could have written *Typee* without having visited the Marquesas.

9. Hugh W. Hetherington, *Melville's Reviewers: British and American, 1846–1891* (Chapel Hill: University of North Carolina Press, 1961), 24, 25, 33.

10. William B. Dillingham (*An Artist in the Rigging: The Early Works of Herman Melville* [Athens: University of Georgia Press, 1972], 24) explores the theme of the "irrecoverable" past in *Typee*; Rowland A. Sherrill (*The Prophetic Melville: Experience, Transcendence, and Tragedy* [Athens: University of Georgia Press, 1979], 7–32) discusses the "retrospective narrator" of the work.

11. Dillingham, 11–12. A summary of treatments of the theme appears in 12n.

12. For a theoretical treatment of authorial functionality see Michel Foucault, "What Is an Author?" in *Language, Counter-Memory, Practice*, ed. Donald F. Bouchard, trans. Donald F. Bouchard and Sherry Simon (Ithaca: Cornell University Press, 1977), 113–138.

13. Herbert (153–180) discusses at length the contradictions and tensions centering on Tommo's view of the natives. Cf. Duban's (9n) suggested revision of Herbert's outlook.

14. *The Letters of Herman Melville*, ed. Merrell R. Davis and William H. Gilman (New Haven: Yale University Press, 1960), 70. Subsequent references to *Letters* will appear in the text.

15. Dryden, *Melville's Thematics of Form*, 38–46.

16. Mary K. Bercaw, *Melville's Sources* (Evanston: Northwestern University Press, 1987), 110. Also see Perry Miller, *The Raven and the Whale: The War of Words and Wits in the Era of Poe and Melville* (New York: Harcourt, Brace & World, 1956), 21.

17. Richard Henry Dana, Jr., *Two Years before the Mast* (1912; rpt. London: Dent, 1972), 169.

18. Edgar Allan Poe, *Poetry and Tales* (New York: Library of America, 1984), 1170.

19. Stern, *Fine-Hammered Steel*, 61.

20. Rogin concludes that "there is no evidence that the Typeeans actually plan to eat Tommo" (47).

21. See Stern, *Fine-Hammered Steel*, 40, and Dryden, 45, on Tommo's corrupting effects on the Typees.

22. Milton R. Stern, "Typee," in *Critical Essays on Herman Melville's "Typee,"* 139; Dryden, 37.

23. Herbert, 189.

24. Joseph Frank, *The Widening Gyre* (New Brunswick: Rutgers University Press, 1963). Frank summarizes the effects of spatialization on narrative as follows: "For the duration of the scene, at least, the time-flow of the narrative is halted; attention is fixed on the interplay of relationships within the immobilized time-area" (15); "past and present are apprehended spatially, locked in a timeless unity that, while it may accentuate surface differences, eliminates any feeling of sequence by the very act of juxtaposition" (59).

25. Charles Feidelson, Jr. (*Symbolism and American Literature* [Chicago: University of Chicago Press, 1953], 165) sees the "topography" of *Typee* as "metaphoric." Focus on the metonymic nature of Tommo's valley experiences has the effect of replacing Feidelson's symbolic perspective with a view of figurative processes in the novel corresponding more closely to Paul de Man's notion of "allegory" developed in "The Rhetoric of Temporality," in *Blindness and Insight*, 2d ed. (Minneapolis, University of Minnesota Press, 1983), 187–228.

26. Stern, *Fine-Hammered Steel*, 59.

27. Michael Clark, "Melville's *Typee:* Fact, Fiction, and Esthetics," in *Critical Essays on Herman Melville's –"Typee,"* 219; Tolchin, 47.

28. John Samson ("The Dynamics of History and Fiction in Melville's *Typee,*" *American Quarterly* 36 [1984]: 276–290, esp. 289) sees in this passage a "typical Wordsworthian motif." He argues that "Tommo's intimations of immortality can at this point come only through recollection of his 'childhood' in Typee." Samson relates the combined retrospective and teleological temporality of Melville's description to the "transcendent, spiritual meaning" which Tommo gives to events rather than to the mediating power of style.

29. Harold Bloom, *A Map of Misreading* (New York: Oxford University Press, 1975), 102–103; see also Gerard Genette, *Narrative Discourse: An Essay on Method,* trans. Jane E. Lewin (Ithaca, Cornell University Press, 1980), 234–237.

30. *Poems of Herman Melville*, ed. Douglas Robillard (New Haven, Conn.: College and University Press, 1976), 203.

31. Paul Witherington, "The Art of Melville's *Typee,*" *Arizona Quarterly* 26 (1970): 136–150, esp. 144.

NANCY FREDRICKS

Melville and the Woman's Story

One way to understand the change in direction that Herman Melville's
work took in the 1850s is to consider his writing from *Moby-Dick* through
The Piazza Tales in relation to the increasing involvement of women in
reading, writing, and publishing. For feminists and traditional critics
alike, Melville's *Moby-Dick* represents a bastion of masculinist aesthetics where women are as out of place as Aunt Charity's ginger beer on
the *Pequod*. Long used to buttress theories of American literature that
valorize male bonding and the romantic quest into the wilderness away
from home and mother, *Moby-Dick* is an exemplary text for its generic
representation from a male perspective of the segregation of the sexes
in nineteenth-century America.[1] Melville himself apparently thought of
Moby-Dick as a man's book and wrote to one of his female friends, Sara
Moorehead, to dissuade her from reading it for fear of offending her
feminine sensibilities:

> Dont you buy it—dont even read it, when it does come out,
> because it is by no means the sort of book for you. It is not a
> piece of fine, feminine, Spitalfield silk—but is of the horrible
> texture of a fabric that should be woven of ship's cables and
> hausers.[2]

Studies in American Fiction, Volume 19 (1991): pp. 41–54. © 1991 Northeastern University.

When Sophia Hawthorne wrote to Melville praising the book, his response was one of astonishment:

> I have hunted up the finest Bath I could find, gilt-edged and stamped, whereon to inscribe my humble acknowledgement of your highly flattering letter of the 29th of Dec:—It really amazed me that you should find any satisfaction in that book. It is true that some *men* have said they were pleased with it but you are the only *woman*—for as a general thing, women have small taste for the sea.[3]

"Next time," Melville tells Sophia, he shall not send her a "bowl of salt water. . . . The next chalice I shall commend, will be a rural bowl of milk." He then inquires politely about the state of her "domestic affairs."[4]

Melville's remarks to these women suggest that he was working under certain gender-determined notions of genre. If genres represent mini-subcultures with their own values, languages, and epistemologies,[5] then it seems understandable that in a period characterized by relatively separate spheres for men and women there would be associated with each sphere types of works that best reflect that group's immediate concerns. Melville had been working most of his career with a predominantly male audience in mind. In the six novels leading up to and including *Moby-Dick*—sea adventures all—women appear as either obstacles to the male romantic quest or as the distant and unattainable object of that quest. *Pierre,* which Melville referred to generically as a "regular romance," marks a definite shift away from the man's world of the sea adventure to the land-locked domestic world of women.[6] In *Pierre,* Melville finally gives his female characters articulation[7] and begins to face, on a generic level, the challenge that the female community presented to male writers like himself who had excluded them for too long. If women barely make it to the margin of *Moby-Dick,* the woman as artist takes center stage in *Pierre.*

Pierre, for many readers, represents Melville's "Waterloo." One cannot help but wonder what could have led Melville, at the height of his creative powers, to plunge into the alien territory of the domestic romance. By following *Moby-Dick* with *Pierre,* he may have been trying to grant equal time to two competing myths of his day.[8] After pursuing the romantic quest into the wilderness to its limits in *Moby-Dick,* it seems that Melville decided to turn to its generic "opposite," the domestic romance, and take that to its limits also. Possibly Melville (who was nothing if not artistically ambitious) wanted to capture the totality of his world and knew he could not hope to do it with the *Pequod* alone as his setting. The familiar trope of the "ship as world," which had served Melville well for years, tended to exclude the female half of the population. The setting of *Pierre* provides Melville with the opportunity to explore the world of women excluded from his earlier works and to address a nineteenth-century female audience largely concerned with domesticity, Christianity, and the position of women in society.

Considered in this light, *Moby-Dick* and *Pierre* appear to form a giant, gender-determined literary diptych. The diptych structure serves Melville as a formal means to represent the totality of his world while at the same time inscribing the gesture of gender exclusion. Melville uses diptychs to represent sexual and economic polarization and exclusion in several pieces of short fiction written immediately after *Pierre:* "Two Temples," "Poor Man's Pudding and Rich Man's Crumbs," and "The Paradise of Bachelors and The Tartarus of Maids." His method in these stories is to juxtapose two separately set tales told by the same first-person narrator. "The Paradise of Bachelors and The Tartarus of Maids" provides the clearest example of Melville's feminism and affords a vantage from which to read, retrospectively, the gender-determined relation between *Moby-Dick* and *Pierre.* On the surface, this short story can be read as a celebration of the homoerotic joys of bachelorhood and, perhaps, as an example of Melville's alleged misogyny. But as the more careful readers of Melville's alleged "racist" texts have demonstrated, Melville likes to set ideological traps to catch the reader in his or her own social prejudices. The methods used by Carolyn L. Karcher in her readings of Melville's texts dealing with racial oppression in *Shadow Over the Promised Land* need to be applied to his texts about sexual oppression as well.[9] As Jane Mushabac has written, "Melville had always been profoundly attuned to the condition of slavery implicit in the human condition; it was only a matter of time before he noticed that women as well as men were slaves."[10]

The gendered juxtaposition in "The Paradise of Bachelors and The Tartarus of Maids" illustrates not only the exclusion of women but their constitutive status in capitalistic, patriarchal society. Their exploitation is presented as inseparable from issues of sexuality, economic power, and representation. The "blank looking girls, with blank, white folders in their blank hands, all blankly folding blank paper" must surrender their reproductive power (the factory only employs maids) in the production of paper that the wealthy bachelor lawyers (in the first tale) will inscribe with the language of money.[11] Melville's use of the diptych structure implies that the extravagant lifestyle of the lawyer bachelors is linked to—even depends upon—the deprivation of the oppressed maids at work in the paper factory.

Melville certainly deserves more credit than he has gotten for addressing the concerns of women readers.[12] He is often judged guilty by association with Hawthorne, whose notorious remarks about "that damned mob of scribbling women" seem to have attached themselves to Melville as well. Jane Tompkins, for example, claims that Melville together with Hawthorne "hated" the popular and critical success of "their sentimental rivals."[13] In contrast to Hawthorne, who fled to Europe expressing disgust with the women writers he believed were edging him out of a writer's living, Melville weathered the storm and even appears to have made a bid for position in the changing market with *Pierre*. Surprisingly, Hawthorne's derogatory remarks about women writers have done little to damage his reputation among male and female readers today who admire his strong female characters. Melville, on the other hand, has been neglected by feminist critics, presumably because of his "inability" to move beyond stereotypes to present realistic, fully developed, strong, and positive female characters.

In the "Agatha" letters written to Hawthorne after Melville completed *Pierre*, Melville appears to be going through a crisis of confidence concerning his ability to represent female characters. He seems especially conscious of this literary "shortcoming" in comparison to Hawthorne, whom he urges to write a story based on information Melville had collected about a woman named Agatha. This woman witnesses the shipwreck of her husband and nurses him back to health only to see him off again. She waits in vain for a letter from him. While she waits the rest of her life for his return, he marries and raises a family in another port.[14] It seems for the first time in Melville's life, his imagination and sympathy are engaged more with the woman left on shore than the sailor at sea. He pesters Hawthorne to write the woman's story because, he says, it is in Hawthorne's "vein." Hawthorne finally loses patience with his friend and tells him to write it himself.[15] It is not clear whether Melville ever did write Agatha's story.[16] A variant of the tale appears in "The Encantadas" in the story of Hunilla, the Chola woman and turtle hunter who witnesses the drowning of her husband and survives alone for years on a remote, uninhabited island.[17]

Perhaps Melville's feminism has often been overlooked because he does not generally represent strong middle-class women triumphing over adversity in a man's world, the kind of woman in Fanny Fern's *Ruth Hall*, the one book by a woman writer that won Hawthorne's praise.[18] Except for Hunilla (the Chola widow in "The Encantadas"), most of the strong women in Melville's work, like Hautia in *Mardi* and Mrs. Glendinning in *Pierre*, are oppressors like the "strong" man, Ahab. Through these "strong" women, Melville explores the darker side of women's political powerlessness that leads in Pierre's mother's case, for example, to excessive control over domestic affairs. Mrs. Glendinning rules supreme over her maternal domain with the church, in the figure of the ineffectual Rev. Falsgrave, at her side, an illustration of the strategic alliance that Ann Douglas has documented and critiqued in *The Feminization of American Culture*.[19] Melville's representation of the darker side of family life in *Pierre* has led one feminist historian, Mary Ryan, to praise him in her book *The Empire of Mother* as his period's "most insightful critic of ante-bellum domesticity."[20] While Ryan gives Melville credit for his cultural awareness, she and other less generous critics place undue emphasis on *Pierre*'s negativity, emphasis that has led to the conclusion that Melville hated sentimentalism.

On the contrary: "I stand for the heart," Melville wrote to Hawthorne, declaring his allegiance in language that echoes *Pierre*'s enthusiastic rhetoric.[21] *Pierre* is a book about righteousness and the transforming power of love, in sentiment comparable to *Uncle Tom's Cabin*, minus the dogmatic optimism.[22] In *Pierre*, Melville explores his deeply ambivalent feelings about Christianity. On the one hand, he is attracted to that embodiment of all love, the Sermon on the Mount; on the other hand, he despairs at the abyss separating the ideal and the practical in this "mammonish" world. It is a distortion to reduce this ambivalence to purely negative parody, just as it is a mistake to reduce *Pierre* to a cynical and mean-spirited attack on the female reading public.

Melville's interest seems to lie primarily in representing women who may very well be strong but who, unlike the Ruth Halls and Fanny Ferns of this world, remain oppressed and excluded by social forces. His texts about women need to be treated in the context of the popular generic tradition that David S. Reynolds has identified as "the literature of misery."[23] Like Isabel's tale in *Pierre*, and like the story of the factory workers in "The Tartarus of Maids," the "literature of misery" tends to focus on the struggles of the impoverished and unrepresented working class, particularly women factory workers and seamstresses. The problem for Melville as a writer is how to represent the unrepresentability of these women, their marginal yet constitutive status in capitalistic, patriarchal society. Excluded from *Moby-Dick* and "The Paradise of Bachelors," these women are elevated by Melville to a position of "equality" as the focus of the second half of the diptych, *Pierre* and "The Tartarus of Maids," respectively. With the creation of Isabel, his first central female character, Melville begins to explore in depth the subversive power of the excluded feminine. *Pierre* may be named for a male character, but the moving force in the book is certainly Isabel. Her initial shriek initiates a chain of events that ultimately pulls all around her to destruction. Her power is not merely negative, however. It is Isabel, Melville writes, who awakens Pierre to the "darker though truer aspect of things."[24] For this alone, she deserves to be ranked among Melville's heroines.

Melville may have found help in dealing with these issues from the texts by women writers that he was reading at the time. Melville purchased Mary Shelley's *Frankenstein* while in London before writing *Moby-Dick*.[25] The obvious parallels between Victor Frankenstein and Ahab suggest that Melville not only read Shelley's book but that he drew heavily on her portrait of the monomaniacal Victor in creating Ahab. In his next writing project, *Pierre*, Melville may have adopted the extremely effective strategy in *Frankenstein* of interrupting the flow of the narrative with a detailed story told in first person by one oppressed and excluded from the previously dominant discourse. Isabel's story of her life in *Pierre*—her extreme loneliness, her awakening sense of self, her struggle to learn to read and write, her search for links with others—reads like the creature's story in *Frankenstein*. Isabel is the sympathetic monster as woman. When Melville decided to present Isabel as a musician and singer, he may also have had in mind another influential book he had purchased in London along with *Frankenstein,* Mme. de Stael's *Corinne*.[26]

These apparent attempts by Melville to reach out to the female reading public of his time were a dismal failure. Perhaps the book's scathing critique of the American class structure told from the point of view of those exploited and excluded, the impoverished servant class, together with the prominent theme of incest cut the book off from the appreciation of the more genteel, middle-class audience. The highly wrought and densely allusive language may have cut it off as well from the under-educated lower classes. Furthermore, Melville's language in *Pierre* is exceedingly artificial at a time when the dominant aesthetic is beginning to shift towards realism. As Josephine Donovan and Judith Fetterly have recently demonstrated, this shift towards realism in American literature was being spearheaded by women writers associated with the local-color movement like Caroline Kirkland, Alice Carey, and Rose Terry Cooke, to name a few. [27] According to Donovan, these women writers were tapping a "centuries old tradition of women's literary realism opposed to sentimental romance,"[28] a tradition aligned with philosophical empiricism and novelistic critiques of romance aesthetics.

In two short stories written after *Pierre,* "I and My Chimney" and "The Piazza," Melville explored the generic tension between realist and romance aesthetics in terms of gender.[29] In "I and My Chimney," the chimney functions not only as a phallic metaphor but as a metaphor for Melville's art of the sublime, as best exemplified in *Moby-Dick*. The wife and daughters of the narrator conspire against him to bring down his beloved old chimney, which the narrator compares to the pyramids and to a whale, two of Melville's favorite images of the sublime. The women object to the chimney's centralized position from which it dominates the rest of the house like an aristocratic ruler. They wish to tear it down to clear the way for a "grand entrance-hall."[30] As things stand now with the chimney, writes Melville, "almost every room, like a philosophical system, was in itself an entry, or passage-way to other rooms, and systems of rooms" and in "going through the house, you seem to be forever going somewhere, and getting nowhere."[31]

The arguments between the narrator and the women of the house echo debates beginning to surface in the press over the relevance of an aesthetic based on the romance form. Many American women writers were championing realism as an antidote to the excesses of the romance.[32] Solidly middle class and pragmatic, their writing is characterized by a no-nonsense attitude toward reality, emphasis on ordinary people in ordinary settings, simplified language, focus on regionalisms, and a skeptical attitude towards romanticizing. In comparison to the work of these women realists, Melville's writing, with its obscure metaphysics, dense literary allusions, and elaborately figurative language, must have seemed as old-fashioned as the narrator's smokey old chimney.

Although Melville, like the narrator in "I and My Chimney," was not about to give up on his way of writing, he did reflect on the limits of his aesthetic in the title piece to his only published collection of short stories, *The Piazza Tales* (1857). "The Piazza" reads as a retrospective of Melville's writing career. Drawing on the popular genre of the landscape sketch, Melville lays out a literary map of aesthetic ground covered in the author's artistic quest for the sublime. The unnamed first-person narrator tells a story of an "inland voyage to fairy-land. A true voyage; but take it all in all, interesting as if invented."[33] This quest leads to an encounter with a woman, named Marianna, who bears a resemblance to the figure of Isabel in *Pierre*. Both are impoverished orphans living with their "brother" on the margins of society.[34]

"The Piazza" begins with the narrator's tribute to the natural scenery around his farmhouse and his decision to build a piazza or porch from which to view the countryside. After much deliberation he rejects neighborly advice and chooses to build his piazza on the north side facing the sublime Mount Greylock (the mountain to which Melville dedicated *Pierre* and which he thought "very like a whale"). While gazing at the mountain one day, he spots a shining light and thinks to himself, "Fairies there."[35] After an undisclosed illness confines him to his bed for a while, the narrator grows so sensitive that he finds himself disgusted by the beauty immediately surrounding his piazza. He looks closely at the flowers creeping up his post and sees

> millions of strange, cankerous worms, which, feeding upon those blossoms, so shared their blessed hue, as to make it unblessed evermore—worms, whose germs had doubtless lurked in the very bulb which, so hopefully, I had planted.[36]

The narrator feels the need for a cure and decides to launch his "yawl,"[37] in search of the source of light shining from the mountain top. Nourished by his readings in the romance tradition, he dreams of finding his fairy queen there, or at least some glad mountain girl, to ease his weariness.

This story, as critics Richard S. Moore, Helmbrecht Breining, and Klaus Poenicke have convincingly demonstrated, represents an autobiographical journey through the beautiful, the picturesque, and the sublime of nineteenth-century aesthetics.[38] After the narrator rejects the beauty of the carefully cultivated countryside surrounding his piazza because it merely masks an underlying disease, he begins a quest for the sublime hoping to find his Una, or one truth. He travels up the picturesque mountainside where he discovers souvenirs of man's failed attempt to conquer nature: an "old saw-mill, bound down and hushed with vines," a huge block that someone had tried to split but that still contains the "wedges yet rusted in their holes," and finally "apples from a long neglected tree that now taste of the ground."[39] He then reaches the sublime summit:

> No fence was seen, no inclosure. Near by—ferns, ferns, ferns; further—woods, woods, woods; beyond—mountains, mountains, mountains; then—sky, sky, sky. Turned out in aerial commons, pasture for the mountain moon. Nature, and but nature, house and all.[40]

The house he finds on the summit is dilapidated, its north side (the same side as the narrator's piazza) "doorless and windowless, the clapboards, innocent of paint."[41] Instead of meeting his "Una," "Titania," or at least "some glad mountain-girl,"[42] the narrator finds Marianna, an orphaned young woman who has taken up residence on the mountain along with her brother in this abandoned cottage. Here she works sewing by the only paned window, while her brother cuts wood and burns coal on the other side of the mountain most of the day and night. When the narrator speaks of her house as "gilded" (as it has appeared to him from his piazza below), she sharply contradicts him and paints for him a bleak picture in realistic detail of her daily struggle for existence. When she tells him of the sun that shines through the window nearly blinding her at her work, of the flies and the wasps, the rotting roof, and the chimney that fills with snow in the winter, he can only comment inappropriately, "yours are strange fancies, Marianna." "They but reflect the things," she responds.[43] When the narrator suggests that she walk outside to break up the monotony, she tells him that the outdoors lures her not, for being alone by the hearth is better than being alone by a rock. Inside she has her familiar world of shadows to keep her company, shadows she knows by the names she has given them.

Several critics who see Marianna's shadow reading as evidence of her insanity focus their interpretations of this story on the narrator's disappointment at discovering that his hoped-for "fairy queen" is nothing but a poor, mad woman, defeated rather than uplifted by her sublime surroundings. In the interpretation of Marianna lies Melville's ideological trap. Seeing Marianna solely as "possibly demented" or "nearly crushed and extinguished in her humanity" reveals sexist and classist prejudices.[44] "No doubt you think," Marianna says to the narrator,

that, living so lonesome here, knowing nothing, hearing nothing—
little, at least, but sound of thunder and the fall of trees—never
reading, seldom speaking, yet ever wakeful, this is what gives me
my strange thoughts—for so you call them—this weariness and
wakefulness together.[45]

The reader knows, however (and perhaps senses), that the narrator—who
knows a lot and reads a lot and who calls her thoughts "strange"—experiences
the same symptoms of weariness and wakefulness, symptoms that drove him
to her house in the first place to seek a cure.[46] With this identity between the
two characters established, the differences that remain appear determined by
social, economic, and biological factors.

Rather than interpret Marianna as a "victim" of her sublime environment who reveals the "lie" of sublime aesthetics,[47] perhaps she is a victim of a
socio-economic system that has forced her, much like Frankenstein's monster
among the caves of ice, to seek the only dwelling "man does not grudge."[48]
The negative determining factors in Marianna's life seem to be overwhelming
considering her poverty, her lack of education, her harsh environment, her
loneliness, her gender, her work. Yet to reduce her completely to the status of
a "victim" is to deny her any power of self-determination. If she is seen only as
"insane," her dignity as a human being is negated. Surely there is something
to admire in this young woman who strives to make a life for herself along
with her brother under such adverse circumstance. Furthermore, Marianna
possesses the power to render the narrator "mute" on two occasions.[49] For
Melville, who wrote in *Pierre* "silence is the only Voice of our God," Marianna's power to silence the narrator deserves respect.[50]

Rosemary Kenny comes closest among the critics to granting Marianna the dignity she deserves. Drawing on allusions in the story to Plato's
allegory of the cave, she recognizes an artist in the poor woman. Kenny
concludes that through the figure of Marianna, Melville is parodying the
lesser, "mimetic" artist who, in the Platonic sense, takes shadows for the
real things.[51] Kenny's characterization of Marianna as a realist artist is
useful, but Melville allows this character a dignity beyond parody. It is not
the realist artist that Melville is critiquing in his curious twist on Plato's allegory of the cave but the hierarchical dimension of Platonic thought itself.
The narrator in "The Piazza" scales the heights in search of "Una,"[52] the
one truth, and finds at the top of the mountain not the shining light of one
truth but a cave-like dwelling in which sits a woman, chained to her work,
blinded by the sun, reading shadows on the wall. When Marianna says to
the narrator, whom she sees looking out the window at the ground, "You
watch the cloud," he "corrects" her (as she had earlier "corrected" him about
the "gilding" of her house), "No, a shadow; a cloud's, no doubt—though I

cannot see," he says, making the "proper" Platonic hierarchical distinctions between appearance and reality, shadow and thing, distinctions that she is either unable or unwilling to make.[53]

Instead of finding the one truth, Una, the narrator finds himself engaged in an unsettling dialogue that reveals the limits of two points of view: Marianna's "realist" empiricism (which refuses to make distinctions between shadows and things-in-themselves, phenomena and noumena) and the narrator's "romantic" idealism. The story juxtaposes, without resolution, these two perspectives. On a textual level, the narrator's elaborate, richly allusive prose with its dominant trope of personification mediating all the descriptions of nature through imagery drawn from the span of the western cultural tradition, stands in sharp contrast to the stark details of Marianna's story of her struggle to survive on the frontier of nature and culture in this inhospitably sublime setting. Melville does not dismiss or condescend to Marianna's point of view. If Marianna is "deluded" about "reality," she is no more so than the narrator is. She may appear to lack flexibility of perspective (in keeping with her empiricism) when she refuses to accept the possibility that her roof appears "gilded" from a distance like his appears to her; on the other hand, she may be simply rejecting his figurative use of the word "gilded" as an aestheticized misrepresentation of her economic condition and, in that sense, a lie.

During their brief encounter, Melville focuses on two hop vines outside the window that serve as a figure for the irreducible difference between these two perspectives. The vines, in climbing their separate poles and "gaining their tip-ends, would have then joined over in an upward clasp, but the baffled shoots, groping awhile in empty air, trailed back whence they sprung."[54] While these two perspectives are not able to come together, there is a sense in which the two characters are linked through their opposition. Just as the narrator gazes longingly up at her house, she gazes down at his. They both suffer from "wakeful weariness," a condition that neither religion nor drugs ("prayer" or the "fresh hop pillow") has been able to relieve.[55] The narrator had hoped that by gazing on the "queen of fairies at her fairy-window" or at least "some glad mountain-girl," he would be able to "cure" his weariness.[56] She shares the same hope about meeting the inhabitant of the "marble" house (his house) she sees in the distance, at least that is what she tells him. Perhaps she has already guessed where the narrator comes from and is mocking his quest when she says to him,

> "Oh, if I could but once get to yonder house, and but look upon whoever the happy being is that lives there! A foolish thought: why do I think it? Is it that I live so lonesome, and know nothing?"

He cannot help but recognize himself in her words and is compelled to admit

> "I, too, know nothing; and, therefore, cannot answer; but, for your sake, Marianna, well could wish that I were that happy one of the happy house you dream you see; for then you would behold him now, and, as you say, this weariness might leave you."[57]

The narrator may be trying to preserve her "illusions," as some critics have suggested.[58] On the other hand, Marianna may just be testing his mettle to see if he will reveal himself. In the end, he witholds his identity from her. He listens to her story but reveals nothing about himself.

Swearing off all future trips to "fairyland," the narrator retreats to the comforts of his middle-class existence where from his piazza, his "box-royal," the "scenery is magical—the illusion so complete."[59] It appears that one of the effects of his encounter with Marianna is a shift away from the dominant pictorial trope of the opening sequence to the dramatic trope at the end, perhaps an indication of respect for the autonomy of Marianna's voice. From the deck of his piazza, he listens to the song of "Madam Meadow Lark," his own "prima donna." And "drinking in her sunrise note, which, Memnon-like, seems struck from the golden window, how far from me the weary face behind it," he says. The narrator succeeds in appropriating Marianna for the moment through his personification of the singing bird, his art-servant, but only while the sun shines on the stage of his "amphitheatre." "Every night," he tells the reader,

> when the curtain falls, truth comes in with darkness. No light shows from the mountain. To and fro I walk the piazza deck, haunted by Marianna's face, and many as real a story.[60]

Marianna's face and her "real" story ultimately resist appropriation as objects of the narrator's romantic quest for the ideal and, in doing so, they reveal the limits of both sublime and realist aesthetics. For the reader, the character of Marianna can also be said to resist appropriation as an object of interpretation. In contrast to the narrator, she reveals much of her personal life yet remains inexplicable. She can appear in various lights as clever, strong, condescending, naive, pitiful, admirable, ordinary, a fake, a fairy queen, a sorceress, an artist; the list seems endless. Through this indeterminacy, Melville preserves the possibility of his female character's freedom and dignity while giving the reader the opportunity to experience freedom in facing the limits of the power of representation.

Notes

1. For a reading of Melville's critique of the "ideological structures of gender, class, and race underlying the male bond," see Robyn Wiegman, "Melville's Geography of Gender," *ALH*, 1 (1989): 735–753.

2. *The Letters of Herman Melville*, ed. Merrell R. Davis and William H. Gilman (New Haven: Yale University Press, 1960), p. 138; see the letter of December 9, 1851.

3. *Letters*, pp. 145–146 (January 8, 1852).

4. *Letters*, p. 146.

5. For an exposition of this concept of genre, see Rosalie L. Colie's *The Resources of Kind: Genre Theory in the Renaissance*, ed. Barbara K. Lewalski (Berkeley: University of California Press, 1973).

6. In a letter to his publisher, Richard Bentley, Melville writes that his new book (*Pierre*) possesses "unquestionable novelty, as regards my former ones" and treats "of utterly new scenes & characters." He assures Bentley that it is "very much more calculated for popularity than anything you have yet published of mine—being a regular romance, with a mysterious plot to it, & stirring passions at work, and with-all, representing a new and elevated aspect of American life." See *Letters*, p. 150.

7. Melville's inarticulate early female characters include the mute woman in "Fragments from a Writing Desk, No. 2," Fayaway in *Typee*, Yillah in *Mardi*. All represent love objects of the hero.

8. These two competing myths Leslie Fiedler has identified as "Home as Heaven" and "Home as Hell" in his *What Was Literature?: Class Culture and Mass Society* (New York: Simon & Schuster, 1982), p. 145.

9. See Carolyn L. Karcher's *Shadow Over the Promised Land: Slavery, Race and Violence in Melville's America* (Baton Rouge: Louisiana State University Press, 1980), p. xii.

10. See Jane Mushabac, *Melville's Humor: A Critical Study* (Hamden: Archon Books, 1981), p. 149.

11. *The Piazza Tales and Other Prose Pieces, 1839–1860*, ed. Harrison Hayford, Alma A. MacDougal, G. Thomas Tanselle, and others (Evanston and Chicago: Northwestern University Press and the Newberry Library, 1987), p. 328.

12. In 1986, the Melville Society attempted to redress the problem by publishing papers on "Women in Melville's Art" delivered during the Modern Language Association conference. See *Melville Society Extracts*, 65 (1986): 2–16.

13. Jane Tompkins, *Sensational Designs: The Cultural Work of American Fiction, 1790–1860* (New York: Oxford Univ. Press, 1985), p. 148. See also Joyce W. Warren's introduction to *Ruth Hall and Other Writings* (New Brunswick, N.J.: Rutgers University Press, 1986), p. xxxvi.

14. See *Letters*, pp. 154–161.

15. The Agatha letters were written during the time when Hawthorne was trying to distance himself from Melville. Perhaps Melville's apparent identification with Agatha results from his own feelings of being abandoned by the one he tried to force to write her story.

16. Hershel Parker, during the 1988 Melville session of the Northeast Modern Language Association, cited evidence to suggest that Melville did indeed write Agatha's story but that the story has not yet been found.

17. Hunilla's character inspired Melville to write "Humanity, thou strong thing, I worship thee, not in the laurelled victor, but in this vanquished one." See *Piazza*, p. 157.

18. Hawthorne, after reading *Ruth Hall*, amended his previous remark about the "damned mob of scribbling women." He wrote that Fanny Fern "writes as if the devil was in her; and that is the only condition under which a woman ever writes anything worth reading. Generally women write like emasculated men, and are only distinguished from male authors by the greater feebleness and folly; but when they throw off the restraints of decency, and come before the public stark naked, as it were; then their books are sure to possess character and value." *The Letters of Hawthorne to William Ticknor, 1851–1869*, ed. C. E. Frazer Clark, Jr. (Newark: Carteret Book Club, Inc., 1972), I: 78.

19. Ann Douglas, *The Feminization of American Culture* (New York: Knopf, 1977).

20. Mary Ryan, *The Empire of Mother: American Writing and Domesticity, 1830–1860* (New York: Institute for Research in History and Haworth Press, 1982), p. 126.

21. See *Letters*, p. 129.

22. Admittedly, the omission of an ultimately optimistic view makes for a world of difference between the two books. Unlike Stowe, Melville, in *Pierre*, is interested in the limits of the sentimental and melodramatic vision (as he was interested in the limits to the romantic quest in *Moby-Dick*). This interest in limits, however, does not preclude an earnest attachment on Melville's part to melodramatic rhetoric.

23. David S. Reynolds, *Beneath the American Renaissance: The Subversive Imagination in the Age of Emerson and Melville* (New York: Knopf, 1988), pp. 352–353.

24. Herman Melville, *Pierre, or the Ambiguities*, ed. by Henry A. Murray (New York: Hendricks House, 1949), p. 94.

25. See Jay Leyda, *The Melville Log: A Documentary Life of Herman Melville, 1819–1891* (New York: Gordian Press, 1969), I: 351.

26. See *Log*, p. 351.

27. See Judith Fetterly's "Introduction" to *Provisions: A Reader from 19th-Century American Woman* (Bloomington: Indiana University Press, 1985), p. 10.

28. Donovan traces the tradition as far back as the work of Christine de Pisan. See Josephine Donovan, *New England Local Color Literature: A Woman's Tradition* (New York: Ungar, 1983), p. 3.

29. See Naomi Schor, *Reading in Detail: Aesthetics and the Feminine* (New York: Methuen, 1987), for an exploration of the gendered implications of this aesthetic tension.

30. *Piazza*, p. 360.

31. *Piazza*, p. 364.

32. See Fetterly, *Provisions*, pp. 10–11.

33. *Piazza*, p. 4.

34. Both are also identified with music. Melville, in his attempt to represent the unrepresentability of Isabel, personifies her as the spirit of music. The narrator of "The Piazza" tries to do the same with Marianna when he identifies her with a singing bird he hears from his piazza (p. 12). Marianna, by contrast, resists, in the end, any such appropriation by a literary device.

35. *Piazza*, p. 5.

36. *Piazza*, p. 6.

37. *Piazza,* p. 6.

38. See Helmbrecht Breinig, "The Destruction of Fairyland: Melville's "Piazza" in the Tradition of the American Imagination," *ELH,* 35 (1968): 254–283; Klaus Poenicke, "A View from the Piazza: Herman Melville and the Legacy of the European Sublime," *Comparative Literature Studies,* 4 (1967): 267–281; Richard S. Moore, *That Cunning Alphabet: Melville's Aesthetics of Nature* (Amsterdam: Rodopi, 1982).

39. *Piazza,* p. 7.

40. *Piazza,* p. 8.

41. *Piazza,* p. 8.

42. *Piazza,* pp. 8, 5.

43. *Piazza,* p. 10.

44. See Moore, p. 2, and Poenicke, p. 267.

45. *Piazza,* p. 11.

46. The narrator also reads shadows. See *Piazza,* p. 5.

47. See Poenicke, p. 273.

48. Victor discovers the creature among the glacial caverns on the top of the mountain. See Mary Shelley, *Frankenstein, or the new Prometheus* (New York: New American Library, 1965), p. 96.

49. *Piazza,* pp. 9, 10.

50. See *Pierre,* where Melville also wrote "all profound things, and emotions of things are preceded and attended by Silence" (p. 284).

51. Rosemary Austin Kenny, "Melville's Short Fiction; A Methodology of Unknowing," Dissertation, University of Wisconsin, 1980. Cited by Merton M. Sealts, Jr. in *Pursuing Melville 1940–1980: Chapters and Essays* (Madison: University of Wisconsin, 1982), p. 326. Marvin Fisher, in *Going Under: Melville's Short Fiction and the American 1850's* (Baton Rouge: Louisiana State University Press, 1977), also recognizes in the story allusions to Plato's allegory of the cave (p. 25). Fisher focuses on the disillusionment of the narrator and grants little, if any, power and autonomy to the figure of Marianna. See pp. 26–27.

52. *Piazza,* p. 8.

53. *Piazza,* p. 10.

54. *Piazza,* p. 12.

55. *Piazza,* p. 12.

56. *Piazza,* p. 6.

57. *Piazza,* p. 12.

58. See Fisher, p. 26.

59. *Piazza,* p. 12.

60. *Piazza,* p. 12.

STEPHEN MATHEWSON

"To Tell Over Again the Story Just Told": The Composition of Melville's Redburn

In 1849, Melville feverishly and rather joylessly wrote *Redburn,* the first of two books he would complete during that summer in an effort to atone for the financial failure of *Mardi.* He wrote to his English publisher Richard Bentley that he had "enlarged" *Redburn,* "somewhat to the size of Omoo—perhaps it may be a trifle larger."[1] Melville frequently relied upon sources while composing; for example, he enlarged his early work by incorporating exploration and travel narratives into his stories of South Seas adventure. In *Redburn,* however, he expanded his narrative by replicating his own story. The first third of the narrative, the outward-bound voyage from New York to Liverpool, is ingeniously repeated on the return voyage, and the Liverpool section in the middle of the narrative has repeated clusters of three chapters within itself. Apparently, the hurried pace at which Melville wrote *Redburn* precluded much creativity and compelled him to borrow, as it were, from himself.

On 5 June 1849, Melville complained to Bentley about the reviews of *Mardi* and mentioned his initial plans for *Redburn.* Addressing his practical reasons for writing a book with "no metaphysics, no conic-sections, nothing but cakes & ale," he elaborates: "In size the book will be perhaps a fraction smaller than Typee; will be printed here by the Harpers, & ready for them two or three months hence, or before. I value the English Copyright

ESQ: A Journal of the American Renaissance, Volume 37, Number 4 (1991): pp. 311–320. © 1991 ESQ: A Journal of the American Renaissance.

at one hundred & fifty pounds, and think it would be wise to put it forth in a manner, admitting of a popular circulation." Melville wrote *Redburn*, then, to make money from a popular audience, "those who read simply for amusement" (*L*, 86).

The conditions under which Melville wrote his tale of "cakes & ale" in June and July of 1849 were far from ideal. Living in his house were two newborn children—his own son, Malcolm, and Allan Melville's daughter, Maria—and other relatives as well. Melville stayed in New York City the entire summer, giving up his customary August vacation to work, and, despite the very crowded household, was kept indoors because of an epidemic of blue cholera that infected the city from the middle of May until the first of August.[2] Under these oppressive conditions, both physical and economic, he composed *Redburn* in less than two months.

On 20 July 1849, at the plague's height, Melville wrote to Bentley about the novel's progress: "[it] is now going thro' the press, & I think I shall be able to send it to you in the course of three weeks or so." He also accepted Bentley's offer of one hundred pounds for the book, fifty less than asked for. Melville must have been disappointed, especially since the reasons for enlarging *Redburn* were economic; the more volumes "got up" in Bentley's style, the more money paid in advance (*L*, 88). By the end of the summer, Melville had written *Redburn* as well as *White-Jacket*, becoming "a tired and somewhat bitter man."[3]

Still the question remains: how did Melville expand *Redburn* from a book "a fraction smaller than 'Typee'" to a book "somewhat . . . the size of Omoo—perhaps . . . a trifle larger"? Chapters, characters and scenes already appearing in the first section of the book (the voyage to Liverpool) are recycled in the third section (the return voyage to New York). In addition, the book's middle (Liverpool) section is enlarged through the repetition of key scenes. Since he had little time for imaginative invention that summer, Melville recast what he had already written into the latter portions of the book.

1

Melville repeats leave-takings and sailings in the initial land chapters, an indication that he had a hard time getting his novel out to sea in June. Redburn leaves home and sails down the Hudson River to New York City, doubling these actions when he takes leave of the Joneses, a substitute family for his own, and sails from New York City on the *Highlander*. In chapter 4, "How He Disposed of His Fowling-Piece," Redburn goes to two different pawnbrokers to dispose of his gun, retracing his steps to the first pawnbroker. He says, "My best plan then seemed to be, to go right back to the curly-headed pawnbroker, and take up with my first offer."[4] Redburn, though, receives two dollars and a half for his gun rather than the initially offered three. Later, while writing *Moby-Dick,* Melville would encounter the same problem getting his book started.

Harrison Hayford has argued that in *Moby-Dick* "it takes not one but two chapters to do the narrative job of getting Ishmael started out to see the watery part of the world on his first whaling voyage," noting that Ishmael does not sail from the first port he comes to, but the second, thus staying at two separate inns and going to bed twice at the second inn.[5] The same observation applies to Redburn because he, too, sails from his second port. Like Ishmael, Redburn signs aboard his ship in two separate scenes: the day before the *Highlander* sails when he "put[s] down" his "name and beat[s] a retreat" (19), and again when one of the ship's mates asks if he has signed on as "a tailor" (24). In *Redburn,* Melville had the same problems beginning his narrative that he would have in *Moby-Dick,* and in both cases he solved the problem by means of duplication.[6]

While Redburn is in Liverpool, repetition abounds: Melville reuses his own material, and also introduces another source, the guidebook *The Picture of Liverpool;* he then repeats what he writes about the guidebook to further enlarge this middle section of the novel. Here Max the Dutchman serves as an emblem for Melville's method. Forgetting that the Dutchman is a bachelor (79), Melville writes that he has wives performing similar functions in the different ports: "Liverpool, away from the docks, was very much such a place as New York" (202). In chapter 27, "He Gets a Peep at Ireland, and at Last Arrives in Liverpool," Redburn sees a woman come aboard the *Highlander* when it docks in Liverpool. Carrying clean clothes for Max, Sally (his Liverpool wife) exchanges "her bundle of clean clothes for a bundle of soiled ones, and this was precisely what the New York wife had done for Max, not thirty days previous" (128). This is an appropriate opening to the Liverpool section, for here the repetitious composition patterns really begin.

Clearly, Redburn's reason for sailing to Liverpool is to retrace the experiences of his father's visit to that city by following his father's guidebook. Melville employs the guidebook framework in a very sophisticated way, juxtaposing Redburn's and the book's descriptions of Liverpool to expand the section in its first two chapters, 30 and 31. Whether congruous or incongruous, what Redburn finds while walking the streets of Liverpool he finds in the guidebook. In chapter 30, "Redburn Grows Intolerably Flat and Stupid over Some Outlandish Old Guide-Books," Melville repeats *The Picture of Liverpool* verbatim, undercutting his own method when he has the narrator exclaim, "I will *not* quote thee, old Morocco . . . I should be charged with swelling out my volume by plagiarizing from a guide-book—the most vulgar and ignominious of thefts!" (150). Melville, however, continues his method of self-plagiarism in the next chapter, "With His Prosy Old Guide-Book, He Takes a Prosy Stroll through the Town." In effect, Melville spells out how his strategy works in this chapter: "having my guide-book in my pocket, I drew it forth to compare notes" (152). Redburn finds in "Old Morocco" that a fort should be where he stands, but he sees a tavern which stands only in name, "The Old Fort Tavern," for what he reads in the guidebook.

The same compositional pattern appears in the next chapter: Redburn reads the guidebook, sees the existing surroundings, and finally compares his perception to the text. Attempting to follow his father's path, he searches for his father's hotel, the Riddough, and finds his way into the Merchant's Exchange quadrangle. He relates what he has read in the guidebook about the Town Hall, describes what he sees in the square, and then compares what he sees with the guidebook, noting such points of difference as the statue of "Lord Nelson expiring in the arms of Victory" (155). After contemplating the statue, Redburn gets tossed out of a reading room, an action paralleled in another ejection scene in chapter 42, "His Adventure with the Cross Old Gentleman." Eventually he learns that the Riddough Hotel has been pulled down and concludes that "the thing that had guided the father, could not guide the son," since guidebooks are "the least reliable books in all literature" (157).

Though Redburn finds guidebooks unreliable, Melville found them both reliable and helpful when composing rapidly, for he returns to the guidebook and to the same compositional pattern. Redburn uses the book to search for the "Old Docks," and later, in chapter 36 ("The Old Church of St. Nicholas, and the Dead-House"), to supply facts about the old church. In each instance he follows the same pattern of reading, seeing, and comparing. Having Redburn read *The Picture of Liverpool* achieves the same end as plagiarizing it: Melville is "swelling out" his "volume" by using the book in two ways while writing. His use of the guidebook resembles Carlo's accordion playing: he expands the Liverpool section by pulling on his compositional accordion, the guidebook, unfolding a scene that might have been presented from a single point of view into one he can present from at least three perspectives.

The search for the old docks leads to a similar pattern of composition. Chapter 32, "The Docks," describes the area around the Liverpool docks and sets up topic-by-topic descriptions that follow in the next three chapters: chapter 33 ("The Salt-Droghers, and German Emigrant Ships"), chapter 34 ("The Irrawaddy"), and chapter 35 ("Galliots, Coast-of-Guinea-Man, and Floating Chapel"). Melville then repeats this pattern. Chapter 37, "What Redburn Saw in Launcelott's-Hey," introduces the topic of the poor, the human waste of nineteenth-century industrial England. Looking down into a cellar in Launcelott's-Hey, Redburn sees, "crouching in nameless squalor, with her head bowed over . . . the figure of what had been a woman. Her blue arms folded to her livid bosom two shrunken things like children, that leaned toward her, one on each side" (180). The huddled woman and her children resemble the struggling forms Redburn saw earlier at the base of Nelson's statue:

At uniform intervals round the base of the pedestal, four naked figures in chains, somewhat larger than life, are seated in various attitudes of humiliation and despair. One has his leg recklessly thrown over his knee, and his head bowed over, as if he had given up all hope of ever feeling better. Another has his head buried in despondency, and no doubt looks mournfully out of his eyes, but as his face was averted at the time, I could not catch the expression. (155)

Functioning like "The Docks," chapter 37 provides compositional material for Melville. He addresses the topic of the poor in chapter 38 ("The Dock-Wall Beggars"), chapter 39 ("The Boole-Alleys of the Town"), and chapter 40 ("Placards, Brass-Jewelers, Truck-Horses, and Steamers"). Again Melville hints at his method in these two sets of chapters when he writes in chapter 40, "As I wish to group together what fell under my observation concerning the Liverpool docks, and the scenes roundabout, I will try to throw into this chapter various minor things that I recall" (192).

The central chapter in the Liverpool section (37, "What Redburn Saw in Launcelott's-Hey") Melville rewrites in the New York voyage section in chapter 58, "Though the Highlander Puts into No Harbor As Yet; She Here and There Leaves Many of Her Passengers Behind." He recasts the potent description of the poverty seen in Launcelott's-Hey when depicting Redburn's descent into the ship's hold on the way back to New York: "In every corner, the females were huddled together, weeping and lamenting; children were asking for bread from their mothers, who had none to give" (287). Melville's method characterizes, in a sense, the famine and disease on the ship: "But as the dying departed, the places of two of them were filled in the rolls of humanity, by the birth of two infants, whom the plague, panic, and gale had hurried into the world before their time. The first cry of one of these infants, was almost simultaneous with the splash of its father's body in the sea" (289). The social criticism Melville begins when describing the poor in Liverpool he repeats with force when he dwells upon the conditions the Irish emigrants suffer on the Highlander, conditions worse than those they escape.

2

The largest pattern of repetition shows Melville finishing the narrative by using what he had written in the first voyage section. The principal characters on each trip, Redburn on the outward voyage and Harry Bolton on the return voyage, are very much alike. To begin with, they physically resemble each other. Redburn says, "I was young and handsome," and later he calls Bolton "handsome" (58, 216). Melville's handsome sailors also have similar backgrounds: Redburn's father died when he was young and Bolton, too, "was early left an orphan" (217). Both are fallen gentlemen with no financial means, Redburn's fortune collapsing with his father's bankruptcy and death and Bolton's through gambling, which strips him of his "last sovereign" (217). And we read in chapter 56, "Under the Lee of the Long-Boat, Redburn and Harry Hold Confidential Communion," that Redburn "could sympathize with one in similar circumstances," discussing with Bolton their "common affairs" (279).

As Bolton's reasons for sailing resemble Redburn's, so do the circumstances surrounding his going to sea. Bolton finds that the sea has "a dash of romance in it" (218) which is like the "strange, romantic charm" Redburn feels when dreaming of the sea, reading ship advertisements in the New York City newspapers (3). Both are broke, and Bolton's selling of his vests for money to buy sailor's gear resembles Redburn's pawning of his gun for the same purpose. Their signings-on are very similar, as is Captain Riga's behavior in each. In chapter 3, "He Arrives in Town," Mr. Jones aids Redburn in signing-on the *Highlander*, with Captain Riga playing the role of a "fine funny gentleman" (16). Bolton's signing-on in chapter 44 parallels Redburn's so plainly that Melville writes that Redburn "perceived in the captain's face that same bland, benevolent, and bewitchingly merry expression, that had so charmed, but deceived me, when, with Mr. Jones, I had first accosted him in the cabin" (219). In their signings-on, both Redburn and Bolton are forced off the ship, not able to stay onboard until the ship sails: Redburn spends a miserable night in rainy New York City, and Bolton, with Redburn, spends "A Mysterious Night in London" in chapter 46.

Not only do Redburn's and Bolton's port experiences match but their sea experiences do so as well. In chapter 14, "He Contemplates Making a Social Call on the Captain in His Cabin," Redburn dresses to present himself to the "gentlemanly" Captain Riga: "I put on a white shirt in place of my red one, and got into a pair of cloth trowsers instead of my duck ones, and put on my new pumps, and then carefully brushing my shooting-jacket, I put that on over all, so that upon the whole, I made quite a genteel figure" (68). On deck the ship's crew ridicules Redburn's appearance, asking him if he "was dressing to go ashore," which elicits laughter and shouting (68–69). This scene is substantially repeated in chapter 50, "Harry Bolton At Sea," in which "this Bury blade" Bolton comes "on deck in a brocaded dressing-gown, embroidered slippers, and tasseled smoking-cap, to stand his morning watch" (253). The crew mocks Bolton's dress, but not in such a lighthearted manner as in Redburn's case. A mate cries, "Who's that Chinese mandarin?" The mocking continues, the sailors hating Bolton and his mahogany wardrobe chest. In each scene of mockery the sailor Jackson plays the same role. He asks Bolton "to lift up the lower hem of his trowsers, to test the color of his calves" (254), much as he had derided Redburn "with a hideous grin": "'Let him go, let him go, men—he's a nice boy. Let him go; the captain has some nuts and raisins for him'" (69). Thus, despite superficial changes, the Bolton scene is clearly a rewriting of the Redburn scene.

Melville also mirrors Redburn's first experience going aloft in the rigging in Bolton's similar experience. As in the dressing scenes, the outcomes differ: Redburn's scene leads to the crew's acceptance and Bolton's to their further rejection. In chapter 16, "At Dead of Night He Is Sent Up to Loose the Main-Skysail," Max the Dutchman tells Redburn to go aloft in the rigging. "Holding on might and main to the mast," Redburn reflects, "I seemed all alone; treading the midnight clouds; and every second, expected to find myself falling—falling—falling, as I have felt when the nightmare has been on me" (78). He overcomes his fears and completes his task, then descends and receives "something like a compliment from Max the Dutchman" (79). In the Harry Bolton chapter, Melville recasts Redburn's trial in the rigging, but to very different thematic ends. Like Redburn, Bolton is ordered aloft and forced to climb the rigging; like Redburn he experiences fear: "he stopped short, and looked down from the top. Fatal glance! it unstrung his every fiber; and I saw him reel, and clutch the shrouds, till the mate shouted out for him not to squeeze the tar out of the ropes" (256). Like Jackson in the clothing scenes, Max the Dutchman serves parallel functions when Redburn and Bolton climb the rigging. While Max orders Redburn aloft, he literally butts Bolton up: "Max went up the rigging hand over hand, and brought his red head with a bump against the base of Harry's back" (256). Bolton, after unreeving the sail, returns to the deck "pale as death, with bloodshot eyes, and every limb quivering" (257). Unlike Redburn, who is approved by the crew, Bolton again earns "jibes and jeers" (257). The going aloft and clothing scenes repeat, but so does the pattern of acceptance and rejection. In each Bolton scene the end result is the same: the crew rejects him.

Another pattern concerns Jackson, who is ill during each passage. In chapter 12, "He Gives Some Account of One of His Shipmates Called Jackson," Melville writes that Jackson "was being consumed by an incurable malady" (58), and in chapter 55, "Drawing Nigh to the Last Scene in Jackson's Career," the sailor has a "malady which had long fastened its fangs in his flesh" (275). This illness leads to his spectacular death in a fall from the ship's rigging, an enactment of the fear Redburn and Bolton share. Jackson's death also recalls the drunken sailors' deaths onboard the *Highlander* which inaugurate each voyage. Chapter 48, "A Living Corpse," repeats chapter 10, "He is Very Much Frightened; the Sailors Abuse Him; and He Becomes Miserable and Forlorn." Melville writes in chapter 48, "it was destined that our departure from the English Strand, should be marked by a tragical event, akin to the sudden end of the suicide, which had so strongly impressed me on quitting the American shore" (243). One of the three drunks brought onboard, Miguel Saveda, spontaneously combusts and is then thrown overboard. As

Melville indicates, this chapter is "akin" to chapter 10, in which a drunken sailor brought on the ship commits suicide by leaping into the sea, "raging mad with the delirium tremens" (50). Also in each chapter, Jackson strikes fear into the heart of Redburn: Jackson's remarks about each drunk's death freeze Redburn's "blood" and make his "soul stand still" (246).

Rather than create new material to complete *Redburn*, then, Melville used what he had already written to enlarge the book. He fashioned his text in this manner for economic reasons: faster composition meant faster financial return for both *Redburn* and *White-Jacket*. Yet in spite of his haste, Melville knew he had written a good novel. "I have not repressed myself much," he wrote of *Redburn* to Lemuel Shaw on 6 October 1849 (*L*, 92), but he despised the novel for the economic state it was meant to remedy, hence his comment to Evert Duyckinck in a letter from London, 14 December 1849, about "beggarly 'Redburn'" (*L*, 95). The narrative fittingly ends with Bolton and Redburn cheated out of their wages by Captain Riga: like Melville after *Mardi*, they are again broke, repeating the financial states that prompted their sailings.

Notes

1. Melville to Richard Bentley, New York, 20 July 1849, *The Letters of Herman Melville*, ed. Merrell R. Davis and William H. Gilman (New Haven: Yale University Press, 1960), 88; hereafter cited parenthetically as *L*, with page number.

2. Leon Howard, *Herman Melville: A Biography* (Berkeley: University of California Press, 1951), 134.

3. Howard, *Herman Melville*, 134.

4. *Redburn: His First Voyage*, ed. Harrison Hayford et. al, vol. 4 of *The Writings of Herman Melville* (Evanston & Chicago: Northwestern University Press and The Newberry Library, 1969), 22; hereafter cited parenthetically by page number only.

5. Harrison Hayford, "Unnecessary Duplicates: A Key to the Writing of *Moby-Dick*," in *New Perspectives on Melville*, ed. Faith Pullin (Edinburgh: Edinburgh University Press, 1978), 128, 129.

6. Hayford asserts that in *Moby-Dick* "duplicates breed duplicates" ("Unnecessary Duplicates," 129). His purpose, however, is to show "Melville's shifting intentions for some of the central characters in *Moby-Dick*" (128). Thus he argues that the pattern of duplicates arising in *Moby-Dick* signals that "the larger process in which Melville was engaged at this point was a multiple reassignment of roles among four of his central characters" (144). Though *Redburn* and *Moby-Dick* share duplicate beginnings, the pattern of repetition that arises in *Redburn* results from Melville's hurried writing process and not from the reassignment of characters' roles that Hayford finds in *Moby-Dick*.

BILL CHRISTOPHERSON

Israel Potter: Melville's "Citizen of the Universe"

"But who *is* this ere singing, leaning, yarn-spinning chap?"
—Herman Melville, *Israel Potter*

If there was ever a moment when Herman Melville stood a chance of recouping the readership he had lost by publishing *Moby-Dick* and *Pierre*, it may have been with the release, in 1855, of *Israel Potter: His Fifty Years of Exile*. Written at the height of his powers (just after "The Encantadas" and before "Benito Cereno"), this historical romance is based on the ghostwritten autobiography of Revolutionary War veteran Israel R. Potter, whose career as a patriot soldier was thwarted by captivity, poverty, and prolonged exile in England. *Israel Potter* is, among other things, a good read, from its wry send-up of Benjamin Franklin to its rendition of the famous naval battle between the *Serapis* and the *Bon Homme Richard* to its pungent images of eighteenth-century London. Lest the pace flag, Melville imports two Revolutionary War celebrities—Ethan Allen and John Paul Jones—into his tale and improvises, sometimes wildly, sometimes waggishly, on the adventure sequences. Gaudy yet grounded in history, humorous yet insightful, the swashbuckling *Israel Potter* seems as if it should have been the popular success that had been eluding its author since *Typee* and *Omoo*. Yet despite favorable reviews, the novel never quite took off (in fact, it was eclipsed by another Revolutionary War romance, *Kate Aylesford: A Story of the Refugees*,

Studies in American Fiction, Volume 21 (1993): pp. 21–35. © 1993 Northeastern University.

released by Melville's own publisher, Putnam). More surprising still, not even the strip-mining of Melville's *oeuvre* by twentieth-century critics has managed to reclaim what may be Melville's least read book.

Critics who have addressed *Israel Potter* have generally faulted it on one of two grounds. Lewis Mumford, Warner Berthoff and Newton Arvin have found it diffuse, "impromptu to the point of negligence," "hardly more than a heap of sketches"—in short, a victim of its episodic format.[1] George Henry Lewes, Charles Feidelson Jr., and F. O. Matthiessen, meanwhile, have criticized the book's conclusion (Potter's exile) for its vagueness, nihilism, "labored" symbolism, and failure adequately to represent a key part of Israel's history (his destitution in London).[2] Matthiessen, pressing the issue farthest, scores the book's "slurred" climax as a failure of will on Melville's part. The author's over-identification with his protagonist, claims Matthiessen, subverted his artistic purpose.

This second criticism surprises. *Moby-Dick* and *Pierre* are nothing if not testimonies to a writer who faces up to the implications of a tale, whether that means killing off an entire cast of characters save one or grappling with themes such as atheism and incest. And as to Berthoff's and others' felt lack of a unifying organization ("*Israel Potter* gives an impression of exceptional imaginative power scattering its effects more or less at random"—Berthoff, p. 59), the table of contents alone reveals a comprehensive structural principle that belies the charge of "impromptu" execution. "Israel in the Lion's Den," "Samson among the Philistines," "Israel's Flight Towards the Wilderness," "Israel in Egypt": such chapter headings, absent in Melville's source (Henry Trumbull's *Life and Remarkable Adventures of Israel R. Potter*), suggest a figural, or typological, scheme overarching this saga.[3] Melville seems to have framed the novel on his culture's premise that its history and destiny postfigured that of the Biblical Israel; that Americans were a chosen people, brought out of captivity, blessed by God and appointed to a divine spiritual and historical mission. But why should Melville have conceived his historical romance in such figural terms? Even more fundamentally, what was Melville's aim in adapting *Israel Potter*?

His aim, suggested contemporary French critic Emile Montégut, was to portray America's penchant for mythologizing her own history: "*Israel Potter* . . . représente le caractère américain au moment où il était en formation."[4] Montégut's approach has been updated by recent critics like Arnold Rampersad, who argues that Melville's "aim . . . is the illumination of the dark, violent side of the American body."[5] Alexander Keyssar concurs, suggesting that the novel depicts an America that celebrates its heroes while ignoring social realities.[6] Kenny Jackson, taking a similar tack, suggests that "from the opening lines of the Dedication to the Bunker Hill Monument to the closing lines of the novel, Melville finds fault with American values as he presents a penetrating study of American attitudes." Jackson elaborates:

> In order to present his growing concern for the America which was to come, Melville selected three popular folk heroes who represented various phases of the American experience. Yet there is in the novel a suggested antagonism toward some of these heroes.
>
> ... The novel is an indictment against that part of America which could not distinguish between a popular hero and a true patriot.[7]

Jackson's highlighting of the book's concern with the national self is, like Montégut's, Rampersad's and Keyssar's, on target. Surely America's identity is Melville's subject—one he pursues, however, beyond the scope of patriotic sentiment, social justice, or even the contemporary mindset, examining it in light of America's most fundamental, Biblical myth of divine selection. Yet to say so is to be brought up short by the book's pessimism, for Israel Potter seems at last, as Feidelson notes, to be a wanderer whose "life accretes no meaning" (p. 183). Unless, of course, *Israel Potter* holds up America's self-assumed Election as an ironic frame. Unless, that is, Melville's purpose is to scrutinize America's actual identity while deposing her inflated self-image. If these are his intentions, *Israel Potter* is a triumph, not a failure, of will and art—a fiction that pursues its themes to their conclusion, demythologizing America and mythologizing modern man in its stead.

• • •

The figural tapestry Melville weaves in *Israel Potter* identifies America with the Biblical Israel in part by converting America's war heroes into Biblical types.[8] Ben Franklin is a contemporary Jacob, in whom "the diplomatist and the shepherd are blended" (p. 46). John Paul Jones, "like young David of old, ... beard[s] the British giant" (p. 95). The captured Ethan Allen is a Yankee Samson among Philistines; he even courts the role, allowing an "adorable Delilah" to shear a lock of his hair for a kiss (pp. 142, 145). Israel Potter, meanwhile, analogue and amalgam of all the above, is what his name suggests: a one-man recapitulation of Old Testament history. Captured at the outset by a British frigate, he is remanded in irons to the brig, where he languishes for a month "like Jonah in the belly of the whale" (p. 15). Escaping into the countryside, he sheds his English garments for a ditcher's coat of many colors (p. 19). Shortly thereafter, he is befriended by an "Abrahamic gentleman" (p. 27) from whom he unwillingly parts. Forced to labor in the king's garden, Israel refuses, like Daniel, to kowtow, only to gain the king's respect and friendship—and thus is preserved, as it were, in the den of the British Lion.

This motley allegory fades during the battle sequences—although Israel becomes, at one point, immured in a cell for what seems to him like "all the prophetic days and years of Daniel" (p. 71), and participates, later on, in a fiery sea battle likened to the destruction of Gomorrah (p. 130). But following the war episodes, it vigorously resumes. Such chapter headings as "Israel's Flight Towards the Wilderness" and "Israel in Egypt" prophesy Israel Potter's luckless and persecuted wandering through England and his sojourn in London, the smoky "desert" in which Potter, "our Wandering Jew"—blessed, eventually, with a son, "the spared Benjamin of his old age"—abides forty years before repatriating to "the Promised Land, . . . far Canaan beyond the sea" (pp. 165–166). By this time Israel Potter has subsumed his Biblical analogues, has become their apotheosis: a Yankee Christ, "the bescarred bearer of a cross," whose repatriation is "less a return than a resurrection" (pp. 167–168).

One could understand Melville's deciding to season his tale, as it were, with such allusions in order to enhance its cultural appeal. After all, America's seventeenth-century founders had asserted the divine nature of their enterprise in proclaiming New England the site of the New Jerusalem, God's City on a Hill. The exegetes of the Puritan theocracy had literalized the conceit with countless Biblical parallels, inventing an unprecedented rhetorical framework to define and justify their errand. Ursula Brumm and Sacvan Bercovitch have shown both the extent to which New England perceived its history and mission typologically and the extent to which Old Testament types survived in the rhetoric of the republic.[9]

Why Melville chose to feature this rhetoric, though—to make it the structural framework for his novel—is another question, one whose answer is bound up with the author's attitude toward his subject. For several chapters Melville displays a sort of bemused ambivalence toward America. Aware of both the myth and the reality, he adopts the temporary strategy of letting America's textbook heroes diffract her paradoxes, the typological backdrop quietly magnifying their deeds and confirming their significance. Midway through the book, however, the ironies attending his subject begin to overwhelm his story, resisting even the exorcism of burlesque. And as these ironies intensify, ironies the typological backdrop foreshortens, Melville's fascination with America's paradoxes dwindles, overshadowed first by a growing skepticism and then by universal questions of human worth.

Melville, for all intents, begins *Israel Potter* by embracing a romanticized America at face value. The New England of chapter one, page one, is a cross between "heaven" and classical paradise. To be sure, Melville peoples it with charcoal burners and maple-sugar boilers. But it is essentially a mythic world inhabited by mythic folk. In his opening portrait of Eastern Massachusetts, birthplace of his hero and of the American Revolution, Melville cites New England's stone walls, those "herculean undertakings"

at which "the very Titans seemed to have been at work," as an index to
the temper of the men of the Revolutionary era. Mixing mythologies with
abandon, Melville continues:

> To this day the best stone-wall builders, as the best wood-
> choppers, come from those solitary mountain towns; a tall,
> athletic and hardy race, unerring with the axe as the Indian with
> the tomahawk; at stone-rolling, patient as Sisyphus, powerful as
> Samson (pp. 4–5).

Not only divine favor but the whole legacy of Western civilization seems
to have cross-fertilized this mist-covered Arcadia and engendered these
mythical Americans.[10]

Almost at once, however, the picture darkens. Like the woman before
the mirror, whose portrait is simultaneously a grinning skull, the New England summer yields to its counterpart, during which

> the mountains are left bleak and sere. Solitude settles down upon
> them in drizzling mists. The traveller is beset, at perilous turns,
> by dense masses of fog. . . . As he warily picks his way . . . he sees
> some ghost-like object looming through the mist at the roadside;
> and wending towards it, beholds a rude white stone, uncouthly
> inscribed, marking the spot where, some fifty or sixty years ago,
> some farmer was upset in his wood-sled, and perished beneath the
> load (p. 6).

Such two-sidedness—sometimes comic, sometimes tragic—seems for
Melville to characterize both the landscape and its people.

Melville's patriots are all, in fact, paradoxes. Ben Franklin is a "practical
magian in linsey woolsey" (p. 47), a "Machiavelli in tents" in whom "a polished
Italian tact gleam[s] under an air of Arcadian unaffectedness" (p. 46). Ethan
Allen characterizes himself, rather comically, as "a meek-hearted Christian"
among Turks (p. 145), although, to the English ladies who have come to stare,
he looks the reverse: "an Ottoman," albeit one who "talks like a beau in a par-
lor" (p. 145). John Paul Jones, meanwhile—poet and outlaw, rake and ruler,
gentleman and savage, overgrown infant and *enfant terrible*—presents a still
more pronounced paradox. Israel first glimpses him pursuing a chambermaid
up a staircase. Seconds later this same John Paul Jones bursts on the scene,
an incensed patriot demanding ships and endorsement. "When Israel now
perceived him again," writes Melville, "he seemed, while momentarily hidden, to have undergone a complete transformation" (p. 56). Perhaps the most
telling image of John Paul Jones is his tattooed arm, decorated with "large,

intertwisted cyphers . . . such as [are] seen only on thoroughbred savages" (p. 62), but which he conceals beneath the lace and ruffles of his Parisian coat-sleeve. Melville sees this "barbarian in broadcloth" (p. 63) as quintessentially American:

> Intrepid, unprincipled, reckless, predatory, with boundless ambition, civilized in externals but a savage at heart, America is, or may yet be, the Paul Jones of nations (p. 120).

Melville's adroit portraits of Ben Franklin, John Paul Jones, and Ethan Allen, for all their wit, hint perceptively at other American traits: "laby-rinth-minded" plain-spokenness (a trait Melville ascribes to Franklin and his spiritual compatriots, Jacob and Thomas Hobbes, p. 46); authoritarian propensity ("My God, why was I not born a Czar!" shouts John Paul Jones at one point, infuriated at "this shilly-shallying timidity called prudence," p. 57); morbid reverence for the dollar ("Never joke at funerals, or during business transactions," chides a poker-faced Ben Franklin, p. 43); protean versatility and jack-of-all-tradesmanship (Franklin, in this respect the "type and genius of his land," was "everything but a poet," p. 48); sensuous appe-tite—present even when disguised (all three heroes are ladies' men, the sev-enty-two-year-old Dr. Franklin being "the caressed favorite of the highest born beauties of the Court," p. 48); and the "western spirit" (Melville says of Ethan Allen: "His spirit was essentially western; and herein is his peculiar Americanism; for the western spirit is, or will yet be [for no other is, or can be], the true American one," p. 149).

Melville's tone thus far is that of an amused observer intrigued by the puzzle America, in the persons of such eccentric heroes, presents. But de-spite the prevailing comedy, a tragic potential inheres in many of his char-acterizations. The "western spirit," for example, as Israel's eventual ill-fated repatriation suggests, may partake as much of naive self-delusion as of heroic enterprise. Likewise an America that is the "Paul Jones of nations" may prove as vicious and amoral as it is gallant and fearless—as Melville not only sug-gests in the passage cited above, but later shows. An America, meanwhile, whose "genius" is metamorphosis runs the attendant risk of self-*less*ness. The most dramatic example, perhaps, of such dormant irony is John Paul Jones's jaunty characterization of himself as an "untrammelled citizen and sailor of the universe" (p. 56). The nineteenth-century American was, in a sense, pre-cisely that, since America was still undefined, still in the process of becom-ing—hence heir to an identity that, like her people, must finally comprise the world's influences, rather than those of any one people or culture. John Paul Jones's brow, we are told, gleamed with "the consciousness of possessing a character as yet unfathomed" (p. 63). Yet to be "unfathomed," a "sailor of the universe," can be as ambiguous a blessing as it is an identity, as Israel's history demonstrates.

These cameo portraits of the patriots generate insight as well as interest, then, and provide vehicles for Melville's more abstract characterization of a people. But beyond a point, their extraordinariness limits their usefulness as indices. So Melville's attention devolves finally on Israel Potter, who combines many of their traits. Israel is shrewd and brave, devoted and proud: in a word, as illustrious as his celebrated acquaintances. Like Ethan Allen, he is captured, baited and harassed by the British, yet remains, in his own way, defiant. Like Paul Jones, Israel goes to sea young, takes over a ship, and defies an enemy crowd single-handedly, combining grace with daring and civility with savagery in the process. Like Franklin, he serves as a foreign emissary, albeit a secret one; displays a "labyrinth-minded" plain-spokenness on more than one occasion; and even writes a book—whose practical instructiveness, we suspect, might rival some of Poor Richard's sardonic apothegms.

Israel is, in short, the prototypical American: revolutionary, roustabout, and Yankee peddler rolled into one—and christened with a Puritan name to boot. Yet for all his valor and accomplishments, this composite patriot and figural patriarch dies an unknown soldier. And while his history rings truer for his anonymity, we are hard put to cipher its meaning. What are we to make of this cultural antihero whose trials, unlike the Biblical Israel's, lead not to redemption, reward, self-definition, or fulfillment, but to obscurity? It is as if the Biblical Daniel had survived the lion's den only to die a derelict in Babylon.

Nor is Israel's obscurity just luckless coincidence. Rather it suggests an identity vacuum. Israel's career consists largely of his changing clothes (every ten pages, it seems), losing himself in one crowd or another, sailing under different flags and figuratively dying and being reborn. A forerunner of the Confidence Man,[11] his guises include those of beggar, scarecrow and ghost. Melville capitalizes on such occasions for comic relief, but Israel's career is finally tragic, not comic. Like the marginal characters and nonentities he impersonates, Israel seems somehow insubstantial—a fast-talking figment, stopped time and again by the question, "Who are you?"

Melville's treatment of Israel's elusive identity verges on obsession in the "Shuttle" episode. "Who the deuce *are* you?" demands the British officer-of-the-deck when Israel materializes unexpectedly on the foredeck of his ship after a skirmish. (Israel has prematurely climbed aboard, and must now feign membership in the crew or be discovered for an enemy.) "Who *are* you? . . . What's your name? Are you down in the ship's books, or at all in the records of nature?" Israel's outrageous song-and-dance reply ("My name, sir, is Peter Perkins. . . . It might be, sir, . . . that seeing I shipped under the effects of liquor, I might, out of absent-mindedness like, have given in some other person's name instead of my own," p. 137) buys him time and saves his life. But he is peremptorily tagged a "ghost" and a "phantom" (p. 139) and the jape resonates as a cultural caricature—America as a *poseur*, albeit a feisty and inventive one.[12]

The morbid tone the book assumes from this point on lends support to such a reading. What is not immediately apparent, though, is why Melville's essentially good-humored fascination with America's paradoxes lapses into caricature. The key to his souring attitude lies in the episode describing the face-off between the *Bon Homme Richard* and the *Serapis*, the sequence preceding "The Shuttle." Prior to this point, the grimmer ironies of his subject have simmered harmlessly, the typological ground inconspicuously enriching the tale's texture and adding dimension to the heroes' exploits. But during this battle sequence, the ironies erupt; figure and ground come into conflict; history, as it were, subverts typology.a

In the preceding chapters Britain has figured as Babylon, the oppressor nation—hence, for instance, the chapter entitled "Israel in the Lion's Den," in which Israel is unmasked, then befriended by King George III. The *Serapis-Richard* sequence, however, explodes this typology. The battle is introduced portentously: "there would seem to be something singularly indicatory in this engagement. It may involve at once a type, a parallel, and a prophecy" (p. 120). The parallel is disturbing enough: that America, "civilized in externals but a savage at heart, may well be the Paul Jones of nations" (p. 120). But the type, let alone the prophecy, shocks. Instead of a victimized American "Israel" being delivered from Babylon (from the British Lion) Melville presents the battle as a maritime version of the destruction of Sodom and Gomorrah. After limning the fire blazing in the rigging of both ships, he writes:

> A few hours after sunrise the Richard was deserted for the *Serapis* and other vessels of the squadron of Paul. About ten o'clock the *Richard*, gorged with slaughter, wallowed heavily, gave a long roll, and, blasted by tornadoes of sulphur, slowly sank, like Gomorrah, out of sight (p. 130).

The *Richard*, Paul Jones's ship, sinks "like Gomorrah." (The dramatic irony of the phrase is even clearer for the fact that Jones has earlier vowed to "rain down on wicked England like fire on Sodom," p. 56). This image of England and America as mutually wicked cities of the plain jars our expectations and deposes America's sanctimonious self-image.

Melville justifies his renegade typology with frequent reminders that, unlike the Biblical Israel, America is fighting her own kin: "it seemed more an intestine feud, than a fight between strangers. Or, rather, it was as if Siamese Twins, oblivious of their fraternal bond, should rage in unnatural fight" (p. 125). He likewise links the antagonists through formal parallels and similes,[13]

so that "the belligerents [seem] . . . a co-partnership and joint-stock com-
bustion-company" (p. 126) and become, at last, "confounded . . . in one chaos
of devastation" (p. 120). Both literal and figurative kin to "wicked England" (p.
56), America, with her guise of Election, seems sorely deluded. These ironies are
compounded by the savagery her warriors display during the fight.

Until now, Paul Jones has distinguished himself not only by his daring,
but by his humanity, as in his torching of the English ship at Whitehaven:

> Not a splinter was made, not a drop of blood spilled throughout
> the affair. The intentional harmlessness of the result, as to human
> life, was only equalled by the desperate courage of the deed. It
> formed, doubtless, one feature of the compassionate contempt of
> Paul towards the town, that he took such paternal care of their
> lives and limbs (p. 104).

But in the *Serapis* encounter there appears a feral and fanatical Paul Jones,
his bared sword-arm "cabalistically terrific as the charmed standard of
Satan" (p. 126), meting destruction. Moreover, Israel, who earlier forbore,
on principle, to harm the British king, is now shown dropping a grenade
into a hatchway "with such faultless precision" that "more than twenty men
were instantly killed: nearly forty wounded" (p. 127). In light of such atrocities, Melville seems unable to indulge partisan hurrahs. America, the figural
Israel, seems to be just one more warring tribe.

Its pedestal fractured, the republic becomes less an engaging paradox
than a pathological schizophrenic. One minute a raging lion, the next a "poor,
persecuted fellow" (p. 138), America/Israel with its quick-change artistry less
dazzles than disturbs. Hence the extensive, if abortive, cross-examining Israel
undergoes in the following chapter—as if Melville, exasperated by his elusive
subject, sought to extort some straight answers by giving his protean hero the
third degree.

The *Serapis-Richard* episode signals another important change in the
narrative. Henceforth the very notion of national identity begins to evaporate,
to seem irrelevant in the face of a larger paradox. Both sides' ruthlessness established, Melville, after quoting the casualty figures, ends the chapter:

> In view of this battle one may ask—What separates the
> enlightened man from the savage? Is civilization a thing distinct,
> or is it an advanced stage of barbarism? (p. 130).

The *Serapis-Richard* encounter adumbrates a broader, more cynical view of
man than Melville has articulated so far—one he will develop, then leaven
in the remaining chapters.

• • •

So Melville's attempts to unravel the American character net him both
more and less than he bargained for. His insight into America's capacity for
self-delusion horrifies especially, although, as he later intimates, America
has no monopoly on self-deceit. But in the wake of the *Serapis* and *Shuttle*
chapters, the national identity, though more inscrutable than ever, becomes
less consumingly important. It is as if Melville realizes, two-thirds of the way
through his book, that to scrutinize America's mercurial surface is futile, and
to scrutinize its deep self is nothing less than to scrutinize humankind's. This
last insight, a corollary of the Serapis episode, is perhaps the book's most profound revelation. If America, its self-styled Election notwithstanding, is not
special, then it is like other nations: selfish, brutal, disappointingly human.
And though this revelation seems at first to appall, Melville derives from it a
more profound sympathy, a new typology—indeed, a new testament.

The ironic similarities between England and America that first become plain in the *Serapis-Richard* episode are echoed by various rhetorical
ploys elsewhere in the book. Melville, for instance, uses the word "lion"—a
popular characterization of England ("the British Lion")—to characterize
America's prototypes Ethan Allen and Israel Potter (pp. 102, 143). Likewise
the name Richard—as in Ben Franklin's "Poor Richard," and John Paul
Jones' ship, the *Bon Homme Richard*—also recalls England's Richard the
Lion-hearted—who, according to Melville's narrator, is the spiritual sire
of Ethan Allen (149). So too the image of England as a "wilderness" and
London as a "desert" (p. 161) counterpoints Ben Franklin's map of the New
World, on which the then-uncharted America is labeled "DESERT" (p.
38). Melville bolsters these rhetorical devices with formal parallels, playing
off Israel/America's anonymity against that of London's masses and rein-
voking New England's mists in old England's fogs and industrial palls. And
just in case these strategies fail, he dramatizes his irony in the Ethan Allen digression, introducing Allen as a "wild beast" (p. 144) among civilized
Englishmen and then, in the following chapter, putting the shoe on the
other hoof by relating the monstrous treatment accorded the captive Allen
by the British, and concluding, "when among wild beasts, if they menace
you, be a wild beast" (p. 150).

These ironies deprecate not only America's myth of Election, but any
nation's less-than-severe self-appraisal. Humanity, in short, usurps America's
role as preeminent paradox. Following the chapter spotlighting Allen, Melville begins to lace his prose with observations that cut across national lines to
depict a universal sordidness:

> It is among nations as among individuals: imputed indigence
> provokes oppression and scorn; but that same indigence being

risen to opulence, receives a politic consideration even from its former insulters (p. 151).

Israel's sojourn in England continues this trend, Melville signifying Israel's tribulations over and above those commonly associated with national, wealth, and class distinctions. At one point Israel, upon learning that his whole crew is in danger of impressment, leaves the British ship he has successfully infiltrated and flees inland, "hunted by the thought, that whether as an Englishman, or whether as an American, he would, if caught, be now equally subject to enslavement" (p. 152). Shortly thereafter Israel, clad again in beggar's rags, becomes one of a throng of existential brickmakers to whom "men and bricks were equally of clay. 'What signifies who we be—dukes or ditchers?' thought the moulders; 'all is vanity and clay. . . . Kings as clowns are codgers—who ain't a nobody?'" (pp. 155, 157).

By now, the despair of Melville's vision frightens. Like Lot's wife, who looked once too often, Melville seems overcome, immobilized by the desolation he has glimpsed and by the seeming apocalypse at hand. He describes London:

> As in eclipses, the sun was hidden; the air darkened; the whole dull, dismayed aspect of things, as if some neighboring volcano, belching its premonitory smoke, were about to whelm the great town, as Herculaneum and Pompeii, or the Cities of the Plain. And as they had been upturned in terror towards the mountain, all faces were more or less snowed, or spotted with soot. Nor marble, nor flesh, nor the sad spirit of man, may in this cindery City of Dis abide white (pp. 159–160).

Charles Feidelson, Jr. rightly notes the nihilism informing these final pages and captured in the image of London Bridge, over which "that hereditary crowd—gulf-stream of humanity . . . has never ceased pouring, like an endless shoal of herring" (p. 158). The phantom metaphor earlier applied to Israel/America recurs, universalized, in Melville's portrait of these multitudes who "one after the other, . . . drifted by, uninvoked ghosts in Hades" (p. 160). By now, no "disguises," national or otherwise, suffice; no one escapes sordid anonymity. All are ghosts; bricks in a wall; herrings in a shoal.

With America deposed and its importance subsumed, Melville's laboriously woven figural tapestry threatens to become a white elephant. Yet rather than scuttle or revise his typological framework, Melville intensifies it. The final chapters—"Israel's Flight Towards the Wilderness," "Israel in Egypt"—further typify Israel's sojourn in England, although there is little left to tell of his adventures. If anything, Melville overworks his motif, dallying too explicitly in calling his hero "poor Israel! Well-named—bondsman in the English Egypt" (p. 157), and disposing of him with the comment that "encouraged by the exodus of the lost tribes of soldiers, Israel returned to chair-bottoming" (p. 163). Heavy-handed or not, however, these chapters perform their narrative task, which is both to set the stage for Israel's final "deliverance" into America, the Promised Land, and to detail the figural ground anew in relation to Israel's dawning messianic identity. Melville's figuralism in these final chapters acts both as an ironic foil and a reconstituted metaphor. These closing chapters detailing Israel's decline and destitution represent not so much a "slurred climax"[14] as a prelude to the final irony of Israel's repatriation. By revitalizing expectations of an Exodus, a deliverance into Canaan, Melville's reactivated typology foreshortens the downward spiral of Israel's career.

For the American typology Melville borrows was nothing less than the spiritual backbone to a colony, a nation, a people whose City on a Hill was, from the outset, an experiment in brinksmanship. At Massachusetts's founding, and then during the Indian wars and the collapse of Cromwell's Protectorate, and later still during the decline of the New England theocracy, and again during the Revolution, the rhetoric of Election enabled America to survive against enormous odds and to progress, convinced that its very trials, like the Biblical Israel's, were proof of its divine destiny. By identifying its mission with Old Testament Israel's, New England—and later the republic—both fortified itself against the wilderness it had chosen to inhabit and transformed that wilderness into an oasis. The premise of this rhetorical posture was, of course, the notion of a God who chastises to purify and who has made a covenant with His people that will not be broken. But what if the nation's hardships were to prove to be nothing more than the vicissitudes all nations undergo? What if her trials in the wilderness were never to end? What if the covenant were a fiction, and no redemption was to follow? What if Canaan itself were to prove a desert? What, in short, if Israel were to be forgotten?

This, quite literally, is what happens. The implicit time of deliverance having come and gone (as the subtitle—"His Fifty Years of Exile"—hints), Israel arrives in "the Promised Land" only to find himself, as always, a stranger. After almost being run over by a patriotic float in procession (it is July 4th when he disembarks in Boston), the best Israel can manage is to glimpse his father's homestead and the crumbling remains of the ancient hearth. Redemption, grace, reward, all elude him. Even his rightful pension is denied him. Unwelcomed and unremembered, he dies shortly after writing "a little book, the record of his fortunes" (p. 169).

And so Israel-as-America-as-Latter-Day-Israel perishes in the desert, and his testament with him. But the figural grid, active until the end, forces his fate into relief and intensifies the melodrama of his homecoming. Melville's irony is as perfect as it is painful, a hand passing slowly and repeatedly through the pillar of fire that was at once the figment and forestay of the American imagination in its adopted wilderness.

But if, in *Israel Potter,* "Israel" is deposed, "Potter" is not. The tension between Election and obscurity embodied in the protagonist's name from the start undercuts the American myth, but mythologizes man in its stead.[15] This is the second, non-ironic function of the typology Melville resurrects in the closing chapters: to elevate humanity in spite of its apparent worthlessness and abandonment. This time the figure of Israel captive in Egypt typifies not America as British colony, but Everyman as figurative exile in an alien world.

Hence Israel's identification as the "Wandering Jew," for if Israel has an abiding identity, it is that of Exile and Wanderer (p. 165). Hence too his final transformation into a Christ figure, the "bescarred bearer of a cross" (p. 167). Melville, as it were, transfigures his "ghost," makes of him not only a prophet, but a priest and mock king—merging his identity, in the Dedication, with that of "His Highness," the Bunker Hill Monument (p. vii). Hence, finally, Melville's empathy for London's masses of "tormented humanity" (p. 159), and his sympathy in portraying the brickmakers and allegorizing the bricks. (Variously burned according to their placement in the kiln, they suggest that human life is a trial by fire, fatal to some but strengthening to others enabled by their circumstance to withstand the furnace's heat.) Melville's final chapters eulogize "the unupholstered corpse of the beggar": "man, 'poor player,'" who "succeeds better in life's tragedy than comedy" (pp. 161, 160).

This sympathetic, humanist perspective was not unique to *Israel Potter.* It informs much of Melville's short fiction of 1853–1855. The narrator of "The Tartarus of Maids," for example, identifies with the pale-faced drudges laboring in a paper mill. Likewise the narrator of "Bartleby, the Scrivener," meditating on Bartleby's pathetic death, envisions the dead letters it had once been Bartleby's job to sort ("pardon for those who died despairing; hope for those who died unhoping; good tidings for those who died stifled by unrelieved calamities"), then concludes, "Ah, Bartleby! Ah, humanity!"[16]

The same sentiment—expressed, as in *Israel Potter,* through adapted gospel motifs—underpins "Cock-A-Doodle-Doo!" and "The Encantadas." In "Cock-A-Doodle-Doo!" a dejected debtor takes heart from a trumpeting rooster and his owner, a struggling but indomitable wood-sawyer. Melville develops the story as an ironic Easter fable in which not resurrection but death prevails (the wood-sawyer, his ailing wife and children, and finally his rooster all expire in a tragicomic chain reaction). Yet, perhaps because death comes as a blessing if not a crown for these souls who endured so stoically, the Easter text Melville adverts to ("O death, where is thy sting? O grave, where is thy victory?" [p. 288]) takes on a new, if less mystical, grandeur, even as the crowing cock, instead of shaming the doubting and dispirited narrator as its

Biblical ancestor had shamed Christ-denying Peter, fills him with human pride and a glorious insolence.

But perhaps the work closest to *Israel Potter* in tone and trope is "The Encantadas, or Enchanted Isles." At the heart of this fiction is the tale of the Chola Widow, Hunilla, who, with her husband and brother, journeys to the Galápagos Islands to collect tortoise oil. The captain they contract to bring them back betrays his promise. Brother and husband both drown before Hunilla's eyes when their catamaran breaks apart on the reef, and before Hunilla is rescued by the narrator and his crew, a whaling crew discovers her plight, rapes her and abandons her. Melville's portrait pays reverential tribute to this quintessential victim: "humanity, thou strong thing," Melville writes, "I worship thee, not in the laurelled victor, but in this vanquished one" (p. 157). His closing image transforms the widow into a latterday Christ: "the last seen of lone Hunilla she was passing into Payta town, riding upon a small gray ass; and before her on the ass's shoulders, she eyed the jointed workings of the beast's armorial cross" (p. 162).

What sets the humanist gospel of *Israel Potter* apart, though, is precisely the typological context in which the tale is couched, and which Melville so radically debunks and transforms. The island universe of "The Encantadas," which is the same Galápagos Islands Darwin studied as a crucible of evolutionary pressures, is from the start a wasteland of burnt cinders and reptiles in which natural selection determines all, a postlapsarian world in which "naught else abides . . . but unkept promises of joy" (p. 153). The universe of *Israel Potter*, by contrast, is America, a New World Canaan whose fertile soil and thriving culture lend credence to its divine aspirations. Once this promised land becomes, as it were, untransfigured, and all the world stands revealed as a kiln, a desert, the sense of spiritual collapse is overwhelming. The gospel of love that Melville extracts is the more remarkable for this implosion of faith that precedes it.

Potter's field, not Canaan, may be man's portion. But *Israel Potter*, Melville's most compassionate book, dignifies the funeral and makes of Potter's Field a designated resting place (Potter bestowing his name, in effect, on obscure plots the world over). Dedicated to a monument, *Israel Potter* is itself a monument; invoking the Bible, it is itself a bible. It is a monument, however, not to an American myth, but to the human condition; a bible, not of a people, but for all people.

NOTES

1. Lewis Mumford, *Herman Melville* (New York: Harcourt Brace, 1929), p. 167; Warner Berthoff, *The Example of Melville* (Princeton: Princeton Univ. Press,

1962), p. 69; Newton Arvin, *Herman Melville* (New York: William Sloane, 1950), p. 245.

2. George Henry Lewes, review of *Israel Potter* in *The Leader* (May 5, 1855), 428; Charles Feidelson Jr., *Symbolism in American Literature* (Chicago: Univ. of Chicago Press, 1953), p. 183; F. O. Manhiessen, *The American Renaissance* (New York: Oxford Univ. Press, 1941), p. 491.

3. *Israel Potter: His Fifty Years of Exile*, ed. Harrison Hayford, Hershel Parker and G. Thomas Tanselle, vol. 8 of *The Writings of Herman Melville*, gen. eds. Hayford *et al.* (Evanston & Chicago: Northwestern Univ. and Newberry Library, 1982), pp. ix, x; hereafter cited parenthetically in the text.

4. Emile Montégut, review of *Israel Potter, Revue des deux mondes* (July 1, 1855), 7.

5. Arnold Rampersad, *Melville's Israel Potter: A Pilgrimage and Progress* (Bowling Green: Bowling Green Univ. Press, 1969), p. 101.

6. Alexander Keyssar, *Melville's Israel Potter: Reflections on the American Dream* (Cambridge: Harvard Univ. Press, 1969), p. 24.

7. Kenny Jackson, *"Israel Potter:* Melville's '4th of July Story,'" *CLAD*, 9 (1963), 197–198, 204.

8. Nathalia Wright has catalogued the Israel motif in *Melville's Use of the Bible* (Durham: Duke Univ. Press, 1949). Other critics—notably Edgar A. Dryden in *Melville's Thematics of Form: The Great Art of Telling the Truth* (Baltimore: Johns Hopkins Univ. Press, 1968)—have noted the irony of such Biblical analogues in *Israel Potter* but have not related the motif to America's typological self-image (pp. 143–144). Dryden observes merely that "unlike the Biblical figures with whom he is so often associated, [Israel's] physical pain and suffering is no preparation for spiritual cleansing and rebirth" (p. 145).

9. Ursula Brumm, *American Thought and Religious Typology* (New Brunswick: Rutgers Univ. Press, 1970); Sacvan Bercovitch, *The Puritan Origins of the American Self* (New Haven: Yale Univ. Press, 1975), and *The American Jeremiad* (Madison: Univ. of Wisconsin Press, 1978).

10. As Robert Zaller astutely notes, Melville's New Englanders may have been ironically conceived from the outset, the Titans, Sisyphus, and Samson all being "classic heroes of futility." See "Melville and the Myth of Revolution," *SIR*, 15 (1976), 608.

11. Michael P. Rogin sees this comparison as a contrast. See *Subversive Genealogy: Politics and Art in Herman Melville* (New York: Knopf, 1982), p. 230.

12. For a comprehensive discussion of Israel's non-identity, see John Seelye, *Melville: The Ironic Diagram* (Evanston: Northwestern Univ. Press, 1970).

13. Both ships, for instance, suffer the unhelpful approach and retreat of their own consorts. The two ships are depicted, meanwhile, as "a hawk and a crow" (p. 123), and as opposite sides of the same faulted land mass (p. 125). Indeed, Melville's establishing shot of "that bewildering intertanglement of all the yards and anchors of the two ships" (p. 120) signals the extent of their indistinguishability. "The two vessels were as two houses, through whose party-wall doors have been cut; one family (the Guelphs) occupying the whole lower story; another (the Ghibelines) the whole upper story" (p. 126).

14. Matthiessen, p. 491.

15. Ray B. Browne also stresses this apotheosis of the common man in *"Israel Potter:* Metamorphosis of Superman," in *Frontiers of American Culture*, ed. Ray B.

Browne et al. (Lafayette: Purdue Univ. Press, 1968), pp. 89–98. But for Browne, *Israel Potter* is a sort of Jacksonian-democratic deposition of our heroes and gods, a paean to equality and to "America . . . the hope of humanity" (p. 96). Such a nationalistic reading collapses under the irony of Potter's homecoming and death. Melville eschews chauvinistic considerations, so that at the close Potter is less a democratic hero than a bedraggled but deified "citizen of the universe."

16. *The Piazza Tales and Other Prose Pieces, 1839–1860,* ed. Harrison Hayford, Alma A. MacDougall, G. Thomas Tanselle et al., vol. 9 of *The Writings of Herman Melville* (Evanston and Chicago: Northwestern Univ. and Newberry Library, 1987), 1). 45; hereafter cited parenthetically in the text.

JUDITH HILTNER

Disquieting Encounters: Male Intrusions/ Female Realms in Melville

In the second sketch of "The Paradise of Bachelors and the Tartarus of Maids," Melville's male narrator visits an isolated paper mill that employs only women "operatives," and his penetration into the center of appropriated female energy is depicted as a shocking experience that renders him faint and temporarily incapacitated. Using imagery that suggests the violation of a sacred taboo, he compares the effects of what he has witnessed in the factory to the suffering of Actæon, mauled by bloodhounds for viewing the naked Artemis. The narrator records no personal interaction with any of the women after his initial encounters with two pale and miserable workers outside the dormitories; after first faltering at each confrontation, he forcibly dismisses the second woman with the desperate cry, "[I]s there no man about?" He can enter the scene of female labor and survive the experience intact only when the encounter is mediated by the "dark-complexioned," fur-wrapped "Old Bach" and the young "Cupid."[1]

Scenes in which a male curiously observes or intrudes upon a female realm recur in Melville as dramatic and psychically charged experiences: Tommo disrupts a circle of women tappa makers in *Typee;* Ishmael, on one of the *Pequod's* whaleboats, penetrates a school of female whales, some nursing, some in labor; Pierre interrupts a sewing society; the "Encantadas" narrator observes the scene of Hunilla's fruitless labors; the curious narrator of "Poor

ESQ: A Journal of the American Renaissance, Volume 40, Number 2 (1994): pp. 91–111. © 1994
ESQ: A Journal of the American Renaissance.

Man's Pudding" imposes upon Martha Coulter's wash day; Captain Delano intrudes upon a slave mother nursing her child in "Benito Cereno"; and
the "Piazza" narrator startles Marianna at her sewing. In all of these scenes,
the male intruder encounters women engaged in some form of labor in the·
broadest sense; their energies, at the point of his arrival, are channelled into
physical or mental activities, though the "work" may be peripheral to Melville's main focus. This pattern reinforces a persistent patriarchal association
between the female body and a tireless, unstoppable machine—a frequently
appalling organic dynamo that operates independently of male influence. The
scenes, however, are distinguished by the nature of the realm invaded; some
of Melville's observers intrude upon a place of communal female activity, and
others upon an individual woman's private domain. The individual encounters
specify and even exacerbate the psychological malaise pervading the communal scenes, and telling parallels emerge between the observers' reactions in
both types of encounters.

   In *Typee* and *Moby-Dick*, intruder scenes are treated humorously or as a
source of psychic solace for the male. Even in these early texts, however, the
narrator perceives that he is entering a strange and alien world—a world that
threatens him with a sense of confinement. Frequently in such scenes, the
intrusion represents a violation or is otherwise disruptive. In later works, Melville raises increasing doubts about the male's comprehension or interpretation
of what he has observed. The observer is generally rendered faint and speechless, and his intuitive perception of the scene's implications fuels a growing
urgency to resist its effects upon his psyche, to escape in order to remain intact. Increasingly the women are engaged in activities unrelated to their natural gifts or desires, their energies appropriated by forces from which they are
alienated. In some of Melville's texts, the male observer/intruder scene enjoys
a temporary and unstable status as a protest against class distinction and labor
oppression, but soon the political or social indictment is absorbed into literary
and aesthetic tensions, or into an exploration of more abstract psychological
and metaphysical ambiguities. At the same time, the description of the female
realm becomes less realistic, more grotesque and allegorical—a movement that
helps to subvert the thrust of the social critique.[2]

   The differences in these scenes of male intrusion upon female realms
suggest a transition in Melville's assessment of the male's ability to absorb
and interpret female experience. The scenes raise interesting questions about
the male writer's ability to depict female energies without sliding into strategies of detachment; they also trace Melville's rapidly altering associations
with the term "natural." Changes in the male intruder scene may effectively
be assessed by noting striking similarities and telling differences between the
"Tartarus" narrative (1855) and an earlier example, Tommo's unsettling of the
Typee tappa makers (1846).[3] Because the natural abundance of the Typee

Valley satisfies nearly all the necessities of the natives, scarcely any physical exertion is required in Typee, but it is primarily women who perform whatever is demanded, particularly the preparation of breadfruit and the making of tappa cloth. The "only industrious person in . . . the valley" is Kory-Kory's mother, Tinor, who spends her time actively engaged in household crafts and tasks. Tommo suggests that though largely unnecessary, work is joy for Tinor, a natural, rhythmic expression of her abundant energies: she seems to work "from some irresistible impulse; her limbs continually swaying to and fro, as if there were some indefatigable engine concealed within her body which [keeps] her in perpetual motion."[4] In the later "Tartarus" scene, this "indefatigable engine" with which woman's body continues to be associated becomes an externalized machine of torture that joylessly enslaves by "metallic necessity" and "unbudging fatality" (*PT,* 333).

Tommo's realistic description of tappa making reveals that the procedure curiously reverses the process of papermaking in Tartarus, which is described as an allegorical reenactment of gestation and birth. In the paper mill, the "woolly-looking," "albuminous" fluid is rendered increasingly thick and viscous as it moves along the mechanical rollers, until it finally hardens into solid sheets of foolscap (*PT,* 331–332). In tappa making, on the other hand, the initially solid raw material (tree branch fiber) is softened and decomposed by being soaked in water. It is stretched and gently beaten into a thin, malleable substance, until its final formlessness as silky cloth (*Typee,* 147–148).

The reader observes other curious parallels and disturbing differences between the two procedures, as the natural process of tappa making is converted into the mechanical oppression of Tartarus. Both processes involve imprinting: The fine grooves in the mallet used to beat the tree fiber in tappa making account for the "corduroy sort of stripes" visible in the final cloth (*Typee,* 147). In Tartarus, the workers themselves, having become identified with the inanimate product of their labor, are printed upon; the wires used for lining the paper appear in one young woman's "ruled and wrinkled" forehead, and the image of the workers' pale faces, in the narrator's haunting vision, is imprinted on the pulp passing through the mechanical rollers (*PT,* 328, 334). Occasionally the Typee women will add vegetable dye to color their cloth, but they prefer the "natural tint" of "dazzling whiteness" rendered by drying and bleaching the sheets in the sun (*Typee,* 148). By contrast, the whiteness of the final product in Tartarus is not "dazzling." The narrator repeatedly sees a reflection of the foolscap in the dull pallor and "sheet-white" faces of the women, and the rose dye of the tinted paper comes from draining the blood of the operatives: "I looked from the rosy paper to the pallid cheek, but said nothing" (*PT,* 330, 328). Finally, the mallets used to thin out the fibers in tappa making produce at every stroke a musical ringing sound, and when the narrator approaches from a distance, he hears in the simultaneous striking of several mallets a lovely harmony. How far from "the sharp shriek of the tormented steel" that makes the narrator's "unaccustomed blood" curdle in Tartarus (*PT,* 330).

The tappa making house is located in a secluded portion of the Typee Valley, but it is far more accessible than the route to Tartarus. As the entire novel persuades us, the intimate domain of the female is more easily penetrated in the pagan South Seas than in Protestant midcentury America. And because the house is more accessible and familiar, it appears less threatening to the male observer. Tommo has witnessed women making tappa numerous times during his visit and has even "handled the bark in all the various stages of its preparation." In the scene the narrator recounts, the women hardly protest his appearance; they chat with him "gaily" before resuming their work. Only when he "carelessly" picks up some of the bark and "unconsciously" picks it apart do they begin to shriek. The sense of violation perceived by the narrator is reinforced by his allusion to the Roman warriors' rape of Sabine women. When the tappa makers' bosoms swell and they point at him in horror, Tommo assumes that some "venomous reptile" must be concealed in the bark he holds and so examines it more closely, triggering even more desperate screams from the women. Alarmed, he is about to bolt the scene, as the Tartarus narrator does several times during his visit. But Tommo's fear is assuaged by the explanatory cry "Taboo," as the Typee women, unlike those in Tartarus, are empowered to speak to the male observer. Tommo later learns that this particular cloth, "destined" for women's head wear, is taboo to male touch at every stage of its production (Typee, 221–222).

In this text, the narrator gradually associates the intricate system of taboo with oppressive restrictions that undermine the freedom he had begun to relish after first yielding to Typee life and repressing his urgent desire to escape. He begins to see the taboo system as "strange," "complex," and ultimately incomprehensible, even to foreigners who live in Typee for years and master the language (*Typee,* 221). But as other readers have suggested, Tommo never seriously attempts to understand it; he insists upon breaking taboo dictates whenever he can persuade male authority figures to yield to his demands.[5] Even in a relative paradise, then, a place of easier intercourse between men and women, masculine assertion and masculine incomprehension result in violation of a female realm. Moreover, the narrator's impression of the Typee taboo system as an "inexplicable" and "all-controlling power" whose effects "pervad[e] the most important as well as the minutest transactions of life" (*Typee,* 221) persists after his return from the South Seas. The system is in part projected upon the female gender, and most particularly upon the woman's body, inevitably controlling the male's encounters within the feminine realm.

The "Tartarus" narrative of 1855 intensifies the bleaker hints of the earlier tappa scene and petrifies them into inexorable "necessity." Male and female exist in realms so separate that no communication can occur; the complexities and periodic rhythms of the female body are ossified into a steel machine that is inscrutable and oppressively relentless. Female figures are abstract and voiceless. The identification of female anatomy with the inchoate, raw forces of nature renders both equally subject to appropriation by a male-engendered and male-controlled technology. And as the narrative suggests, this impersonal and metallic reification accounts for the seemingly sensitive narrator's inability to endure the scene without mitigating male company and, ultimately, his need to flee it.

Inevitably, the biological allegory circumscribes Melville's laboring women, a circumscription that has generated modern debate over whether the story is primarily about human bondage to technology or to the female reproductive machine.[6] As Michael Paul Rogin notes, Melville's pallid "waifs" bear little resemblance to the actual factory women of Lowell, Massachusetts, "who wrote letters and verse, and organized to protest their regimentation." According to Rogin, "Melville ignores such autonomous subjects, who gained individual voices in the course of their collective struggle."[7] In "Tartarus," women's economic and social plight has been soldered to a male vision of their anatomy, rendering their predicament irresolvable. And it is this "unbudging fatality" that severs the male narrator's sympathy with the female laborers. Repeatedly in Melville's stories throughout this period, his narrators express the futility of sympathy and compassion when the object of pity is beyond help.[8] The "Bartleby" narrator, for example, concluding that the scrivener is a victim of an "innate and incurable disorder," says that "when at last it is perceived that such pity cannot lead to effective succor, common sense bids the soul be rid of it" (*PT,* 29). Similarly, the narrator of "Poor Man's Pudding," overwhelmed by what he perceives as the irremediable condition of Martha Coulter, argues that he can "stay no longer to hear of sorrows for which the sincerest sympathies could give no adequate relief" (*PT,* 295). "The Tartarus of Maids," then, suggests how the problematic circumscription of female possibility by physiological allegory can accommodate male surrender to the "hopelessness" of women's social and economic oppression.

The "Tartarus" observer's threatening identification of female energies with nature's primal, inexorable forces is reinforced by the hyperbolic gynecological imagery he uses to recount his difficult journey through the narrow "Mad Maid's Bellows'-pipe" to the "Dungeon" of a hollow in which the mill is situated (*PT,* 323–325). But a far more positive association between female energies and natural forces had been rendered several years earlier in *Moby-Dick* (1851). Ishmael's encounter with nursing mother whales at the center of "The Grand Armada" (chap. 87) identifies maternal labor with an

omphalic core of nature that is pacific and loving—an identification parodi-
cally subverted in "Benito Cereno" (1855) by Captain Delano's impression of
a nursing slave mother aboard the *San Dominick*. In *Moby-Dick,* the passage
into the maternal scene recalls Tommo and Toby's entry into the Typee Valley (chap. 9); "glid[ing] between two whales into the innermost heart of the
shoal" is metaphorically linked with sliding down a "mountain torrent . . .
into a serene valley lake."[9] Just as Tommo is struck by the lack of apocryphal
violence during his residence among the allegedly brutal Typees (*Typee,* 128),
so Ishmael tells us that at the inner heart of the shoal, "the storms in the
roaring glens between the outermost whales [are] heard, but not felt" (*MD,*
386–387). And just as Tommo feels oppressed by the mountainous enclosure
that locks him into the valley, so Ishmael notes that the dense concentration
of whales guarding the inner circle forms a "living wall that hem[s] [them]
in," affording "no possible chance of escape" (*MD,* 387).

In the center of the shoal, baby whales, innocent of the harpoon, nuzzle
against Ishmael's boat, just as the females of Nukuheva, "[u]nsophisticated
and confiding," first swim to the *Dolly* to welcome their western exploiters
(*Typee,* 14–15).[10] The narrator of *Moby-Dick* gazes beneath the surface, where
the baby whales are sporting, into a deeper and "still stranger" world of nursing mothers, who eye the mariners suspiciously, while the newborn infants
gaze away in blissful reminiscence of the womb, referred to, significantly, as
"foreign parts." The tranquillity of the scene, however, is suddenly shattered by
the harpooner's screams, echoing those of the Typee tappa makers. Queequeg
has mistaken the umbilical cord of a newly born whale for a harpoon line and
is alarmed that mother and cub have been lanced. The narrator explains that
such violations frequently occur in the chaos of the chase; the whale line may
get entangled with an umbilical cord, trapping an infant (*MD,* 387–388).
Once again, masculine penetration into a strange and hitherto unfamiliar
world violates a sacred taboo.

In this scene the intruder is not compelled to flee, but he does instantly
repress the image of violation. Ishmael turns, without transition, from pictur-
ing the trapped cub to an allegorical parallel between this external scene of
peace in the center of turbulence and the tranquillity that he experiences deep
within his own soul, even in the midst of life's "tornadoe[s]." He marvels that
he can still "disport" himself in "mute calm" deep down in this "inland" realm
while "planets of unwaning woe revolve around [him]" (*MD,* 389). In the abstract association between this peaceful feminine realm and an "insular Tahiti"
within his own being, the narrator demystifies the world of female "strange-
ness" by absorbing it into himself, a process in which he seems to repress,
temporarily, the knowledge of its vulnerability to his own aggressive impulses.
However, his latent hostility toward this domain, which he associates with
a landed spot in the midst of tempestuous ocean, continues throughout the

novel. Repeatedly, Ishmael insists that all noble and "earnest thinking" is an effort to remain free of the "treacherous, slavish shore" (*MD*, 107).

This violation of the female realm and the narrator's spontaneous repression of the crime in order to promote his own psychic gratification is reiterated in Ishmael's cavalier footnote, after he speaks of viewing the "subtlest secrets of the seas" and "young Leviathan amours in the deep." His note explains that frequently the harpooner's lance inadvertently pierces a nursing whale's breasts, the "pouring milk and blood . . . discolor[ing] the sea for rods." The lurid picture is followed by the observation, delivered with seemingly callous cupidity, that the milk has been sampled by men, and as it is remarkably "sweet and rich," "might do well with strawberries" (*MD*, 388). The transition dissolves the butchery of the maternal breast into an image of male oral gratification.

This unstable linking of maternal energies with some benign core of nature to provide psychic solace for the male is exploded in the later "Benito Cereno," when Captain Delano stumbles upon a slave woman, lying beneath the bulwarks nursing her infant. Just as Ishmael's whaleboat is engulfed in chaos before entering the tranquil inner core of the shoal, Delano's mind is spinning in currents of confusion before he encounters this "pleasant sort of sunny sight; quite sociable, too" (*PT*, 73). The suspicions that he has begun to entertain regarding the true state of affairs aboard the *San Dominick* are contaminating his optimistic assumptions about humanity, beneficent providence, and the harmony of nature. But his alarms are dispelled at the sight of the woman nursing, just as his anxieties repeatedly are quelled whenever he sees other slaves dutifully engaged in shipboard labors, which they execute with such natural grace and alacrity (*PT*, 83). The animal imagery of a "dam" nursing her "wide-awake fawn," who reaches for the nipple with his "two paws," recalls the nursing whales in *Moby-Dick*. Noticing her observer, the woman at first "start[s] up . . . facing Captain Delano," as if she initially feels violated at being caught in such a vulnerable pose; but then she immediately collects herself and assumes an air of nonchalance. She sweeps up her child as if transported by maternal rapture and covers him with kisses. The effect of the gesture is not wasted upon Delano, who is pleased and soothed by what he perceives as "naked nature . . . pure tenderness and love," mirroring Ishmael's "Leviathan amours in the deep." "These natural sights" reinforce the captain's earlier observations of the tenderness of the slave women aboard, "insensibly deepen[ing] his confidence and ease" (*PT*, 73).

The woman's transported gesture is, of course, merely another act in the histrionic tour de force masterminded by Babo. In fact, when Delano first approaches her the mother is sound asleep, oblivious to the nursing child, who awakens her only with his "vexatious half-grunt" (*PT*, 73). Her loving embrace of the infant, which so tranquilizes Delano, is part of the scenario orchestrated to allay the white captain's suspicions. The deposition that concludes the narrative suggests that Delano has made no contact with the real nature of the women whose loving tenderness so eased his fears. Throughout the revolt and execution of the Spaniards, the women allegedly "sang melancholy songs" designed to intensify the violence of the slaughter; and had the male slaves not restrained them, they would have insisted on torturing their white captors before killing them (*PT,* 112). In this scene, Melville seems intent on deconstructing the association between female energy and a "natural" realm of tranquillity, cutting off a source of psychic support for the masculine ego.

Pierre (1851), the exceptional male intruder in Melville, demonstrates an unmitigated and defenseless openness to the female realm when he interrupts the two Miss Pennies' sewing circle and first gazes upon Isabel's face. He does not repress the implications of the encounter, nor does he view it in a way that gratifies his own ego. Incapable of resisting its powerful effects, he sinks into the scene instead of fleeing it. Melville begins the episode by linking the intrusion to aristocratic social control. According to his mother, Pierre tends "to be a little impatient . . . of these sewing scenes," but she insists that he accompany her to survey the wives and daughters of the Glendenning estate's tenant farmers, the "pretty . . . dames and girls" over whom he "shall one day be lord."[11] Her seemingly innocent promise that he will witness "a rare display of rural red and white" ominously recalls the blood and milk spilling from the harpooned whale's breast, an image that also anticipates the rosy sheets and pale cheeks in the paper mill.

In this scene, Pierre apparently violates some taboo the moment he enters the "room full of [female] faces." As soon as one of the elderly seamstresses welcomes him by name, the tranquillity and concentration of the busy circle is shattered by a "sudden, long-drawn, unearthly girlish shriek," echoing the screams of the tappa makers and Queequeg's cry in *Moby-Dick.* But in this scene the violating lance is cast in the opposite direction: "[T]he sudden shriek seem[s] to split its way clean through [Pierre's] heart, and leave a yawning gap there," suggesting an irreversible psychic effect. Bewildered, Pierre first clutches his mother's arm, just as the "Tartarus" narrator clings to "Old Bach," but he recovers his self-possession and begins to circulate among the women, chatting with them, although far more self-consciously than Tommo among the tappa makers (*Pierre,* 45).

The narrator emphasizes Pierre's profound embarrassment, cloaked by his air of uneasy assurance. Although future lord of the manor, he is victimized by the rigid sexual and class bifurcation of his environment; the women blush and he stammers. Pierre's awkwardness anticipates the far more oppressive uneasiness of Melville's later intruder in "Poor Man's Pudding," who, curious about how the poor really live, imposes himself upon a humble tenant wife but is unprepared to absorb what he discovers. Melville reinforces

Pierre's class consciousness by referring to the women with generic peasant names in the plural; the "Betties, Jennies, Nellies . . . who [skim] the cream, and ma[k]e the butter of the fat farms of Saddle Meadows" are valued solely for their ability to enhance the wealth of the estate by converting its rich resources into marketable products. But Pierre's uneasiness is intensified by his sensitivity to their sexual power, as he curiously feels himself pierced by *their* gaze: "[T]here he stood, target for the transfixing glances of those ambushed archers of the eye" (*Pierre*, 46).

When Pierre's gaze finally falls upon Isabel, his blush turns to pallor. Melville's imagery suggests a powerful force about to erupt from her seemingly placid form as she sits steadily sewing. The velvet border around her neck contracts and expands "as though some choked, violent thing were risen up there within from the warming region of her heart." She betrays her efforts to suppress its release by occasional furtive glances, until "yielding to the irresistible climax of her concealed emotion, . . . she lifts her whole marvelous countenance" and fixes her gaze "unreservedly" upon Pierre's face. For the first time in Melville's intrusion scenes, the male focuses intently upon the face of an individual woman who returns his gaze. He sees an image of "Anguish . . . contend[ing] with Beauty" (*Pierre*, 46–47).

Absorbed, Pierre feels no impulse to flee; instead he "surrender[s]" himself entirely to an "incomprehensible curiosity" and attempts to move nearer to Isabel, longing to hear her voice, some "audible syllable," some words that might make intelligible her ineffable attraction. But his efforts are arrested by his mother's voice calling him away. On the carriage ride home he realizes that "never in his whole existence ha[s] he been so profoundly stirred"; Isabel's face has triggered emotions that take hold of "the deepest roots and subtlest fibres of his being," suggesting both a sexual and spiritual awakening, as well as an unprecedented penetration into his unconscious: "[S]o much the more that it was so subterranean in him, so much the more did he feel its weird inscrutableness" (*Pierre*, 47–49). For the first time in Melville's male intruder scenes, the observer yields entirely to the strange influences that trigger his unconscious energies instead of repressing them, fainting, or resorting to cavalier ego defenses. He is also the last to surrender so completely. The scene suggests what becomes a pattern in the remaining intrusion scenes in Melville's fiction: a "sliding" from social critique of class and labor exploitation to an exploration of the effects of the female on the male psyche. But as numerous critics observe, the rest of the novel traces Pierre's hopeless endeavor to channel the conflicts that Isabel's gaze has awakened into intellectual abstractions and ultimately into a work of art, a project that involves the psychic and physical banishment and petrifaction of the human influence that inspired it.[12]

Male intrusion scenes after *Pierre* continue to render vividly the woman's power to evoke male empathy and pity, as well as a haunting sense of his complicity with the seemingly inexorable forces responsible for her plight. Significantly, except for "Tartarus," the later scenes focus on encounters with individuals, who are more difficult to objectify than groups of women; but like "Tartarus," they dramatize the observers' various strategies for evading the threatening effects of the experience, as if Melville's narrators were refining techniques for resisting the influence to which Pierre succumbs. In these later intrusion scenes, Melville depicts the woman with increasing detachment, implying that the male is incapable of reaching or accurately reading her.

In "Poor Man's Pudding and Rich Man's Crumbs" (1854), Melville attempts to expose the faulty reasoning employed to rationalize poverty and to reconcile the destitute to their own condition. But following the pattern of the *Pierre* scene, the ostensible critique of class and labor oppression in this episode is overshadowed by the male observer's personal struggle to survive the powerful psychic effects of his encounter with an anguished woman, a pattern repeated in "Tartarus." The narrator sets out to test the sanguine conviction of his wealthy host Blandmour that nature bountifully satisfies all the needs of the poor. He calls upon humble tenant farmers, startling Martha Coulter as she quits her washtub in order to prepare the midday meal. This meal is a sacred one for Martha, the only time during the day that she can spend with her laboring husband. The narrator attributes her embarrassment upon his arrival to his fine dress, oblivious to her uneasiness about being imposed upon by a male stranger. But the reader senses the genuine source of her dismay when her husband stands "stock-still" and turns toward her "inquiringly" upon arriving home to find a male visitor (*PT,* 291, 293). His response is understandable if, as one critic argues, Martha already is prostituting herself to their landlord, Squire Teamster, in order to make ends meet.[13] The narrator is struck by her paleness, which he attributes to the penetrating dampness of the cottage and also to a "more secret cause," her visible pregnancy. But there is some other "fathomless heart-trouble" he cannot penetrate (*PT,* 291).

While he gains all the evidence he needs to explode Blandmour's philosophy, during the dinner scene the narrator's curiosity about the life of the poor degenerates from mild discomfort into loathing. Throughout the meal he finds himself unable to swallow their moldy pork and unsavory rice, but the most unpalatable part of the experience is his private interview with Martha after her husband leaves. As she begins to tell him the painful facts of her life, particularly about the death of her children, the narrator resorts to strategies of resistance, including the specious argument that "[w]hen a companion's heart of itself overflows, the best one can do is to do nothing." We sense some struggle as he attempts to avoid sympathetic engagement, first plunging a spoonful of pudding into his mouth to keep from responding,[14] and then finally mastering the impulse by proclaiming that he can "stay no longer to hear of sorrows for which his sincerest sympathies [can] give no adequate relief." He is able to exert an uneasy mastery as voyeur but not as auditor of Martha's story. He flees and purges his guilt in a subsequent indictment of the wealthy Blandmour for presuming to understand the plight of the poor (*PT,* 295, 296).

In "The Piazza" (1856), a disquieting encounter with the female provokes more than guilt or feelings of inadequacy in confronting irremediable sorrow; the threat that Marianna poses is metaphysical. The encounter in this story is triggered solely by the observer's psychic malaise, and in the female realm he enters, physical energies have been absorbed entirely by the mind. It is neither the awesome intricacies of the female body nor Marianna's isolation and economic duress, but her accommodation to an appalling epistemological void that ultimately spurs the narrator's flight.

The narrator's spiritual angst prompts his voyage to "fairy-land" and his fantasy that an encounter with the female who presides there—"the queen of fairies [or] at any rate, some glad mountain-girl"—will provide solace for his discontent, an illusion bolstered by literary associations. The intruder's appearance startles the woman, as in Melville's earlier scenes, and triggers an unlikely association: "She shyly started, like some Tahiti girl, secreted for a sacrifice, first catching sight . . . of Captain Cook" (*PT,* 6, 8–9). Though as Edgar A. Dryden notes, Marianna "is obviously no Fayaway" who will yield graciously and sensuously to the stranger's violation of a taboo that he cannot understand,[15] she *is* sacrificed by the narrator, at least figuratively. Like the intruders in "The Tartarus of Maids" and "Poor Man's Pudding," this narrator is unprepared to witness the expenditure of relentless but fruitless female energy. The unstoppable machine to which the factory women are pinioned in "Tartarus" operates as inexorably in "fairy-land," but it has been severed from the body in order to appropriate the mind. Marianna is condemned to a life of "[t]hinking, thinking—a wheel [she] cannot stop; pure want of sleep it is that turns it." Deprived of active physical or reproductive labor and engaged in endless sewing, "dull woman's work—sitting, sitting, restless sitting," she channels her energy into a ceaseless mental engine (*PT,* 12).

Marianna's substitution of shadows for things suggests that she, like the narrator, has severed her sense impressions from any connection to an "objective" reality, making from them a world of her own. A passing shadow of a cloud becomes a dog she has never seen, just as for the narrator a "strawberry mole" on the hillside becomes Una's cottage in fairy-land (*PT,* 4, 8). But unlike the narrator, Marianna admits that the status of her associations may be purely subjective. When she gazes down the mountainside from her chair by the window, "the white" that shines out against the blue of the fields becomes the home of some "happy being." But even she considers the association a "foolish thought" born of loneliness. Her mental images have as little chance of connecting to any substantial reality as the two hop vines that, "baffled" in their efforts to clasp, grope in "empty air" and fall "back from whence they sprung" (*PT,* 9, 12). It is her unresisting acceptance of the human psyche's inability to connect to any "reality" beyond its own ego-sustaining projections that appalls the narrator, who cannot tolerate the exposure of his own subjective illusions.[16] His refusal to shatter her fantasy about the "happy being" who lives down the mountainside is prompted, not by compassion, but by his own psychic resistance to the truth with which she forever haunts him.

The tale concludes with the narrator's retreat into illusion; he will maintain his view of fairy-land from a distance. As Pierre discovers, the solace of aesthetic detachment is shattered when one penetrates the "Delectable Mountain" too deeply (*Pierre,* 342–346). The observer realizes that his detached perspective is artificial; his piazza chair is a theater box, and the lovely performance is merely his own composition that conceals the "weary face behind it." Only when night falls, dimming the stage lights, is he haunted by a return of the repressed: the "truth [that] comes in with darkness . . . Marianna's face, and many as real a story" (*PT,* 12).

This final distancing of the anguished female through strategies of aesthetic detachment had been anticipated two years earlier in "Sketch Eighth" of "The Encantadas" (1854), in the observer's response to the weary Hunilla. In the narrator's rendering of her story, the adventurous labor of tortoise collecting on an unpopulated island is a source of joy for Hunilla and her husband and brother, despite the hard work. But adventure turns to soulless drudgery after she loses the men she loves; she digs her husband's grave, then spends monotonous days fruitlessly searching for her brother's corpse and gathering sea fowl eggs and small tortoises for her own survival (*PT,* 152–157).

From the moment he first encounters her, the narrator struggles with his alleged inability to depict Hunilla adequately and to convey her misery. In *Israel Potter,* written within months of this story, the narrator resists providing the painful details of Israel's forty-year servitude in London, arguing that "just as extreme suffering, without hope, is intolerable to the victim, so, to others, is its depiction, without some corresponding delusive mitigation."[17] Realistic depiction of pain repels the reader, while sentimentality, as Melville insists in *Pierre,* falsifies the reality. As numerous critics observe, Melville had begun to doubt the writer's ability to convey truth in anyway that is "readable."[18] We witness the aesthetic struggle in "The Encantadas" when the narrator refuses to describe the "two unnamed events" that befell Hunilla during her isolated labors (*PT,* 158). Most readers have assumed that Hunilla was raped by passing seamen, drawing upon the narrator's indirect hints, which even he compares to "sporting with the heart of him who reads," like a cat dallying with a lizard before devouring it (*PT,* 156). The narrator's unwillingness to report the facts resonates with his strategies for distancing Hunilla from himself and the reader throughout the episode.

The observer never hears Hunilla's story from her own lips, since she speaks a "strange language" that must be translated by an intermediary. The narrator explains that he would like to present her to the reader as a work of art, since "crayons, tracing softly [her] melancholy lines, would best depict the mournful image of the dark-damasked Chola widow" (*PT*, 152). Throughout the sketch, he attempts to render Hunilla's real experience inaccessible, just as unknowable as the life of the model who poses for the chair portrait in *Pierre* (*Pierre*, 197, 353). The narrator tells us that in his encounter with Hunilla, he sees only her "soul's lid, and the strange ciphers thereon engraved," that "all within" is withheld. But the actual agents of concealment must be his own strained repression and narrative detachment from her emotions, since he withholds facts that Hunilla must have divulged. Despite his insistence that her "pride's timidity" kept her from revealing her strongest emotions, the narrator records the release of her passionate grief: "[She] struggled as against the writhed coilings of a snake, and cringing suddenly, leaped up, repeating in impassioned pain, 'I buried him, my life, my soul!'" (*PT*, 155). It is the narrator, in fact, who represses Hunilla's grief. He reports that she buried her husband with "half-unconscious automatic motions," an account that could not come from Hunilla herself (*PT*, 155). Nor is it likely that she would describe the deaths of her husband and brother with the imagery of aesthetic detachment that the narrator employs: "Death in a silent picture ... [s]o instant was the scene, so trance-like in its mild pictorial effect ... that Hunilla gazed and gazed, nor raised a finger or a wail" (*PT*, 154). He focuses upon her "Spanish and Indian grief, which would not visibly lament," and sees "nature's pride subduing nature's torture." While Marianna's and Martha's unlocking of the "soul's lid" spurs the narrators' flight, Hunilla's enforced silence enables the narrator in this case to continue sketching her portrait until she rides out of sight (*PT*, 162).

In *Pierre*, Isabel's grief ultimately triggers the abstract intellectual struggle that painfully, slowly, but inexorably dissolves her role in the protagonist's drama; but in "The Encantadas," the woman's painful story is repressed altogether through strategies of narrative detachment, enabling the observer to appropriate her from the start as a symbol for his own abstract theme. In his rendering, Hunilla represents faithful humanity deserted by the faithless heavens, a suggestion reiterated in the narrator's allusions to the vain rituals of her "Romish faith" and her "crucifix worn featureless, like an ancient graven knocker long plied in vain" (*PT*, 155, 161). The sequence of male intrusion scenes in Melville traces a similar pattern of exposure, suppression, and consequent abstraction. Melville moves his intruder figure from the experience of violating a realm perceived as sacred and alien, through a devastating openness to its influence, and finally to the mastery of strategies for psychic and aesthetic detachment. This sequence of episodes suggests a pattern of evasion of the feminine on the part of Melville's male characters, triggered by combined feelings of fear and guilt. The fear appears to be rooted in the threat of confinement, arrest, and ego dissolution—the same threats that prompted Melville's first intrusive observer, Tommo, to flee the bower of the Typees. All of the female domains in these episodes are enveloped in images of enclosure (with the possible exception of Norfolk Island in "The Encantadas," although it too is enclosed by miles of ocean that Hunilla cannot traverse). The fear of ego dissolution is exacerbated by an unsettling perception that the female body is energized by forces that are vital, relentless, impersonal, and indifferent to human will or desire—as awesome, sacred, and alien as nature herself. Finally, the women in Melville's later stories appear to provoke dread by their accommodation to conditions that strike the observer as philosophically intolerable.

The narratives suggest two sources of the intruders' guilt: a haunting sense of complicity with the forces that victimize or oppress women and a more deeply rooted, less conscious suspicion that male penetration of the female domain is, by definition, an act of aggression. In stories like "Tartarus," where the narrator is a client who profits from the cheap envelopes produced by the factory women, or in "Poor Man's Pudding," where he is a curious aristocrat hosted by a wealthy landlord, the grounds for complicity and guilt are self-evident. The voyeurs are compelled to evade recognition of their own contributions, however indirect, to the seemingly irremediable anguish that they encounter. But because in almost all of these scenes the male intrusions are unsolicited and uninvited by the women, who are preoccupied with activities and concerns that exclude men, the reader may suspect that merely to enter is to intrude, and that to penetrate is to violate.

To what extent does Melville identify with the guilt and fear that motivates his characters, or to what extent does he subject their anxious evasions to authorial critique and irony? The recurrence of motifs described in these eight scenes, in stories that, according to most critics, vary in degree and extent of authorial distance, suggests that Melville is vividly dramatizing the full range of gender anxieties rooted in his own experience in mid-nineteenth-century American culture, and especially in female-dominated households. He appears equally illuminating in his display of the range of ego defenses unconsciously triggered by these anxieties.

Notes

1. Herman Melville, "The Paradise of Bachelors and the Tartarus of Maids," in *The Piazza Tales and Other Prose Pieces, 1839–1860,* ed. Harrison Hayford et al.,

vol. 9 of *The Writings of Herman Melville* (Evanston and Chicago: Northwestern University Press and The Newberry Library, 1987), 326–330. All references to prose in *The Piazza Tales* are hereafter cited parenthetically as *PT*.

2. David S. Reynolds argues that Melville's increasingly sensational and grotesque assaults on his narrators is a strategy that furthers his "bitter aim of attacking America's Conventional culture." The grotesque represents his transition from traditional reform literature to the "suprapolitical literary realm in which he uses popular sensational imagery to assault the staidly Conventional" (*Beneath the American Renaissance: The Subversive Imagination on the Age of Emerson and Melville* [Cambridge: Harvard University Press, 1988], 292–294). This discussion in part explores some of the unsettling implications of increasing aesthetic detachment inherent in Melville's depiction of male encounters within the female realm.

3. Even though I am tracing the development of a motif in Melville over time, I do not discuss the eight intrusion scenes in the order of publication. Instead, my organization is designed to highlight comparisons and contrasts that I consider most significant for my thesis. As the discussion will indicate, I see distinctions between intrusion scenes written before *Pierre* and those written after, although there are continuities throughout the eight. I first analyze two pairs of thematically related scenes, each juxtaposing one scene from the earlier and one from the later group. Then I discuss the pivotal scene from *Pierre* and comment upon scenes in three stories published later.

4. Herman Melville, *Typee: A Peep at Polynesian Life*, ed. Harrison Hayford, Hershel Parker, and G. Thomas Tanselle, vol. 1 of *The Writings of Herman Melville* (Evanston and Chicago: Northwestern University Press and The Newberry Library, 1968), 85; hereafter cited parenthetically as *Typee*.

5. See, for example, Mitchell Breitwieser, "False Sympathy in Melville's *Typee*," *American Quarterly* 34 (1982): 408.

6. Two recent articles represent the divergent implications that the allegory has suggested to critics. Philip Young argues that the female anatomy/gestation imagery of the papermaking process, read in the context of Melville's own concerns regarding birth control, explodes the claim that the story has anything to do with "the enslavement of females to mills and factories" ("The Machine in Tartarus: Melville's *Inferno*," *American Literature* 63 [1991]: 223). For Robyn Wiegman, on the other hand, the papermaking machine, which is fertilized by an albuminous fluid flowing from testicular vats, represents not the female body alone but heterosexuality. In this reading, the male appropriates the female body for both biological and economic re-production ("Melville's Geography of Gender," *American Literary History* 1 [1989]: 743–744).

7. Michael Paul Rogin, *Subversive Genealogy: The Politics and Art of Herman Melville* (New York: Knopf, 1983), 205.

8. In some of Melville's tales that do not primarily involve encounters with women (e.g., "Bartleby, the Scrivener," "Benito Cereno," "Cock-A-Doodle-Doo!"), the narrator or protagonist similarly appears to repress, retreat from, or evade the darker implications of suffering, despair, or incomprehensibility in others. The response is not gender determined; rather, it appears to be gender intensified. (Many readers, however, have identified what they consider distinctively "feminine" qualities in both Bartleby and Cereno.)

9. Herman Melville, *Moby-Dick; or, The Whale*, ed. Harrison Hayford, Hershel Parker, and G. Thomas Tanselle, vol. 6 of *The Writings of Herman Melville*

(Evanston and Chicago: Northwestern University Press and The Newberry Library, 1988), 386; hereafter cited parenthetically as *MD*.

10. Laurie Robertson-Lorant associates the nuzzling whales with the "amphibious young creatures" with whom Tommo plays in the Typee lagoon ("Melville's Embrace of the Invisible Woman," *Centennial Review* 34 [1990]: 401). But unlike the lagoon episode, where the Typee maidens control the sensuous encounter, both "The Grand Armada" and the *Dolly* scenes terminate in imagery of violation on the part of the male intruder.

11. Herman Melville, *Pierre; or, The Ambiguities*, ed. Harrison Hayford, Hershel Parker, and G. Thomas Tanselle, vol. 7 of *The Writings of Herman Melville* (Evanston and Chicago: Northwestern University Press and The Newberry Library, 1971), 45; hereafter cited parenthetically as *Pierre*.

12. See, for example, Kris Lakey, "The Despotic Victim: Gender and Imagination in *Pierre*," *ATQ*, n.s., 4 (1990): 67–76; and Leland S. Person Jr., *Aesthetic Headaches: Women and a Masculine Poetics in Poe, Melville, and Hawthorne* (Athens: University of Georgia Press, 1988), 70–87.

13. Beryl Rowland, "Sitting Up with a Corpse: Malthus according to Melville in 'Poor Man's Pudding and Rich Man's Crumbs,'" *Journal of American Studies* 6 (1972): 76–78.

14. The narrator's impulse toward orality, in order to repress the scene of female suffering, parallels Ishmael's fantasy of strawberries and cream, which obscures the harpooned breast of the nursing whale. I would like to acknowledge my colleague, Maire Mullins, for calling my attention to this association.

15. Edgar A. Dryden, "From the Piazza to the Enchanted Isles: Melville's Textual Rovings," in *After Strange Texts: The Role of Theory in the Study of Literature*, ed. Gregory S. Jay and David L. Miller (University: University of Alabama Press, 1985), 57.

16. Nancy Fredricks argues that Marianna's "realist" empiricism is juxtaposed to the narrator's "romantic" idealism ("Melville and the Woman's Story," *Studies in American Fiction* 19 [1991]: 50). The fact that Marianna's sense impressions are more real to her than any abstractions they may signify supports this observation. But Melville, I would argue, suggests that the things she does not literally perceive, such as the shaggy dog Tray or the "happy being" down the mountainside, become for her, as for the idealist, the most significant entities in life. The starkness of her vision lies in the fact that she, unlike the idealist, entertains no confidence regarding their ontological status. Fredricks notes that "[i]f Marianna is 'deluded' about 'reality,' she is no more so than the narrator is" (50), but Melville wants to insist that, unlike Marianna, the narrator will not acknowledge the implications and extent of his delusion.

17. Herman Melville, *Israel Potter: His Fifty Years of Exile*, ed. Harrison Hayford, Hershel Parker, and G. Thomas Tanselle, vol. 8 of *The Writings of Herman Melville* (Evanston and Chicago: Northwestern University Press and The Newberry Library, 1982), 161.

18. See, for example, Nina Baym, "Melville's Quarrel with Fiction," *PMLA* 94 (1979): 909–923.

JOHN WENKE

Narrative Self-Fashioning and the Play of Possibility

And though essaying but a sportive sail, I was driven from my course, by a blast resistless.

—*Mardi*

As he "wrote right on; and so doing, got deeper and deeper into himself" (*Mardi* 595), Melville became more confident of his purpose and less tolerant of any impingement on his designs. Irked by Murray's continuing suspicion that Herman Melville was "an imposter shade" and fixed on the right "determinations" of his self-vaunted instinct, Melville informed Murray of a design to be "blunt." Melville's third work would "in downright earnest [be] a 'Romance of Polynisian Adventure'—But why this? The truth is, Sir, that the reiterated imputation of being a romancer in disguise has at last pricked me into a resolution to show those who may take any interest in the matter, that a *real* romance of mine is no Typee or Omoo, & is made of different stuff altogether" (*Correspondence* 105–106, Melville's emphasis). Melville was intent upon engaging "that play of freedom & invention accorded only to the Romancer & poet," thereby mining Polynesia's "rich poetical material." In explaining his artistic evolution, Melville registered "invincible distaste" for his "narrative of *facts*":

Well: proceeding in my narrative of *facts* I began to feel an invincible distaste for the same; & a longing to plume my pinions

Melville's Muse: Literary Creation and the Forms of Philosophical Fiction (Kent: Ohio State University Press, 1995): pp. 27–46. © 1995 The Kent State University Press.

for a flight, & felt irked, cramped & fettered by plodding along
with dull common places. . . . My romance I assure you is no dish
water nor its model borrowed from the Circulating Library. . . .
It opens like a true narrative . . . & the romance & poetry of the
thing thence grow continually, till it becomes a story wild enough
I assure you & with a meaning too. (106)[1]

Even in this "blunt" manifesto, Melville fails to do justice to the extremity
of *Mardi*'s departure. It does not, for example, open like a "true narrative."
Rather, from the earliest chapters, Melville's "play of freedom & invention" issues in the narrator's wild, rhapsodic speculations. From the outset
the overreaching philosophical self appears full-blown: the narrator takes
center stage, decries his boredom, and vents his disgust with the everyday
commonplace actualities of ship and crew. The way of the *Arcturion* was "a
weary one . . . Never before had the ocean appeared so monotonous; thank
fate, never since" (4). Because of his education, the narrator is estranged
from the crew; his "occasional polysyllable . . . [and] remote, unguarded
allusions to Belles-Lettres affairs" (14) make the narrator a learned outcast.
Accepting his isolation, he repays the favor by dismissing the "flat repetitions of long-drawn yarns. . . . Staler than stale ale." He eschews "Bill
Marvel's stories" and "Ned Ballad's songs" (5). Melville projects his own
impatience with high-sea adventure yarns into a narrator who distinctly
defines his aspirations in terms of intellectual fulfillment. If Tommo in
Typee deserts the *Dolly* because his belly is not satisfied, then the narrator
of *Mardi* resolves to desert the *Arcturion* because his mind is malnourished.
Even the captain, a fine nautical man in all respects, cannot "talk sentiment
or philosophy." Nor can his shipmates "page [him] a quotation from Burton
on Blue Devils" (5). No one on board is "precisely to [his] mind" (4).

Like Ahab in *Moby-Dick,* the narrator redefines the purpose of the voyage. While not heaped and tasked by the inscrutable malignity of brute forces,
the narrator of *Mardi* is impelled by ennui to figure himself as an explorer on
the high seas of consciousness and erudition. In a "willful mood" (7) he climbs
the masthead, and in a passage that prefigures Ishmael's masthead reverie in
Moby-Dick, the narrator divorces himself from the day-to-day concerns of
life at sea. If "The Mast-Head" examines the death-dealing incompatibility
between workaday actuality and mystical meditation, especially as the slip of
an inch can bring one to plunge into "Descartian vortices" (*Moby-Dick* 158–
159), then the "Foot-in-Stirrup" chapter of *Mardi* examines the exhilarating
attraction of the mystical world of mind, especially insofar as the visionary
lure provides an experiential displacement of the same old song of social contexts. In his frenzied vision, the narrator spins the materials of the ensuing
fiction. His romantic vision counterpoints the forecastle yarns. The source of

the succeeding tale is to be found more in mind than in extrinsic fact. In craving a world of expansive consciousness, he imagines a "dream-land" (*Mardi* 7) located on the magical margins of mind. Somewhere to the west, "loosely laid down upon the charts" (*Mardi* 7), this imaginary space displaces his present tedium. He imagines what the ship could never give him—a new, unexplored world exotic enough to engage, if not satisfy, his voracious appetite for the unknown.

Significantly, this visionary world ranges into view through a series of exotic images:

> In the distance what visions were spread! The entire western horizon high piled with gold and crimson clouds; airy arches, domes, and minarets; as if the yellow, Moorish sun were setting behind some vast Alhambra. Vistas seemed leading to worlds beyond. To and fro, and all over the towers of this Nineveh in the sky, flew troops of birds. Watching them long, one crossed my sight, flew through a low arch, and was lost to view. My spirit must have sailed in with it; for directly, as in a trance, came upon me the cadence of mild billows laving a beach of shells, the waving of boughs, and the voices of maidens, and the lulled beatings of my own dissolved heart, all blended together. (7–8)

As in the "Time and Temples" chapter, the moment of imagined transcendence is depicted through the Platonic image of a bird. Here the "low arch" through which the bird flies separates two competing experiential realms and two competing forms of narrative. The narrator's spirit soars with the bird, creating the spiritual imperative that will lead the body to follow. As in Rabelais's travelogue, one gets the sense in *Mardi* that new worlds are being spun out of the mind. Indeed, the narrator's visionary trance manifests how *ideas* determine not merely the exotic nature of place but the perimeters of behavior. Here Melville presents the creative moment of transfer. The quotidian is left behind, and the narrator figuratively loses hold, though he does not tumble into the Cartesian swirl but instead lifts into poetic rapture. For the narrator, the desire for philosophic vent cannot be dissociated from the mind-moving medium of poetic invention. What is most crucial here—and what will serve Melville in multiple ways not only in *Mardi* but in *Moby-Dick, Pierre, The Confidence-Man,* and *Clarel*—is the self-defining and self-realizing reach of the narrator's play of mind. His visionary experience both displaces the quotidian and imbues him with the psychological authority to pursue a life dedicated to his adventurous muse. The power of intuition makes pictures in the seer's mind. In this masthead moment, such visionary manifestations are peculiarly without foundation. Nevertheless, the vision supplies the narrator's imperative to desert, though each momentous step away from historical context creates its own ironic entanglement: he leaves a doomed ship but feels guilt; later he rescues the mysterious maiden Yillah but commits murder to do so; and, subsequently, Yillah's disappearance binds him as both pursuer and pursued.

The lesson deriving from the narrator's vision is clear: the imperatives of the starved philosophical self can only be answered by the narrator's attempt to estrange himself from his personal, cultural, and historical past. Even though this leap into romance leads frequently to the spinning out of tedious abstractions, Melville's great discovery in *Mardi* resides in the fictional possibilities inherent in the dramatization of ideas. Melville's career-long alternating expression or repression of this urge becomes a means for measuring his standing with the book-buying public. What Melville called *Mardi*'s "metaphysical ingredients (for want of a better term)" did in fact repel his audience. This was followed by his conscious, though not complete, suppression of "metaphysics . . . [and] conic-sections" in favor of "cakes & ale" in *Redburn*, which allowed him to recapture the confidence of reviewers and readers (*Correspondence* 131–132). Similarly, following the commercial disaster of *Pierre*, Melville's success as, for the most part, an anonymous author in the relatively lucrative periodical market derived from his ability to contain his materials within the acceptable generic confines of sketch and tale.[2] In *Mardi*, Melville had trouble with his readers largely because he was trying to invent his own form: he sought to adapt the conventions of the exotic romantic voyage of search and discovery to the cause of metaphysical improvisation and satirical anatomy. In the resulting hybrid form—a compendium of competing if not self-defeating intentions—action and character were either subservient to, or representations of, the narrator's effusive, unfolding consciousness. *Mardi*'s action essentially provides the excuse or point of departure for presenting the narrator's *experience* of his own consciousness, a concern that Melville successfully balances throughout *Moby-Dick*, especially in Ishmael's presentation of the cetology material as basis for analogy and symbol.

The early chapters of *Mardi* most fully depict the narrator's experience of consciousness as he confronts extreme physical situations. On the masthead, his elevated perspective and isolation lead him to mystical visions. Twice the narrator must contend with an oppressive meteorological condition, a calm at sea. While the narrator is still on the *Arcturion*, the calm induces a wildly skeptical flurry of thought; later adrift with Jarl in an open boat, the narrator meditates briefly on the relationship between objective and subjective frames of reference. As with the scene on the masthead, Melville uses these set pieces to explore the metaphysical implications of the narrator's circumstance. Each scene demonstrates the presentation of actions that exist solely to showcase the narrator's cogitations. Melville thus elevates the flux of consciousness itself to a principle of narrative self-fashioning; these moments offer extensions of his earlier preoccupation with Tommo's limitations of perspective in *Typee*, and they point ahead to Ishmael's inquisitive excursions in *Moby-Dick* and to the narrator's verbal gymnastics in *The Confidence-Man*.

A chapter in *Mardi*, "A Calm," succinctly dramatizes the fusion of the narrator's intellectual aspiration and the author's aesthetic experimentation. The dullness of workaday life at sea (and for Melville the banality of the travel narrative) stand in direct opposition to the possibilities for pursuing wild, speculative vistas (and for Melville the profundity of writing Truth). A calm at sea provides the quintessential intensification of all that the narrator most abhors. Its vacuity diametrically opposes his intellectual ferment. The calm appears as a static meteorological counterpoint to the involuted world of psychological flux. The physical locale ironically stirs a whirl of thought; the calm "unsettles his mind; tempts him to recant his belief in the eternal fitness of things; in short, almost makes an infidel of him" (9). In this suspended state, the narrator grows "madly skeptical" and begins to doubt his senses. In the face of the blank sea, he thinks of "Priestley on Necessity" and seeks the solace of philosophical determinism. Such a posture, however, is of no avail to the skeptic. He knows that the thing to do is to endure the calm; but he cannot bring himself to accept such a compromise. Indeed, the play of mind feeds on itself, frustrating the thinker with repeated admissions of his unacceptable impotence. This scene presents the first self-conscious expression in Melville's work of the tangled relationship between skepticism and stoicism, on the one hand, and the opposing psychological imperative to pursue a condition of absolute felicity, on the other. The calm functions as a foil for Melville to engage the complex he most wishes to consider: the metaphysical implication of an oppressive moment.

The second "trying-out" of the calm extends Melville's interest with placing his center of narrative consciousness in the experiential context of sheer vacancy and existential blankness. After deserting the ship, the narrator and Jarl become caught in the doldrums, an area conspicuously missing what Sir Thomas Browne calls "flux and reflux," the ebb and flow of process (20, 78–79). Here the natural world lacks gradation, distinction, dynamism: "Every thing was fused into the calm: sky, air, water, and all. Not a fish was to be seen. The silence was that of a vacuum. No vitality lurked in the air. And this inert blending and brooding of all things seemed gray chaos in conception" (48). Figuratively, the calm threatens the life of the intellect. Melville's fusion of fiction and philosophy depends not on "inert blending" but on an active interpenetration of extrinsic and cognitive realms. And that is what the narrator attempts as the tale develops: he takes an experiential dead end and brings it to intellectual life. The calm may originally be "gray chaos in conception," but the thinking mind re-forms such recalcitrant material and uses it to focus *Mardi*'s central concern: the revelation of the thinking mind, now in solipsistic isolation, later in a dialogue of projected intellectual abstractions.

What animates these two scenes, and provides unity not of execution but of purpose, is Melville's commitment to rendering the active play of intelligence. The narrating mind comes to know itself in the act of forging relationships that seem true or valid in the moment. In *Typee* such a process is implicit in Tommo's engagement with epistemological quandaries; the mystery surrounding Tommo's condition provides the basis of action and meditation. In *Mardi* the mind's very process of thinking constitutes the generative force of action. In *Mardi*'s paradigmatic scenes, the narrator's experience of a particular phenomenon suggests possibilities for thought, possibilities for reaction. As the scene changes, the thinker's very engagement with a new set of circumstances displaces the previous moment of insight. With these scenes on the calm, Melville has it both ways, for the encounter with nothingness is in itself an experience that stirs thought. Though there is a danger that the calm, by its very inertness, may never deliver the thinker to the next moment, a calm at sea partakes of an encompassing meteorological process and will eventually pass.

Nevertheless, Melville's interest in dramatizing the narrator's response to vacancy highlights the symbiotic relationship between phenomena and consciousness, with the preeminent focus on reaction over action. Later in the narrative, Taji's very phrase, "the world of mind" (557), suggests what has been implicitly true all along: there exists a vital link between object and subject, between the world of phenomena and the realm of perception.[3] Behind this strategy is the desire to make knowledge of the self through knowledge of the world the locus of interest. At stake here is Melville's ongoing attempt, first fully dramatized in *Mardi,* to present as an explicit fictional subject the protean qualities of human consciousness, with the distinct expectation that the formulation of one moment might be undone by the next. Melville's absolutists—among them Taji, Ahab, Pierre, Celio, Mortmain, Ungar, and possibly, Vere—become dangerous precisely because they refuse to adjust, or reformulate, the relation of subject to the changing world of objects. For Taji to insist that he must regain Yillah or for Ahab to insist that the White Whale has one fixed signification is for both men to preempt the potential validity of future experiences and future perceptions. Their kind of consciousness can be characterized as "inert blending" (*Mardi* 48). They eschew the challenge of what Redburn calls "a moving world" (157), in which the "flux and reflux" of experience presents repeated possibilities for reseeing the world and reconstituting the self. In *Mardi* the two depictions of the calm at sea, then, allow Melville to explore the reciprocity between phenomena and epistemology, brute fact and the pursuit of self-knowledge. The treatments of the calm are, in fact, early renderings of the epistemological centers of *Moby-Dick*—the "story of Narcissus" and "The Doubloon" chapter (5, 430–435). Any perception is one version of a multitude of self-reflecting configurations. The horror is that no further reading may be possible unless the world resumes its protean condition.

Early in *Mardi*, then, Melville was experimenting with developing techniques that would allow him to marry fiction and metaphysics. As we have seen, the narrator's trance on the masthead and the two renderings of a calm provide set pieces in which psychological reaction takes precedence over the complexities of the action itself. In fact, these scenes are bereft of dramatic activity, for instead Melville focuses on the mind's capacity to create meaning or, better yet, to create the speculative form within which meaning takes shape. Central is the critical intelligence responding to impressions from the human eye. For Melville the world is alive with teasing, though shifting and perhaps unknowable, signification; without the assurance of transcendental beneficence, the perceiver is loosed into a realm of perceptual "flux and reflux."

The outgrowth of using narrative as a vehicle for rendering conciousness leads Melville to make consciousness itself the source of dialectic. In the early sequences of *Mardi*, Melville develops two distinctly identifiable narrative voices that stand in dialectical tension. The narrator oscillates between speaking as a fraternal genialist and a solipsistic isolationist. Prior to the narrator's loss of Yillah, both voices appear intermittently. A moment's mood tends to determine one's perceptions; one's reading subsequently informs behavior. While the narrator's fraternal strain, which links him to communal life in a historical and social context, appears in his highly selective federation with Jarl, his solipsistic strain, which reflects anticommunal life in an ahistorical absolutistic context, becomes manifest in his bitter estrangement from ship life.

The narrator's genial voice celebrates the unifying nature of humor and verbal play. At one point the narrator, gushing effusively over the amiable side of a shark, brings his meditation to a joyous close: "Now hate is a thankless thing. So, let us only hate hatred; and once give love play, we will fall in love with a unicorn" (41). The narrator also engages in a whimsical display of learning. Commenting on Jarl's grave demeanor, the narrator reflects, "But how account for the Skyeman's gravity? Surely, it was based upon no philosophic taciturnity; he was nothing of an idealist; an aerial architect; a constructor of flying buttresses" (36). Later the narrator forces a comparison between Jarl and Bishop Berkeley, thereby debunking an idealist who also keeps a matter-of-fact eye on the main chance: "[H]onest Jarl was nevertheless exceedingly downright and practical in all hints and proceedings concerning [the ship]. Wherein, he resembled my Right Reverend friend, Bishop Berkeley—truly, one of your lords spiritual—who, metaphysically speaking, holding all objects to be mere optical delusions, was, notwithstanding, extremely matter-of-fact in all matters touching matter itself" (63).

The narrator is at other times given to visionary and self-isolating ful-minations. Related to his solipsism is the desire to assert his will and thereby dominate others. He takes control of the *Parki* and turns Jarl, Samoa, and Annatoo into subservient crew members. He speaks in the

> mild, firm tone of a superior; being anxious, at once to assume the unquestioned supremacy. . . . Our course determined, and the command of the vessel tacitly yielded up to myself, the next thing done was to put every thing in order. . . . I felt no little importance upon thus assuming for the first time in my life, the command of a vessel at sea. The novel circumstances of the case only augmented this feeling . . . I was owner, as well as commander of the craft I sailed. (96–97)

In *Mardi*, Melville does not maintain anything approaching consistency of voice. Instead, these conflicting voices help him to extend the possibilities of fictional form, especially as the genialist or the solipsist come to suggest metaphysical qualities of consciousness. Exemplifying this are two parallel narrative excursions—articulations of the genialist and the solipsist, respec-tively—each dealing with states of existence outside the diachronic movement of the narrative. In each instance, the narrator employs the allusive catalog to show his relationship to the great thinkers of the past.[4] In both cases Melville uses the present tense to separate his materials from the ongoing retrospec-tive narrative. In the chapter "A King for a Comrade," the narrator presents a vision of a congenial afterlife. The contrasting case occurs in the "Dreams" chapter, where the solipsistic narrator, by now named Taji, suffers miserably in a prison. The scene could only take place sometime after the narrative con-cludes with Taji being chased "over an endless sea" (654).

In a fascinating passage in "A King for a Comrade," which echoes ele-ments of style and theme in *Religio Medici*, the genial narrator seeks to merge (rather than dissociate) the immediate time-bound world of sense experience with the exotic, rhapsodic world of transcendent thought. Rather than try-ing to escape the commonplace, the narrator takes the strange and invests it with the homely and familiar. In effect he personalizes an imagined afterlife.[5] The narrator's meditation on Jarl's ancestry and the interrelationship among mortals culminates with a densely allusive vision of a federated and congenial afterlife, replete with cameo appearances by many of the great dead:

> All of us have monarchs and sages for kinsmen; nay, angels and archangels for cousins. . . . Thus all generations are blended: and heaven and earth of one kin. . . . All things form but one whole; the universe a Judea, and God Jehovah its head. Then no more let us

start with affright. In a theocracy, what is to fear? . . . No custom is strange; no creed is absurd; no foe, but who will in the end prove a friend. In heaven, at last, our good, old, white-haired father Adam will greet all alike, and sociality forever prevail. Christian shall join hands between Gentile and Jew; grim Dante forget his Infernos, and shake sides with fat Rabelais; and monk Luther, over a flagon of old nectar, talk over old times with Pope Leo. . . . Then shall the Stagirite and Kant be forgotten, and another folio than theirs be turned over for wisdom; even the folio now spread with horoscopes as yet undeciphered, the heaven of heavens on high. (12–13)

This vision of a happy afterlife finds an experiential counterpoint in the "Dreams" chapter. "Dreams" is a digressive chapter that functions as a set-piece divorced from the ongoing action. By offering a self-portrait of Taji, "Dreams" succinctly presents the culmination of Melville's use of the solipsistic, absolutistic voice in *Mardi.* Taji's self-exhaustion has derived explicitly from his overindulgence in philosophical speculation. The unrestricted search for truth, which initiated his flight from the *Arcturion,* not only leaves him physically imprisoned but psychologically wasted. Indeed, Melville's first philosophical narrative demonstrates the danger of the unimpeded metaphysical quest, a danger emphatically reinforced in *Moby-Dick* and *Pierre.* Taji's extreme dedication to learning comes at the expense of his relationship to the limited, but life-sustaining, domain of social contexts. Whirled by the hyperactive flights of his soul, the megalomaniac Taji experiences panoramic vistas that paradoxically become self-restricting:

And my soul sinks down to the depths, and soars to the skies; and comet-like reels on through such boundless expanses, that methinks all the worlds are my kin, and I invoke them to stay in their course. Yet, like a mighty three-decker, towing argosies by scores, I tremble, gasp, and strain in my flight, and fain would cast off the cables that hamper. (367)

Falling prey to the competing claims of contentious, unintegrated voices, Taji journeys into the world of mind and gains access to many nations, times, places, and authors.[6] Consequently, he not only "reels on through such boundless expanses" but comes to identify with the sources of all knowledge. He becomes, as it were, lost in an intellectual vortex. "[F]ull with a thousand souls," Taji struggles with a library of voices. The theater of the mind engages in an endless, self-defeating drama of dialectic. It is here that Melville's use of the allusive catalog becomes more than a technique for learned display, a means of evoking a litany of ideational contexts, for here Melville dramatizes the debilitating psychological effects of the solipsistic and absolutistic intellectual pursuit. Taji winds up talking interminably to himself in a grim repetition of ruminative thought. Such broad knowledge becomes in itself the imprisoning force. Taji consorts with Homer, Anacreon, Hafiz, Shakespeare, Ossian, Milton, and Petrarch. In his mind "St. Paul . . . argues the doubts of Montaigne; Julian the Apostate cross-questions Augustine; and Thomas-a-Kempis unrolls his old black letters for all to decipher" (367). His play of mind includes such figures as Zeno, Democritus, Pyrrho, Plato, Proclus, Verulam, Zoroaster, Virgil, and Sidney. Taji's "memory is a life beyond birth; my memory, my library of the Vatican, its alcoves all endless perspectives" (367–368). In this remarkable chapter Melville reveals that Taji's mind has become self-restrictive, his intellectual absolutism self-exhausting. His mental growth, while perhaps stunning in its allusive reach, succeeds finally in accentuating Taji's estrangement from other human beings. Total immersion in the "Vatican" of knowledge severs him from social experience.

Melville's congenial and solipsistic narrative voices reflect polarized attributes of being. In the two cases just examined, the narrator constructs a world that mirrors his informing psychological disposition. His vision of the afterlife depicts a socially democratizing world in which great differences in viewpoint become the prelude to an all-encompassing communalism. Taji's imprisonment in "Dreams" derives from a paradoxically willed necessity. He becomes the victim of what he most longed to be: "My cheek blanches white while I write; I start at the scratch of my pen; my own mad brood of eagles devours me; fain would I unsay this audacity; but an iron-mailed hand clenches mine in a vice, and prints down every letter in my spite" (368).

Throughout his career, Melville refined his ability to bring into dialectical relationship characters that can be identified through voices and visions that are, on the one hand, genial and relativistic and, on the other, solipsistic and absolutistic. The narrative voices of *Mardi* prefigure the more finely realized conflicts in voice and vision that are later expressed in Ishmael and Ahab, young Pierre (with Lucy) and the older Pierre (with Isabel), the lawyer and Bartleby, Claret and Nathan, Rolfe and Ungar. Through these distinct voices, Melville makes character, perception, and behavior sources for dialectic. In "Bartleby, the Scrivener," for example, the mystery underlying Bartleby's naysaying absolutism releases in the lawyer a nagging series of interpretations, no one of which answers, any one of which conducts him to the next unsatisfying attempt.[7]

While Melville's experiments in *Mardi* with the ideational play of possibility and the dramatization of competing voices can certainly be viewed as part of the emerging intellectual process that later generates Ishmael and Ahab, we are nevertheless closer to Melville's creative rhythms in *Mardi* if we see these voices as emerging from spontaneous, unintegrated impulses seeking expression in narrative form. The competing voices are attempts to dramatize distinctly philosophical moods. In *Mardi,* Melville grafts philosophical aspirations to his tried technique of the first-person narrative, persistently accommodating philosophical concerns to the demands of his plot. Whereas in the early sequences of *Mardi* the narrator inhabits a state of psychological free fall between the demands of geniality and solipsism, Melville moves the plot to the moment at which the two voices will no longer be reflected in the narrator's diachronic rendering of events.

In presenting *Mardi*'s major dramatic action—the discovery and rescue of Yillah—Melville allows his narrator to undergo a self-generated and self-fashioned ontological revolution that estranges him from the social world and its rhetoric of fraternal interactions. In repudiating his historical past, the narrator aspires to cosmic status. Melville's presentation of the Yillah episodes can be seen as the means whereby he brings his first absolutist into full figure. If the narrator's boredom on the *Arcturion* launches his philosophical quest and Taji's incarceration in "Dreams" stands as a paradoxically never-ending ending of this process, then the irreversible moment of ontological, intellectual, and rhetorical transfer begins when the narrator meets the high priest Aleema, who is conducting the mysterious Yillah toward sacrificial death. The narrator intervenes, kills Aleema, and rescues the maiden.

The creation of Yillah marks a crucial moment in Melville's career. The figure of Yillah fuses a host of literal and symbolic attributes. Merrell R. Davis links Yillah's literary antecedents with La Motte-Fouqué's Undine, Moore's Lily, Von Hardenberg's Mathilde, Southey's Oneiza, Coleridge's Geraldine, Keats's Lamia, and also the enchanting fays of medieval legend (75–76). With her "reminiscences of her shadowy isle" (158), Yillah represents the Platonic realm of the soul's preexistence (Sealts, "Platonic Tradition" 291). Yillah can also be seen as an all-alluring ideal, a symbol of the Absolute, a sign of primordial perfection—once enjoyed, now regained, soon to be lost.

This reading of Yillah's symbolic attributes, however reflective of Melville's expansive learning, tends to make her little more than an abstract lure for the four questers to pursue. What tends to be overlooked, and what characterizes Melville's fictionalization of the philosophical ideal in Yillah and later in Moby Dick and Isabel, is that these romantic, religious, and philosophical entities have no intrinsic supernatural qualities whatsoever. The ideal attributes of Yillah, Moby Dick, and Isabel generate explicitly from *stories* told by human beings on the hunt for mythic patterns that will explain the unusual and mysterious. Yillah's tale of deific origin, for example, derives from Aleema's religious contexts; Moby Dick's putative ubiquity in time and space evolves from the fertile speculations of superstitious mariners; Isabel's legend falls from her own lips. Quite possibly a lunatic, Isabel gives narrative form to images of her shadowy past. Her controlling desire is to regain the figure of a lost father through entanglements with a supposed half brother. In *Mardi,* Yillah believes Aleema's stories; she relates these tales to the narrator, who not only seconds but embellishes them, writing himself into the script of her biographical delusions. Thanks to Aleema's sons, we discover that the biological and historical creature yclept Yillah is the daughter of adventuring missionaries of European descent who were slaughtered by islanders after these missionaries slew three suspected thieves (307–308). Aleema, however, obliterates her cultural origins. All she has left are vague memories of Taji's language and the creation myth imposed on her by Aleema.

Yillah purports to be "more than mortal, a maiden from Oroolia, the Island of Delights." One day, she became entangled in a vine and transformed into a flower, her "conscious soul folded up in the transparent petals" (137). In due time, the blossom found its way to Aleema, who "by a spell" returned Yillah to maiden form. According to Aleema, the exiled spirit was then called home to Oroolia. She was to travel there by way of the vortex at Tedaidee. Significantly, in Aleema's tale Melville draws on Platonic and Cartesian complexes, bringing them directly into collision. On the one hand Yillah symbolizes the ideal, the Absolute, the ethereal soul cast temporarily into earthly form; on the other, Yillah's fate is prefigured by the "whirlpool" (138). She must plunge into the vortex and thus be purged of mortal qualities. According to Aleema, Yillah would "follow thy bird" and enter the "vortex on the coast of Tedaidee" (157). Melville links Yillah not only to the Platonic image of the soul's preexistence but also to the Platonic figure that depicts the soul's transcendence. As the bird enters the whirlpool, Platonic and Cartesian, ideal and material entities collide. Like the young Platonist on the masthead in *Moby-Dick,* who hovers over "Descartian vortices" (159), Yillah stands to be killed by the brute facts of material existence.

The narrator originally sees Yillah as a poor manipulated victim. He "was almost persuaded that the luckless maiden was some beautiful maniac" (137). At the same time he has no trouble seeing Aleema as a fiction-making charlatan who acts for "ulterior purposes connected with . . . sacerdotal supremacy" (139). Not only does the narrator understand that Yillah's metaphysical identity was applied from without, but he clearly recognizes that this fiction undermines her essential humanity. As the narrator points out, the Aleemas of the world kidnap infants and

> craftily delude them, as they grow up, into the wildest conceits.
> Thus wrought upon, their pupils almost lose their humanity in the constant indulgence of seraphic imaginings. . . . Beguiled with some fairy tale about revisiting the islands of Paradise, they are led to the secret sacrifice, and perish unknown to their kindred. (139)

Put simply, the narrator comprehends fully the extent to which Yillah fell victim to a religious confidence game. Her deliverance could be accomplished, the narrator realizes, by weaning her from the fiction of godliness. And he has every opportunity to restore her to herself. Yillah has distant recollections of her native tongue: "She started, and bending over, listened intently, as if to the first faint echo of something dimly remembered. . . . [W]ith much earnestness, she signed to me to address her as before" (137). Later, the narrator reports, "Often she entreated me to repeat over and over again certain syllables of my language" (152). In an instinctual attempt to recapture her lost identity, Yillah pronounces these words "even as if recalling sounds long forgotten." Instead of telling her the historical facts of her past—"she had not the remotest conception of her real origin" (153)—the narrator appropriates and extends Aleema's fiction:

> In relating her story, the maiden frequently interrupted it with questions concerning myself.—Whence I came: being white, from Oroolia? Whither I was going: to Amma? And what had happened to Aleema? For she had been dismayed at the fray, though knowing not what it could mean. . . . These questions for the time I endeavored to evade; only inducing her to fancy me some gentle demi-god, that had come over the sea from her own fabulous Oroolia. And all this she must verily have believed. For whom, like me, ere this could she have beheld? Still fixed she her eyes upon me strangely, and hung upon the accents of my voice. (140)

When the narrator fashions a fiction of their past acquaintance, Melville is again drawing on the Platonic notion of knowledge as reminiscence of primordial spiritual unity. The narrator tells her, "Those little spirits in your eyes have seen me before. They mimic me now as they sport in their lakes. All the past a dim blank? Think of the time when we ran up and down in our arbor, where the green vines grew over the great ribs of the stranded whale" (143). Using distinctly Platonic figures, the narrator identifies her as "the substance of this spiritual image, . . . the earthly semblance of that sweet vision, that haunted my earliest thoughts" (158). Just as they were married, so should they *now* marry.

The narrator, however, realizes that this fictionalized, metaphysical kinship is inimical to his desire for earthly, physical love. He finds himself in a quandary: how can he continue to impose his self-deifying fiction while at the same time leading her to love him with the repressed passion of her buried human nature? He wants Yillah to think of him as a fellow god, but to do so might also "teach her to regard him as some frigid stranger from the Arctic Zone, what sympathy could she have for him? and hence, what peace of mind, having no one else to cling to?" (142). This dilemma characterizes Melville's metaphysical questers: self-identification with the Absolute freezes the emotions and destroys human sympathy. To what limits, then, should the narrator carry the fiction? And what are the contingencies of becoming trapped within the deific terms of his self-dramatization? At first, Yillah "had wildly believed, that the nameless affinities between us, were owing to our having in times gone by dwelt together in the same ethereal region. But thoughts like these were fast dying out" (158). She begins to look into his human eyes and listen to the sound of his human voice. Falling in love would demythify their divine status; but in order to enhance his stature, the narrator feels he must "prop my failing divinity; though it was I myself who had undermined it. . . . I perceived myself thus dwarfing down to a mortal" (159).

In adopting the identity of Taji, a demigod from the sun, the narrator effectively renounces his place among fellow mortals. Like Yillah's fabled deification, the fictional status of demigod generates from self-serving imperatives. Its fundamental purpose is to magnify the self, thus providing ontological warrant for his claim to special privilege. As revealed on the *Arcturion*, the narrator essentially longs for an idealized state (7–8). Consequently, his fiction making with Yillah serves his narcissistic self-love. He does not so much love Yillah the maiden as he loves the concept of a fit companion for his invented god-self. In *Mardi*, Melville does not directly engage the tensions between the demands of Taji's absolutistic yearnings and his sensual compulsions. Instead, he dissociates the romance and philosophical plots into elements of his quest saga. The missing Yillah becomes no more than a lost ideal; the moral and sexual contingencies of Taji's rescue of Yillah erupt only when Aleema's avenging sons and Hautia's seductive heralds occasionally appear. As a character, Taji virtually disappears. The play of philosophical rumination no longer has its center in the tension between his genial and solipsistic voices. In effect, the disappearance of Yillah completes Taji's estrangement from the realm of commonplace experience—a process that began with his boredom on the *Arcturion*.

Since mythic Yillah reflects a narcissistic projection of Taji's deific aspirations, and his physical love is inimical to his desire for transcendent status, then Yillah's disappearance eradicates Taji's place in the narrative. For Taji, to have lost Yillah is to have lost the capacity for presenting himself through the tension between two voices and two modes of existence. The congenial voice, figuratively speaking, becomes lost in the vortex that presumably swallows flesh-and-blood Yillah. In the post-Yillah chapters, Taji *never* engages his companions in their seemingly endless discourses. Seldom do his companions speak to him. With the unpredictability of a spirit rapper, he makes long declamatory speeches in the interpolated digressions. As a third-person narrator he records the conversations of his companions, every now and then duly noting that Yillah is not to be found.

Having eschewed the social axis, Taji finds himself condemned to solipsism; he then adopts the appropriate rhetorical mode of soliloquy. In his most self-revealing monologue, "Sailing On," Taji sums up the uncompromising single-mindedness of the absolute idealist:

> Oh, reader, list! I've chartless voyaged. With compass and the lead, we had not found these Mardian Isles. Those who boldly launch, cast off all cables; and turning from the common breeze, that's fair for all, with their own breath, fill their own sails. Hug the shore, naught new is seen. . . .
>
> And though essaying but a sportive sail, I was driven from my course, by a blast resistless; and ill-provided, young, and bowed to the brunt of things before my prime, still fly before the gale. (556–557)

In this moment of reflexivity, Taji depicts his "bold quest" both in terms of his protean compositional method and his attending intellectual exhaustion:

> But this new world here sought, is stranger far than his, who stretched his vans from Palos. It is the world of mind; wherein the wanderer may gaze round, with more of wonder than Balboa's band roving through the golden Aztec glades.
>
> But fiery yearnings their own phantom-future make, and deem it present. So, if after all these fearful, fainting trances, the verdict be, the golden haven was not gained;—yet, in bold quest thereof, better to sink in boundless deeps, than float on vulgar shoals; and give me, ye gods, an utter wreck, if wreck I do. (557)

This passage specifically points ahead both to "The Lee Shore" chapter of *Moby-Dick* and to the more extreme megalomaniacal rants of Ahab and Pierre.

In *Mardi*, however, Melville's interest is focused more on exploring "the world of mind" than on depicting the "utter wreck" of the Promethean quester. Ironically, except in the digressions, Taji reveals very little of what he discovers on his sallies through intellectual space. Given the fact that his actions and thoughts have the same focus—regaining Yillah—Melville must invent a strategy whereby the narrator's futile quest can impel Melville's preoccupation with intellectual play, improvisation, and dialectic. Though Taji has one thing on his mind, Melville has many. Melville displaces Taji as the center of consciousness and focuses his ideational concerns through the questers—four characters who represent four distinctly adumbrated modes of knowledge and being: Media is Political Authority; Babbalanja is Philosophy; Yoomy is Poetry; Mohi is History. Each character speaks for his own special interest. Wrangling over abstract issues as they encounter a multitude of allegorical contexts, Taji's four companions allow Melville to explore the "chartless . . . world of mind" (556–557). The narrative's dramatic action thus provides a series of counterpoints to the dead-end issue of Yillah's discovery. The journey through *Mardi*, ostensibly a quest for the maiden, provides both form and forum through which Melville can try out narrative techniques capable of containing his speculations.

NOTES

1. In *New England Literary Culture*, Buell identifies the centrality of romantic art to be not in an ideology of the self-deification of the artist but in a notion of the artist as iconoclastic transformer of existing literary structures, what Buell calls "form breaking": "Romanticism . . . starts with a destructive, ground-clearing impulse that easily moves from the level of mere protest against received forms to the level of an anti-aesthetic impulse of protest against the constraints of art itself" (70). The terms of Buell's discourse clarify the nature of Melville's drive to dissociate himself from the narrative form wherein he achieved initial success. In protesting against the limits of the travel narrative, Melville plunged into philosophical romance, which is synonymous in his view with artistic freedom and invention. His pursuit of Truth within this iconoclastic aesthetic, then, must not be seen as representing a search for the practicability of staid, conservative platitudes of mid-nineteenth-century Christian moralism. Truth seemed for Melville to encompass whatever one found after diving beneath the surfaces of quotidian formulations. Truth came to be grounded in dark, possibly nihilistic, formulations that related to the human domain of instinct, compulsion, vent, and irrationality. Buell goes on to describe the way the iconoclastic artistic impulse emerges: "This impulse is manifested in two principal ways: first, in celebrations of the creative process, as opposed to the aesthetic product, the 'poetic' being located in the realm of experience rather than in the artifact; and second, in Romantic irony, the systematic breaking of the poetic illusion in order to call attention to it as artifice" (70). In the first instance, Melville celebrates the creative process not in terms of the narrator's actions but in the ranging play of his reactions. *Mardi*'s opening sequences, as will be argued, are generally devoid of dramatic activity. In the second case, which is not explicitly within the limits of this study, Melville's political satire reflects Buell's notion of romantic irony.

2. For Melville's view that great literary artists write in a kind of doublespeak—to popular tastes and, simultaneously, to a deeper reader—see "Hawthorne and His Mosses" (*Piazza Tales* 244–245).

3. Melville's concern in *Mardi* with the interpenetration of subject and object places him at the center of Romantic attempts to link the self with the world of experience. In *Biographic Literaria*, Coleridge discusses the basic Socratic dictum,

KNOW THYSELF! . . . And this at once practically and speculatively. For as philosophy is neither a science of the reason or the understanding only, nor merely a science of morals, but the science of BEING altogether, its primary ground can be neither merely speculative nor merely practical, but both in one. All knowledge rests on the coincidence of an object with a subject. (162–163)

For discussions of related issues, see Cascardi; Greenberg; and Chai 308–312.

4. The allusive catalog serves Melville well in *Mardi* and in subsequent works. This technique allows him to combine learned reference with the dialectical play of competing positions. It is a favored technique of Plato, Rabelais, Sir Thomas Browne, and Burton. See Wenke, "Ontological Heroics" 569–570, for a discussion of how invoked names tend to function for Melville as synoptic metaphors, which resonate with associational possibilities.

5. In the 1(?) June 1851 letter to Hawthorne, Melville pens a similarly speculative scenario about a congenial afterlife:

It is a rainy morning; so I am indoors, and all work suspended. I feel cheerfully disposed, and therefore I write a little bluely. Would the Gin were here! If ever, my dear Hawthorne, in the eternal times that are to come, you and I shall sit down in Paradise, in some little shady corner by ourselves, and if we shall by any means be able to smuggle a basket of champagne there (I won't believe in a Temperance Heaven), and if we shall then cross our celestial legs in the celestial grass that is forever tropical, and strike our glasses and our heads together, till both musically ring in concert,—then, O my dear fellow-mortal, how shall we pleasantly discourse of all the things manifold which now so distress us,—when all the earth shall be but a reminiscence, yea, its final dissolution an antiquity. Then shall songs be composed as when wars are over. . . . [Y]es, let us look forward to such things. Let us swear that, though now we sweat, yet it is because of the dry heat which is indispensable to the nourishment of the vine which is to bear the grapes that are to give us the champagne hereafter. (191–192)

6. A passage in Burton might well be a direct source for the technique, ideas, and characterization in "Dreams." Burton uses the allusive catalog, but unlike Melville, he celebrates study as a means to exorcise melancholy. Burton's passage is an inversion of Melville's exposition. Burton writes:

Seneca prefers Zeno and Chrysippus . . . before any Prince or General of an Army; and Orontius the Mathematician so far admires Archimedes, that he calls him a petty God, more than a man; and well he might, for ought I see, if you respect fame or worth, Pindar of Thebes is as much renowned for his Poems, as Epaminondas, Pelopidas, Hercules, or Bacchus, his fellow citizens, for their warlike actions . . . the delight is it which I aim at; so great pleasure, such sweet content, there is in study. . . . Sir Thomas Bodley . . . brake out into that noble speech: If I were not a King, I would be an University man; and if it were so that I must be a prisoner, if I might have my wish, I would desire to have no other prison than that Library, and to be chained together with so many good Authors and dead Masters. (457)

Burton goes on to offer a caution that Taji could well have observed:

> Whosoever he is . . . that is overrun with solitariness . . . I can prescribe him no better remedy than this of study, to compose himself to the learning of some art or science. Provided always that his malady proceed not from overmuch study, for in such cases he adds fuel to the fire, and nothing can be more pernicious; let him take heed he do not overstretch his wits, and make a skeleton of himself. (458–459)

7. See Stern, "Towards 'Bartleby'" for a discerning overview of the story's unresolved critical complexes.

WORKS CITED

Melville, Herman, *Correspondence.* Evanston, IL: Northwestern University Press/Newberry Library, 1993. Vol. 14 of *The Writings of Herman Melville,* Ed. Lynn Horth. 15 vols. to date, 1968– .

———. *Mardi and A Voyage Thither.* Evanston, IL: Northwestern University Press/Newberry Library, 1970. Vol. 3 of *The Writings of Herman Melville,* Ed. Harrison Hayford, Hershel Parker, and G. Thomas Tanselle. 15 vols. to date, 1968– .

———. *Moby-Dick: or, The Whale.* Ed. Harrison Hayford and Hershel Parker. New York: Norton, 1967.

Sealts, Merton M., Jr. "Herman Melville's Reading in Ancient Philosophy." Diss. Yale University, 1942.

MERTON M. SEALTS, JR.

Whose Book Is Moby-Dick?

I have written a wicked book, and feel spotless as the lamb.
—Melville to Nathaniel Hawthorne, [17?] November 1851

During the early years of the Melville Revival, which began in this country in the aftermath of World War I, roughly a hundred years after Melville's birth in 1819, there was much discussion of *Moby-Dick* as a rediscovered masterpiece. But then as now, many people merely talked about the book instead of actually reading it. When Harold Ross founded the *New Yorker* magazine in 1925, according to James Thurber in *The Years with Ross* (1959), he was "unembarrassed by his ignorance of the great novels of any country," including his own. One day, Thurber reports, "he stuck his head into the checking department of the magazine . . . to ask 'Is Moby Dick the whale or the man?'"[1] But whether or not they've ever read the book, most literate Americans today know that it was Ahab who pursued the White Whale and are also well aware of another character in *Moby-Dick:* the one who speaks that memorable opening line, "Call me Ishmael."

Whose book, then, is *Moby-Dick?* Should we award it to the title character, the invincible whale himself? Or to Captain Ahab, who dooms his ship and crew in his desperate quest to slay the monster who had reaped away his leg? or to narrator Ishmael, the one human survivor of the

Beyond the Classroom: Essays on American Authors (Columbia: University of Missouri Press, 1996): pp. 175–188. ©1996 Curators of the University of Missouri.

inevitable catastrophe, who alone escapes to tell the story? Since the book was first published in 1851 the question has been posed repeatedly, but the answers to it, as we shall see, have been various indeed. For the entire book is like that gold doubloon, the coin of great value that Ahab nailed to his ship's mainmast, promising it as a reward to the first man who should sight the White Whale. Witness these words of Ahab: "this round gold is but the image of the rounder globe, which, like a magician's glass, to each and every man in turn but mirrors back his own mysterious self" (chap. 99, "The Doubloon," 431). So with the book—and so too with its principal characters. All of them mirror back the reader and whatever he or she has brought to the experience of reading.

But Melville's contemporaries saw little of themselves in either the characters or the book, despite all that he had put into it for those possessing eyes to see. Like two other innovative literary works of the 1850s in America, Thoreau's *Walden* and Whitman's "Song of Myself," Herman Melville's *Moby-Dick* had to wait the better part of a century for the readership that we now think it deserves. What each of the three writers had to say in these works and the unique way in which he said it seemed somehow foreign to their contemporaries, who had other ideas about what literary productions should be and do. We see a similar divergence in our own day between popular taste and the groundbreaking work of new artists in various media, not only in poetry and prose but also in music and painting, or in architecture and interior design. Indeed, every creative artist, if he is "great and at the same time *original,* has had the task of *creating* the taste by which he is to be enjoyed." So Wordsworth, speaking from experience, put it as long ago as 1815, for he and Coleridge as innovators in poetry had faced the same problem in England since publishing their *Lyrical Ballads* in 1798.[2]

Different as they are in both subject matter and form from the poetry of Wordsworth and from one another, *Walden,* "Song of Myself," and *Moby-Dick* as innovative works have much in common with the pervasive Romantic spirit that had animated European art and literature long before its influence was felt on this side of the Atlantic, but they also draw on experience that we recognize immediately as uniquely American. Like much Romantic art, moreover, they are intensely subjective in character. Each of the three employs what Wayne Booth has called a "dramatized narrator," an "I" who not only tells the reader about events of the past but also addresses him directly in the narrative present, as in the opening paragraphs of *Walden:* "In most books, the *I,* or first person, is omitted; in this it will be retained; that, in respect to egotism, is the main difference.... I should not talk so much about myself if there were any body else whom I knew as well."[3] Here are the first three lines of "Song of Myself":

I celebrate myself,
And what I assume you shall assume,
For every atom belonging to me as good belongs to you.[4]

And here too are the familiar opening lines of chapter 1 of *Moby-Dick,* also addressed directly to the reader—to "you": "Call me Ishmael. Some years ago—never mind how long precisely—having little or no money in my purse, and nothing in particular to interest me on shore, I thought I would sail about a little and see the watery part of the world. It is a way I have of driving off the spleen, and regulating the circulation" (3).

Again in Romantic fashion, each of the three works proceeds to take both the "I" and the reader into nature and the open air: with Thoreau to "the shore of Walden Pond, in Concord, Massachusetts," there to transact what he calls some private business; with Whitman "to the bank by the wood," there to "loafe and invite my soul"; with Melville's Ishmael, again "waterward"— since "as every one knows, meditation and water are wedded for ever"—and ultimately to sea, motivated chiefly by "the overwhelming idea of the great whale himself," for "only on the profound unbounded sea, can the fully invested whale be truly and livingly found out" (4, 7, 454).

To speak now about Melville's book in particular, are we to read it as a story both by and about its narrator, like *Walden,* or is it about what Ishmael calls "the fully invested whale"—specifically the title character, though Moby Dick himself does not appear until the third chapter from the end? Or is it really about still another character, one linked both to Moby Dick and to Ishmael—Captain Ahab? Ahab, that "grand, ungodly, god-like man," as Captain Peleg describes him to Ishmael (79), makes his entrance only after Melville has given us a hundred pages of Ishmael's story, but he seemingly dominates the action thereafter. Is it then Ahab's book, or the Whale's, or narrator Ishmael's? Contemporary reviewers first raised these questions; twentieth-century readers have raised them again.

On the evidence of the original titles, *The Whale* in the first English edition of 1851 and *Moby-Dick; or, The Whale* in the first American, a reader might well infer that Melville himself thought of whales and especially of one White Whale—Moby Dick—as central to the book. As a persuasive twentieth-century reader put it in 1966, Melville presents Moby Dick as "the crown and consummation of the imperial breed of whales"; moreover, "the logic of the book as a whole works to give whales in general, and him in particular, a mythic and heroic stature. He gains this stature only by having whalers and whaling share it; but because they do, he gains it more triumphantly. . . . Moby Dick *is,* in the most relevant sense, the book's protagonist."[5]

At first hearing you may be inclined to agree with this eloquent statement and say that the book is indeed Moby Dick's. But before you go that far, consider as well these differing opinions from three other twentieth-century essays, also by readers of the 1960s:

> *Second Reader:* "I say 'Call me an Ishmaelite' because I assume that this is primarily Ishmael's book. The drama of Ahab and the whale is most significant when seen in relation to Ishmael experiencing that drama. . . . Ahab never would (nor could) have written this book; Ishmael does (and must)."[6]

> *Third Reader:* "But this is not Ishmael's story. He is a delightful narrator in the beginning, and for a time at sea plays the role admirably, but when Melville becomes truly engrossed in telling the story of Ahab, he pushes Ishmael aside and gives insights denied his first-person narrator."[7]

> *Fourth Reader:* "But is Ahab then the 'hero' of *Moby Dick?* To answer with an unqualified affirmative is to neglect just half of the book. For if it is the tragedy of Captain Ahab, it is also the novel of Ishmael."[8]

On a purely literal level, one must grant, Ahab certainly couldn't have written such a book, if only because it describes his own death, and Ishmael does indeed disappear from our view in later chapters when Ahab comes to the fore and at last encounters Moby Dick. The narrative as we have it gives readers not only "insights" but also basic information that sailor Ishmael could not conceivably have obtained aboard the *Pequod:* for example, Ahab's statements either in his private soliloquies or in exchanges with Stubb, Starbuck, and Pip that no other member of the crew would have easily overheard. To the question "Whose book is *Moby-Dick?*" there is still no generally accepted answer among those who variously name the White Whale, Ishmael, or Ahab as its principal figure. Moreover, there has been further disagreement over the genre and form of *Moby-Dick:* can a book be considered aesthetically unified if it is at once "the tragedy of Captain Ahab," "the novel of Ishmael," and what one early reviewer called it, a "Whaliad"[9]—meaning a prose epic treating learnedly and exhaustively, or exhaustingly, of whales and whaling?

i

For an indication of how and when these associated questions first arose, let us begin with a glance at aspects of the nineteenth-century response to *Moby-Dick.* None of the three principal figures—Ishmael, Ahab, and the White Whale—attracted many readers to the book during Melville's lifetime—to his deep disappointment, as we know, for he had composed

Moby-Dick with the sense that a literary masterwork might well be taking form under his hand. The initial reviews had been mixed. Even those British critics who had high praise for some attributes of the book were troubled nevertheless by what they considered its faults of style and structure: for example, they noted that Melville did not consistently maintain Ishmael's first-person point of view and, since the London edition did not include the Epilogue, they complained that the book offered no explanation of Ishmael's survival after the sinking of the *Pequod;* how, they asked, could he be alive to tell his story?

The first American reviewers were less concerned with such technical matters, partly because the first New York edition not only provided the Epilogue but also carried "Etymology" and the "Extracts" on whales and whaling at the beginning of the narrative rather than at the end, where they had appeared in the earlier London edition. But Americans too were uncertain about how to classify the new work, and several of them objected to its general tone. One leading journal, the *New York Literary World,* published by Melville's friends Evert and George Duyckinck, dealt with it as "two if not three books ... rolled into one." Their two-part review praised Melville's "brilliantly illustrated" account of the great Sperm Whale and identified Moby Dick as his "hero," going on to express reservations about both the characterization of Ahab and the prominence given Ishmael and his inveterate philosophizing.[10] To the Duyckincks, Ahab's story seemed melodramatic rather than tragic, and with other American critics of the 1850s they considered Ishmael's speculations to he shockingly irreverent. Melville, wrote a representative critic in 1857, should give over his "metaphysical and morbid meditations" and return to the vein of *Typee* and *Omoo,* the books of adventure that had so pleased the public a decade earlier.[11]

With the decline of the whaling industry in later years of the century, when petroleum, natural gas, and electricity in turn replaced whale-oil in American and European households, interest in books about whales and whaling declined as well. But a small band of admirers in England kept Melville's name alive there, and with the conclusion of World War I a new generation of American readers found that *Moby-Dick,* along with *Walden* and "Song of Myself," was speaking to them in a way that most nineteenth-century readers had simply failed to understand and enjoy. By 1951, the book's centennial year, *Moby-Dick* had become a standard work on American college reading lists and a subject for proliferating critical and scholarly study.

ii

The one twentieth-century work that in effect legitimated an aesthetic approach to Melville and his American contemporaries was F. O. Matthiessen's *American Renaissance: Art and Expression in the Age of Emerson and Whitman,* first published in 1941.[12] Other scholars writing during the 1950s and 1960s significantly broadened the context of both research and teaching by relating the work of our nineteenth-century authors to the Romantic and symbolist movements in both America and Europe. One example is Morse Peckham, a theorist of Romanticism who dealt with Melville and *Moby-Dick* in terms of the perennial Romantic themes;[13] another is Charles Feidelson, whose *Symbolism and American Literature* (1953) traced the affiliations of American writers not only with their European predecessors but with their modern heirs and successors as well.[14]

These studies and others like them had a remarkable effect on ways of reading *Moby-Dick*. Where some commentators since the 1850s had seen the book as a structural hybrid, an uneasy juxtaposition of epic and essay, or of novel and tragedy, that failed to conform to the accepted rules of any one literary genre, others writing in the spirit of Matthiessen and Peckham were now praising it as a highly successful example of Romantic art, creating its own form not mechanically, after some existing model, but organically— again like *Walden* and "Song of Myself." As Ishmael puts it at the beginning of chapter 63, "Out of the trunk, the branches grow; out of them, the twigs. So, in productive subjects, grow the chapters" (289). And as Walter Bezanson remarked in his "*Moby-Dick:* Work of Art," a landmark essay first read as a lecture in the centennial year of 1951, "Organic form is not a particular form but a structural principle. In *Moby-Dick* this principle would seem to be a pe- culiar quality of making and unmaking itself as it goes. . . . Ishmael's narrative is always in process and in all but the most literal sense remains unfinished. For the good reader the experience of *Moby-Dick* is a participation in the act of creation."[15]

The approach to *Moby-Dick* represented by Bezanson's essay brought with it a reconsideration of two of the interrelated issues under discussion here: whether or not the book has a unified structure and whom to iden- tify as its central character. During the early stages of the Melville revival the usual emphasis of both readers and critics was clearly on Ahab and his struggle with the whale, with lesser regard for Ishmael and what were often objected to as his philosophical "digressions." Interpreters as late as the 1940s tended to see the opposition between Ahab and Moby Dick in allegorical terms, praising Ahab as a self-reliant, Promethean individual confronting in Moby Dick the embodiment of all the forces of evil—physical or metaphysi- cal—that beset oppressed humanity. For Melville, wrote one representative commentator, "the essence of the world is a dualism between good and evil," and man's appointed role is "to fight evil without compromise and without respite." So Ahab is fated "to spend his life pursuing Moby Dick, knowing that the master of the *Pequod* could never conquer the whale. In the end Ahab saved his soul, maintained inviolate his personal integrity by going down in unconquered defeat while Moby Dick swam on for other Ahabs to pursue. Ahab was the personification of Melville's philosophy of individualism."[16]

Much can be said for such a reading, as for most serious approaches to any complex book, but there are also other factors to be considered. What, for instance, are we to make of a monomaniac captain, repeatedly denominated as "crazy" or "mad," and his willful dedication of his ship and her crew to the fulfillment of his private quest for what his chief mate calls "vengeance on a dumb brute" (163)? Isn't Melville offering an implied *criticism* of self-reliant individualism—perhaps of capitalist entrepreneurs generally—rather than an endorsement? Even so, Ishmael's admiration of the man informs the portrait he is essaying. As a "tragic dramatist who would depict mortal indomitableness in its fullest sweep and direst swing," he must acknowledge that Ahab lacks "all outward majestical trappings and housings." Therefore, "what shall be grand" in the resulting portrait "must needs be plucked at from the skies, and dived for in the deep, and featured in the unbodied air!" (148).

Melville's presentation of Ahab through Ishmael's words shows him as a commanding figure of tragic stature, flawed by "fatal pride" (519) yet not incapable of compassion, as we see in his treatment of Pip and even of Starbuck; he is no mere cardboard "personification." As Leon Howard wrote as long ago as 1950, when critics were beginning to deal with the book in a more searching and understanding way, "It was the author's emotional sympathy" for Ahab as "a character of whom he intellectually disapproved which gave *Moby Dick* much of its ambiguity and dramatic intensity."[17]

In the newer readings of *Moby-Dick* the White Whale emerged as more than that fixed allegorical embodiment of pure evil which Ahab persisted in seeing; instead, critics after the 1950s came to write of the whale's function in the overall structure of the book as that of a dynamic and ever-changing symbol, a cynosure that gradually accumulates not only meaning but multiple significance. From "Etymology" and "Extracts" through what Howard Vincent called its "cetological center"[18] to its concluding Epilogue, the book is filled with the lore of whales and whaling, showing how whales have figured in time and place over the centuries, how they appear not only to artists and scientists but to men actually risking their lives in the whale fishery. As a former whaleman, Melville well knew that "the only mode in which you can derive even a tolerable idea of [the whale's] living contour, is by going a whaling yourself; but by so doing, you run no small risk of being eternally stove and sunk by him" (264).

As Ishmael revealed at the outset, "the overwhelming idea of the great whale" had been a leading motive for his own decision to go a whaling. But as his narrative progresses we learn with him how Captain Ahab had projected his rage and hate upon one particular White Whale, and we begin to understand as well how Ishmael came first to share and later to distance himself from Ahab's obsession. And in due course, as initiated readers we are at last prepared to confront Moby Dick himself, in all his magnitude and surpassing beauty:

> Not the white bull Jupiter swimming away with ravished Europa clinging to his graceful horns . . . ; not Jove, not that great majesty Supreme! did surpass the glorified White Whale as he so divinely swam. . . . No wonder there had been some among the hunters who namelessly transported and allured by all that serenity, had ventured to assail it; but had fatally found that quietude but the vesture of tornadoes. Yet calm, enticing calm, oh whale! Thou glidest on, to all who for the first time eye thee, no matter how many in that same way thou may'st have bejuggled and destroyed before. (548)

However any one critic may view Moby Dick—as "the deepest blood being of the white race," in the words of D. H. Lawrence, or the Freudian super-ego, as Henry A. Murray suggested,[19] or Deity, or Death, or Nature, or the universe itself, to cite some other interpretations—there is likely to be no more agreement about his ultimate meaning than there was among the crews aboard the various ships we as readers encounter in the nine gams of the *Pequod*. "Shall we ever identify Moby Dick?" Harry Levin once asked. "Yes," he answered—"when we have sprinkled salt on the tail of the Absolute; but not before."[20]

iii

During the 1950s, while critics were still thinking of Ahab as Melville's protagonist confronting his antagonist in Moby Dick, Bezanson and other scholars had also begun to write of Ishmael and his point of view as the unifying center of the story. Although there was minimal reference to *Moby-Dick* in Wayne Booth's influential book of 1961, *The Rhetoric of Fiction*,[21] Booth's work inspired others to undertake a close examination of the technical aspects of Melville's fiction—notably his use of narrative point of view and his employment of dramatized narrators. With *Moby-Dick* in particular this approach of course involved a reappraisal of Ishmael's role.

Bezanson had already distinguished between the younger Ishmael who had once sailed aboard the *Pequod* and the older Ishmael who is telling his story; in 1962 Warner Berthoff in *The Example of Melville*—the best book to date on Melville as a literary craftsman—demonstrated how artfully Melville used Ishmael first to set the nautical scene and then to prepare its for both Ahab and the whale. As Berthoff explained, Ishmael conducts us as readers through "four distinct 'worlds.'" We meet him first in the world of "the dry land, or at least the thronged edges of it: New York, New Bedford, Nantucket."

Next, Melville and Ishmael take us aboard the *Pequod,* herself "a virtual city of the races and talents of men," and there, through a great opening-out, into "the non-human world of the sea and the indifferent elements." Then at last we are prepared to enter "the final, furthest 'world' set out in *Moby Dick,*" one that "communicates to men only in signs, portents, and equivocal omens, and seems intelligible only to madmen like Ahab and Pip."[22]

Into the fourth of these worlds, the realm beyond physical nature, it is fair to add that Melville himself could never have conducted us directly. Instead, speaking by indirection—first through Ishmael's voice and later through Ahab's—he "craftily says, or sometimes insinuates," what would be "all but madness" for an author to utter or even to hint to us "in his own proper character." So Melville himself had once written of Shakespeare, at the very time when *Moby-Dick* was taking form; so Emily Dickinson would enjoin us to "Tell all the Truth but tell it slant— / Success in Circuit lies."[23] Even as truth-teller Ishmael is leading us out of our everyday world into the world of ships and the sea, where at last we meet Ahab and ultimately Moby Dick, he is at the same time securing for Melville the needed aesthetic distance from those two antagonists that as their creator he had to establish and maintain.

When any writer becomes "identified with the objects of [his] horror or compassion," as in our own century Scott Fitzgerald would declare in *The Crack-Up,* the result, as Fitzgerald had learned, to his own cost, is "the death of accomplishment."[24] An author who fails to guard against such identification risks artistic disaster, and perhaps a psychological crisis as well—witness Melville in his next book, *Pierre, or the Ambiguities* (1852), where there is no Ishmael to stand between him and his title character: reviewers unanimously condemned *Pierre,* and some readers and critics even questioned its author's sanity. In *Moby-Dick,* by contrast, Ishmael as intervening narrator had provided Melville with essential insulation, as Nick Carraway would do for Fitzgerald in *The Great Gatsby* and Marlow for Joseph Conrad in *Heart of Darkness,* each narrator distancing the creator from his creation. Were there no Ishmael in *Moby-Dick,* we may feel sure, Melville would never have been able to give us his protagonist and antagonist—or to purge himself of his own pity and terror by doing so. That is why he could say, with relief, to Hawthorne, "I have written a wicked book, and feel spotless as the lamb" (*Correspondence,* 212).

iv

Ishmael's dual role as narrator and as actor has been profitably explored by several critics since Bezanson distinguished between "the enfolding sensibility . . . , the hand that writes the tale, the imagination through which all matters of the book pass," and that "young man of whom, among others, narrator Ishmael tells us in his story." The older narrator looking back upon his younger self had been a feature of Melville's earlier works, the differences between the

two growing sharper in *Redburn* (1849) and *White-Jacket* (1850), the immediate predecessors of *Moby-Dick*. Now in a fully dramatized Ishmael, we
witness "the narrator's unfolding sensibility," Bezanson observed. "Whereas
forecastle Ishmael drops in and out of the narrative . . . , the Ishmael voice
is there every moment."[25]

The fullest exploration of "the Ishmael voice" is Paul Brodtkorb's "phenomenological reading" of the book, *Ishmael's White World* (1965), which pre-
supposes that narrator Ishmael is not only "the vessel that contains the book,"
but "in a major sense he *is* the book."[26] In 1961 Glauco Cambon had written
of Ishmael as "the artist in the act of telling us, and struggling to understand,
his crucial experience";[27] in 1970 Barry A. Marks further pointed out that like
other "retrospective narrators" in Thoreau and Whitman, Ishmael is in fact
presenting two stories simultaneously: one, his "past-time story," is about his
recollected experience that is now over and done; the other, his "writing-time
story," is about experience still in progress—an ongoing story of "a narrator's
telling about his past."[28]

Like speakers in Thoreau and Whitman, Ishmael too addresses his
reader directly; he frequently pauses in his narration to consider the larger
implications for the narrative present of something in the past that he had
just described or related. "Yes, there is death in this business of whaling," he
remarks after telling of the memorial tablets in Father Mapple's chapel (37).
Again, in concluding his chapter on "The Line," he observes that "All men
live enveloped in whale-lines. All are born with halters round their necks; but
it is only when caught in the swift, sudden turn of death, that mortals realize
the silent, subtle, ever-present perils of life" (281). And at the end of "The Try-
Works" he specifically warns the reader: "Give not thyself up, then, to fire, lest
it invert thee, deaden thee; as for the time it did me. There is a wisdom that is
woe; but there is a woe that is madness" (425).

As for his ongoing story, Ishmael makes us fully aware of the challenge facing "a whale author like me" who is presently engaged in "writing
of this Leviathan" and earnestly striving "to produce a mighty book" on such
"a mighty theme" (456). So daunting an enterprise, he contends, demands "a
careful disorderliness" as "the true method" (361). "I promise nothing complete," he tells us in his chapter on "Cetology"; he holds the typical Romantic
view that "any human thing supposed to be complete, must for that very reason infallibly be faulty. . . . God keep me from ever completing anything. This
whole book is but a draught—nay, but the draught of a draught" (136, 145).

Concerning Ishmael's several departures from his original first-person
point of view, that unconventional practice that so troubled nineteenth-
century reviewers and twentieth-century formalist critics as well, and other
instances of what have been called "formal discontinuities" in *Moby-Dick*,
Cambon has argued that Ishmael's supposed disappearance from the story

is a legitimate rhetorical device that has its parallels both in the classical poets and historians and in twentieth-century fiction. Thus Ishmael's "imaginative reconstruction" of the other characters anticipates what Quentin Compson was to do in Faulkner's *Absalom, Absalom!*, where "memory modulates into imagination," and where once again the reader "share[s] the experience of creation in progress."[29]

v

Emphasis on Ishmael as narrator rather than actor—and on Ishmael-like observers in contemporary American criticism, fiction, and intellectual life generally—has dismayed other commentators. "Ahab and the whale do not appear in our novels," one of them complained in 1959; "we write only about Ishmael."[30] A decade later, in the midst of the campus activism of the late 1960s, an angry black contributor to *Partisan Review* blasted narrator Ishmael as "the precursor of the modern white liberal-intellectual" that he found infesting American universities. If Ishmael were really an active "character" in the story, according to Cecil Brown, he "would have repelled Ahab"![31]

More recently, historicist and contextualist critics of *Moby-Dick* have indeed been shifting their focus from Ishmael back to Ahab, at the same time exploring what they see as the book's political implications rather than the cetological, metaphysical, and literary elements that variously engaged their predecessors. Meanwhile, scholars investigating the origins and textual development of the book have once again cast doubt on its artistic unity, citing a panoply of minor inconsistencies in Melville's text and even suggesting "unnecessary duplicates" among his characters.[32] Such instances of apparent disunity in the book can of course be cited against Bezanson and other champions of organic form—a concept which its opponents in an age of deconstruction dismiss as a convenient mask for hiding both minor and major artistic failings.[33]

To the degree that the Ishmaels of this world overshadow its Ahabs and White Whales, the anti-Ishmaelites do indeed have a point. But it also seems fair to say that in the last analysis the book is not the story of any one or even two of its characters. The only feasible way *to* Ahab and at last to the White Whale is *through* Ishmael, Melville's necessary surrogate and the reader's veritable guide, philosopher, and friend; and *all three figures* are equally indispensable to the author, to his book, and to its readers. As for the question of unity or disunity, the real test comes in the very act of responsive reading. In Brodtkorb's words, "literary unity is in the mental set of the reader as much as in the literary work,"[34] and in the case of *Moby-Dick* that "mental set" is powerfully influenced and shaped by Ishmael—favorably so, as for Bezanson and his followers, or unfavorably, as for Cecil Brown.

For further guidance from Ishmael himself, consider his distinctions in chapter 89 between Fast-Fish and Loose-Fish, based on "the laws and regulations of the whale fishery" with respect to harpooned whales:

I. A Fast-Fish belongs to the party fast to it.
II. A Loose-Fish is fair game for anybody who can soonest catch it. (395–396)

Whose book, then, *is* this much-hunted Loose-Fish? It cannot he just Ahab's, or the whale's, or Ishmael's, nor is it entirely Melville's, since you and I as individual readers have genuine claims of our own as well. "There is then creative reading, as well as creative writing," as Emerson long ago observed,[35] and modern critics such as Bezanson and Cambon have applied his idea to *Moby-Dick.* "For the good reader," Bezanson told us, "the experience of *Moby-Dick* is a participation in the act of creation." In Cambon's phrasing, such a reader "will share the experience of creation in progress"—the same experience that Barry Marks has illustrated for us in Melville along with Thoreau and Whitman.

Once you as reader share that experience, then you have indeed made fast to *Moby-Dick,* and in a real sense it has become *your* book—*your* Fast-Fish, as I feel it to be very much mine. But if this comment sounds like an endorsement of what is now called reader-response criticism, we must nevertheless remember that there is a reciprocal corollary: Melville, reaching out through Ishmael as his surrogate, has at the same time figuratively harpooned *us* as his readers, making us fast to his book and therefore belonging to it. As narrator Ishmael, once again turning directly to each of us, pointedly asks, "What are you, reader, but a Loose-Fish, and a Fast-Fish, too?" (398).

At the conclusion of *Moby-Dick,* the fated *Pequod* has been lost—lost with all her crew save one. Protagonist Ahab has met his lonely death on lonely life, while the White Whale, his invincible antagonist, swims on victorious. It is Ishmael, survivor of the *Pequod's* wreck, who escapes alone to tell their story. And by addressing us indirectly through Ishmael's omnipresent voice, Melville himself persuades us, like the authors of *Walden* and "Song of Myself," to assume what he has assumed in this mighty book and to celebrate, with him and with Ishmael, its mighty theme.

NOTES

1. James Thurber, *The Years with Ross* (Boston: Little, Brown, 1959), 77.
2. William Wordsworth, "Essay Supplementary to Preface (1815)," in *Wordsworth's Literary Criticism,* ed. Nowell C. Smith (London: Humphrey Milford, 1905), 195. Wordsworth credited the idea to Coleridge.

3. Henry D. Thoreau, *Walden,* ed. J. Lyndon Shanley (Princeton, N.J.: Princeton University Press, 1971), 3.

4. Walt Whitman, *"Leaves of Grass": The First (1855) Edition,* ed. Malcolm Cowley (New York: Viking Press, 1959), 25.

5. Vincent Buckley, "The White Whale as Hero," *Critical Review* (Melbourne) no. 9 (1966): 12.

6. Gordon Roper, "On Teaching *Moby-Dick,*" *Emerson Society Quarterly* no. 28, pt. 3: Melville Supplement (1962): 2, 3.

7. William Braswell, "The Main Theme of *Moby-Dick,*" *Emerson Society Quarterly* no. 28, pt. 3: *Melville Supplement* (1962): 16–17.

8. John Halverson, "The Shadow in *Moby-Dick,*" *American Quarterly* 15 (Fall 1963): 444.

9. *New York Daily Tribune,* quoted in Hershel Parker and Harrison Hayford, eds., *Moby-Dick as Doubloon: Essays and Extracts* (1851–1970) (New York: W. W. Norton, 1970), 47. *Moby-Dick as Doubloon,* as its editors remark, "contains most of the best and some of the worst that has been written about *Moby-Dick*" through 1970 (xv). A full listing of reviews and criticism through 1960 will be found in Brian Higgins, *Herman Melville: An Annotated Bibliography, 1846–1930,* and *Herman Melville: A Reference Guide, 1931–1960* (Boston: G. K. Hall, 1979, 1987).

10. See *Moby-Dick as Doubloon,* 50–51, 35, or the Norton *Moby-Dick,* 613–615. For other contemporary identifications of the Whale as "hero," see *Moby-Dick as Doubloon,* 24, 39, 56, and 61. Another reviewer chose Ahab (11) and still others named Ishmael, or Melville (4, 53, 85, 87); for Ishmael, see also Hershel Parker, "Five Reviews Not in *Moby-Dick as Doubloon,*" *English Language Notes* 9 (March 1972): 183.

11. Fitz-James O'Brien, "Our Authors and Authorship: Melville and Curtis," *Putnam's Monthly Magazine* 9 (April 1857): 390.

12. F. O. Matthiesse, *American Renaissance: Art and Expression in the Age of Emerson and Whitman* (New York: Oxford University Press, 1941).

13. See in particular Morse Peckham, "Toward a Theory of Romanticism," *PMLA* 66 (March 1951): 5–23; R. P. Adams, "Romanticism and the American Renaissance," *American Literature* 23 (January 1952): 419–432; and Morse Peckham, "Hawthorne and Melville as European Authors," in *Melville and Hawthorne in the Berkshires,* ed. Howard P. Vincent (Kent, Ohio: Kent State University Press, 1968), 42–62. In the last essay cited, pp. 58–59, Peckham surveys "the great Romantic themes" as they appear in *Moby-Dick,* suggesting that by 1851 "Melville had absorbed . . . all stages of Romanticism up to his own time, and had presented them in *Moby-Dick* in inextricable confusion." This is the reason, he speculates, that "the interpretation of *Moby-Dick* is so difficult and why in all probability it will never be understood with clarity or agreement."

14. Charles Feidelson, Jr., *Symbolism and American Literature* (Chicago: University of Chicago Press, 1953). Feidelson observes that mid-nineteenth-century American writers "inherited the basic problem of romanticism: the vindication of imaginative thought in a world grown abstract and material . . . ; their solution . . . is closer to modern notions of symbolic reality than to romantic egoism" (4). He credits Edmund Wilson as the first critic to note their affinity with "the symbolist aesthetic that produced modern literature."

15. Walter E. Bezanson, *"Moby-Dick:* Work of Art," in Tyrus Hillway and Luther S. Mansfield, eds., *Moby-Dick: Centennial Essays* (Dallas: Southern

Methodist University Press, 1953), 56. Bezanson's essay is reprinted in part in the Norton Critical Edition of *Moby-Dick,* ed. Harrison Hayford and Hershel Parker (New York: W. W. Norton, 1967), 651–671, and in *The Merrill Studies in Moby-Dick,* comp. Howard P. Vincent (Columbus, Ohio: Charles E. Merrill, 1969), 87–103.

16. Ralph H. Gabriel, *The Course of American Democratic Thought: An Intellectual History since 1815* (New York: Ronald Press, 1940), 74. For other representative comments which regard Moby Dick as symbolizing evil, see Yvor Winters, "Herman Melville and the Problems of Moral Navigation" (1938), reprinted in his *In Defense of Reason* (New York: Swallow Press and William Morrow and Co., 1947), 201: "the chief symbol and spirit of evil"; Henry Alonzo Myers, "The Meaning of *Moby Dick,*" in his *Tragedy: A View of Life* (Ithaca, N.Y.: Cornell University Press, 1956), 77: "the white whale of evil."

17. Introduction to *Moby Dick* in the Modern Library Edition (New York: The Modern Library, 1950), xiii.

18. See Howard P. Vincent, *The Trying-Out of Moby-Dick* (Boston: Houghton Mifflin, 1949), part IV.

19. D. H. Lawrence, "Herman Melville's '*Moby Dick*'" (1923), and Henry A. Murray, "In Nomine Diaboli" (1951), as reprinted in Vincent, *Merrill Studies in Moby-Dick,* 50, 61.

20. Harry Levin, *Symbolism and Fiction* (1956), quoted in *Moby-Dick as Doubloon,* 265.

21. Wayne C. Booth, *The Rhetoric of Fiction* (Chicago: University of Chicago Press, 1961). Booth's book was immediately influential, especially among younger scholars. John Bryant, *Melville Dissertations, 1924–1980: An Annotated Bibliography and Subject Index* (Westport, Conn.: Greenwood Press, 1983), singled out "the shift to rhetorical criticism, narrative, and point of view" as perhaps the most significant trend among dissertators of the 1960s (xvii).

22. Warner Berthoff, *The Example of Melville* (Princeton, N.J.: Princeton University Press, 1962), 79–86 passim.

23. Melville in "Hawthorne and His Mosses" (1850), as reprinted in *"The Piazza Tales" and Other Prose Pieces 1839–1860,* 244; Dickinson in *Complete Poems,* ed. Thomas H. Johnson (Boston: Little, Brown, 1960), 506 (no. 1129).

24. F. Scott Fitzgerald, "Pasting It Together" (1936), as reprinted in *The Crack-Up* (1945), ed. Edmund Wilson (New York: New Directions, 1956), 81.

25. Bezanson, *"Moby-Dick:* Work of Art," 36, 41.

26. Paul Brodtkorb, Jr., *Ishmael's White World: A Phenomenological Reading of "Moby-Dick,"* (New Haven: Yale University Press, 1965), 4.

27. Glauco Cambon, "Ishmael and the Problem of Formal Discontinuities in *Moby Dick,*" *Modern Language Notes* 76 (June 1961): 523.

28. Barry A. Marks, "Retrospective Narrative in Nineteenth Century American Literature," *College English* 31 (January 1970): 366–367. This neglected essay, which is especially valuable for classroom teachers and is well worth the attention of literary critics as well, contains a provocative analysis of the "two stories" that Ishmael tells in *Moby-Dick.* According to Marks,

> The shape, and finally the meaning also, stems from the fact that Ishmael's changing manner of narration is more than mere aimlessness; rather it is a significantly patterned search for efficacious speech. . . . The writing-time story of the retrospective narrative parallels the essential shape and meaning

of its related past-time story. The narrative present is a metaphoric or mimetic version of the narrative past. . . .

The writing-time story is a means of showing directly and immediately meanings which the author despairs of being able to communicate by conventional language and literary forms. (374)

29. Cambon, "Ishmael and the Problem of Formal Discontinuities," 523.

30. Robert Hazel, speaking at the December 1959 meeting of the Modern Language Association of America.

31. Cecil M. Brown, "The White Whale," *Partisan Review* 36 (1969): 459, 457. "The white whale" in Brown's view "is none other than you, Ishmael—the white, disembodied, overliterate, boring, snobbish, insipid, jew-bastard, nigger-lover, effete, mediocre, assistant-professor type, liberal" (454).

32. See Harrison Hayford, "Unnecessary Duplicates: A Key to the Writing of *Moby-Dick*," in Faith Pullin, ed., *New Perspectives on Melville* (Edinburgh: Edinburgh University Press; Kent, Ohio: Kent State University Press, 1978), 128–161, and "Discussions of Adopted Readings" in the Northwestern-Newberry *Moby-Dick*, 809–906 passim.

After beginning *Moby-Dick* with high hopes for its success, Melville finished writing it only under great difficulties, complaining to Hawthorne of his "ditcher's work" with the book and his fear that all his books were "botches" (*Correspondence*, 212, 191). Although some present-day critics profess to discuss *Moby-Dick* as a virtually seamless narrative web—one, Paul Brodtkorb, going so far as to charge Ishmael rather than Melville himself with the "mistakes and inconsistencies" observable in the narrative (*Ishmael's White World*, 4–5, 7)—others such as Hayford have taken such occurrences as possible clues to the compositional history of the book. For a succinct review of various theories concerning its genesis and development, see section 5 of Historical Note, Northwestern-Newberry edition, 648–659.

33. In 1951, the centennial year of *Moby-Dick*'s publication, when Walter Bezanson first described the book as a work of organic art, James Benziger remarked that "modern organic critics use their theory to check the pretensions of the biographical and historical critics," adding that *any* theory must be "applied with judgment"; see his "Organic Unity: Leibniz to Coleridge," *PMLA* 66 (March 1951): 48. His caution is applicable today, now that successive generations of historically minded critics have reacted in turn against the organicists.

34. Brodtkorb, *Ishmael's White World*, 4.

35. Ralph Waldo Emerson, "The American Scholar," in *Nature, Addresses, and Lectures*, ed. Alfred R. Ferguson and Robert E. Spiller (Cambridge: Harvard University Press, Belknap Press, 1971), 58.

Work Cited

The Writings of Herman Melville, edited by Harrison Hayford, Hershel Parker, and G. Thomas Tanselle, 15 vols. (Evanston and Chicago: Northwestern University Press and the Newberry Library, 1968–).

STANTON GARNER

Naples and HMS Bellipotent:
Melville on the Police State

Herman Melville's visit to Naples from February 18 to February 24, 1857, affected him deeply. It was an epiphany: he saw there, for the first time, a tyranny in which, in contrast to most of Europe, a population was still being held in thrall by an unenlightened monarch whose reign depended upon subjugation by a large and alien soldiery, subversion by informers, and wholesale imprisonments of citizens only suspected of disloyalty. While another man might have dismissed this revelation as a regrettable local phenomenon, Melville, whose imagination tended instead toward global synthesis, saw the police state of Naples as a type which may recur in any era of human existence and in any human community. Thus, the repression of the citizen of Naples was the potential repression of every man, and for this reason it is echoed in a number of Melville's later works. It is the purpose of this essay to show how, after attempting to speak of it in several poems about Naples, Melville made forceful, tragic, and final use of it in *Billy Budd, Sailor.*

At the time of his arrival, the city was ruled by "Bomba," or Ferdinand V, the latest in a dynasty of Bourbon monarchs whose rule had provoked repeated insurrections. It had been less than nine years since the last great uprising, when royal cannon had fired into the streets and Sicilian troops and Swiss mercenaries had attacked civilian barricades on the streets and

Leviathan: A Journal of Melville Studies, Volume 1, Number 2 (1999): pp. 53–61. © 1999 Blackwell Publishing.

had swept through shops and homes, massacring citizens and throwing men, women, and children out of windows.[1] Visiting the city in its aftermath, future British prime minister William Gladstone, learning that there were 20,000 political prisoners held indiscriminately in cells with the basest of felons, condemned the regime publicly.[2] In the three months prior to Melville's arrival, Baron Francesco Bentivegna and some others had been executed for participating in a Sicilian conspiracy to establish a united, republican Italy, and during a military drill in Naples an infantryman had broken ranks in an attempt to impale the king on his bayonet. In obedience to "the fourth degree of public example," the soldier had been tortured and executed, both in public view. In addition, a powder magazine on a military pier had exploded and a frigate had blown up in the harbor, though the authorities were unable to link these events directly to subversion. Both the British and French governments had become so disgusted with the royal barbarity that they had broken off diplomatic relations and deployed warships lest their citizens in Naples be endangered.[3]

In his journal, Melville noted the ominous military presence: "Palace—soldiers—music—clang of arms all over city. Burst of troops from archway Cannon posted inwards," and, later, "Military continually about streets."[4] His remarks about the oppressive political climate end with that: much of the rest of the journal entries record his investigations of fabled sites in the area, as he dared the fates by descending into the crater of Vesuvius and as he walked through a grotto at Posillipo, which, he might have imagined (especially since his guide told him that it was the entrance to the "Infernal regions") was Virgil's model for the passage to the Underworld into which Aeneas had ventured. As a coda to his journal entries, before he left for Rome he jotted down some notes for future literary use:

> enumerate the mementoes of the remorselessness of Nature—ravages of war &c.—burned city. Solfatara &c.—Now, one would think if any *modern* city were here built &c, they would be sober in view of these things. But no. Gayest city in the world. No equipages flash like these; no beauties so haughty. No cavaliers so proud, no palaces so sumptuous. &c. &c.—Apt representation of that heedlessness, benignly ordained, of man which prevents him one generation from learning from a past.—"Let us eat, drink & be merry, for tomorrow we die." Such seems the lesson learned by the Neapolitans from their scenery. (*NN Journals* 105)

But when he did write about Naples—two poems unpublished in his lifetime "Naples in the Time of Bomba" and "At the Hostelry" (since paired under the title "Marquis de Grandvin") and another poem, "Pausilippo (In the Time of Bomba)" published in *Timoleon* (1891)—he wrote instead about the police state there.[5]

"Naples in the Time of Bomba" is a versified carriage ride through Naples and its environs by the narrator, Jack Gentian, in which some of Melville's own experiences are compressed into a single day. As the tour proceeds, the familiar Melville drama of darkness subverting light is played out. Naples *appears* to be a paradise of light, a place of ineffable beauty and joy inhabited by friendly, cheerful, colorful, free-spirited inhabitants who respond to his gesture of friendship with a merry ovation. Gentian is encouraged to doubt the stories he heard in England of Neapolitan oppression, but soon the darkness reveals itself in a city fortress where the cannon "seem trained / Less to beat alien foemen off / Than awe the town. 'Rabble!' they said, / Or in dumb threatening seemed to say, / 'Revolt, and we will rake your lanes!'" (*Poems* 342) and where the portals daily spew forth thousands of soldiers "To threaten, intimidate, and cow" (343). Was the apparent joy of the citizens "mirth's true elation? / Or even in some a patched despair, / Bravery in tatters debonair, / True devil-may-care dilapidation" (*Poems* 344)? Does the human heart prosper here, or is it a victim of the tyrant's oppression? After all, he muses, the Church provides a succession of festive holidays the year around.

One answer is provided by a rose thrust upon Gentian by a local "Peri."[6] A symbolic emissary of the light (a "festive flower"), the rose encourages an optimistic belief in a natural, unrepressed humanity—quite likely, what Melville meant by the "heart"—but it itself is afflicted by manifestations of the dark as they recur. The next such manifestation appears on Gentian's visit to Pausilippo (as Melville spelled it in the poem) where he seeks what the ancient Greek settlers had promised he would find there, "ease to pain." But the sight of Vesuvius, set between Pompeii and Herculaneum, both of which had been buried in its famed eruption, reminds him that periodically Nature exhibits a seeming malice of its own over which men have no power, as he later indicated by a subterranean eruption in his Civil War poem "The Apparition" (*Poems* 102). The people of Naples, he decides, live between a "Bomb-King" on the one hand, and on the other Vesuvius, which, as a result of ages of its own bomb-throwing, has made the area a "Vined urn of ashes, bed on bed" (350).

Melville expands the point about the Bomb-King in "Pausilippo," an excerpt from "Naples in the Time of Bomba" which he eventually recast into an independent poem. Visiting the hill, a narrator encounters a bard, Silvio, with his daughter.[7] Silvio is not old, but he is pallid, "bleached through strange immurement long." He has been a victim of "Clandestine arrest abrupt by night; / The sole conjectural cause / The yearning in a patriot ode / Construed as treason; trial none; / Prolonged captivity profound; / Vain liberation late" (*Poems* 243). Unmanned by his long imprisonment, he is a voiceless bard who plays his harp but cannot sing: his daughter must supply the voice that suffering has stilled. In the face of this reminder of tyranny, Pausilippo provides no soothing balm for the visitor. As Melville had said of his own encounter with the hill, "At Posilipo found not the cessation which the name expresses" (NN *Journals* 102).

Back in the city with a juggler and a tumbler to delight him, Gentian's thoughts are drawn to the dark past of Naples. However, it is a history re-shaped in Melville's imagination to emphasize that darkness. Gentian thinks first of the Angevin Queen Joanna I, who was suspected of complicity in her husband's 1345 strangulation at an inland city well north of Naples. In the poem, the murder is fictionalized by relocating it to the shore of Naples and suspicion becomes certainty as Joanna weaves an (apocryphal) noose of "three strands of silk and gold" with which to hang her Andrea (*Poems* 353).[8] Then Gentian's thoughts move on to an exemplary wife who was herself a victim, the Roman Agrippina, "The truest woman that ever wed" (359). The wife of Germanicus, she had responded to his murder in 19 AD by shaming the perpetrator into suicide, but was ten years later exiled by the apprehensive emperor Tiberius to what is now Ventone, an island over the horizon from Naples, where she starved to death. In the poem, however, her place of exile is so situated that she could "gaze on Naples' sunny bay," though Melville may or may not have been aware of the geographical error. Confronted with these thoughts, the rose complains, "Ah, let time's present time suffice, / No Past pertains to Paradise" (355), and reminds him that her bloom will fade.

Despite an offer of red ripe tomatoes ("love-apples") from a songstress peddler, Gentian's somber thoughts persist, taking him back to July 7, 1647, when the Neapolitan populace, led by the legendary young fisherman Ma-saniello, rose in protest against the wrongs of the Spanish viceregency, es-pecially its crushing taxes on fruit and flour, the food of the poor. Gentian remembers that the battle-painter Aniello Falcone and his sometime pu-pil, Salvator Rosa, took part in the uprising. Barricades were erected, blood was shed, and, as the rebellion began to spread to the outlying territories, the viceroy surrendered, pardoning the rebels, granting the citizens some rights, and removing some of the taxes. Some days later, Masaniello was assassinated and his head, impaled on a pike, was carried to the delighted viceroy. Again, Melville may not have known that neither Rosa nor Falcone participated in the uprising, since that was a persistent historical error.[9] Still, it was an uplifting idea, that art and freedom are allies, even if only in the poem. Gentian responds to the recollection by ruing that the uprising was as bloody as was the tyranny from which it sought redress.

It is interesting that, although Gentian speaks of Naples's "Red after-years" (the "red" of continued and futile struggle against tyranny, one imag-ines) he abbreviates his mention of the brief experiment, of 1799, in citi-zen government known as the Parthenopean Republic and the subsequent hanging of Admiral Prince Caracciolo, which has been cited as a source of *Billy Budd*.[10] One might have expected that this brief and ill-fated attempt at popular rule would have excited Melville's sympathy, and that he would have regarded its tragic suppression by the king and the summary execution of the gallant Caracciolo by Admiral Nelson with disapproval. Instead, according to the poem, the Republic was invalidated because of its sponsorship by French republican invaders, who brought with them *"The Terror,"* symbolized by the "Carmagnole" (a French revolutionary costume). Instead of a blow struck for freedom, Gentian sees it as a period of the "cannibal hymn" and "Mad song and dance," "Hell's cornucopia crammed with crime!" (*Poems* 357). Of the general European Revolution of 1848, which had its inception in this king-dom, there is not a word. Like Melville a stoic, Gentian clearly disapproves of violence, however noble its aim.

Returning to the Naples of the present, the darkness persists as Gen-tian's tour takes him through civilians outside a fence watching soldiers within "With eye-lids squeezed, yet letting out / A flame as of quick lightning thin." The soldiers, in turn, glance distrustfully back at the citizens. Then, as a boy wanderer sings to a crowd gathered in a street, a blind man, who may be one of Bomba's agents in disguise, listens, as do a pair of bystanders, a Jesuit and a lawyer. These, too, are suspect: the lawyer is "A useful man to lawless pow-er, / Expert to legalise the wrong" (360). Next another contingent of troops marches down the street, led by a *miles glorioso* drum-major, a caricature of Bomba's tyranny:

> Arch whiskerando and gigantic
> A grandiose magnifico antic
> Tossing his truncheon in the van.
> A hifalutin exaggeration,
> Barbaric in his bearskin shako,
> Of bullying Bomba's puffed elation
> And blood-and-thunder proclamation,
> A braggadocio Bourbon-Draco! (*Poems* 363)

Gentian's description is the kind of burlesque that Lord Shaftesbury had identified as the most appropriate artistic response to tyranny, a response also employed by the boy-singer who, after the parade has passed, sings mock-ingly of both the soldiers and the king. An alarmed citizen hastens to warn him of the risk of imprisonment, not for "patriots only, plotters deemed, / But talkers, rhymesters, every kind / Of indiscreetly innocent mind."[11]

Gentian's final view of Naples in chains comes when a robed priest and his entourage pass through the crowd bearing the communion host to the bedside of a dying parishioner. The reverent citizens fall silent and kneel in

what, in his journal, Melville had called "Romish superstition." Despite his earlier satisfaction with the ample calendar of religious festivities, Gentian muses
in prose that the Church is more effective in bringing a "semi-insurgent populace to their knees" (*Poems* 365) than is all of the military might of the monarch.
With this, the rose expires and Gentian's tour has ended. But in a later note, he
celebrates the fall of Naples to the liberator Garibaldi, the rose returned in the
person of the Red Shirt, who, on September 7, 1860, arrived alone to proclaim
the freedom of the city. In memory of Garibaldi, Gentian proclaims that "down
time's aisle, mid clarions clear / Pale glory walks by valor's bier" (367) only to
regret, in an "After-Piece," that his poem had ended with the catafalque rather
than the rose.

"At the Hostelry" is an imaginary symposium in which an assortment
of painters of various nationalities and of various eras meet at Delmonico's,
in Melville's time an opulent New York City restaurant and banquet house,
to discuss their art. There the narrator, the Marquis de Grandvin, uses the occasion to amplify the portrait of Garibaldi, who was "knightly" despite living
in a paladin age," and to compare him to El Cid. This modern knight was
heroic in ending the tyranny in Naples without bloodshed: "he the hero was
a sword / Whereto at whiles Cavour was guard. / The point described a fiery
arc, / A swerve of wrist ordained the mark. Wise statesman, a ruling star /
Made peace itself subserve the war" (*Poems* 314). In retrospect, the Marquis
also remarks on the role of the church in supporting the rule of "the preda-
tory band / Of shyster-princes." Italy, he says, was "Nigh paralysed, by cowls
misguided" (315).

• • •

Melville's experience in Naples, and the poems he wrote about it, echo in his
later works, as early as his Civil War poems dealing with civilians victimized by military imperatives, the Southerners at Vicksburg and Charleston
and along the line of Sherman's march and the Northern draft rioters of
New York, and as late as 'Timoleon,' which deals directly with tyrannous
rule. But their influence on *Billy Budd, Sailor* is particularly strong. In terms
of the title character, it would be difficult to find a more apt model than
Masaniello, the low-born blond youth who leapt from the obscurity of the
Neapolitan fishery to the unquestioned leadership of the 1647 Neapolitan
uprising with no greater qualification than his charisma. He was a cynosure, indeed, but, like Billy, Masaniello paid with his life for his role as
a Handsome Sailor. Furthermore, Melville's depiction of Bomba's Naples-
world is strongly suggestive of the world-ship *Bellipotent*. Like Naples, the
man-of-war is characterized by its ubiquitous cannon, its military guards,
and its government by a less barbarous, but equally unforgiving, tyranny,
while the omnipresent danger of informers on the Naples streets is paralleled

by the wires of underground influence that are strung through Captain Vere's crew. The daily terror of the Neapolitans is echoed in the terror that seizes young Billy when he first witnesses a flogging and realizes that the threat of the cat-o'-nine-tails hangs constantly over "the people," and the caution through which the inhabitants of Bomba's streets survive is echoed by the wariness of the Dansker, who, after an adulthood of shipboard submission, dares not speak frankly to the young sailor, even when, by doing so, he might save him.

Another salient similarity can be found in the suggested complicity of the lawyers and clergy in the Naples police state. There are no lawyers in *Billy Budd*, but the law proves to be, nevertheless, a deadly instrument for exacting a punishment which is not adjudicated but is pronounced by Captain Vere before Billy's court-martial is even convened—a way to "legalise the wrong." But it is the role of religion which is the most telling.

From the time of Billy's impressment into the man-of-war world until the events following his execution, religion abets the military rule on the world-ship—parodying Christ's Beatitudes, Lieutenant Ratcliffe blesses the warship's guns as "peacemakers."[12] Again, in a notorious disquisition, the narrator remarks that the ship's chaplain "indirectly subserves the purpose attested by the cannon" and "lends the sanction of the religion of the meek to that which practically is the abrogation of everything but brute Force" (*BB* 122). This passive complicity becomes active when the sailors react to Billy's burial at sea with "encroachment" (127), only to be subdued by a call to battle-stations, where they stand under the watchful eyes of the sworded officers listening to sacred music from the ship's band and a religious service. With that, the men are "toned by music and religious rites subserving the discipline and purposes of war" (128).

The same point is made symbolically in chapter three of *Billy Budd*, in the allusion to the mutiny at Spithead and the Nore, that brilliantly-executed uprising that first brought a soupçon of recognition by the British admiralty of the humanity of the navy's seamen. There, with a flag invented by Melville for the purpose,[13] the sailors remove symbols of church and state (a cross and a British "union") which had been superimposed on a red field, thus liberating the heart color of Jack Gentian's rose and of Garibaldi's shirt. The narrator refers to that red as "the enemy's red meteor of unbridled and unbounded revolt" (*BB* 54), but that is a red herring, so to speak: since Britain's enemy, revolutionary France, was symbolized by a tricolor flag rather than a red one, the only remaining enemy is the sailors who defied entrenched tyranny in order to gain a pathetically small modicum of decent treatment. Some readers may give little importance to the dehumanizing effect of the alliance of government and religion in feudal times, but the American founders understood it perfectly when they demanded the separation of the two, and certainly Melville did.

The complex process through which Melville toyed with elements of two existing naval ensigns until he had created one of his own which allowed him to attach new symbolic meanings to the union and the cross, on one hand, and a solid red background, on the other, is, again, an example of irony deployed to expose tyranny. To refashion established, harmless symbols into a new one with a subversive meaning is the essence of protest against the police state and its almost unassailable structure. In *Benito Cereno*, as John Bryant points out, Melville had "the need to retreat within unstable narrative ironies because his nation could not bear plain speaking" (*Melville and Repose* 48) Not the least of those ironies is another flag conversion, in which tyranny bleeds a Spanish flag of its reds and its heraldic animal life, thus anticipating the heraldic swap in *Billy Budd* by three and a half decades. [14]

But, it might be argued, what Melville experienced and wrote about much earlier in life is irrelevant to *Billy Budd*. In the long, exhausting, and indecisive division of opinion about that work, those who defend the actions of Captain Vere on the ground that his highest duty was to preserve order on his ship, and that it was necessary to sacrifice Billy to that end, do so in defiance of the fact that, taken all in all, Melville's earlier works defend the common seaman (the common man) against the tyrannies of his captains (those in authority over him). They explain that incongruity by claiming that during the intervening years his views underwent a complete reversal: that in his last years he came to believe that society must be governed rigidly according to immutable "forms, measured forms" (*BB* 128) by leaders who preserve those forms.

But the Naples poems refute that idea. Considering the impact that Melville's visit had on him, it is quite possible that he began writing about his experiences there soon after the end of his trip, when he turned his attention to poetry. It is especially suggestive, in relation to "At the Hostelry," that he began lecturing on art then.[15] Whether or not he began the poems before the Civil War by the mid-1870s, when he worked on prose sketches to accompany them, "he had already composed [the Naples poems], at least in part."[16] At that time, he had ample opportunity to revise the poems he had written earlier to reflect any change of heart that he might have experienced. We know that he took up the poems again as late as mid-1882, after Garibaldi died, but his eulogy of the Red Shirt, introduced then, would have given Captain Vere no comfort. Sealts believes that he went back to "Hostelry" and "Bomba" again in 1890 ("Burgundy Club Sketches" 79), when he excerpted "Pausilippo," but in that poem Silvio still suffers the blight of his dungeon years, and still Posillipo is powerless to hear him. It may be that Melville finally abandoned the Naples poems because what he had to say in them had already been incorporated in *Billy Budd*.[17]

Billy did not know who his parents were, but *Billy Budd, Sailor* was not an orphan: it was a legitimate child of Melville's earlier works and attitudes. They track his thinking and his art through the years, showing us continuing similarities in situations, symbols, and concerns in a way that nothing else can: the cannon with which the French fleet threatens the natives of Nuku Hiva are the same cannon that White Jacket hopes will never be turned inboard, the same cannon that roll through the streets of New York during the draft riots, and the same "peacemakers" between which Billy Budd is shackled awaiting execution. Naples is Naples, but it is also the *Bellipotent*. Prepared with the lessons which Melville's lifetime of composition teaches, we are in a strong position to understand one of his most opaque and seemingly contradictory works and to avoid misleading speculation about Melville's aberrant state of mind as he wrote it.

Notes

1. Pietro Colletta, *History of the Kingdom of Naples, 1734–1825,* with suppl., 1825–1856, trans. S. Horner, 2 vols. (Edinburgh: T. Constable, 1858), 2: 548–552.

2. Lacey Collision-Morley, *Naples Through the Centuries* (London: Methuen, 1925), p. 163.

3. Gordon Poole, "Naples in the Time of Melville: Italian Politics 1857," *Melville Society* Extracts, no. 105 (June 1996), 8–9. I am indebted to Professor Poole for sharing with me his extensive knowledge of Naples and Melville's relationship to the city, and for guarding me, to the extent possible, from historical error.

4. Herman Melville, *Journals,* ed. Howard C. Horth, Lynn Horsford, Harrison Hayford, and G. Thomas Tanselle (Evanston and Chicago: Northwestern University Press and The Newberry Library, 1989), pp. 101 and 103. Hereafter cited as NN Journals.

5. Herman Melville, *Collected Poems of Herman Melville,* ed. Howard P. Vincent (Chicago: Hendricks House, 1947), p. 311. Hereafter cited as *Poems.* There is no generally accepted text or title of the two unpublished poems. A recent, impressive edition (of all three poems) is *At the Hostelry* and *Naples in the Time of Bomba,* ed. Gordon Poole (Naples: Istituto Universitario Orientale, 1989), which includes valuable annotations and textual notes. Hereafter cited as *Hostelry* and *Naples.*

6. In Persian lore, a fairy of a sort; in this case, a sprite-like, very beautiful woman.

7. According to Gordon Poole, this is Silvio Pellico (1789–1854), an author who was imprisoned for ten years (*Hostelry* and *Naples,* p. 90).

8. An invention. Collison-Morley states that Andrea was strangled (not hanged) with a silken (but not gold) cord, then thrown out of a window (49). W. C. Stafford and Charles Ball, *Italy Illustrated: A Complete History of the Past and Present Condition of the Italian States,* 2 vols., vol. 1 (London: London Printing and Publishing Co., 1860–1861), 1:156, admit that Giovanna might have consented to an assassination plot hatched by her Neapolitan courtiers, but Collison-Morley claims that she was shocked by the crime and retreated to the castle, where her son was born.

9. Luigi Antonio Lanzi, *The History of Painting in Italy, from the Period of the Revival of the Fine Arts to the End of the Eighteenth Century,* trans. Thomas Roscoe, 6 vols. (London: Simpkin and Marshall, 1828), 2:421, states confidently that Falcone formed the "Band of Death," made up of fellow-artists, which "committed the most revolting and sanguinary excesses" and was protected by the Spanish painter Spagnoletto (Giuseppe Ribera). Other English-language sources available to Melville list the soldier-painters (Alfred de Reumont, *The Carafas of Maddaloni: Naples under Spanish Dominion* [London: Bohn, 18541, p. 332], and give a detailed account of Rosa's activities (Lady [Sydney] [Owenson] Morgan, *Life and Times of Salvator Rosa,* 2 vols. [London: Colburn, 1824], 1:383–389, and 2:5). However, Collison-Morley speaks for modern scholarship when she says that the "Band of Death" and the participation of Falcone and Rosa "appears to be altogether mythical" (113).

10. Kay S. House, "Francesco Caracciolo, Fenimore Cooper and Bully Budd," *Studi Americani* (Rome), no. 19–20 (1976), 83–100.

11. *Poems* 365. Shaftesbury's formulation, as transmitted through the American critic William A. Jones, is discussed in John Bryant, *Melville and Repose: The Rhetoric of Humor in the American Renaissance* (New York: Oxford University Press, 1993), p. 48.

12. Herman Melville, *Billy Budd, Sailor,* ed. Harrison Hayford and Merton M. Sealts, Jr. (Chicago: University of Chicago Press, 1962), p. 48. Hereafter cited as *BB.*

13. Stanton Garner, "Fraud as Fact in Herman Melville's *Billy Budd,*" *San José Studies,* 4 (May, 1978): 88–91.

14. Stanton Garner, "A Vexillogical Key to Melville's Attitude Toward Slavery," unpublished paper, Melville Society meeting (New York, December, 1978).

15. In November, 1859, Melville borrowed the Lanzi history from Evert Duyckinck. See Merton M. Sealts, Jr., *Melville's Reading,* rev. (Columbia: University of South Carolina Press, 1988), p. 192.

16. Merton M Sealts, Jr., "Melville's Burgundy Club Sketches," *Pursuing Melville, 1940–1980* (Madison, University of Wisconsin Press, 1982), p. 78.

17. Poole reports that even after he had removed "Pausilippo" for inclusion in *Timoleon,* Melville continued work on "Naples—the Time of Bomba" ("Manuscript and Transmissions," p. xliv).

THOMAS HOVE

Naturalist Psychology in
Billy Budd

One of the most important cultural debates of the late nineteenth century was the status of morality in the wake of Darwinism and other naturalist accounts of human development. If Darwin's theories were correct, many Victorian moralists worried, there might be no strong foundation for traditional Christian values like altruism and benevolence.[1] According to traditional Christianity's dualist view of human nature as a mix of pure spirit and corrupt matter, these values were justified by their location in the higher realm of the spirit. Instances of human error and evil could be blamed on the limitations our bodily existence puts on our spiritual aims. Melville explored the ethical problems of this dualist view most thoroughly in *Pierre* (1852): "Pierre, though charged with the fire of all divineness, his containing thing was made of clay."[2] Even though his other fictions of the 1850s foreground various cognitive and ethical impasses of dualism, it would take several decades for him to entertain a naturalist outlook disassociated from cynical and pessimistic characters like the Fiddle passengers in *The Confidence-Man* (1857) and Margoth in *Clarel* (1876).

In *Billy Budd*, Melville explores a naturalist view of action more thoroughly and sympathetically than in any of his previous works.[3] In doing so, he challenges the traditional dualist metaphysics of the person and the absolutist normative framework it supports. *Billy Budd* manifests a post-Darwinian

Leviathan: A Journal of Melville Studies, Volume 5, Number 2 (2003): pp. 51–65. Copyright © 2003 Melville Society.

philosophical tendency to rank passions not according to a dualist hierarchy of pure spirit and corrupt matter but according to a pragmatic sense of what actions are appropriate for achieving a goal within a specific situation. According to this naturalist ethics, deeming what's appropriate depends not on some accurate perception of truth but rather on interpretations of situations that can guide human energies toward desired ends. Although the narrator of *Billy Budd* suggests that we can never directly perceive these energies, and although he characterizes thought as a latecomer on the scene of action, he nevertheless affirms intelligence's efforts to understand action's laws and mechanisms. Such efforts are most apparent in his speculations on the origins and mechanisms of Claggart's antipathy toward Billy.

Analyzing *Billy Budd* from a naturalist standpoint offers several theoretical and interpretive advantages over readings that either insist upon a correspondence theory of knowledge or reaffirm traditional dualist ethics. Readings that try to resolve the novel's cognitive and ethical problems tend to assume that accurate assessment of a character's motivations will allow us to attribute determinate moral or political positions to the text. This obsession with both epistemological and ethical certainty appears even in deconstructive readings, which emphasize how the novel's historical and normative claims fail to live up to standards of absolute certainty. But if we reject these standards as inappropriate remnants of a dualist metaphysics, we can begin to place the novel in the intellectual context of late nineteenth-century efforts to reconceive morality from a materialist standpoint. In addition, to get around the impasses that have plagued ethical and political interpretations of *Billy Budd*, we can reject the assumption that the text itself strives for certainty, and we can avoid measuring the text's ethical and political content up against external normative frameworks like Christian altruism or Marxist anti-authoritarianism.[4] To list other advantages of an epistemologically modest and ethically neutral reading strategy: it enables us to take fuller account of the variety of impulses that motivate characters' actions; it cautions us against assigning too great a role to rational self-control in the normative conclusions we might draw from the text; it avoids the conceptual impasses typical of mind-body, spirit-matter, idea-sensation dualism; and it offers a method for ranking motivations and actions according to naturalist values like health and appropriateness rather than absolutist values like good and evil, truth and falsehood.

Ethics without Spirit, Knowledge without Representation

Ever since the 1920s, Melville scholarship has commented on the ambiguities permeating the portraits of Billy, Claggart, and Vere.[5] But naturalist theories of action can help us read *Billy Budd* in a way that does not simply reiterate the obvious fact that these ambiguities complicate our knowledge of the characters' motivations and our judgments of their actions. Instead, we can follow the lead of pragmatist and Nietzschean action theories, which take these conditions of uncertainty as a given, thereby sidestepping epistemological questions that have no answers and no necessary relation to motivation and action. As in the psychological explorations of his younger American contemporaries William James and John Dewey, Melville's naturalistic picture of human existence attempts to reconceive traditional moral values from within a materialist metaphysics. Although it pays tribute to Hawthorne's "The Birthmark," *Billy Budd* does not reproduce Hawthorne's Romantic, dualist assumption that one kind of motivation comes from corrupt material sources and a different, "higher" kind comes from pure spiritual sources.[6]

Although Melville initially shared this dualist metaphysics of the person, he wrote *Billy Budd* after decades of public debate over the ethical implications of Darwinism and naturalism. Like many of his Victorian contemporaries, Melville tries to preserve a place within naturalism for ethical values formerly justified by their association with a higher realm of spirit. But like every ethical theorist who has tackled this problem up to the present day, he fails to supply a satisfactory alternative justification.[7] Instead, the modest goal he and other naturalist thinkers manage to achieve is to challenge the reductive tendencies of traditional dualism and crude materialism. Melville issues these antireductive challenges through thick, polyvalent descriptions of motivation, and through a narrative technique that manifests circumspection, self-correction, tentativeness, and ambivalence.

Scholarly commentary on *Billy Budd* tends to treat these techniques as demonstrating the impossibility of attaining certainty about motivation. But the text invites us to disregard the assumption which underlies much of this commentary—that knowledge must consist of representational accuracy.[8] If we read Melville's descriptions of motivation from a pragmatic rather than an absolutist or even a radically skeptical perspective, we can set aside epistemological and normative debates that will always remain unresolved. Questions about the "essential" moral natures of Billy, Claggart, and Vere cannot be resolved because they assume habits of absolutist ethical thought that the text tries to get past. Rather than read the text as a challenge to discern moral reality behind deceptive and ambiguous appearances, we can take up its invitation to extrapolate from its speculations on the link between physiology and psychology. Significantly, these speculations make no pretensions to accurate representation of the sources and laws of motivation and action. One of Nietzsche's unpublished notebook entries offers an apt justification for this epistemologically modest orientation:

> In the tremendous multiplicity of what happens within an organism, the part we become conscious of is merely a little corner; and the

rest of the totality of what happens gives the lie to the little scrap of 'virtue', 'selflessness' and similar fictions in a perfectly radical way. We do well to study our organism in its perfect immorality.[9]

Although Melville's skeptical narrator would agree with these observations, neither his nor Nietzsche's assumptions about the human organism's "perfect immorality" can make better claims to objectivity than the traditional "fictions" they challenge. In proposing an amoral study of human motivation, however, their shared aim is to open up speculations about human action to possibilities excluded from traditional dualist views.

The naturalist psychology of *Billy Budd* lies in the narrator's tendency to describe motivation and action with terminology borrowed from physics and mechanics. He often labels characters' motivations as different kinds of "energies." This vague label can refer to a variety of phenomena: e.g., impulses, passions, emotions, habits, virtues. For each character, the narrator specifies one or two energies that serve as primary motivational forces: Billy is driven by unself-conscious exuberance; Claggart, by envy and antipathy; Vere, by military custom and an urgent fear of mutiny. Dualist morality would treat each of these energies as a blind force that overpowers the conscious, spiritual, "better" part of one's nature. But Melville's metaphysics of the person does not privilege particular kinds of energy over others—except to the extent that some of them are more appropriate than others in certain situations and for certain ends.

By lacing this purported "inside narrative" with so much uncertainty, the narrator suggests that normative judgments cannot ground themselves in an accurate perception of human psychology and social situations. Like Nietzsche and the pragmatists, he rejects the view that knowledge must reflect, represent, or correspond with the world "out there" beyond our minds. As in his famous remark that "Truth uncompromisingly told will always have its ragged edges,"[10] he pre-empts the concern for epistemological certainty by having his narrator foreground his cognitive tools of tentative speculation, self-correction, and an openness to a variety of viewpoints. Accordingly, we can read his narrative technique as aiming at a goal other than the representational accuracy emphasized in both conventional and deconstructive readings. In a brilliant instance of the latter, citing the narrator's admission that he cannot "hit" Claggart's portrait, Barbara Johnson wonders, "how reliable can a description be if it does not hit its object?"[11] But as the narrator's constantly shifting frames-of-reference suggest, reliable representation is not the only purpose of description. Instead, descriptions can provide understanding of action even when they cannot lay claim to representational accuracy. Like Melville's younger contemporaries William James and John Dewey, we need to jettison the hope that accounts of action can provide us with a "reliable" picture of moral existence that might help us "accurately" judge action. Nevertheless, the narrator's analytical efforts in *Billy Budd* suggest that accounts of action can provide tools for the tentative assessment of past and present action, and the possible control of future action.

Elements of Naturalist Motivation

Rather than normative ethical and political judgments, the narrator assesses energies according to their situational appropriateness.[12] His choice of standards for judging their appropriateness depends on the evaluative framework he brings to bear on the characters' actions viewed as adaptations to their environments. By including multiple frames of reference within his descriptions of the characters, the narrator highlights the inevitable plurality of overdetermined motivations relevant to a given action. Billy's exuberance competes with his prudent fear of punishment; Claggart's envy competes with his admiration of Billy's goodness; Vere's fear of mutiny competes with his compassion for Billy. Avoiding dualism, the narrator does not rank these competing motivations according to a hierarchy of greater and lesser degrees of spirituality or materiality. Nor does he insist on the ontological difference and superiority of motivations originating in the realm of spirit. To be sure, he does speculate about the positive and negative effects certain energies may have on the mind, soul, body, and society at large. But he does so according to pragmatic considerations of health, proper functioning, and goal achievement rather than normative considerations of right and wrong.

From the narrator's descriptions, we can formulate the following picture of moral existence on board the *Bellipotent*. He classifies the characters' motivations as different kinds of energies that manifest themselves in their temperaments and actions. The temperaments of Billy, Claggart, and Vere differ because they possess varying combinations of energies in varying amounts. In addition, as a substitute for dualist notions of good and evil, the narrator refers to two contrasting poles of motivation. On one hand, there is "natural virtue," which he associates with Billy and describes as a positive, expansive vitality: "a virtue went out of him, sugaring the sour ones" (*BB* 47). On the other hand, there is "natural depravity," which he associates with Claggart and describes as an "unreciprocated malice" that opposes natural virtue's positive vitality and sometimes even seeks to destroy it (80). Setting aside the more complicated case of Vere, we can use this materialist formula to make sense of the interactions between Billy and Claggart, which are determined primarily by these conflicting energies of depravity and vitality.

In dramatizing this formula, Melville exposes a crucial problem at the heart of normative frameworks that rely on the notion of a pure spirit. Traditionally, the spirit is the source of thought, which commands the body to carry out its higher laws by means of action. In contrast to this view, the interactions between Billy and Claggart illustrate the utter subordination of thought to action. What occurs between Billy and Claggart is like a chemical reaction. Rather than produce a chemical bond, Claggart's and Billy's "natures" react to each other like sodium and water. Billy's vitality is expansive, and it emanates positive influences on anything in its path that does not obstruct it. But Claggart's depravity is destructive, and it happens, for no apparent reason, to single out Billy as its "special object" of destruction (76). Each man's vital or depraved energies lie beyond thought's conscious control. To make sense of this conflict, the narrator does not rely on dualism's notions of motivation and action. Instead, he portrays action as an interplay of rival but ontologically similar energies.

This view of action bears striking affinities not only to Nietzsche's theories of action but to those of the young John Dewey. Around the time Melville was writing *Billy Budd,* Dewey was beginning to work out his refutation of the dualist psychology of action. Dewey rejected the model of "reflex action" as a series of disjointed arcs consisting of physical stimulus, followed by mental idea, followed by physical response. Instead, taking his lead from William James's *The Principles of Psychology* (1890), Dewey's seminal essay "The Reflex Arc Concept in Psychology" (1896) portrays action as "one uninterrupted, continuous redistribution of mass in motion. In the physical process, as physical, there is nothing which can be set off as stimulus, nothing which reacts, and nothing which is response. There is just a change in the system of tensions."[13] But this materialist view of action raises the following question: if there is no spirit that stimulates action, and if action consists of nothing but a redistribution of tensions within matter, what is the role of thought?

Instead of mirroring the world, thought in *Billy Budd* entails the ex post facto interpretation and indirect regulation of human energies. While the narrator knows that he cannot pretend to representational accuracy in his accounts of Billy's and Claggart's conflicting energies, he nevertheless attempts his own interpretations of their actions. These interpretations reflect his efforts to arrive at a new understanding of action in light of the challenges posed by this story of "certain phenomenal men" (*BB* 75). This endeavor is most apparent in the blend of emotional and physiological terminology he uses to describe motivation and action. Although he associates "vitality" mainly with Billy, both Billy's and Claggart's bodies function as vessels for particular kinds of vitality. In Claggart's case, vitality takes the form of "depravity"—specifically, his self-destructive envy. But Claggart's envy is not just self-destructive. It also seeks to eradicate the external objects of its antipathy, even if the effort to do so destroys its human host in the process. By contrast, the narrator usually refers to Billy's vitality as "exuberance." While his exuberance is not necessarily destructive, it can burst forth at tragically inopportune moments and destroy whatever lies in its path.

The narrator describes Billy and Claggart acting under the sway of these forces in a neutrally scientific rather than a normative tone. When he does use terms like "good" and "evil," their sense is not normative but figurative. He alludes to moralistic hierarchies, but he uses moral terms and concepts without their traditional implications, of judgment according to absolute standards.[14] This is not to say that he leaves normative standards out of his descriptions altogether, for he obviously uses morally inflected words like "innocence" and "evil" to describe Billy and Claggart. But the narrative's standards of virtue are more Aristotelian and pragmatic than absolutist. They appeal to health, appropriateness, and the proper functioning of organisms in their environment rather than pure values existing in a spiritual realm above and apart from bodily existence.

In addition to contrasting two kinds of vitality in his descriptions of Billy and Claggart (exuberance and depravity), the narrator contrasts two kinds of virtue. Each virtue has its relative advantages and disadvantages, and the narrator assesses these advantages according to their situational function and the interpretive frame that defines that function. First, there is "conventional" virtue, which is derived from civilized custom but can often lead to hypocrisy. It can even foster something like Claggart's natural depravity: "Civilization, especially of the austerer sort, is auspicious to [depravity]. It folds itself in the mantle of respectability" (*BB* 75). This conventional virtue works at cross purposes to the second kind of virtue, which the narrator labels "unsophisticated" virtue. Unsophisticated virtue has little to do with natural depravity and more to do with something like Billy's natural exuberance or vitality. It expresses itself through actions that appear to be "frank manifestations in accordance with natural law" (52).

The narrator also classifies circumstantial forces that either help or hinder these different types of virtue. In cases where civilized life cannot tolerate manifestations of unsophisticated virtue, "custom" appears in the form of acquired habits that restrain natural exuberance for the purpose of social order. Two obvious forms of customary restraint are morality and law. But the most prominent form it takes in the narrative is military discipline, which the narrator describes as capable of being internalized as instinct: "True martial discipline long continued superinduces in average man a sort of impulse whose operation at the official word of command much resembles in its promptitude the effect of an instinct" (*BB* 127). Ironically, custom and conventional virtue foster depravity better than they tolerate exuberance. This neutral, psycho-social equation of forces begins to explain why an exuberant nature like Billy's cannot function properly in a situation ruled by military discipline and law. Contrary to certain critical traditions, Melville does not describe this situation moralistically. Billy is not an innocent victim of corrupt social practices. Instead, to use naturalist terminology characteristic of pragmatist normativity, he is an organism maladapted to his environment.

To place Billy's and Claggart's motivations within a meaningful frame of reference, the narrator alludes to Judeo-Christian tradition. While this is obvious enough, Melville deploys the morally loaded terms of religious tradition in a contrastive rather than an absolutist sense. As Robert Milder notes about Melville's use of Christian imagery in the late stages of writing, "the language functions more as a resonant gloss on characters and events than as symbols within an articulated religious parable."[15] When the narrator introduces Billy and Claggart, he uses Christian imagery to portray them as two extremes of human vitality and depravity. He describes Billy as a prelapsarian Adam not to mark him as a moral innocent but to emphasize how his exuberance is not impeded by rational self-consciousness: "By his original constitution aided by the co-operating influences of his lot, Billy in many respects was little more than a sort of upright barbarian, much such perhaps as Adam presumably might have been ere the urbane Serpent wriggled himself into his company" (*BB* 52). As for the serpent in this story, "something such as one was Claggart, in whom was the mania of an evil nature, not engendered by vicious training or corrupting books or licentious living, but born with him and innate, in short 'a depravity according to nature'" (76). In spite of this morally essentialist rhetoric, Melville characteristically allows ambiguities to creep into the portraits of both men. Several commentators including Johnson in "Melville's Fist" have pointed out that these ambiguities force us to question the traditional reading of Billy and Claggart as moral opposites. More significantly, though, they force us to question the appropriateness of using moralistic terms like "good" and "evil" to characterize their motivations and actions in the first place.

Indirection, Antireductionism, and the Evasion of Epistemology

The descriptions of Claggart in Chapters 8, 10, 11, and 12 epitomize the link between Melville's naturalist view of motivation and his indirect narrative technique.[16] The narrators' skeptical, self-questioning speculations about Claggart's motivations reflect Melville's unwillingness to affirm reductive conclusions that presume to represent what "really" happens between Claggart and Billy. The narrator begins his psychological investigations with a skeptical examination of the evidence available to him. Second, he supplements this skepticism with tentative speculations about Claggart's nature. At this point, he attempts to synthesize these speculations with his preexisting assumptions about the laws of human nature. Third, he subjects his new speculations to further skepticism. Finally, he appeals to circumstance and settles upon a comparatively modest claim about Claggart that cannot be reasonably doubted. But this modest claim still fails to resolve his confusion about the source of Claggart's intense antipathy toward Billy. This narrative technique suggests that the sources of action cannot be inferred with any degree of completeness or accuracy. Instead of striving for epistemological certainty, the narrator's speculations reflect his ongoing attempt to understand energies that must always lie beyond his cognitive grasp—in this case, vitality and depravity. This perpetually incomplete, experimental pursuit of understanding resembles what Dewey would later call "intelligence" in moral inquiry:

> intelligence treats events as moving, as fraught with possibilities, not as ended, final. In forecasting their possibilities, the distinction between better and worse arises. Human desire and ability cooperates with this or that natural force according as this or that eventuality is judged better. We do not use the present to control the future. We use the foresight of the future to refine and expand present activity.[17]

Through a close analysis of the narrator's attempts to understand Claggart's antipathy toward Billy, we can begin to see what this view of narrative technique as the "intelligent" analysis of action entails.

Before conjecturing anything specific about Claggart's motivations, the narrator acknowledges the impossibility of making his portrait correspond with the man himself. He sidesteps this epistemological concern by admitting that his descriptions cannot reproduce Claggart according to standards of representational accuracy: "his portrait I essay, but shall never hit it" (*BB* 64). In addition, the contradictory rumors about Claggart's past history make the narrator's efforts to pin him down even more difficult. Yet he offers the following conjectures anyway. Like Billy and Vere, Claggart seems to come from a noble background. He may, for example, be a chevalier "keeping incog" (64). But such rumors are trivial historical by-paths, not significant enough to interrupt the narrator's more pressing inquiry into Claggart's nature. In spite of his doubts about achieving certainty, the narrator's attempts to explain Claggart affirm the importance of reaching some sort of understanding of another person's motivations. Since understanding cannot achieve the type of certainty aimed at in the correspondence theory of knowledge, it needs a different goal.

Setting aside the goal of representational accuracy, the narrator aims at interpretive consistency. If his goal in "essaying" this portrait is a better understanding of human action, he can at least strive for an understanding that is theoretically consistent with his preexisting assumptions about the laws of action, i.e., its differing degrees and kinds of "virtue" and "vitality." One insight about Claggart's nature can be gleaned from his overly enthusiastic zeal in the role of master-at-arms. His enthusiasm on the job can be attributed to a prudent conformity with "conventional" virtue. This insight, however, is not consistent with Claggart's behavior after the antipathy toward Billy possesses him. From that point on, Claggart's behavior conforms less and less to the narrator's standards of conventional virtue. Instead of maintaining order, Claggart sows chaos and destruction. This destructive impulse is hinted at in the rumors that Claggart had been a criminal before his impressment, one of those "drafts culled direct from the jails" (*BB* 66). A prudent historian, the narrator points out that the people most likely to credit these shadowy rumors are the sailors who fear and resent Claggart's "official rattan" (65). But he also admits that these rumors are partially supported by the definite, albeit circumstantial, fact of Claggart's impressment. At this point in his description, the narrator's return to concrete fact indicates that he is not a radical skeptic when it comes to understanding motivation. At the very least, this fact sheds some light on the mystery of Claggart, for his having been impressed lends plausibility to the vague impression of his criminality. But a contingent circumstance like impressment does not fully explain the intensity of Claggart's perversity and "spontaneous" antipathy. Accordingly, the narrator sets aside these reflections on circumstance and returns to speculations about Claggart's nature.

These metaphysical speculations further bear out the narrator's doubts about dualist notions of action. Strictly speaking, Claggart is not entirely evil, and he certainly cannot be said to consciously "will" evil. He suffers from natural depravity, but he also possesses impulses that could be called naturally virtuous. Claggart's "elemental evil" is simply a more powerful kind of energy than his relatively low degree of natural virtue. He can appreciate Billy's natural vitality (particularly when it expresses itself in Billy's exuberance), but he cannot emulate that vitality in his own actions. This is a naturalist way of reading Claggart as "apprehending the good, but powerless to be it." Most tragically for Claggart, his natural depravity threatens to destroy him: "a nature like Claggart's, surcharged with energy as such natures almost invariably are, what recourse is left to it but to recoil upon itself and, like the scorpion for which the Creator alone is responsible, act out to the end the part allotted it" (*BB* 78). If we evaluate Claggart from a naturalist-pragmatic rather than a dualist-absolutist standpoint, what makes him tragic is not some inner conflict between a lesser spiritual good and a more powerful bodily evil. Instead, his tragedy lies in a distribution of energies that threatens his physical and psychological well-being, and in his unfortunate placement within a situation that brings forth these harmful energies. Like Billy, he is an organism maladapted to a hostile environment. But what makes Claggart's case of maladaptation more dire is that this environment consists of not only his social circumstances but his own body.

Claggart's case shows Melville returning to the problem he and Hawthorne wrestled with in their earlier fiction—the dilemma of being pulled in opposite directions by competing impulses that are equally compelling yet, from a normative standpoint, seem qualitatively different. Melville's early works typically contrast the spiritually pure impulses of the "heart" with the calculating interests of the "head." But Melville's idea of the heart in *Billy Budd* differs from that earlier view of it as the seat of our better, higher, spiritual natures. In his portraits of Claggart, Melville complicates this view by suggesting that the heart can also be the source of depravity and malice—not a unitary source of good but rather something heterogeneous in nature. This different view of the heart corresponds with a naturalist theory of action, one that does not postulate higher spiritual sources that motivate good action from some divine chamber of the heart. In Claggart's case, his heart seems to consist of "natural depravity," not because he is evil but because he has such a small amount of the energy Melville labels "natural virtue." Trying to account for his apparent perversity, the narrator "invents" a reason or two to explain Claggart's antipathy toward Billy. As usual, his method of explanation is tentative, and he tries not to founder in the "deadly space between" his own mind and Claggart's mind. Again, he suspects that the effort to represent Claggart's mind accurately will lead him into an epistemological bottomless pit. For this reason, the task of understanding rather than representing Claggart "is best done by indirection" (74).[18]

To understand Claggart's antipathy, the narrator entertains two speculations about its origins: the "romantic" theory and the "realistic" theory. According to the romantic theory, Claggart may have known Billy in a different walk of life, and he may still harbor a grudge against him for some past offense. But, plausible as this theory may be, the narrator immediately rules it out because it supplies yet another trivial, circumstantial explanation that does not satisfy him. Even though he knows he cannot achieve certainty, he wants to base his understanding on available facts that he cannot reasonably doubt.[19] According to the "realistic" theory, Claggart feels his antipathy toward Billy for the perverse reason that Billy is innocent: "For what can more partake of the mysterious than an antipathy spontaneous and profound such as is evoked in certain exceptional mortals by the mere aspect of some other mortal, however harmless he may be, if not called forth by this very harmlessness itself?" (*BB* 74). Manifesting his antireductive habits of thinking, the narrator claims that this theory is particularly realistic because it is charged with "mysterious" elements similar to those in Gothic romance. Truth, he suggests, must be stranger than "romance" because the truth never admits of easy explanations—especially when the phenomenon in question is human motivation. This conflation of mystery with psychological "fact" becomes the primary ground for the narrator's understanding of the interactions between

Billy and Claggart. This understanding has no firm basis in historical evidence, but it does an adequate job of satisfying the narrator's expectations of psychological consistency.

Forms of Self-Control

One important element to add to this portrait of Claggart is the psychological capacity of self-control. In keeping with the novel's anti-representational approach, "self-control" does not refer to some discrete capacity actually existing in the mind. Instead, the narrator treats it as yet another energy competing with, but ontologically similar to, other physiological energies like vitality, exuberance, and depravity. In contrast to Billy and Claggart, Captain Vere has a highly developed capacity for self-control. Although he too is susceptible to involuntary impulses, he can exercise the restraint characteristic of "conventional" virtue more successfully: "At the presentation to him then of some minor matter interrupting the current of his thoughts, he would show more or less irascibility; but instantly he would control it" (*BB* 61). Even in his descriptions of Vere, the narrator subordinates thought to action: self-conscious control comes only after an act has begun. For example, when Claggart approaches Vere to insinuate Billy's mutinous intentions, "a peculiar expression" produced by a "vaguely repellent distaste" comes over Vere's face as soon as he senses Claggart's presence (91). Even though Vere momentarily succumbs to this impulse, he is able to control it as soon as he becomes conscious of its outward manifestation. Incidents such as this demonstrate that Vere does not essentially differ from Billy or Claggart, for his "nature" is equally driven by involuntary impulse. With respect to self-control, Vere's nature differs from theirs only in his greater ability to restrain the expression of impulse. (Vere's exclamation "Struck dead by an angel of God! Yet the angel must hang!" [101] is a notable exception.) Furthermore, Vere's restraint is not the instantaneous exertion of some special mental faculty but rather the cumulative consequence of habits instilled by military training and social conditioning.

While Claggart shares Vere's ability to maintain a socially respectable exterior, his self-control arises from a different source and performs a different function. To distinguish Claggart's self-control from Vere's, the narrator describes it as arising not from a concern for military decorum but rather from his depravity's self-preservational need to conceal itself. Both forms of self-control are the by-products of unconscious habit. But while Vere's habit is the product of military training, Claggart's is the product of his depravity's struggle for survival. As the narrator points out, "An uncommon prudence is habitual with the subtler depravity, for it has everything to hide" (*BB* 80). Claggart's depravity acts like a hostile parasite, and its self-protective prudence merely conceals the destructive energies that consume its unfortunate human host. The most vivid contrast between Claggart's and Vere's forms of self-control appears in Claggart's reactions to Billy. In contrast to Vere's relatively strong self-control, Claggart's cannot fully master the antipathy he feels whenever he encounters Billy. Most significantly, in the pivotal soup-spilling incident, once Claggart notices it was Billy who spilled the soup, his antipathy betrays itself in an "involuntary smile, or rather grimace." Although Claggart soon tames this outward manifestation, his tardy self-control fails to maintain concealment:

> Meantime [Claggart], resuming his path, must have momentarily worn some expression less guarded than that of the bitter smile, usurping the face from the heart—some distorting expression perhaps, for a drummer-boy heedlessly frolicking along from the opposite direction and chancing to come into light collision with his person was strangely disconcerted by his aspect. (72–73)

As this incident illustrates, Claggart's body acts before he is even conscious of its doing so. His unguarded expression "usurps the face from the heart," and his habits of self-control kick in too late to stop this socially inappropriate betrayal of depravity.

In this and similar instances, most notably Billy's fatal blow to Claggart's forehead, the narrator questions the role of conscious, deliberate thought in theories of action. His point, however, is not to affirm fatalism but rather to achieve a coherent understanding of action that might serve as a tool for the intelligent channeling and regulation of energies. In rejecting both dualism and deterministic materialism, Melville does not fall back on traditional moral absolutism. Instead, he fashions a contrastive ranking of energies that takes account of determinism but allows for the possibility of ethical judgment. As William James proposed around the time Melville was writing *Billy Budd*, "The physiological study of mental conditions is the most powerful ally of hortatory ethics."[20] Melville's attitude toward Claggart's depravity is obvious enough: he sees it as utterly harmful and self-destructive. But since he also understands it as something beyond Claggart's control, he avoids moralistically portraying Claggart as an "evil" person. Instead, his characterizations attempt to naturalize ethics by basing moral judgments on the appropriate expression of human energies in particular situations.

In its portrayals of motivation as both unknowable and heterogeneous, Melville's narrative technique attempts to get around the impasses that dualist frameworks of moral evaluation run up against. Such frameworks rely on the possibility of epistemological certainty, whether the object of that certainty is an identifiably pure or corrupt motivation, or a projected outcome that a particular action is intended to produce in a direct cause-effect relation.

But in spite of the uncertainties that surround ethical judgment in *Billy Budd,* and contrary to the tone of even deconstructionist readings, the novel insists that uncertainty does not render efforts to understand motivation and action pointless. To be sure, Melville shows how uncertainty complicates moral evaluation, and how it can contribute to tragic outcomes like Claggart's and Billy's deaths. But the indirect narrative technique in *Billy Budd* suggests that moral judgments need not depend on the cognitive ideal of representational accuracy that dualist normative frameworks aim at. New avenues for assessing the theoretical and cultural backgrounds and implications of *Billy Budd* might be opened up by further internal and contextual examinations of Melville's late works in relation to post-Darwinian theories of action.[21] We still have much to mine from Melville's ambiguities, and naturalist approaches to psychology and the theory of action might allow us to get beyond the conceptual and normative impasses those ambiguities expose.

Notes

1. For a broad philosophical discussion of this crisis of Victorian ethics, see Charles Taylor, *Sources of the Self* (Cambridge: Harvard University Press, 1989), 393–418.

2. Herman Melville, *Pierre; or, The Ambiguities,* ed. Harrison Hayford, Hershel Parker, and G. Thomas Tanselle (Evanston and Chicago: Northwestern University Press and The Newberry Library, 1971), 107.

3. For a different account of Melville's turn to naturalism, see Milton R. Stern, *The Fine Hammered Steel of Herman Melville* (1957; Urbana: University of Illinois Press, 1968).

4. Christian and anti-Christian readings of the novel abound, but a recent, well-known Marxist reading is Brook Thomas. "*Billy Budd* and the Judgment of Silence" in *Literature and Ideology,* ed. Harry R. Garvin. (Lewisburg: Bucknell University Press, 1982), 51–78.

5. A recent, succinct summary of the traditions of critical response to *Billy Budd* appears in Lee Yearle; "Heroic Virtue in America: Aristotle, Aquinas, and Melville's *Billy Budd,*" in *The Greeks and Us: Essays in Honor of Arthur W. H. Adkins,* ed. Robert B. Louden and Paul Schollmeier (Chicago: University of Chicago Press, 1996), 70–73. Yearley lists five typical ways of reading the narrative, and his classifications rely heavily on the 1962 overview of scholarship in the "Perspectives for Criticism" section of the Hayford-Seahs edition. For other useful overviews, see Introduction to *Critical Essays on Melville's "Billy Budd, Sailor,"* ed. Robert Milder (Boston: G. K. Hall, 1989), 1–21; and Merton M. Sealts, Jr., "Innocence and Infamy: *Billy Budd, Sailor*" in *A Companion to Melville Studies,* ed. John Bryant (New York: Greenwood Press, 1986), 421–424.

6. Hawthorne himself shows signs of abandoning this assumption by the time he became a full-fledged novelist, for example in the final chapters of *The Scarlet Letter* (1850) that emphasize the various passions, impulses, tastes, and habits of Hester and Dimmesdale rather than their obedience to so-called higher principles.

7. The most ambitious recent attempt to establish new grounds for normative justification is the work of Jurgen Habermas, especially *The Theory of Communicative Action*, trans. Thomas McCarthy (1981; Boston: Beacon Press, 1984; 1987).

8. For a philosophical history and critique of this correspondence theory of knowledge, see Richard Rorty, *Philosophy and the Mirror of Nature* (Princeton: Princeton University Press, 1979).

9. Friedrich Nietzsche, *Writings from the Late Notebooks*, ed. Rudiger Bitmer, trans. Kate Sturge (New York: Cambridge University Press, 2003), Notebook 11 [83], 214.

10. *Billy Budd, Sailor: An Inside Narrative*, ed. Harrison Hayford and Merton M. Sealts, Jr. Chicago: University of Chicago Press, 1962), 128. Hereafter cited as *BB*.

11. Barbara Johnson, "Melville's Fist" in *The Critical Difference* (Baltimore: Johns Hopkins University Press, 1980), 92.

12. For a sophisticated materialist reading that assesses these energies according to a metaphysical schema Melville would have encountered in the work of Balzac, see Leon Chai, *The Romantic Foundations of the American Renaissance* (Ithaca: Cornell University Press, 1987), 210–241.

13. John Dewey, "The Reflex Arc Concept in Psychology," in *The Philosophy of John Dewey*, ed. John J. McDermott (Chicago: University of Chicago Press, 1981), 142. On the historical and cultural background of this essay, see Robert B. Westbrook, *John Dewey and American Democracy* (Ithaca: Cornell University Press, 1991), 65–71.

14. For a different but insightful treatment of absolute morality in *Billy Budd*, see Wendell Glick, "Expediency and Absolute Morality in *Billy Budd*," *PMLA* 68 (March 1953): 103–110. Glick argues that Billy represents absolute morality and therefore cannot survive in a political system based on "social expediency" (103–104). This is similar to the brief comments on *Billy Budd* in Hannah Arendt's *On Revolution* (New York: Viking, 1963), pp. 83–88. Both accounts, however, accept the traditional dualist distinction between absolute morality on one hand and worldly expediency (Glick) or politics (Arendt) on the other.

15. Robert Milder, "Old Man Melville: The Rose and the Cross," in *New Essays on Billy Budd*, ed. Donald Yannella (New York: Cambridge University Press, 2002), 100.

16. For the compositional genesis of this indirect narrative technique, as well as its philosophical and interpretive implications, see John Wenke, "Melville's Indirection: Billy Budd, the Genetic Text, and the 'Deadly Space Between'" in *New Essays on Billy Budd*, ed. Donald Yannella (New York: Cambridge University Press, 2002), 114–144.

17. John Dewey, *Human Nature and Conduct* (1922), in *The Middle Works, 1899–1924*, ed. Jo Ann Boydston (Carbondale: Southern Illinois University Press, 1988), 215.

18. Also see Johnson's and Wenke's treatments of the process of indirection.

19. This method of inquiry resembles the "scientific" method famously defined in C. S. Peirce's essay of 1877 "The Fixation of Belief" in *The Essential Peirce, vol. 1*, ed. Nathan Houser and Christian Kloesel (Bloomington: Indiana University Press, 1992), 109–123.

20. William James, *The Principles of Psychology*, vol. 1 (New York: Henry Holt, 1890), 128.

21. For a brief but wide-ranging sociological overview of theories of action since the Victorian era, see Mustafa Emirbayer and Ann Mische, "What Is Agency?" *American Journal of Sociology* 103 (January 1998): 962–1023.

CINDY WEINSTEIN

We Are Family:
Melville's Pierre

Despite the fact that, today, Melville's reputation and readership is greater than those of Caroline Lee Hentz's or Mary Jane Holmes's, two very popular antebellum writers, and despite Pierre's harangues against "the countless tribes of common novels," Pierre was (and is) desperate to be one of them.[1] On the most practical level, Melville wanted to write a popular novel that would make money. On a more theoretical level, "common novels" begin with absent parents who leave their children alone, a condition to which Pierre aspires. Although the separation between parents and children is painful and often inexplicable—why can't Ellen Montgomery in Susan Warner's *The Wide, Wide World* go with her mother and father? What takes Gerty's father in Maria Susanna Cummins's *The Lamplighter* so long to find her?—these young girls become women. They develop precisely because they have been freed from their biological parents. Gerty and Ellen grow, they learn, they live. If we can use Pierre as counter-factual evidence, we find that Pierre shrivels up, deludes himself into thinking he's learned something about "the all-comprehending round of things" (*NN Pierre* 111), and dies. Why the difference?

One decisive reason is that the plots of many sentimental novels depend upon their protagonists' ability to create new affections based on choice, allowing the scope of the novel to extend beyond the limitations of

Leviathan: A Journal of Melville Studies, Volume 7, Number 1 (2005): pp. 19–40. Copyright © 2005 Melville Society.

consanguinity. By contrast, Pierre tries and fails to generate voluntary relations, painfully constricting the novel to a world of "blood relation" (*NN Pierre*
218). For some critics, *Pierre's* inability to be a sentimental novel registers
Melville's own success as an author of novels not plagued by the ideological
and characterological problems of sentimental fictions, undoubtedly a conclusion Melville would have been happy to embrace. But Melville's relation to
sentimental novels is more complicated than this scenario suggests. One look
at the novel and its critical reception reveals that there is enough evidence to
prove that *Pierre* is as much a sentimental novel as it is not, and both positions are, paradoxically, correct. Because *Pierre* is neither a sentimental novel
nor an anti-sentimental novel, and yet both, I would like to approach the text
from a slightly different vantage point to argue that the story *Pierre* offers us
is a pre-history of the sentimental novel. *Pierre* is the story that takes place
before most sentimental novels begin, and this pre-condition helps to explain
not only why a sentimental protagonist like Gerty might be happier not being
enmeshed in a biological family but also the necessity of the family's absence.
At *Pierre's* end, there is no alternative to the family; there is no Gerty-figure
with which to start. Pierre, Isabel, and Lucy are dead, taking with them the
nightmare of consanguinity, which is the nightmare of *Pierre*. *Pierre* conducts
an archeology of the sentimental novel; it lays bare the novel's foundations,
and in the process, destroys it. But Why?[2]

All of the children in *Pierre* seek to embrace an ideal of choice only to
find that biology, indeed incest, awaits them. The novel thus begins to attack
itself because the only available choices are negations of relation. But even
the negations become attestations of consanguinity. Children choose not to
have parents, and parents choose to disown children, thus setting the stage
for a reconstitution of family based on choice, but the "unimpairable blood-
relation" (*NN Pierre* 224) survives. This survival kills Pierre, the character and
the novel. Unlike Ellen's or Gerty's recovery, Pierre's is not from the loss of
parental relation, but a failed recovery from never having lost them. From
Pierre's point of view, most sentimental protagonists are in the enviable position of having lost their parents. They begin (or quickly become) free from
parental ties, whereas Pierre must divest himself of all "kith and kin" (89).
They get to choose new parental figures, whereas Pierre can only disown his.
Pierre's story is one where mothers refuse to go away and die, where fathers
won't leave town, even though they are dead. *Pierre*/Pierre cannot get started
because he will not be orphaned, left alone, forced to choose a new, unrelated
family. All that remains for him to do is destroy the consanguineous bonds
that destroy him. If Ellen thinks that reunification with her mother is her ut-
most desire, Pierre reveals it to be the child's worst nightmare. What is most
outrageous about *Pierre* is its utter assault on the parent/child relation, and

the novel's (not so) underlying contention that a dead or disowned parent is better than any parent at all.

Pierre reveals Melville's understanding of the radical origins of sentimental novels, which is to say that without the biological family in shards, such novels cannot work, and as much as protagonists mourn the family's wreckage, their very lives depend upon it. Sentimental novels cannot exist without this destructive donnee; that donnee is itself Pierre's story, but paradoxically, Melville's novel can barely exist with it. As a text bent on its own self-destruction, Pierre admirably succeeds. This essay explores how it succeeds: I begin with Pierre's experimentalism, in which repetition is the constitutive though self-canceling principle, and conclude with its social experimentalism, which makes chosen affection the foundational, though unrealizable, principle of the family. Chosen love in the world of Pierre is impossible because virtually everyone in Pierre is related to everyone else; all attempts to get outside of consanguinity only reproduce it.

"And but beginningly as it were"

Pierre can barely begin, or, more precisely, it begins again and again. There is the novel's bizarre opening, the story of Isabel's origins, the history of Pierre's friendship with his cousin, Glendinning Stanley, the account of Pierre's authorship, and Plinlimmon's pamphlet. Both the plot and language of Pierre can be said to begin only "as it were," as it strives to conjoin the narrative continuity of the word "and" with the narrative suspension of the word "but." The beginnings of the novel promise the start of a narrative, which is then blocked.[3] Godey's Magazine and Lady's Book captures the novel's negative reception, and goes a step further in "imitation of [Melville]'s style": "in the insignificant significances of that deftly-stealing and wonderfully-serpentining melodiousness, we have found an infinite, unbounded, inexpressible mysteriousness of nothingness" (NN Pierre 313). If some antebellum reviewers responded to Melville's "long brain-muddling, soul-bewildering ambiguity" (308) by parodying it, more recent critics, such as Eric Sundquist, have focused on the significance of parody itself: "no one can fail to be struck by Pierre's insanely pastoralized opening."[4] This insane opening situates Pierre and Pierre in a temporal zone which immobilizes both novel and character: characters "suppose it is afternoon" because time is never certain; they "swiftly pause," and they are "stilly" (NN Pierre 3, 25, 60, 178).

Time is on the narrator's mind in Pierre's first chapter, as he remarks upon the strange resemblance between Mrs. Glendinning and Pierre, suggesting that "the mother seemed to have long stood still in her beauty," while the son "almost advanced himself to that mature stand-point in Time" (NN Pierre 5). Time is at a stand point in Saddle Meadows, where "Not a flower stirs; the trees forget to wave; the grass itself seems to have ceased to grow"

(3) as virtually everything exists in a "half-unconscious" state. Although the narrator meditates upon these oddities of time, his narrative is not immune to them. The degree to which *Pierre*'s language stalls, gets obstructed, and repeats itself suggests that the "trance-like aspect" of Saddle Meadows is something with which virtually every character, including the narrator, must contend. Words pile up without accreting meaning and prose has difficulty getting out of its own way. We read the dialogue and inner thoughts of characters who use the same words over and over again, such as Lucy's initial greeting to Pierre, "'Pierre;—bright Pierre!—Pierre!'" (4), or Mrs. Glendinning's soliloquy in which she refers to the docility of Pierre and Lucy no less than eight times in one paragraph. The characters' penchant (or compulsion) for repetition is also reflected in the narrative voice. The narrator refers to Pierre's grandfather as "grand old Pierre" five times in a single paragraph, repeating the name and its epithets as if "he" were an insufficient mode of designation: "'I keep Christmas with my horses,' said grand old Pierre. This grand ole Pierre always rose at sunrise" (30). Such verbal excess (pleonasm) signals not only the grandiosity of Pierre's grandfather but Pierre's diminishment. The more room taken up by the grandfather—on the page, in the psyche, in Saddle Meadows—the less room for Pierre. Words and their variants are repeated, such as "descended" (7, 9, 17) "endless descendedness" (9), "blood-descent" (10), "far-descended" (11), "descending" (12), and "double-revolutionary descent" (20), or the title of Book IX, "More Light, and the Gloom of That Light. More Gloom, and the Light of That Gloom" (165). The words that are *Pierre* act like the novel's characters, incapable of doing much more than repeating, mirroring, or descending from themselves.

Just as individual words get in each other's way, so too the narrative of *Pierre* is constantly bumping into itself. The narrator repeats descriptions, ideas, and passages while calling attention to those repetitions, and has difficulty restraining its foreshadowing, as if his narrative can only either circle around itself or lurch forward, unable to find a stable, temporal rhythm through which to tell its story. As early as section three of the opening chapter, the narrator repeats himself, "it has been said that the beautiful country round about Pierre appealed to very proud memories" (*NN Pierre* 8). At the start of section four, he asserts, "we poetically establish the richly aristocratic condition of Master Pierre Glendinning, for whom we have before claimed some special family distinction" (12). He then alludes to Pierre's grandfather as "the same grandfather several times herein-before mentioned" (13) and concludes the section with a phrase from its second paragraph, "we shall yet see again, I say, whether Fate hath not just a little bit of a word or two to say in this world" (14). The narrative is made up of obstructions to itself, as evidenced in this quotation from section four: "In conclusion, do not blame me if I here make repetition, and do verbally quote my own words in saying that it had been the choice fate of Pierre to have been born and bred in the country" (13). This passage offers itself as a conclusion—as if the narrative has progressed from point A to point B—when the passage is, in fact, a citation from section two, a kind of self-quotation indicating that the narrative has circled back upon itself. But the narrator is not hiding that fact, because this "conclusion" refers to its status as a moment in an earlier part of the text. The sentence acknowledges itself as an act of tautology, or citationality, through italics and with the phrase, "do verbally quote my own words in saying." The sentence is a conclusion only insofar as it occurs last in a series of repetitions. To put the point a bit differently, the conclusion and the origin are distinguishable not because of some substantive difference between them, but because of a temporal one. The conclusion is the origin repeated a bit later.[5]

The opening chapter even has trouble maintaining this temporal distinction, as the narrator seems unable to tell the origins of Pierre/*Pierre* without giving away his/its ending. The constant use of foreshadowing supplies another indication of the bizarre rhythms of life in Saddle Meadows—time grinds to a halt, repeats itself in a discursive stutter, lurches ahead—as well as the narrative that represents that life. The foreshadowing begins right away, as in this example where the narrator describes Pierre's "romantic filial" love for his mother: "but as yet the fair river had not borne its waves to those sideways repelling rocks, where it was thenceforth destined to be forever divided into two unmixing streams" (*NN Pierre* 5). Almost every paragraph ends in a similar fashion: "Pierre glide[d] toward maturity, thoughtless of that period of remorseless insight, when all these delicate warmths should seem frigid to him, and he should madly demand more ardent fires".[6] This is foreshadowing taken to such an extreme so as to become a mockery of itself. The fictional device meant to hint at the text's future ends up competing with the narration of the text's present tense and divulging its outcome: "Now Pierre stands on this noble pedestal; we shall see if he keeps that fine footing" (12). The foreshadowing accretes so intensely, so quickly, that one cannot help but conclude that the narrator is either having an ordinate amount of difficulty restraining himself from disclosing Pierre's misfortunes or, more likely given the narrator's hostility toward his main character, has no interest in self-restraint. Either way, the results are the same; *Pierre* barely begins and it is over, and both happen at virtually the same time.

"But not thus . . . yet so like"

Melville's novel self-destructs in a variety of ways—language coagulates, plots unravel, and characters die—so as to insure the impossibility of family reunification. The specific goal is the disintegration of anything remotely representing a family, including not only the bonds of consanguinity and the relations that are entered into by choice, but even the words on the page. The novel's experimental language not only calls attention to the fact that words have roots from which variations descend as in a philological family tree but exemplifies how those roots entangle, even strangle, the production of new words which cannot escape their "hereditary syllables" (*NN Pierre* 287). *Pierre* is laced with passages such as "in the minutest moment momentous things are irrevocably done" (83) or "not that at present all these things did thus present themselves to Pierre" (106), or Isabel's farm-house with "its ancient roof a bed of brightest mosses; its north front (from the north the moss-wind blows), also moss-incrusted" (110). The words, like the characters, are related, which is tantamount to a death sentence in *Pierre*.

The logic and language of the biological family finds its way into the very fabric of the narrative as kinship provides an especially powerful and corrosive discourse through which the narrator describes his characters' thoughts as well as his own. In "Retrospective," the narrator says this about Pierre's memory of his father's death-bed words, "'My daughter! my daughter! . . . God! God!'": "into Pierre's awe-stricken, childish soul, there entered a kindred, though still more nebulous conceit" (*NN Pierre* 71). At the very moment that the text begins to engage the issue of Isabel's paternity and potential biological relation with Pierre, the word "kindred" appears as if to settle the question. Later, when Pierre jealously meditates upon Lucy's alleged affection for his cousin, Glendinning Stanley, the narrator again uses the language of kinship not only to describe the content of Pierre's thoughts, which seems logical enough given the subject matter under consideration, but the very way they come into being: "Many commingled emotions combined to provoke this storm. But chief of all was something strangely akin to that indefinable detestation which one feels for any imposter who has dared to assume one's own name and aspect in any equivocal or dishonorable affair; an emotion greatly intensified if this impostor . . . be almost the personal duplicate of the man whose identity he assumes" (289). The narrator painstakingly charts the mental development of Pierre's outraged sense that an act of substitution has taken place whereby the cousins' "peculiar family resemblance" (288) has fostered a willingness on Lucy's part to accept Glen, Pierre's "kinsman" (289), as her paramour, and had made Glen "almost seem Pierre himself—what Pierre had once been to Lucy."

These reflections on Glen's "blood propinquity" illustrate how Pierre experiences kinship as the annihilation of his identity. To "possess a strong related similitude" (*NN Pierre* 288) to someone else is the first step towards death, which is why the language of *Pierre* is, quite literally, so defensively and aggressively self-referential—"self-same" (34–35), "self-willed" (41, 199), "in me myself" (65), "self-suggested" (178, 316), "in himself absolutely" (244), "self-supposed" (294)—as if the self could remain safe only by being unrelated to anything but itself, by being its only point of reference. This "self-conceit" (136) is a dreadful miscalculation for the simple reason that people do exist in relation to each other and for the more complex reason that as soon as they try to cut off those relations, to "own no earthly kith or kin" (89), they, hydra-like, multiply. It is only a matter of time until Pierre divides in order to establish a principle of relation, even if it is only to himself. "He himself" (63, 173) becomes "he himself, as it were" (289) or "the seeming semblance of himself" (289). Pierre's attempt to "spurn and rend all mortal bonds" (106) only necessitates that a new site of "correlativeness" (85) be produced, and that is, of course, his self.

The final point to make about the passage is its use of the term "akin" to characterize Pierre's meditations. As in the first example, where the word "kindred" describes the thought process at the same time as it insinuates the reality of Isabel's sisterly claims, here Pierre's fantasies of Lucy's alleged incapacity to distinguish between him and Glen are written so as to confirm that lack of distinction. Pierre's thoughts, then, are akin to an analogy produced by the narrator, which means that the experience of losing himself to Glen gets reproduced in Pierre's relation to the narrator. As critics have observed, the narrator wildly vacillates between cudgeling Pierre for his naivete and sympathizing with his pain. Sometimes the distance between them is clear; more often, it is not. What makes this relationship so hard to untangle is that in exploring a young man's attempt to make himself by unmaking his relations with others, the narrator uses the language of kinship to describe the process; and this use of kinship language has the effect of undoing Pierre's attempts to strike out on his own; it recreates a family drama in the narrator's relation with Pierre. Here, the narrator reflects upon Pierre's feelings about Lucy's "unearthly evanescence" by positing a set of possibilities not considered by Pierre: "Not into young Pierre's heart did there then come the thought, that as the glory of the rose endures but for a day, so the full bloom of girlish airiness and bewitchingness, passes from the earth almost as soon" (58). The narrator establishes this analogy as his and not Pierre's, but the distance between them collapses. "Pierre's thought was different from this, and yet somehow akin to it" (58).[6]

Moments like this, in which difference is asserted only to be absorbed by what in another context is called "catching likenesses" (*NN Pierre* 330), pervade the text: "But not thus, altogether, was it now with Pierre; yet so like, in some points, that the above true warning may not misplacedly stand" (70); and of Pierre's father, Isabel says, "His face was wonderful to me. Something strangely like it, and yet again unlike it, I had seen before . . . But one day, looking into the smooth water behind the house, there I saw the likeness— something strangely like, and yet unlike, the likeness of his face" (124). No one, including the narrator, is capable of sustaining the difference between difference and similitude. The recognition of difference, which often is registered through the use of analogies, dissipates so as to validate the primacy of "unmistakeable likeness" (351).[7] Analogies in *Pierre* work (or do not) like foreshadowing. They are undone by their inability to withstand the pressure of the difference upon which they are found. If foreshadowing implies temporal disjunction in the act of bringing the future into the present, in *Pierre* the effect of introducing the future is the destruction of the past. Similarly, if analogies imply likeness on the conceptual level even as they are founded on conceptual difference, here the effect of introducing similarity is the evacuation of difference. Both devices operate dysfunctionally and, in doing so, assist in the demise of the biological family.

The narrator thwarts Pierre's attempts to find a haven from the heartless world of family by linguistically arresting him in the discourse of kinship. But it seems perfectly logical in this novel of ubiquitous consanguinity that the narrator gets caught, too. He cannot withstand the perverse principle of "related love" (*NN Pierre* 189) that governs Pierre, and even though phrases such as, "but ignorant of these further insights" (60) or "so at least he thought" (93), work to accentuate the difference between his knowledge and Pierre's, the fact is that they arrive at the same temporal and conceptual place. This is registered by the prolonged use of the present tense in later sections of the novel and by the fact that, whereas early in the novel the narrator could confidently point to Pierre's "ignorance at this time of the ideas concerning the reciprocity and partnership of Folly and Sense" (167), by the novel's end "Pierre saw the everlasting elusiveness of Truth; the universal lurking insincerity of even the greatest and purest written thoughts" (339). Like Pierre and his mother, like Pierre and Isabel, like Pierre and Lucy, Pierre and the narrator merge. They must because this is the inevitable consequence of relations in this novel.

Which is why Pierre has to be an author. Although critics have questioned the plausibility of Pierre's writerly disposition, the logic of "linked correspondence" (*NN Pierre* 36) makes it impossible for him to be anything else.[8] The narrator, however, does anticipate the reader's potential surprise upon learning of Pierre's authorial aspirations in a passage which features just about every peculiarity of the novel's narrative voice: "in the earlier chapters of this volume, it has somewhere been passingly intimated, that Pierre was not only a reader of the poets and other fine writers, but likewise—and what is a very different thing from the other—a thorough allegorical understander of them, a profound emotional sympathizer with them" (244). The narrator alludes to an earlier section of the novel; he deploys the terms "likewise" and "different," as if they did not contradict each other, and he (likewise) combines "but" with "and," as if those conjunctions operated similarly.

In the opening of Book XVII, "Young America in Literature," the narrator offers a statement about his own method of writing. The desire to renounce the psychic pressure of kinship, even as it provides the very terms of that renunciation, binds narrator and protagonist: "Among the various conflicting modes of writing history, there would seem to be two grand practical distinctions. . . . By the one mode, all contemporaneous circumstances, facts, and events must be set down contemporaneously; by the other, they are only to be set down as the general stream of the narrative shall dictate; for matters which are kindred in time, may be very irrelative in themselves. I elect neither of these; I am careless of either; both are well enough in their way; I write precisely as I please" (*NN Pierre* 244). Time is very much on the narrator's mind, especially how his narrative intentionally scorns "various conflicting modes" of writing, which he separates into two narrative categories. The first narrates events synchronically, the second diachronically. With much bravado, the narrator refuses both, electing instead the "careless" mode. Such carelessness, however, is the only narrative mode that the story permits. To write "contemporaneously . . . [or] as the general stream of the narrative shall dictate" is to be capable of sustaining the difference between events that happen at the same time and those that do not. Not only is the narrator telling a story about the inability to keep those differences intact, as the first chapter of *Pierre* so insistently demonstrates, but the narrator is losing that ability as well.

When Pierre becomes an author, the reader begins to sense that the narrator is falling victim to "this age-neutralizing Pierre" (*NN Pierre* 264), as if the neutralization which the narrator had earlier parodied is now neutralizing him. "I write precisely as I please" might be read as the narrator's attempt to declare his independence from conventional modes of writing and from writers, such as Pierre, just as the text is about to plunge both narrator and Pierre into one of its most profound "entanglements" (191). As critics have pointed out, it is often difficult to distinguish between Pierre's tortured book and *Pierre*, the book we are reading. The narrator writes: "It is impossible to talk or to write without apparently throwing oneself helplessly open; the Invulnerable Knight wears his visor down" (259). Ironically, the narrator's assertion of an independent writing style could just as easily be Pierre's, who writes "careless" sentences such as "Now I drop all humorous or indifferent disguises, and all philosophical pretensions. . . . Away, ye chattering apes of a sophomorean Spinoza and Plato, who once didst all but delude me that the night was day, and pain only a tickle" (302). It is no surprise when Book XVIII, "Pierre, as a Juvenile Author," hurls us back to the beginning: "It is true, as I long before said, that Nature at Saddle Meadows had very early been as a benediction to Pierre" (257). We have begun again, only now the strangulating effects of Saddle Meadows' temporality and its regime of "mutual reflections" (4) have caught up with the narrator as "the ineffable correlativeness" (85) of relationships in the novel comes closer to home.[9]

Thus, Pierre's authorial identity is doing to the narrator what Pierre's fictitious marriage to Isabel does to Pierre; to "eternally entangle him in a fictitious alliance which though in reality but a web of air yet in effect would prove a wall of iron" (*NN Pierre* 175). Like Pierre, who "most carefully and most tenderly egg[s]" Isabel (189), the narrator "preambillically examines [Pierre] a little further" (260). As so often happens with words in the novel, the narrator's "preamble" (260) has become "preambillical"; instead of maturing as the narrative progresses, Pierre is becoming "a little toddler" (296), a "baby toddler" (305) who is preumbillicaly (a pun Melville must have found irresistible) connected to the narrator. Just when Pierre imagines himself to "be not only his own Alpha and Omega, but to be distinctly all the intermediate gradations" (261), the narrator turns Pierre into an utter dependent, discursively producing a parental relation between himself and Pierre. Throughout, the narrator has tried to keep himself separate from these correlations by adopting a weirdly aggressive stance toward his protagonist, which now becomes all the more important to maintain as the distinctions between them threaten to dissolve. He derides Pierre's youthful compositions as "the veriest common-place" (257), and even when he applauds Pierre's efforts to write "his deep book" (305), he keeps his temporal and experiential distance by revealing the gap between his knowledge about the writing process and the "young" (244) Pierre's "immature" (282) and "juvenile" (257) attempts. "While Pierre was thinking that he was entirely transplanted into a new and wonderful element of Beauty and Power, he was, in fact, but in one of the stages of the transition" (283). Or, "yet now, forsooth, because Pierre began to see through the first superficiality of the world, he fondly weens he has come to the unlayered substance" (285). Foreshadowing like this is familiar, but here the foreshadowing has everything to do with the status of the narrator vis a vis Pierre, rather than, say, the impending demise of Pierre and Lucy's relationship or the potential appearance of a sister for Pierre.

In what might be the text's definitive paradox, the narrator tries to separate himself from Pierre through the language of relatedness. The methodological statement with which Book XVII begins reveals that Pierre's dilemma is the narrator's: "for matters which are kindred in time, may be very irrelative in themselves" (*NN Pierre* 244). Yes, events that take place at the same time may be not be related, "may be very irrelative," but the fact is that something is always "kindred," at least temporally. This concession speaks volumes, both because the narrator is preoccupied with the breakdown and stabilization of discrete temporal frames and because his desire to maintain a theory of "irrelativity" is voiced in the language of kinship. The conceptualization of the narrative method of *Pierre* assumes the verbal lineaments of family. And because all things akin in *Pierre* must die (and because all things must become akin), the loathing and aggression that once was directed so clearly at the "pellucid and merry romance" (305) of sentimental fiction, now turns inward, as *Pierre* loathes and destroys itself.[10]

"I love my kind"

Early in the novel, Lucy is reunited with her brothers. Her exclamation, "my darling brothers!" is reiterated and extended by Pierre's, "my darling brothers and sister!" (*NN Pierre* 29). In the verbal act of translating his potential brothers-in-law into brothers, Pierre cannot maintain an exogamous connection with Lucy. In a world where even horses "were a sort of family cousins to Pierre" (21), Pierre cannot love someone to whom he is not related. Thus, when Isabel appears and declares herself his sister, he must believe her because he loves her; his capacity for loving her depends upon his ability to identify his feelings as signs of "our related love" (189). All love, like all language, is related. Thus, Lucy and Pierre's initial encounter, as well as the narrator's description of it, is a virtuoso mirroring performance of emotions and words: "As heart rings to heart those voices rang . . . the two stood silently but ardently eying each other, beholding mutual reflections of a boundless admiration and love" (4). The "mutual reflections" of the characters reflect themselves in the repetition of words. "With Lucy's hand in his, and feeling, softly feeling of its soft tinglingness; he seemed as one placed in linked correspondence with the summer lightnings; and by sweet shock on shock, receiving intimating foretastes of the etherealest delights of earth" (36). Like those "mutual reflections," Pierre's experience of "linked correspondence" is registered in the narrator's description, as words and their sounds reverberate. No wonder he wants to "spurn and rend all mortal bonds" (106).

Pierre's attempted destruction of family ties—"cast-out Pierre hath no paternity"—perhaps leaves him "free to do his own self-will" (*NN Pierre* 199). But "his own self-will," surely a desperate description of self-sufficiency that marks its own insufficiency, nonetheless wills itself a family in the form of Isabel, Delly, and eventually Lucy. In fact, when Lucy writes to Pierre in New York, requesting "to re-tie myself to thee" (309), Pierre not only accepts her "angelical" (311) offer without hesitation, but embraces her suggestion that there may be "some indirect cousinship" (311) between them. His decision to "spurn and rend all mortal bonds" leaves him pleasantly vulnerable, if not more willing than ever to be bound.

That Pierre's bond of choice is an incestuous relationship with his (possibly) half-sister gave antebellum readers pause. To make matters even more bizarre, Pierre insists on protecting his mother from the hypothetical knowledge of her husband's pre-marital sexual transgression by announcing that Isabel is his wife; that is, not his sister. In their more benign moments, Melville's reviewers were puzzled; in their more aggressive moments, they were outraged. Especially fulsome was his treatment of incest: "when he strikes with an impious, though, happily weak hand, at the very foundations of society, we feel it our duty to tear off the veil with which he has thought to soften the hideous features of the idea, and warn the public against the reception of such atrocious doctrines" (317). Such atrocious doctrines were, however, not solely a feature of Melville's novel. They were standard fare in the antebellum debate about family reform, and it is to this context that I want to turn in order to indicate the ways in which *Pierre* both engages in and undermines the reformist critique. The fact is that while the home was being crowned as "the sanctuary of all that is most sacred in humanity," to quote E. H. Chapin's *Duties of Young Women* (1848), that same sanctuary was condemned as the source of "apathy and intellectual death." Celebrations of marital relations are ubiquitous, as in William Alcott's *The Young Wife, or Duties of Woman in the Marriage Relation* (1837), where he imagines domestic bliss to be when "your souls seem to be but one," but so are indictments, such as T. L. Nichols and Mrs. Mary S. Gove Nichols's *Marriage: Its History, Character, and Results:* "Running through many families are secret amours. Children are born of these, the parents die, and the marriage of half-brothers and sisters is always possible, and doubtless of frequent occurrence." A startlingly but appropriate epigraph for *Pierre*.[11]

Melville (and *Pierre*) are not alone in pursuing new types of community, Melville's comic representation of utopian life in "The Church of the Apostles" reveals his familiarity and impatience with experiments such as Brook Farm, New Harmony, or Oneida. In an 1843 article, "The Consociate Family Life," English progressive Charles Lane offers this description of the "pure reform principles" practiced at Bronson Alcott's Fruitlands: "Shall I sip tea or coffee? The inquiry may be.—No. Abstain from all ardents, as from alcohol drinks. Shall I consume pork, beef, or mutton? Not if you value health or life. . . . Shall I warm my bathing water? Not if cheerfulness is valuable. Shall I clothe in many garments? Not if purity is aimed at."[12] Supporters of such "insane heterodoxical notions about the economy of the body" (*NN Pierre* 299) are easy targets for Melville. One group of reformers, though, seems to have piqued Melville's interest, and that is the Shakers, whose villages in Hancock and Lebanon, Massachusetts he visited no less than five times in a two year period. Intriguing are the possible connections between Shaker dances and "the hair-shrouded form of Isabel [which] swayed to and fro with a like abandonment, and suddenness, and wantonness" (126). I am, however, less interested in correlating specific Shaker ritual with characters in *Pierre,* than with reading Pierre's desire and failure to destroy the ties of consanguinity in relation to reformers of the period who share both the desire and the failure.[13]

When Pierre, "the young enthusiast" (*NN Pierre* 175) decides to "gospelize the world anew" (273), he goes to the Church of the Apostles, a half-way house for New York City radicals. Because families are few and fragmented in the Church, the building perfectly accommodates Pierre's domestic experiments, which "take no terms from the common world, but do make terms to it, and grind thy fierce rights out of it!" (160). Plotinus Plinlimmon, guiding spirit of the Church, "seemed to have no family or blood ties of any sort" (290), and Charlie Millthorpe, Pierre's childhood friend, sings the praises of non-consanguinity: "The great men are all bachelors, you know. Their family is the universe" (281). Pierre believes this too because if everyone is related to everyone else, then there is no such thing as incest or, more precisely, everyone is always committing incest ("by heaven, but marriage is an impious thing" [58]). Incest is not against the law; "it is the law" (274). In instructing Isabel to "call me brother no more.... I am Pierre and thou Isabel, wide brother and sister in the common humanity" (273), Pierre seems to be suggesting that the difference between incestuous and exogamous love can be dispensed with by replacing the term "brother" with "wide brother in the common humanity." If this is what it means to "take no terms from the common world," he is in trouble.

In fact, characters in *Pierre* treat consanguineous relations as if they could be assumed and dispensed with at will, as if brothers and sisters, parents and children could choose or disown one another. Virtually every character of Pierre's generation, from the ignominious Delly, whose "own parents want her not" (*NN Pierre* 163) to the angelic Lucy, whose mother declares, "I forever cast thee off . . . I shall instruct thy brothers to disown thee" (329), are renounced by their parents. Mrs. Glendinning, the character most committed to biological kinship is keenest to destroy it when she learns of Pierre's betrayal: "He bears my name—Glendinning. I will disown it; were it like this dress, I would tear my name off from me, and burn it till it shriveled to a crisp!" (193). Pages later, Pierre declares his sovereignty from his name in a passage that echoes his mother's words. While committing his father's portrait to the "crackling, clamorous flames" (198), he proclaims, "Cast-out Pierre hath no paternity, and no past" (199). Characters are forever choosing to have or to disown biological relationships, as if these were choices to be made; as if relations that are freely entered into cannot, by definition of being chosen, be incestuous. But of course, they are. In Pierre, virtually all relations are not only chosen, but they are always incestuous. The only choice one has is whether the relationship is chosen to be biological or is biological, whether incest is committed knowingly or unknowingly.

Pierre's domestic experiment follows a trajectory from utopian community to communal disintegration that is familiar to the student of antebellum reform. Like John Humphrey Noyes's Perfectionists, Pierre's followers worship him and "the manly enthusiast cause of his heart" (167). Like Noyes, who both regarded "the whole Associate as one family, and all children as the children of the family" while striving "to get [their] freedom from any claims of kindred, etc.," Pierre's community is organized according to blood relations in a world desperate to be free of them. And like Noyes who developed a theory of sexuality whereby men refrained from ejaculating during sexual intercourse so that "there is no risk of conception without intention," Pierre muses, "from nothing proceeds nothing, Isabel! How can one sin in a dream?" (274).[14] And like Pierre, leaders such as Noyes, Shaker founder Mother Anne Lee, and Mormon Joseph Smith were accused of rape and incest. Critics warned, "Stop these Shakers from creeping about, like the Serpent of old, destroying many a fair Eden of domestic happiness." The Mormon practice of polygamy would have resonated for readers of *Pierre;* moreover, Reverend Hubbard Eastman's 1849 attack on Noyes—"Monogamy is the true basis of all Democratic institutions. . . . If that root is rendered corrupt, the whole fabric of society becomes polluted"—could easily find its way into reviews of *Pierre:* "[Perfectionism] not only contemplates a complete annihilation of the conjugal relations, but it designs to sever the ties of consanguinity, and its ultimate object is to make a clean sweep of all the social relations!" These attacks on alternative family arrangements confirm that if, as Michael Rogin claims, "*Pierre* assaulted the family," he was not alone.[15]

However, as much as *Pierre* is a scathing analysis of the biological family, it also scathingly analyzes attempts to reform it. Unlike the ideal and expanding communities imagined by reformers, where persons decide that "the[ir] neighbor is most truly our brother,—nay, more than brother, he is our other self," Pierre's world of choice ("I will no more have a father" [*NN Pierre* 87]) is one of contraction ("I own myself a brother of the clod" [302]).[16] The Church of the Apostles contains the experiment in reform and its inevitably disastrous consequences; inevitable because the family Pierre chooses reproduces the one he inherited. Every time Pierre rejects the language and logic of blood—"Call me brother no more! How knowest thou I am thy brother?" (273)—he re-embraces it. He laments the "unrelated hands that were hired" to attend to his dead mother "whose heart had been broken by the related hands of her son" (286). At the very moment that Pierre declares that he "will not own a mortal parent" (106), he pleads, "bind me in bonds I can not break" (107). Those bonds assume the form of a new family, with himself as the brother / husband, and Isabel as the sister / wife, Lucy as the "very strange cousin" (313) whom Pierre looks upon "with an expression illy befitting their singular and so-supposed merely cousinly relation" (337). Lucy, in fact, declares Pierre to be the principle of family itself: "thou art my mother and my brothers and all the world and all heaven and all the universe to me" (311). Like Pierre, who in the very act of renouncing family, produces another one, reformers desirous of challenging conventional domestic relations, ended up replicating them, whether in Alcott's "consociate" family at Fruitlands, "Mother" Anne Lee, "Father" William Lee (the brother with whom she was accused of committing incest), and the "brethren" and "sisters" of the Shaker "families." If their aim was the elimination of conventional family arrangements, to "engage collectively . . . as children of one family," to quote Owenite

Frances Wright, Pierre's experiment suggests that reformers did little more than justify and, in some cases, institutionalize the incestuous impulses within the biological family.[17] Pierre thus takes up the challenge issued by reformers like T. L. Nichols and his wife, Mrs. Mary S. Gove Nichols, who complained in their 1854 book, *Marriage: Its History, Character, and Results,* that "now a woman can have no brother, unless he is born such," (Nichols 369), and imagines a world where brothers are not born but made only to discover that the making turns the "fictitious title" into "the absent reality" (7). *Pierre* literalizes the familial metaphors governing reform efforts and reveals the "nameless" and "latent" feelings, code words for incest in *Pierre,* at the center both of the biological family and attempts to reform it.

The language of voluntary bonds pervades the novel, as if the ideal family could be organized around love not blood, only to reveal the "blood relation" (*NN Pierre* 218) that motivates all of its characters' choices. If consanguinity can be destroyed, it can also be produced. Both actions depend upon viewing blood as if it were a matter of choice, a matter of a speech act, the only difference being whether one wants to disown or choose it. Thus, Pierre's announcement that "aunts, uncles, cousins innumerable [are] dead henceforth to me" (196) is theoretically no different from his conversation with his mother where he says, "Mother, stay!—yes do, sister" (96) or his claim that Lucy is "some pretty aunt or cousin" (309). Pierre conjures those relations into being as swiftly as he rejects them, and how he names those relations is crucial. The strain between Pierre and his mother is twice registered by their disagreement about what to call each other, "sister me not, now Pierre, I am thy mother" (95) and "why don't you call me brother Pierre?" (130). Even Isabel, who concedes that "the word father only seemed a word of general love and endearment to me . . . it did not seem to involve any claims of any sort, one way or the other," learns how powerful the words denoting consanguinity are, as well as the claims that go along with them. She calls attention to the designation: "yes, Pierre, Isabel calls thee her brother—her brother," and as if that weren't enough to make the relation stick, she adds, "Dearest Pierre, my brother, my own father's child! . . . Oh, sweetest of words . . . Oh, my brother!" (64). To call someone a brother or a sister is to make that person "thy related brother" (192) or "my best sister" (191), which is the penultimate step to committing incest. But the choice is a sham—one only ever chooses to make someone a brother or sister or cousin who already is one.

The proof is that Pierre is never tempted by Delly, who, like Charlie, signifies a principle of difference with which the novel ultimately cannot or will not come to terms. The distance between Pierre and Delly remains surprisingly consistent for a novel that thrives on the disintegration of boundaries. Never does it cross Pierre's mind to call her sister or cousin.[18] It is in a conversation with Delly that Pierre attempts to stabilize the sexual vertigo into which the narrative has descended. Pierre announces, "my cousin Miss Tartan is coming here to live with us" to which the panicked Delly replies, "Good heavens!—coming here?—your cousin?—Miss Tartan?" Sensing her confusion, Pierre restates the fact of Lucy's imminent appearance and redefines their relation, "My cousin,—mind, my cousin, Miss Tartan, is coming to live with us." Having nailed down that relation, they turn to Isabel and Pierre's and the confirmation of that bond. Delly asks Pierre, "does Mrs. Glendindin—does my mistress know this?" and he replies, "My wife knows all" (*NN Pierre* 320).

The dialogue takes a familiar turn when Pierre asks Delly, "How is my wife, now?":

> Again startled by the peculiar emphasis placed on the magical word wife, Delly, who had long before this, been occasionally struck with the infrequency of his using that term; she looked at him perplexedly, and said half-unconsciously—
> "Your wife, sir?"
> "Ay, is she not?"
> "God grant that she be—Oh, 'tis most cruel to ask that of poor, poor Delly, sir."
> "Tut for thy tears! Never deny it again then!—I swear to heaven, she is!" (321)

This exchange makes clear that just as Pierre's sexual radar fails to pick up Delly because of her non-consanguinity, Delly never imagines that Pierre's relationship with Isabel is anything but what they have presented themselves as being—husband and wife in "secret marriage" (202). It is both odd and entirely proper that Delly, herself an unmarried woman who has an affair with a married man, becomes the standard bearer of conventional notions of sexuality, which is to say that she remains outside of the incestuous menage a trois comprised of Pierre, Isabel, and Lucy.

In fact, Delly's conversation with Pierre follows an exchange between Pierre and Isabel that demonstrates just how unhinged relationships and the words designating them have become. Upon receiving Lucy's letter informing him of her arrival, Pierre informs Isabel that "some pretty young aunt or cousin" is on her way. Lucy's position as cousin, however, troubles Isabel because "that is not wholly out of the degree," by which she means that being a cousin does not keep Lucy safe from Pierre's affections. Of course not. Being a cousin, even "a very strange cousin . . . almost a nun in her notions" (*NN Pierre* 313), guarantees Pierre's ardor. The inability of Pierre or Isabel to control the meaning of their words (and the "wild" passions behind them) becomes palpably obvious as he instructs her not to "have any sisterly jealousy then, my sister," to which she inquires, "would it be well, if I slept with her, my brother?" (314).

The destabilization of the terms designating the biological family begins the process of destroying it. Relentlessly, the language suggests feelings that are not only suspect, but if and when acted upon, illegal. The narrator muses, "much that goes to make up the deliciousness of a wife already lies in the sister" (*NN Pierre* 7). Similarly, Pierre's "romantic filial" (5) relationship with his mother tantalizes him with the possibility that his mother is not really his mother. But the speech act of calling a mother a sister, or a son a brother, has grave consequences. Not calling people by their proper designations has the effect of making a person incapable of knowing the difference between a mother and a sister, a brother and a husband, a cousin and the girl next door. As the narrator says, a "fictitious title" (7), a "fictitious alliance" (175), even (and especially) a "fictitious wife" (180) may as well be real. A "nominal conversion of a sister into a wife" (177) is a conversion. There is no such thing as "empty nominalness" (192). *Pierre* is a novel in which what you call someone is what they are, which is why, when Pierre "assume[s] before the world that by secret rites Pierre Glendinning was already become the husband of Isabel Banford" (173), it is irrelevant whether or not they have actually committed incest. The speech act has made it so. The power to designate the desired relation to someone through a speech act represents both the possibility of individual free will and the moment of its self-destruction because the novel's logic of ubiquitous consanguinity requires that the only available names designate kinship—and so the promise of freedom turns into its nightmare.[19] Pierre and his mother can call each other anything they want, and they choose brother and sister; Pierre can name Lucy anything he wants, and he chooses cousin. *Pierre* is a novel whose protagonist is determined to destroy consanguinity, but whose every move proliferates it.

For every consanguineous relation spurned by Pierre, another one, which combines the attractions of "voluntary election [and] blood propinquity" (*NN Pierre* 288), takes its place. As much as Pierre, and the "too much generous blood in his heart" (222), wants to destroy the "blood relation" (218), it refuses to go away. Blood permeates the text, whether it be the "blood-red" (92) sunrise of Saddle Meadows or the "the blood-shedding times" (75) of the French Revolution. Pierre's mother, upon suspecting him of leaving Lucy, declares, "I feel my blood chemically changing in me" (131), and Pierre, in thinking about the "unproven fact of Isabel's sisterhood," notes that "his very blood seemed to flow through all his arteries with unwonted subtileness, when he thought that the same tide flowed through the mystic veins of Isabel" (139). Isabel's fateful letter to Pierre, in which she declares their relatedness, is blotted with tears that "assume a strange and reddish hue—as if blood and not tears had dropped upon the sheet" (64–65). The only way to end this regime of consanguinity is to "let out all thy Glendinning blood and then sew up the vile remainder" (239). Blood functions as a metonymy for the family relations which persist in spite of the novel's continuous bloodletting as the "black vein" (358) is opened and "the dark vein's burst" (362). But there's always more. Even when "spatterings of his own kindred blood were upon the pavement" (360) as Glen's body lies prone, the novel ends with "more relations coming" (361) to see the bodies of Pierre, Lucy, and Isabel.[20]

"It is the law."

Isabel exists outside of the law. Had she been protected by it, perhaps she would know if she had lived in a place "five, six, perhaps, seven years" (*NN Pierre* 119), or if events took place when she was "nine, ten, or eleven years" (122). Perhaps she would know the difference between "Virtue and Vice" (274). It is precisely her place outside of the law that produces her unstable sense of time and her inability to distinguish between moral categories. And if these attractions were not enough for Pierre (in addition to her "wonderfully beautiful ear" [119]), her complete incomprehension of the meanings and consequences of consanguinity seals his commitment to and desire for her, thus sending him into an incestuous free-fall.

At issue here is not just Isabel as the object of Pierre's desire but also Isabel's relation to the objects of her desire. The incest taboo means nothing to her: because the only distinction she is capable of making is a "general feeling of my humanness among the inhumanities" (*NN Pierre* 123), any relation with a human being would be incestuous. Her perspective undercuts the raison d'etre of the incest taboo, for it makes incest itself something that everyone does; it therefore frees Pierre from the constraints of the law against it. As much as Pierre wants Isabel, then, he also wants Isabel's relation to the terms that signify consanguinity. When she tells him, "I called the woman mother" (123) and "the word father only seemed a word of general love and endearment to me . . . it did not seem to involve any claims of any sort" (145), she has no idea what claims or constraints are incumbent upon the person with whom one has that relation. To "seem not of woman born" (114) is the condition in which Isabel exists and to which Pierre aspires because with it comes the inability to distinguish virtue from vice, or, for that matter, exogamy from endogamy.

But this knowledge, once possessed, cannot be forgotten. "It is the law," Pierre tells Isabel when she asks him to define virtue and vice. In response to her query, he claims that these words have no meaning, declaring them both to be "nothing" (*NN Pierre* 274). Unable to dissolve the law, Pierre chooses the dissolution of himself, Isabel, Lucy, and the world. Isabel will believe virtually anything Pierre tells her about these words, but rather than giving her his vision, he turns the world and words into a meaningless dream. Pierre's opportunity to "gospelize the world anew" (273) has come and gone because he has to keep at bay the full import of having committed incest with the woman he believes is his sister. The law, however, with its "ink unobliterable as the sea" (11) and its "wax ... inexorable [as] bars and bolts" (224) refuses to be wiped out by Pierre's nihilism.

The tangibility of the law is confirmed by the fact that when Pierre visualizes Lucy's brother, Frederic, murdering him, Pierre also hears a jury declaring his guilt: "if such a brother stab his foe at his own mother's table, all people and all juries would bear him out, accounting everything allowable to a noble soul made mad by a sweet sister's shame caused by a damned seducer" (*NN Pierre* 336). This passage is telling for several reasons, not least of which is that Pierre, "thoroughly alive to the supernaturalism of that mad frothing hate which a spirited brother forks forth at the insulter of a sister's honor," imagines the scenario as "if he were actually in the position which Frederic so vividly fancied to be his" (336). For a moment, the terms "brother and sister" have been stabilized, giving Pierre a glimpse into the legal implications of his behavior; but Pierre's imaginative appropriation of Frederic's position also begins to corrode the signifying coherence of those terms as the correspondences between Pierre and Frederic unfold. If Pierre is himself and Frederic, at once seducer and defender of the seduced, the only option is that both die, which is exactly the conclusion Pierre reaches: "murder ... seemed the one only congenial sequel to such a desperate career" (337).

Living with three women who would die for him, Pierre feels "utterly without sympathy from any thing divine, human, brute, or vegetable" (*NN Pierre* 338). How is it that sympathy, the key affect of the sentimental novel, has no place in *Pierre?* At its most basic, sympathy in Melville's text requires a recognition of difference; more specifically, the precondition for sympathy is that there are other people in the world who are not you. Pierre cannot achieve even this most elementary recognition. Every aspect of the novel—the narrative voice, the temporal frame, the words on the page—seems unable to sustain alterity. The only principle the novel can endorse is consanguinity, a principle that is finally and ironically the very antithesis of sympathy. Critiques of sentimental fiction frequently begin with an argument about how sympathy is limited because it is based on the notion that sympathy depends upon the twinned principles of identification and consanguinity. But what *Pierre,* with its polarization of blood and sympathy, demonstrates by negative example is that sentimental novels succeed precisely because of their decoupling of sympathy and blood, sympathy and similarity. Sympathy flourishes because of, not in spite of the fact that, chosen relations have replaced consanguinity. Pierre/*Pierre* escapes the "endless descendedness" (9) of its characters and words by destroying himself/itself. Virtually everyone dies, except two characters whose fates are deemed irrelevant given their lack of blood relation to the main characters and to each other. They are Delly and Charlie, who possess the singular characteristic of being strangers in a book of "ineffable correlativeness" (85). Although both have skewed views of marriage—Delly, a fallen women, Charlie, a devoted bachelor—they survive, bearing with them the possibility of a sentimental novel to come.[21]

Notes

1. Herman Melville, *Pierre, or The Ambiguities*, ed. Harrison Hayford, Hershel Parker, and G. Thomas Tanselle (Evanston and Chicago: Northwestern University Press and The Newberry Library, 1971), 141. Hereafter cited as *NN Pierre* in the text.

2. Richard Brodhead makes a similar point about Melville's complicated relation to the genre of the sentimental novel: "The odd combination of straightforwardness and secret mockery inherent in his handling of the style, characters, and characteristic situations of sentimental romance is evidence of his ambivalence, his desire both to make use of this genre and to assert his independence from it." The distortedness and chaos of *Pierre* are productions of a tension, present from the first and explosive at the end between the author and the literary form he has chosen to work in *Hawthorne, Melville, and the Novel* (Chicago: University of Chicago Press, 1973), 164. For a reading of *Pierre* in relation to sensational fiction, see Sheila Post-Lauria's *Correspondent Colorings: Melville in the Marketplace* (Amherst: University of Massachusetts Press, 1996).

3. Samuel Otter notes a similar effect, describing the novel as "filled with structures that entice and recede," in *Melville's Anatomies* (Berkeley: University of California Press, 1999), 244.

4. Eric J. Sundquist, *Home as Found: Authority and Genealogy in Nineteenth-Century American Literature* (Baltimore: The Johns Hopkins University Press, 1979), 150.

5. Other examples include: "It has been said, that always when Pierre would seek solitude in its material shelter and walled isolation, then the closet communicating with his chamber was his elected haunt" (*NN Pierre* 86); "Wonderful, indeed, we repeat it, was the electrical insight which Pierre now had into the character of his mother" (90); "In the earlier chapters of this volume, it has been passingly intimated" (244).

6. The narrator uses this device in his description of Pierre's correspondence with Glen about the New York house: "Now, if it were not conscious considerations like the really benevolent or neutral ones first mentioned above, it was certainly something akin to them" (223). My argument is indebted to Wai Chee Dimock's point that "a figure of difference is impossible in *Pierre,*" which "affirm[s] a world of likeness, a world of kinship and only kinship" (*Empire for Liberty: Melville and the Poetics of Individualism* [Princeton: Princeton University Press, 1989], 173). Also influential has been Gillian Brown's analysis of the novel's "aesthetics of incest" in relation to antebellum theories of individualism (*Domestic Individualism: Imagining Self in Nineteenth-Century America* [Berkeley: University of California Press, 1990], 152). In contrast to Dimock's and Brown's focus, I adopt a more formalist perspective and examine how the very grammar of the text struggles with this principle of kinship.

7. As Plinlimmon puts it, "by their very contradictions they are made to correspond" (*NN Pierre* 212). The text calls attention to its bizarre use of analogies

when Pierre offers the following comment on Isabel's hand: "But hard and small, it by an opposite analogy hints of the soft capacious heart that made the hand so hard with heavenly submission to thy most undeserved and martyred lot" (154).

8. See Brian Higgins and Hershel Parker, "The Flawed Grandeur of Melville's *Pierre*," in *New Perspectives on Melville*, ed. Faith Pullin (Kent State University Press, 1978): 162–196. Elizabeth Renker similarly notes the difficulties in separating the narrative voice from Pierre's, although she explores this through the novel's tropes of vision; see *Strike through the Mask: Herman Melville and the Scene of Writing* (Baltimore: The Johns Hopkins University Press, 1996), 24–48.

9. At this point in the novel, not only have the distinctions between the narrator and Pierre become blurred almost beyond recognition, but Melville, too, appears to have fallen victim to the novel's relentless logic of "seeming semblance" (289) and "catching likenesses" (330). Thus, when the narrator tells us that Pierre "seems to have directly plagiarized from his own experiences, to fill out the mood of his apparent author-hero, Vivia" (302), we recognize that passages from *Pierre*, especially those having to do with the composition and reception of Pierre's work, have been plagiarized from Melville's own authorial experiences. "Corporations have no souls" (302) is one particularly illustrative example of Melville collapsing into *Pierre*. Clearly, Pierre has less reason to be thinking about corporations than Melville, whose negotiations with Harper's for the publication of the novel were proving difficult, indeed. Unlike his earlier dealings, this contract didn't provide the financial and psychological boost he had been anticipating. According to Hershel Parker, the fact that the Harper's contract "stipulate[d] that for the first 1,190 copies sold . . . the author was to receive no royalties," may have "enforced upon the realization that he might have to abandon the hope of earning a living as a writer" ("Why *Pierre* Went Wrong," *Studies in the Novel* 8 [1976]: 12–13). This realization is precisely Pierre's once he receives the note from the publishing firm of Steel, Flint & Asbestos labeling him "a swindler" and demanding that he pay the "bill for printing thus far, and also for our cash advances" (356). These difficult negotiations seem to be propelling Melville toward a collapse of the distinctions between himself, his narrator, and protagonist.

10. See Wyn Kelley's, "*Pierre*'s Domestic Ambiguities," in *The Cambridge Companion to Herman Melville*, ed. Robert S. Levine (Cambridge: Cambridge University Press, 1998): 91–113.

11. E. H. Chapin, *Duties of Young Women* (Boston: George W. Briggs, 1850), 169; William A. Alcott, *The Young Wife, or Duties of Woman in the Marriage Relation* (New York: Arno, 1972), 58; T. L. Nichols and Mrs. Mary S. Gove Nichols, *Marriage: Its History, Character, And Results; Its Sanctities and Its Profanities; Its Science and Its Facts. Demonstrating Its Influence, as a Civilized Institution, On The Happiness of the Individual and the Progress of the Race* (New York: T. L. Nichols, 1854), 325.

12. Charles Lane, "The Consociate Family Life," *The New Age and Concordium Gazette* 1 (1843): 120.

13. See Merton M. Sealts, Jr., "Melville and the Shakers," in *Studies in Bibliography* 2 (1949): 105–114.

14. John Humphrey Noyes, *Bible Communism: A Compilation from the Annual Reports and Other Publications of the Oneida Association and Its Branches; Presenting, in Connection with Their History, a Summary View of Their Religious and Social Theories* (Brooklyn: Office of the Circular, 1853), 13, 17, 50.

15. Hubbard Eastman, *Noyesism Unveiled: A History of the Sect Self-Styled Perfectionists; with a Summary View of Their Leading Doctrines* (Brattleboro: B. D. Harris and Co., 1849), 117; Michael Paul Rogin, *Subversive Genealogy: The Politics and Art of Herman Melville* (New York: Knopf, 1983), 160.

16. Parke Godwin, *A Popular View of the Doctrines of Charles Fourier* (New York: J. S. Redfield, 1844). 28.

17. Frances Wright, *Course of Popular Lectures, as Delivered by Frances Wright* (New York: Office of the Free Enquirer, 1829), 45. Myra Jehlen argues that it is both Pierre's and Melville's inability to produce a social, familial, or novelistic order different from the one they have inherited that leads to *Pierre*'s (and Pierre's) tragic ending. She concludes that "[Reform] emerges in Melville's novel as a fatally missing term" *American Incarnation: The Individual, the Nation, and the Continent* [Cambridge: Harvard University Press, 1986], 204). My reading, by contrast, insists that reform is very much at the novel's center, quite explicitly in chapters such as "Young America in Literature" and "The Church of the Apostles," which Brodhead has identified as "enormously expand[ing] Melville's book's frame of reference" (182).

18. Other reasons may help explain Pierre's attitude toward Delly, including her class affiliation (although she and Isabel may share this) and the fact of her adultery.

19. Marc Shell writes, "Between perfect liberty and death, which the optimistic American revolutionary Patrick Henry set forth as comedic alternatives, there is, tragically, no essential difference—as probably there was not for Melville himself" (*Children of the Earth: Literature, Politics and Nationhood* [Oxford: Oxford University Press, 1993], 16).

20. Through a close reading of the scene in which Pierre's hand is blackened at the Black Swan Inn, Robert S. Levine intriguingly links the presence of blood and other moments of racialized discourse in the novel with anti-slavery accounts of the miscegenated origins of American society and Western culture in general. In tracing the obsessive interest in racial mixture and purification, Levine is careful to note that Melville "points more generally to the ultimate reality of miscegenated (and unknown) genealogies rather than offering some specific 'proof' of Pierre's 'black' blood" ("Pierre's Blackened Hand," in *Leviathan: A Journal of Melville Studies* 1 [1999]: 34–35). It seems entirely correct to argue that the ubiquitous presence of blood has to do with the matter of race, but I believe that this is only one among many of Pierre's anxieties regarding blood. Black or white, consanguinity must be destroyed.

21. I am grateful to Cambridge University Press for permission to reprint an adapted version of Chapter Six from Cindy Weinstein, *Family, Kinship, and Sympathy in Nineteenth-Century American Literature* (Cambridge: Cambridge University Press, 2004).

PETER BELLIS

Discipline and the Lash in
Melville's White-Jacket

In his 1975 study, *Discipline and Punish*, Michel Foucault speaks of an early nineteenth-century transition between two different concepts of "penality"—from one regime based on the spectacular display of physical punishment to another founded on incarceration, surveillance, and control. The former is publicly enacted on the body and is epitomized by public torture and execution; the latter is withdrawn from public view and relocated within the disciplinary structures of school, factory, and prison.[1]

In *White-Jacket, or The World in a Man-of-War*, published in 1850, Herman Melville depicts a shipboard world in which Foucault's two systems operate not in opposition but in an uneasy tandem. One strand of Melville's book, its narrative thread, condemns the arbitrary and brutal punishment inflicted by autocratic captains. But another more descriptive aspect considers the frigate in quite different terms, as a rigidly determined system based on mechanistic discipline and spatial organization.[2]

My interest here is not primarily in Foucault's model for its own sake, or in a test of its applicability to the antebellum American Navy. Rather, it is in the way that Foucault's categories intersect with and highlight other divisions: first, the structural split within Melville's text and, second, a larger fault line in the political discourse of his time. Written in the midst of campaigns for naval reform, *White-Jacket* registers and responds to the changing forms

Leviathan: A Journal of Melville Studies, Volume 7, Number 2 (2005): pp. 25–40. Copyright © 2005 Melville Society.

of shipboard power in two contrasting ways. Its narrative uses the rhetoric of American democracy and egalitarianism in a forceful attack on corporal punishment, but its descriptive survey of the ship, as a space governed by discipline and surveillance, lacks that critical edge. The book's inability to confront such disciplinary power is symptomatic, I would suggest, of an increasing gap between older kinds of political discourse and the forms of economic and social control that were emerging in the 1840s and 1850s.[3] *White-Jacket*'s ideology of Revolutionary republicanism, with its emphasis on the representation and empowerment of individual citizens, cannot finally come to grips with an order based on the management and control of groups and categories of persons—be they blacks, whites, workers, or slaves.

The Lash

Foucault describes "a certain mechanism of power" that was enacted in public punishments through the late eighteenth century (*Discipline*, 57). Under this regime, the body was "the major target of penal repression," displayed and destroyed in public rituals of torture and execution (8):

> in monarchical law, punishment is a ceremonial of sovereignty; it uses the ritual marks of the vengeance that it applies to the body of the condemned man; and it deploys before the eyes of the spectators an effect of terror as intense as it is discontinuous, irregular and always above its own laws, the physical presence of the sovereign and his power. (130)

In breaking the law, the offender has "touched the very person of the prince," so punishment must be wrought upon his body in the most literal of terms (49). Essential to such punishment is not just its publicity but its theatricality, its demonstration or enactment of authority in the administration of violence.

This form of power was still very much in evidence aboard both the frigate *United States*, on which Melville served, and the *Neversink*, his fictional creation in *White-Jacket*. Under the US Navy's Articles of War—passed by Congress in 1800 and in effect (in revised form) until the mid-twentieth century—authority was concentrated in the hands of a ship's captain.[4] Melville describes him as a virtually unlimited monarch, almost a despot, with his power based on a monopoly of authorized violence aboard ship.[5] "'I allow no man to fight on board here but myself. I do the fighting,'" Captain Claret proclaims—and the first men flogged in the novel are indeed being punished for taking part in an unsanctioned fight (*NN WJ*, 136, 134). The captain's rhetoric makes ship and men extensions of himself, absorbing them into his own symbolic body. He regards the ship's officers, Melville later notes, as "disintegrated parts of himself" (217). Any disruption of the ship's order thus becomes a violation of the captain's person.

The primary instrument and symbol of the captain's power—his means of taking "vengeance" for such violation—is the lash or "cat-o'-nine-tails." Only he can order a flogging, but he can do so "for nearly all degrees of transgression," depending simply on his mood (*NN WJ*, 139). All in all, there were 163 floggings aboard the *United States* during the fourteen months of Melville's service in 1843–1844, seven in his first two days aboard, while the ship was still in port.[6] Men could be flogged for offenses ranging from "stealing poultry" to "being lousy," "spitting," and "cursing the master at arms" (Valle, 80). Scourging serves as a deliberate, almost choreographed display of force; with captain, officers, and accused all occupying fixed positions around the base of the ship's mainmast, all hands are "summoned" to "witness punishment" as a spectacular performance.[7]

The most stylized and extended form of punishment is "flogging through the fleet," in which a portion of the sentence is carried out on board each of several vessels, in order "to strike terror into the beholders" (*NN WJ*, 371). The effect is to make punishment seem "inevitable" and the captain himself "omnipotent"; or, to use Foucault's term, a "super-power" above the law itself.[8]

Even as the lash inscribes the captain's authority on the body of the seaman, the ceremonial and public nature of the act reinforces other facets of the ship's power structure. First, the ritual aspect of the proceedings at "captain's mast" suggests the theatrical or performative elements characteristic of naval life. In peacetime, a warship's primary function would be to "show the flag" in foreign ports, its drills and ceremonies designed to display hierarchical order for its own sake.[9] Such duties were also intended simply to keep the sailors occupied—for while a frigate like the *Neversink* required a crew of more than five hundred to man its guns in battle, as few as fifty would be needed to operate the vessel on a daily basis (Valle, 15–16). Second, it thrusts into relief the navy's rigid class divisions, under which officers remain exempt from the lash, while ordinary seamen ("the people") live under its constant threat (*NN WJ*, 146). The antebellum officer class remained thoroughly aristocratic in outlook and temperament, "gentlemen" ostensibly above "personal malice," but prone to dueling amongst themselves and indulging in prolonged personal vendettas.[10]

Flogging has its legal underpinnings in the Articles of War, and they are asserted in another ritual, the monthly reading of the Articles, for which the crew are mustered around the capstan. Melville's description conflates the text with the violence it authorizes:

"Shall suffer death!" This was the burden of nearly every Article read by the Captain's clerk . . . "Shall suffer death!" The repeated

> announcement falls on your ear like the unremitting discharge of
> artillery . . . [like a] minute-gun . . . and it is a tougher morsel,
> believe White-Jacket when he says it, than a forty-two-pound
> cannon-ball. (*NN WJ*, 293)

Melville, or perhaps, the clerk, takes some liberties with the Articles here, for he several times omits the modifying phrase "or other such punishment as a court martial shall inflict."[11] But this chapter does convey the reality of naval practice, since many commanders customarily administered floggings immediately after the Articles were read (Valle, 81).

Melville's attack on flogging and, less directly, on the Articles themselves, is based on two assumptions: first, that history is progressive, and American democratic institutions will necessarily displace English monarchical ones; and second, that naval law should be continuous with, not distinct from, civilian law. He argues that "flogging in the navy . . . is utterly repugnant to the spirit of our democratic institutions; indeed, that it involves a lingering trait of the worst times of a barbarous feudal aristocracy" (*NN WJ*, 146).

White-Jacket's history is, however, a selective one. For Melville, the authority given by the Articles is autocratic and tyrannical, an "obsolete barbarism" that he traces back to the British navy of the Restoration (*NN WJ*, 282, 297–298). The Articles themselves, he says, are "opposed to the genius of the American Constitution" (143). But in simply opposing the monarchical Articles to the Constitution, he deemphasizes the American Congress's repeated adoption of the British model (in 1775, 1797, and again in 1800), mentioning it only in a footnote (298). Erased from the story is the Federalist affirmation of class and partisan interests in the Articles, the reinscription of class privilege into American democracy even within its first generation.[12] An historical analysis of just this kind was offered in an article in the *United States Magazine and Democratic Review*, part of a series that appeared as Melville was completing his manuscript, but his rhetoric depends upon a myth of the Revolution as both democratic and egalitarian.[13]

Melville's approach is also problematic when he invokes civilian law as a model. Naval codes "should conform to the spirit of the political institutions of the country," he insists; otherwise, for the sailor, "our Revolution was in vain; to him our Declaration of Independence is a lie" (*NN WJ*, 144). His focus is on Article XXXII, which leaves all unspecified crimes to "'be punished according to the laws and customs in such cases at sea'" (143). This is the one that "above all other, puts the scourge into the hands of the captain," he says: it "leaves to his discretion to decide what things shall be considered crimes, and what shall be the penalty; whether an accused person has been guilty of actions by him declared to be crimes; and how, when, and where the penalty shall be inflicted" (143–144). Melville's objections to this Article are two-fold.

First, in procedural terms, it makes the captain simultaneously "a legislator, as well as a judge and an executive" (143). Second, instead of being universally applied, it is "oppressive, and glaringly unequal in its operations," reinforcing the class hierarchy of the ship (146).

Melville goes back to Blackstone to argue for the equal application of law to all citizens (145). But once again, he bypasses the actual choices made by the Founding Fathers: the Constitution, in both Article II and the Fifth Amendment, explicitly distinguishes between civilian and military jurisprudence, leaving the military under the jurisdiction of Congress and the executive, with no appeal to the judicial branch (Valle, 31–32). It would not be until 1950, and the adoption of the Uniform Code of Military Justice, that military justice would be brought into alignment with civilian (Valle, 29).

If *White-Jacket* thus offers a falsely unified version of the founding generations, Melville also overlooks or downplays the sectional divisions of his own time, divisions all too evident in Congressional debates on flogging. Support for abolition came overwhelmingly from the North, opposition primarily from the South, suggesting a link to broader reforms such as anti-slavery (Langley, 193). Melville glosses over the split, however, with a blend of Revolutionary millennialism and Manifest Destiny: "we Americans are the peculiar, chosen people—the Israel of our time; we bear the ark of the liberties of the world. Seventy years ago we escaped from thrall . . ." (*NN WJ*, 151).[14]

White-Jacket's argumentative strategy here is quite different from those of Melville's sources and of the naval reform movement in general. A common approach—used by Richard Henry Dana, Jr., William McNally, and others—was to compare oppressed white seamen to black slaves.[15] Participants in Congressional debates spoke of an ongoing process of social and humanitarian reform, often linking the abolition of flogging to the end of the navy's spirit ration, and even the abolition of slavery.[16] "Why is it," asked Senator John Hale, "that, while humanity is lifting up her voice . . . for every other class of the unfortunate and oppressed, the sailor alone shall be left . . . as the only man, as the only creature that walks erect with the image of God upon his countenance, that is still subjected to this degradation?"[17]

Melville, however, cites the analogy between flogging sailors and beating slaves only in passing, and does not place it at the center of his argument. Instead, he repeatedly emphasizes the sailor's identity as "an American-born citizen, whose grandsire may have ennobled him by pouring out his blood at Bunker Hill" (*NN WJ*, 146). (In so doing, he also disregards the high number of foreign-born seamen in the Navy.) The tactic is, moreover, especially striking in the context of the House debate, for the Congressmen who invoked Revolutionary precedents were generally doing so in support of flogging.[18]

Repeatedly, then, Melville builds his case on a double movement, invoking the Revolution as myth but eliding the post-Revolutionary period as historical fact, sidestepping or displacing the historical realities of economic, racial, and sectional difference. Captain Claret is enough like the vengeful absolute monarch of Foucault's model that the dramatic exercise of his power—flogging—can be attacked using the language of egalitarian democracy. But the result is a decided narrowing of focus. Unlike the author of the series in the *United States Magazine and Democratic Review,* Melville targets only the lash, and not the broader framework of the *Articles* as a whole.[19] In the end, he asks only for a fuller supervision of naval officers and their practices (*NN WJ*, 231–232). And unlike Congressional reformers, he does not emphasize a link between flogging and the more divisive issue of slavery.[20]

Melville's revolutionary rhetoric may be a conservative strategy, a carefully modulated retreat from the antislavery position taken in *Mardi,* for example.[21] But it also suggests the limits of the republican tradition itself, in which the common good depends upon the economic and political independence of individual citizens, that independence forming the basis of civic virtue.[22] Such a discourse does enable Melville to speak on behalf of sailors as individuals: the lash, after all, enforces the captain's power by singling out and marking the particularized body of the sailor. But by the 1850s, the extent and meaning of citizenship itself was now at issue. Faced with the systematic objectification and dehumanization Melville describes—of men both native and foreign-born, white and black—egalitarian republicanism had begun to founder. It might persist in ritual or ceremonial forms, or in conservative or reactionary movements such as Know-Nothingism or "herrenvolk" working-class republicanism, but its progressive political force was spent.[23] The Declaration of Independence might be "the RING-BOLT to the chain of your nation's destiny," Frederick Douglass acknowledged in 1852, but he went on to describe antebellum republicanism as "flagrantly inconsistent," an utter "sham," in its failure to respond to the slavery crisis.[24]

Discipline

There is, as I have noted, also a second order aboard the frigate, one that both contrasts and dovetails with aristocratic privilege and public punishment. It is not, however, an alternative political order, such as the one Melville demands; rather, it is a system of physical confinement and regulation according to function—in short, a version of Foucault's disciplinary enclosure. It is a regime that resists both a historicizing critique and the terms of Melville's Revolutionary ideology, for it is, in some ways, already aligned with the goals of antebellum reform.

"[D]iscipline," according to Foucault, "proceeds from the distribution of individuals in space," using several techniques: First, "Discipline sometimes requires enclosure, the specification of a place heterogeneous to all others and closed in upon itself"; "disciplinary machinery" then divides up this space "on

the principle of elementary location or partitioning ... into functional sites":
"Each individual has his own place; and each place its own individual" (*Discipline*, 141, 143). Ultimately, "[i]n discipline, the elements are interchangeable.
... The unit is, therefore, neither the territory ... nor the place ... but the rank,
the place one occupies in a classification" (*Discipline*, 145). Activity is strictly
controlled, as time is regulated and bodily movement rigidly ordered, almost
mechanized (*Discipline*, 149–153, 164–165). In an earlier essay from the late
1960s, Foucault had described such an enclosed, "heterogeneous" space as a
"heterotopia," and the ship as "the heterotopia par excellence."[25]

Melville's *Neversink* is indeed a virtually sealed space, which he repeatedly compares to a prison; it is "a sort of sea-Newgate, from which [the sailor]
can not escape," except to the bottle (*NN WJ*, 176). As a result, the regulations
are most severe regarding "the smuggling of grog, and being found intoxicated," the most common of minor offenses throughout the fleet.[26] But the
efforts of the master at arms to suppress smuggling are only the most extreme
examples of a generalized surveillance that covers almost every moment of
the seaman's life: "No privacy can you have; hardly a moment's seclusion. It
is almost a physical impossibility, that you can ever be alone," Melville's narrator, laments; "[a]lmost every inch is occupied; almost every inch is in plain
sight; and almost every inch is continually being visited and explored" (*NN
WJ*, 35, 41).

This open and always visible space is also partitioned according to rank
and function. Under the naval rules and regulations of 1818, captains were
required to

> examine and rate [the seamen] according to their abilities . . .
> [and] without loss of time to make arrangements for quartering
> the officers and men; distributing them to the guns, musketry,
> rigging, &c.; to divide them into watches; make out his quarter,
> station, and watch bills, with bills of the names of men stationed
> at every gun; to muster and exercise them frequently.[27]

Melville's description adds specificity to the language of the regulations, but
remains consistent with them: "particular bands," he says, are

> assigned to the three tops, but in getting under weigh, or any other
> proceeding requiring all hands, particular men of those bands are
> assigned to each yard of the tops. . . . [E]very man of a frigate's five-
> hundred-strong, knows his own special place, and is infallibly found
> there. He sees nothing else, attends to nothing else, and will stay
> there till grim death or an epaulette orders him away. (*NN WJ*, 8)

Melville devotes a number of chapters to descriptions of the various sections of the vessel and the different groups of men assigned to each. This "endless subdivision of duties" is summed up for the sailor in a series of "numbers": "White-Jacket was given the number of his mess; then, his ship's number, or the number to which he must answer when the watch-roll is called; then, the number of his hammock; then, the number of the gun to which he was assigned; besides a variety of other numbers" (11). When, late in the novel, White-Jacket is brought to the mast and directly threatened with a flogging, it is for forgetting one of these numbers, and being out of place (277–278). The heart of the *Neversink*'s spatio-temporal order is here, on

> the uppermost deck, round about the main-mast, [which] is the Police-office, Court-house, and yard of execution, where all cases are lodged, causes tried, and punishment administered. . . . The main-mast, moreover, is the only place where the sailor can hold formal communication with the captain and officers. . . . [he] stands there—generally with his hat off—waiting the pleasure of the officer of the deck, to advance and communicate with him. (*NN WJ*, 131)

On the one hand, this is a space in which a sailor may speak to his superiors, but it is also, as White-Jacket finds, the site of his most complete and arbitrary silencing, for he cannot answer if a charge is brought against him during the proceedings at "captain's mast." Officers and seamen may, for a moment, share a physical space, but only so that the lines of authority can be more sharply drawn.

If space is thus strictly controlled, so, too, is time: within the system of four-hour watches, meals are served according to an arbitrary schedule, with the sequence determined strictly according to rank (*NN WJ*, 30), and it is not twelve o'clock until the captain orders "'Make it so'" (23). The ship even has a calendar of its own, as the days of the week are renamed by the sailors, according to the meals served on each. Smoking among the men is limited to thirty minutes after meals—a "sumptuary law" that leads White-Jacket to give up his pipe entirely "rather than enslave it to a time and place" (387). Nothing, in short, is allowed to "mar the uniformity of daily events" (84).

Chapter 18, "A Man-of-War Full as a Nut," depicts the crew as an assortment of varied tradesmen and skilled artisans, but such attributes are erased or overwritten by the multiple classifications aboard ship. Their variety of backgrounds and skills does not work to individuate or empower the seamen; it actually does the reverse, making any one among them easily replaceable (*NN WJ*, 74). At several points in his survey, White-Jacket suggests that a seaman's character is, in fact, reshaped by his shipboard assignment and duties: "[T]heir being so much among the guns is the very thing that makes a gunner's gang so cross and quarrelsome," for example (45), while "holders" are "gloomy" (47), and "'steady-cooks'. . . a narrow-minded set; with contracted souls; imputable, no doubt, to their groveling duties" (47–48). Individual temperament and agency are replaced by an identification through place and function.

In any case, most sailors are little more than unskilled or semi-skilled laborers, and this makes them potentially malleable and manipulable-reducible to undifferentiated labor power. In the end, the men do become "interchangeable," as Foucault predicts—their pea coats make it impossible to tell one from another when they are aloft in the darkness (120)—and the officers use them like "checker-men," or, during a race, as "make-weights" (173, 272).

There may or may not be a legal continuity between the ship and civilian society, but there seems a clear parallel with the emerging disciplinary orders of prison and factory: if Melville compares the ship to Sing-Sing and Newgate prisons (174–176), he also likens it to a "market" or "manufactory" (35). The frigate's meticulous division of labor, along with strict supervision to ensure speed, efficiency, and the maximum use of space, resembles what Sean Wilentz has termed the "bastard artisan system" of antebellum manufacturing unskilled younger workforce—a situation not unlike that in the navy (Stott, 141). The *Neversink* may be a largely proto-industrial order, but at those moments when the entire crew is mobilized (at "general quarters," for example), the ship does seem almost a single mechanism—"a machineless factory" or "manufactory."

There remains a gap between the intensity of wartime mobilization (or drilling for it) and the sometimes purely theatrical aspects of the *Neversink's* peacetime cruise, with the pace of work diminishing when the ship reaches harbor, but this, too, is reminiscent of the seasonal cycles of urban manufacturing. In any case, shipboard routines are designed to make activity as constant and regular as possible. The decks are washed and "holy-stoned" each day, and each man has a piece of "bright-work" to keep polished (*NN WJ*, 86–87, 171). And every ship prides herself on the speed and efficiency with which its crew can handle her sails (193–197).

"The social state in a man-of-war" is ultimately, in Melville's words, "a system of cruel cogs and wheels," more of a rationalized economic order than one based on political representation or community (*NN WJ*, 373, 374–375). The class divisions upheld by the *Articles* of the old order are not done away with in the new; instead, the class antagonism between officers and men becomes "incurable" (208), a structural conflict that is both managed and reinforced by the disciplinary order of the ship.

Melville does not offer a direct attack on this regime, as he has against flogging. For the power of this disciplinary order does not reside in a single location or person, or even a particular practice, but is dispersed throughout the systems and processes of the ship. There are thus no clear targets for a politi-cally-based critique. Instead, he is content to note a number of sites or modes of resistance among the men. Besides their recourse to drinking as a means of escape, and the smuggling that follows from it, man-of-war's-men are also, for instance, inveterate gamblers. Games of uncertainty and chance are at the op-posite pole from the regimentation of the ship, in which numbers and positions are rationally ordered and predetermined. Out of the play of cards and dice springs a counter order of a sort, a covert exchange of money and goods, and the creation of networks of lookouts and spies, shadow doubles of those of the master at arms, his assistants, and informers (*NN WJ*, 306–307).

Just as gambling is hidden below deck, in the dark margins of the vessel, other activities such as reading, sewing, daydreaming, and checker-playing emerge to fill marginal time, to "kill" it in personal or deliberately unproduc-tive ways (*NN WJ*, 170–174). But such activities remain strictly limited, tol-erated or co-opted by the officers as discipline requires. Sailors may dress up and "promenade" along the gun deck, for instance, but only on the starboard side, since the larboard is reserved for officers (83, 172). Fighting is allowed only "under the direct patronage of the captain," as a form of "'play'" for his entertainment (274, 276). And the exuberance of "skylarking" appears only when ordered, during a frigid calm off Cape Horn (102–103).

The pervasiveness of physical regulation aboard ship is perhaps best il-lustrated by what White-Jacket terms "the great Massacre of the Beards" (*NN WJ*, 355). The sailors have sought to assert a degree of control over their bod-ies; they give and receive tattoos, for example, as a chosen alternative to the scars of the lash, and thus also as a form of resistance to naval discipline. As the ship rounds Cape Horn and heads for home, they also begin to cultivate their beards, as signs of both individuality and masculinity. Late in the cruise, however, the Captain suddenly orders all hair cut short and whiskers trimmed "'according to the Navy regulations'" (357). If their beards are signs of the sail-ors' anticipation of a return to life outside the ship, the captain's order insists upon their continued enclosure within it, and their continued identification by ranks and duties alone. Their initial response is a near mutiny; at last, how-ever, all the men but one comply. The lone holdout, Ushant, the Captain of the Forecastle, insists simply that "'my beard is my own,'" a kind of property inseparable from the self and beyond such regulation (365). At this moment, the ship's two structures of power converge: the captain tries to force Ushant to comply by having him publicly flogged, and then by demoting and confin-ing him to the brig (reducing both his rank and his spatial mobility) until the ship reaches port.

This shift, from public punishment to private confinement, from the first of Foucault's models to the second, is precisely the one advocated by reformers of the period, like the anonymous writer for the *Democratic Review*.[28] Such a change did not immediately occur in naval practice, even after the abolition of flogging in 1850; commanders continued to experiment with different forms of bodily punishment—tattooing, branding, forcing sailors to wear signs (Valle, 83). But the "Massacre of the Beards" makes clear that such reforms, while humanitarian in one respect, served to further rather than to limit the extension of shipboard discipline.

White-Jacket does not, then, suggest a neat transition between different forms of penality; nor does it show a retrograde system being superseded by a more enlightened and democratic one, as Melville's rhetoric demands. In both the novel and the antebellum navy, theatricalized physical punishment continued to undergird the personal authority of the captain, even as the space of the ship and the functions of the sailors became more fully rationalized and controlled. The progressive view of history that Melville invokes against the Articles of War yields an equally undemocratic disciplinary regime as their complement.

If Melville's recourse to a mystified republicanism gives him only a limited basis for an attack on flogging, it offers no means of engagement with this new disciplinary order. His continued allegiance to such rhetoric may be strategic, part of a "job" "done for money," but it may perhaps also reflect a deeper psychological investment.[29] Michael Rogin has suggested that both *White-Jacket* and its predecessor, *Redburn,* describe their protagonists' confrontation with class stratification in the wake of their loss of familial identity and inheritance.[30] Melville himself seems to cling to the Revolutionary tradition as his own paternal inheritance: he is the sailor whose "grandsire," Thomas Melville, fought at Bunker Hill.[31] And in a letter of March 1849 to Evert Duyckinck, he had insisted both that "we are all sons, grandsons, or nephews or great-nephews of those who go before us" and that "the Declaration of Independence makes a difference" (*NN Correspondence,* 121,122).

Melville's relation to that ancestry becomes increasingly troubled (his mother's father, Peter Gansevoort, was both a war hero and a slave owner [Robertson-Lorant, 3]), with his ambivalence surfacing clearly in *Pierre* and *Israel Potter.* But in *White-Jacket,* those reservations have only begun to appear, as a sense of loss or diminishment, or even, at moments, an ironic distance from the patriarchs, and from Revolutionary ideology as well.

The momentum of the narrative line does, of course, lead toward an act of rebellion in the scene in which White-Jacket himself is threatened with the lash. He describes himself as about to act from "instinct," to lunge toward the Captain and sweep them both over the side: "The privilege, inborn and inalienable, that every man has, of dying himself, and inflicting death upon another, was not given to us without a purpose," he says (*NN WJ,* 280). But before he can choose between submission and revolt, a petty officer's intervention makes the question moot. White-Jacket's resistance is not simply erased, however. It is displaced and deferred, to return in an altered, twisted form in the "Massacre of the Beards." Here it is a father-figure, Ushant, the "Nestor of the crew," who refuses to have his "manly beard" taken off as the Captain has ordered (360, 363), and is flogged for doing so. The son's impulse toward violent resistance is deflected onto a patriarch, who then passively suffers in the son's place; it is once more the Fathers' Revolution, not the belated son's, lingering into the present only in severely diminished form.

In the end, though, it is naval discipline that mutes and recontains the Revolutionary political tradition. Perhaps the best example of this comes on July 4, when, rather than allowing the men a double ration of grog, Captain Claret gives them permission to put on "theatricals . . . to honor the Fourth" (*NN WJ*, 90). "The people" as audience offer "uncontrollable bursts of applause" when Jack Chase as "Percy Royal-Mast rescues fifteen oppressed sailors from the watch-house, in the teeth of a posse of constables" (94). The response to such a represented liberation is a "terrible . . . commotion," in which "all discipline seemed gone forever" (94). But the breakdown is only temporary—and illusory. As David Suchoff notes, the play has been given "in the same social space" in which floggings are administered, and "the same old scene [is] enacted at the gangway" the next day.[32] His performance as liberator notwithstanding, Chase will later prove unable to prevent (or even speak out against) the flogging of Ushant (*NN WJ*, 365).

In this context, terms such as "liberty" and "the people" take on an ironic undertone. The crew is referred to as "the people," but the phrase always appears in italics or quotation marks (*NN WJ*, 93–95, 213, 225). The term may imply a political identity or authority, but seamen are stripped of such political rights at the moment they join the ship. And the "liberty" Jack Chase seeks— "'we've struck for liberty, and liberty we'll have! I'm your tribune, boys; I'm your Rienzi'" (225)—is only twenty-four hours ashore. Back aboard the *Neversink*, the sailor's reality remains one of constraint and disempowerment.

If Melville can be said to envision any alternative to the frigate's disciplinary order, it is aloft, in the main-top. The foot of the main-mast may be the symbolic center of the vessel, where its hierarchies are made visible, and the captain's authority exercised in public view. But directly above it hangs the platform of the maintop—the post assigned to both White-Jacket and the charismatic Chase. This is the one point aboard ship that Melville exempts from the surveillance and control that enclose and dominate the remainder. The "top," by way of contrast, is a democratic, egalitarian space where speeches and judgments can be delivered unchecked: "'there's no law up aloft here,'" proclaims one of White-Jacket's companions, in the course of a "fierce . . . republican" diatribe against monarchs and noblemen (*NN WJ*, 235– 236).

Larry J. Reynolds has described White-Jacket's privileging of the maintop as "anti-democratic" and elitist,[33] but it may be as much an artisan republican vision as an aristocratic one. According to Sean Wilentz, the early nineteenth century saw the development of a distinct form of republican ideology among urban workers, one that blended democratic, libertarian ideals with egalitarian cooperation and identified political citizenship with the economic independence of skilled labor.[34] By the late 1840s, such "mechanics" were struggling with increasing difficulty to differentiate themselves from unskilled workers and preserve their political identity (Wilentz, 95, 102).

Melville's main-top-men are in many ways such a fraternity of experienced workers, freed for a time from the regimentation of the deck below: "we loaned ourselves to each other with all the freedom in the world," White-Jacket says (*NN WJ*, 15). Singing, for instance, may be forbidden while the men are at work (sea chanteys could be a means of controlling the pace and rhythm of work in the merchant service),[35] but poetry and song are staples of evenings aloft. So too are battle "yarns," war stories told from a seaman's rather than an officer's perspective (*NN WJ*, 311–321). The top becomes both a communal space for free speech and a stage for spontaneous performance, home to a fraternal order based upon shared labor and skill rather than an official hierarchy.

If some shipboard assignments can shape a sailor's character negatively, White-Jacket claims that being a main-top-man has given him his "free, broad, off-hand, bird's-eye, and more than all, impartial" perspective—has, in other words, made the book itself possible (*NN WJ*, 47). The assertion is, however, ultimately self-defeating, for to make it, Melville's narrator must accept the shaping force of the *Neversink*'s disciplinary order.[36] In the end, White-Jacket's freedom on the main-top is a wished-for exception to the rule, while the rule remains intact. Melville ends the book by simply suspending his narrative, leaving the "main-top-men ... aloft in the top ... a brother-band, hand in hand, all spliced together" (396). The maintop can only be a "Pisgah," offering an anticipated—or, more accurately, nostalgic—egalitarian ideal (397).

Why such a visionary but evasive ending? The campaign to abolish flogging was already nearing success before *White-Jacket* appeared, but Melville's democratic and legal arguments do not enable him to go further; they do not give him a language adequate to respond to either the class issues or the disciplinary processes on the decks below. How to reconcile The Declaration of Independence with the realities of industrial capitalism? The language of revolutionary citizenship and individual virtue is no longer sufficient to the task, and, almost reluctantly, *White-Jacket* registers that exhaustion.

A year later, in *Moby-Dick*, Melville would return to the problem, depicting it in terms both starker and more complex. Ahab's authoritarian and theatrical command is, of course, explicitly based on public vengeance to be exacted on the creature that has so directly "touched the very person of the prince," in Foucault's phrase (*Discipline*, 49). But the captain's pursuit is now clearly in conflict with both Starbuck's rational capitalism and the functioning of the whale ship as factory. In this model, with the crew working for "lays" or shares of the voyage's profits, all become members of a "joint stock company," a capitalist enterprise that is in turn quite different from the ecstatic fraternity of "A Squeeze of the Hand" or the bond of friendship between Ishmael and Queequeg. Unlike *White-Jacket*, *Moby-Dick* does not evade the tragic consequences of such oppositions; but it, too closes with the conflicts between democracy and authority, egalitarianism and capitalism, unresolved.

Notes

1. *Discipline and Punish: The Birth of the Prison*, trans. Alan Sheridan (New York: Vintage, 1979); hereafter cited as *Discipline*. In a later formulation, Foucault substitutes for these two terms "a triangle, sovereignty-discipline-government, which has as its primary target the population and as its essential mechanism the apparatuses of security" ("Governmentality," *The Essential Foucault*, ed. Paul Rabinow and Nikolas Rose [New York: New Press, 2003], 243). Naval order, however, seems better described by his earlier model, since it is based on the control of the ship as a space more than of its a crew as a "population."

2. Samuel Otter terms this aspect of the text an "anatomy"; see his *Melville's Anatomies* (Berkeley: University of California Press, 1999), 4–6.

3. In *Modernity at Sea: Melville, Marx, Conrad in Crisis* (Minneapolis: University of Minnesota Press, 2002), Cesare Casarino also contrasts Melville and Foucault, as he locates *White-Jacket* within the genre of the nineteenth-century sea narrative. For him, the genre registers the transition from mercantile to industrial capitalism, and these two orders overlap aboard the *Neversink* (3–5). I would agree that the problem of the emerging industrial order is broached in *White-Jacket*, but my focus here will be on the inadequacy of Melville's political discourse as a response to it.

4. James E. Valle, *Rocks and Shoals: Order and Discipline in the Old Navy 1800–1861* (Annapolis: Naval Institute Press, 1980), 44, 76; Valle also quotes a similar description given by Commodore David Porter in the 1830s (36).

5. Herman Melville, *White-Jacket: or The World in a Man-of-War*, ed. Harrison Hayford, Hershel Parker, and G. Thomas Tanselle (Northwestern University Press and the Newberry Library: Evanston and Chicago, 1970), 23; hereafter cited as *NN WJ*.

6. Charles R. Anderson, *Melville in the South Seas* (New York: Columbia University Press, 1939), 349. Valle describes the *United States* as "an acknowledged 'hell ship'" during these years, and thus not really representative of the navy as a whole (44).

7. *NN WJ*, 134. See also Howard P. Vincent, *The Tailoring of Melville's White-Jacket* (Evanston: Northwestern University Press, 1970), 91.

8. *NN WJ*, 135, 301; Foucault, 57.

9. See especially *NN WJ*, Ch. 39, "The Frigate in Harbor," 160–163.

10. *NN WJ*, 222; Valle, 88. The class gulf between officers and men is registered most clearly in Ch. 59, "A Man-of-War Button Divides Two Brothers."

11. As qtd. in Valle, 287.

12. Valle, 43; see also Harold Langley, *Social Reform in the United States Navy, 1798–1862* (Urbana: University of Illinois Press, 1967), 138–139.

13. "Flogging in the Navy," *United States Magazine and Democratic Review* 25.134 (August, 1849), 101.

14. Wai-Chee Dimock links this expansionist rhetoric to what she sees as the "differential" and thus limited character of Jacksonian reform, but Melville's language, as I have suggested, may be idiosyncratic rather than representative in this regard. See her *Empire for Liberty: Melville and the Poetics of Individualism* (Princeton: Princeton University Press, 1989), 101.

15. See Vincent, 88–106; and Otter, 67–77.

16. See, for instance, the House debate of September 21, 1850. *Congressional Globe*, 31st Congress, 1st Session, XIX, 1906; and Valle, 64.

17. February 12, 1849. *Congressional Globe*, 30th Congress, 2nd Session, XVIII, 507.

18. *Congressional Globe*, 30th Congress, 2nd Session, XVIII, 511.

19. See in particular the fourth installment of the series, "Substitutes Detailed," *United States Magazine and Democratic Review* 25.137 (November, 1849), 417–432.

20. The limits of Melville's version of reform are noted by both Priscilla Allen Zirker in "Evidence of the Slavery Dilemma in *White-Jacket*," *American Quarterly* 18 (Fall, 1966): 477–492; and in John Samson, *White Lies: Melville's Narratives of Facts* (Ithaca: Cornell University Press, 1989), 128–172. Zirker links Melville's ambivalence to that of the Democratic Party in the late 1840s, while Samson describes it as a Whig position on the issue.

21. See Ch. 162, "They Visit the Extreme South of Vivenza," in *Herman Melville, Mardi: and a Voyage Thither*, ed. Harrison Hayford, Hershel Parker, and G. Thomas Tanselle (Northwestern University Press and the Newberry Library: Evanston and Chicago, 1970).

22. The best known formulation of the republican ideal is J. G. A. Pocock's. See, for instance, his "Virtue and Commerce in the Eighteenth Century," *Journal of Interdisciplinary History* 3 (1972): 121; or the final chapter of his *The Machiavellian Moment* (Princeton: Princeton University Press, 1975), 506–552.

23. On the shift of republicanism to the level of cultural practice, see Jean Baker, "From Belief into Culture: Republicanism in the Antebellum North," *American Quarterly* 37.4 (Autumn, 1985): 532–550; on Republicanism and the Northern working class, see David R. Roediger, *The Wages of Whiteness: Race and the Making of the American Working Class* (London: Verso, 1991), 55–60, 80–87.

24. "What To the Slave Is the Fourth of July?" in *The Oxford Frederick Douglass Reader*, ed. William L. Andrews (New York: Oxford University Press, 1996), 112, 125, 126.

25. Foucault, "Of Other Spaces," trans. Jay Miskowiec, *Diacritics* 16.1 (Spring 1986): 24, 27.

26. *NN WJ*, 177; Valle, 5.

27. *Rules, Regulations, and Instructions, for the Naval Service of the United States* (Washington: E. de Krafft, 1818), 51.

28. See "Flogging in the Navy," 97.

29. Letter of October 6, 1849, to Lemuel Shaw, Correspondence, ed. Lynn Horth, Harrison Hayford, Hershel Parker, and G. Thomas Tanselle (Evanston and

Chicago: Northwestern University Press and The Newberry Library, 1993), 138; hereafter cited as *NN Correspondence*.

30. Michael Paul Rogin, *Subversive Genealogy: The Politics and Art of Herman Melville* (Berkeley: University of California Press, 1983), 89.

31. See Laurie Robertson-Lorant, *Melville: A Biography* (New York: Clarkson Potter, 1996), 3; *NN WJ*, 146.

32. *Critical Theory and the Novel: Mass Society and Cultural Criticism in Dickens, Melville, and Kafka* (Madison, WI: University of Wisconsin Press, 1994), 107; *NN WJ*, 95.

33. "Antidemocratic Emphasis in *White-Jacket*," *American Literature* 48.1 (1976): 13–28.

34. Wilentz, 95, 102.

35. See Margaret S. Creighton, "Fraternity in the American Forecastle, 1830–1860," *New England Quarterly* 63.4 (1990): 546–547.

36. John Bryant suggests that such a perspective gives the maintop the privileged viewpoint of Foucault's Panopticon—again, such an assertion of privilege would reinforce rather than escape the order of the ship. See his "The Native Gazes: Sexuality and Self-Colonization in Melville's *Typee*," *Melville Among the Nations*, ed. Sanford E. Marovitz and A. C. Christodoulou (Kent, OH: Kent State University Press, 2001), 256. In any case, White-Jacket seldom looks down onto the deck from his position aloft; his gaze is most often directed up or out over the waves.

Chronology

1819	Herman Melville (or Melvill) born on August 1 in New York City, the third child of Allan Melville, an importer, and Maria Gansevoort Melville.
1826	Melville attends the New York Male High School.
1830–1832	Allan Melville's importing business fails, and he moves the family to Albany. Herman becomes a student at the Albany Academy until his father's death in 1832. Then he works at various jobs: a bank clerk, a helper on his brother's farm and an assistant in his brother's fur factory and store.
1835–1838	Continues his education at various high schools; supplements the family income by teaching.
1839	"Fragments from a Writing Desk" published May 4 and May 18 in the *Democratic Press* and *Lansingburgh Advertiser*. Melville works his way to Liverpool and back on the *Saint Lawrence*, a merchant ship.
1841–1844	Melville leaves Fairhaven, Massachusetts as a sailor on the whaler *Acushnet*, bound for the South Seas. Jumps ship in the Marquesas Islands, where he lives among the natives for about a month. After a series of adventures, travels home as a passenger on the frigate *United States*.
1846	Publishes *Typee*. Brother Gansevoort dies.
1847	Publishes *Omoo*. Marries Elizabeth Shaw, daughter of Chief Justice Lemuel Shaw of Boston.

1847–1850	Melville tries to earn a living as a writer, producing occasional articles and reviews. Makes acquaintance of George and Evert Duyckinck, and other New York literary figures.
1849	Publishes *Mardi* and *Redburn*. Travels to Europe. Son Malcolm born.
1850	Publishes *White-Jacket*. Purchases Arrowhead, a farm near Pittsfield, Massachusetts. Begins his friendship with Nathaniel Hawthorne, who lives in nearby Lenox.
1851	Publishes *Moby-Dick*. Son Stanwix born.
1852	Publishes *Pierre*.
1853–1856	Daughter Elizabeth born. Writes stories and sketches for *Putnam's Monthly Magazine* and *Harper's New Monthly Magazine*.
1855	Publishes *Israel Potter* as a book, after serialization in *Putnam's*. Daughter Frances born.
1856	*The Piazza Tales* published. Melville travels to Europe and the Near East for his health.
1857	*The Confidence Man*, which Melville has left with his publisher before he began traveling, is finally published. Melville returns to the United States.
1857–1860	Melville supports family by lectures on such topics as "Statuary in Rome," "The South Seas" and "Travelling."
1863	Melville sells Arrowhead, and moves his family to New York City.
1866	Publishes a collection of poems, *Battle-Pieces and Aspects of the War*. Son Malcolm shoots himself; son Stanwix runs away to sea.
1876	Publishes *Clarel*.
1886	Son Stanwix dies.
1888	*John Marr and Other Sailors* privately printed.
1891	*Timoleon* privately printed. Melville dies on September 28.
1924	First publication of *Billy Budd*.

Contributors

HAROLD BLOOM is Sterling Professor of the Humanities at Yale University. He is the author of 30 books, including *Shelley's Mythmaking* (1959), *The Visionary Company* (1961), *Blake's Apocalypse* (1963), *Yeats* (1970), *A Map of Misreading* (1975), *Kabbalah and Criticism* (1975), *Agon: Toward a Theory of Revisionism* (1982), *The American Religion* (1992), *The Western Canon* (1994), and *Omens of Millennium: The Gnosis of Angels, Dreams, and Resurrection* (1996). *The Anxiety of Influence* (1973) sets forth Professor Bloom's provocative theory of the literary relationships between the great writers and their predecessors. His most recent books include *Shakespeare: The Invention of the Human* (1998), a 1998 National Book Award finalist, *How to Read and Why* (2000), *Genius: A Mosaic of One Hundred Exemplary Creative Minds* (2002), *Hamlet: Poem Unlimited* (2003), *Where Shall Wisdom Be Found?* (2004), and *Jesus and Yahweh: The Names Divine* (2005). In 1999, Professor Bloom received the prestigious American Academy of Arts and Letters Gold Medal for Criticism. He has also received the International Prize of Catalonia, the Alfonso Reyes Prize of Mexico, and the Hans Christian Andersen Bicentennial Prize of Denmark.

MILTON R. STERN is emeritus professor of English at the University of Connecticut. A former editor of *American Literature Survey*, he has written or edited five volumes on Melville, including *The Fine Hammered Steel of Herman Melville* (Urbana: University of Illinois Press, 1957).

SANFORD E. MAROVITZ retired as professor of English at Kent State University in 1991. With Clarence Ghodes he compiled the fifth edition of

A Bibliographical Guide to the Study of the Literature of the U.S.A. (Durham, N.C.: Duke University Press, 1984).

SANDRA A. ZAGARELL is Donald R. Longman Professor of English at Oberlin College. She was senior editor of *The Heath Anthology of American Literature,* 4th edition. (Boston: Houghton Mifflin, 2001).

JOHN BRYANT is professor of English at Hofstra University. He has written extensively on Melville. His books include *The Fluid Text: A Theory of Revision and Editing for Book and Screen* (Ann Arbor: University of Michigan Press, 2002); *Melville and Repose: The Rhetoric of Humor in the American Renaissance* (New York: Oxford University Press, 1993); and *.A Companion to Melville Studies* (Westport, C.T.: Greenwood Press, 1986). He is editor of *The Typee Manuscript Leviathan: A Journal of Melville Studies* in the Melville Electronic Library.

BRYAN C. SHORT was professor of English at Northern Arizona University and treasurer of the Melville Society at the time of his death in 2003. Between 1971 and his death, he wrote extensively about Melville.

NANCY FREDRICKS is author of *Melville's Art of Democracy* (Athens: University of Georgia Press, 1995).

STEPHEN MATHEWSON wrote his dissertation on Melville, "The Canonical Whale: 'Moby-Dick' and American Literary History" (1990). He has also written articles on Melville and the painter, Thomas Hudson.

BILL CHRISOPHERSEN is author of *The Apparition in the Glass: Charles Brockden Brown's American Gothic* (Athens: University of Georgia Press, 1993).

JUDITH HILTNER is professor of English at St. Xavier University in Chicago. She has written several scholarly articles on Melville, including studies on *Israel Potter* and his short fiction.

JOHN WENKE is professor of English at Salisbury State University. He is author of *Melville's Muse: Literary Creation and the Forms of Philosophical Fiction* (Kent, Ohio: Kent State University Press, 1995).

MERTON M. SEALTS, JR. was Henry A. Pochman Professor of English, emeritus, at the University of Wisconsin, Madison. Among his many respected books on nineteenth-century literature is the *Pursuing Melville, 1940–1980* (Madison: University of Wisconsin Press, 1982); *Melville's Reading,* revised and enlarged (Columbia: University of South Carolina Press,

1988); and *Beyond the Classroom: Essays on American Authors* (Columbia: University of Missouri Press, 1996). Professor Sealts died in 2000.

STANTON GARNER is retired professor of English at the University of Texas. He is secretary of the Melville Society and author of *The Civil War World of Herman Melville* (Lawrence: University of Kansas Press, 1993).

THOMAS HOVE earned his Ph.D. at the University of Illinois, Urbana; his dissertation was "Ethical Ideals, Nonrational Forces: Melville's Critique of Morality" (1999). He has written articles on Toni Morrison, William Gass, and *Billy Budd*.

CINDY WEINSTEIN is professor of English at the California Institute of Technology. Her books include *Family, Kinship, and Sympathy in Nineteenth-Century American Literature* (Cambridge and New York: Cambridge University Press, 2004) and *The Literature of Labor and the Labors of Literature: Allegory in Nineteenth Century American Fiction* (Cambridge and New York: Cambridge University Press, 1995).

PETER BELLIS is professor of English and department chair at the University of Alabama, Birmingham. He has written *No Mysteries Out of Ourselves: Identity and Textual Form in the Novels of Herman Melville* (Philadelphia: University of Pennsylvania Press, 1990) and *Writing Revolution: Aesthetics and Politics in Antebellum American Literature* (Athens: University of Georgia Press, 2003).

Bibliography

Bergmann, Johannes D., "Melville's Tales," in *A Companion to Melville Studies*, edited by John Bryant (New York: Greenwood Press, 1986), pp. 241–278.

Brodhead, Richard H., *Hawthorne, Melville, and the Novel* (Chicago: University of Chicago Press, 1976).

Bryant, John, *Melville and Repose: The Rhetoric of Humor in the American Renaissance* (New York: Oxford University Press, 1993).

Cook, Jonathan A., *Satirical Apocalypse: An Anatomy of Melville's* The Confidence-Man (Westport, Conn.: Greenwood Press, 1996).

Davis, Merrell R., *Melville's* Mardi*: A Chartless Voyage* (New Haven: Yale University Press, 1952).

Detlaff, Shirley, "Ionian Form and Esau's Waste: Melville's View of Art in *Clarel*," *American Literature*, 54 (May 1982): 212–228.

Dillingham, William B., *Melville and His Circle: The Last Years* (Athens: University of Georgia Press, 1996).

Dimock, Wai-chee, *Empire for Liberty: Melville and the Poetics of Individualism* (Princeton: Princeton University Press, 1989).

Finkelstein, Dorothee Metlitsky, *Melville's* Orienda (New Haven, Conn.: Yale University Press, 1961).

Garner, Stanton, *The Civil War World of Herman Melville* (Lawrence: University Press of Kansas, 1993).

Goldman, Stan, *Melville's Protest Theism: The Hidden and Silent God in* Clarel (Dekalb: Northern Illinois University Press, 1993).

271

Hayford, Harrison, "'Unnecessary Duplicates': A Key to the Writing of *Moby-Dick*," in *New Perspectives on Melville,* edited by Faith Pullin (Kent, Ohio: Kent State University Press, 1979), pp. 128–161.

Higgins, Brian, *Herman Melville: A Reference Guide, 1931–1960* (Boston: G. K. Hall, 1987).

Higgins and Hershel Parker, eds., *Herman Melville: The Contemporary Reviews* (New York: Cambridge University Press, 1995).

Howard, Leon, *Herman Melville: A Biography* (Berkeley: University of California Press, 1951).

Kenny, Vincent, "Clarel," in *A Companion to Melville Studies,* edited by Bryant (New York: Greenwood Press, 1986), pp. 375–406.

Lawrence, D. H., *Studies in Classic American Literature* (New York: T. Seltzer, 1923).

Levin, Michael E., "Ahab as Socratic Philosopher: The Myth of the Cave Inverted," *American Transcendental Quarterly,* 41 (Winter 1979): 61–73.

Leyda, Jay, ed., *The Melville Log: A Documentary Life of Herman Melville, 1819-1891* (New York: Harcourt, Brace, 1951; with supplement, New York: Gordian Press, 1969).

Miller, Edwin Haviland, *Herman Melville: A Biography* (New York: Braziller, 1975).

Parker, Hershel, *Herman Melville: A Biography, Volume I, 1819–1851* (Baltimore: Johns Hopkins University Press, 1996).

———. "Herman Melville's *The Isle of the Cross:* A Survey and a Chronology," *American Literature,* 62 (March 1990): 1–16.

Post-Lauria, Sheila, *Correspondent Colorings: Melville in the Marketplace* (Amherst: University of Massachusetts Press, 1996).

Ricks, Beatrice, *Herman Melville: A Reference Bibliography, 1900–1972, with Selected Nineteenth-Century Materials* (Boston: G. K. Hall, 1973).

Robertson-Lorant, Laurie, *Melville, A Biography* (New York: Clarkson N. Potter, 1996).

William H. Gilman, *Melville's Early Life and* Redburn (New York: New York University Press, 1951).

Robillard, Douglas, *Melville and the Visual Arts: Ionian Form, Venetian Tint* (Kent, Ohio: Kent State University Press, 1997).

Samson, John, *White Lies: Melville's Narratives of Facts* (Ithaca, N.Y.: Cornell University Press, 1989).

Schultz, Elizabeth A., *Unpainted to the Last:* Moby-Dick *and Twentieth-Century American Art* (Lawrence: University Press of Kansas, 1995).

Sealts, Merton M. Jr., *Melville's Reading* (Columbia: University of South Carolina Press, 1988).

Short, Bryan C., "Form as Vision in Herman Melville's *Clarel*," *American Literature*, 50 (January 1979): 553–569.

Shurr, William, *The Mystery of Iniquity: Melville as Poet, 1857–1891* (Lexington: University of Kentucky Press, 1972).

Sten, Christopher, *The Weaver God, He Weaves: Melville and the Poetics of the Novel* (Kent, Ohio: Kent State University Press, 1996).

————, ed., *Savage Eye: Melville and the Visual Arts* (Kent, Ohio: Kent State University Press, 1991).

Stern, Milton R., *The Fine Hammered Steel of Herman Melville* (Urbana: University of Illinois Press, 1957).

————. "Toward 'Bartleby the Scrivener,'" in *The Stoic Strain in American Literature*, edited by Duane J. Macmillan (Toronto: University of Toronto Press, 1979), pp. 19–41.

Titus, David K., "Herman Melville at the Albany Academy," *Melville Society Extracts*, 42 (May 1980): 4–10.

Vargish, Thomas, "Gnostick Mythos in *Moby-Dick*," *PMLA*, 81 (June 1966): 272–277.

Vincent, Howard P., *The Tailoring of Melville's* White-Jacket (Evanston, Ill.: Northwestern University Press, 1970).

————. *The Trying-Out of* Moby-Dick (Boston: Houghton Mifflin, 1948).

Wallace, Robert K., *Melville & Turner: Spheres of Love and Fright* (Athens: University of Georgia Press, 1992).

Wenke, John, *Melville's Muse: Literary Creation and the Forms of Philosophical Fiction* (Kent, Ohio: Kent State University Press, 1995).

Wright, Nathalia, *Melville's Use of the Bible* (Durham: Duke University Press, 1949).

Acknowledgments

Milton R. Stern, "Towards 'Bartleby the Scrivener'"; *The Stoic Strain in American Literature,* edited by Duane J. Macmillan (Toronto: University of Toronto Press, 1979): pp. 19–41. © 1979 University of Toronto Press. Reprinted with permission of the publisher.

Sanford E. Marovitz, "Melville's Problematic 'Being'"; *ESQ: A Journal of the American Renaissance,* Volume 28, Number 1 (1982): pp. 11–13. © 1982 Sanford E. Marovitz. Reprinted with permission of the author.

Sandra A. Zagarell, "Reenvisioning America: Melville's 'Benito Cereno'"; *ESQ: A Journal of the American Renaissance,* Volume 30, Number 4 (1984): pp. 245–259. © 1984 Sandra A. Zagarell. Reprinted with permission of the author.

John Bryant, "Allegory and Breakdown in *The Confidence-Man:* Melville's Comedy of Doubt"; *Philological Quarterly,* Volume 65 (Winter 1986): pp. 113–130. © 1986 University of Iowa.

Bryan C. Short, "'The Author at the Time': Tommo and Melville's Self-discovery in *Typee*"; *Texas Studies in Literature and Language,* Volume 31, Number 3 (Fall 1989): pp. 386–405. © 1989 University of Texas Press.

Nancy Fredricks, "Melville and the Woman's Story"; *Studies in American Fiction,* Volume 19 (1991): pp. 41–54. © 1991 Northeastern University.

Stephen Mathewson, "'To Tell Over Again the Story Just Told': The Composition of Melville's *Redburn*"; *ESQ: A Journal of the American Renaissance,* Volume 37, Number 4 (1991): pp. 311–320. © 1991 Washington State University.

Bill Christophersen, "Israel Potter: Melville's 'Citizen of the Universe'"; *Studies in American Fiction,* Volume 21 (1993): pp. 21–35. © 1993 Northeastern University.

Judith Hiltner, "Disquieting Encounters: Male Intrusions/Female Realms in Melville"; *ESQ: A Journal of the American Renaissance,* Volume 40, Number 2 (1994): pp. 91–111. © 1994 Washington State University.

John Wenke, "*Mardi:* Narrative Self-Fashioning and the Play of Possibility"; *Melville's Muse: Literary Creation and the Forms of Philosophical Fiction* (Kent, Ohio: Kent State University Press, 1995): pp. 27–46. © 1995 Kent State University Press.

Merton M. Sealts, Jr., "Whose Book Is *Moby-Dick?*"; Reprinted from *Beyond the Classroom: Essays on American Authors* by Merton M. Sealts, Jr. by permission of the University of Missouri Press. © 1996 by the Curators of the University of Missouri.

Stanton Garner, "Naples and *HMS Bellipotent:* Melville on the Police State"; *Leviathan: A Journal of Melville Studies,* Volume 1, Number 2 (1999): pp. 53–61. © 1999 Blackwell Publishing. Reprinted with permission.

Thomas Hove, "Naturalist Psychology in *Billy Budd*"; *Leviathan: A Journal of Melville Studies,* Volume 5, Number 2 (2003): pp. 51–65. © 2003 Blackwell Publishing. Reprinted with permission.

Cindy Weinstein, "We Are Family: Melville's *Pierre*"; *Leviathan: A Journal of Melville Studies,* Volume 7, Number 1 (2005): pp. 19–40. © 2005 Blackwell Publishing. Reprinted with permission.

Peter Bellis, "Discipline and the Lash in Melville's *White-Jacket*"; *Leviathan: A Journal of Melville Studies,* Volume 7, Number 2 (2005): pp. 25–40. © 2005 Blackwell Publishing. Reprinted with permission.

Index